the Awkward Yeti presents

Heart and Brain

ONWARD TO GOOD THINGS

Andrews McMeel
PUBLISHING®

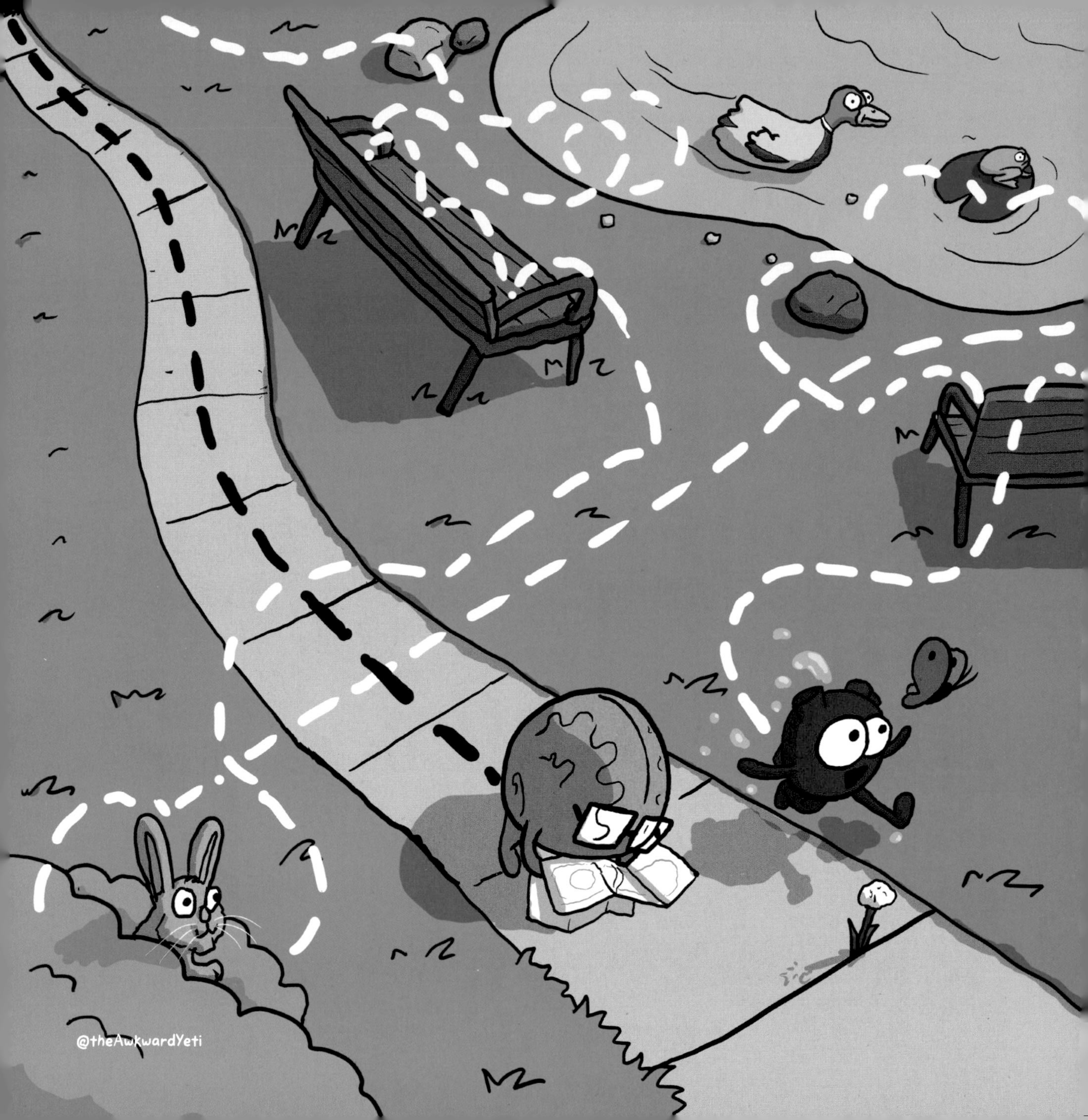
@theAwkwardYeti

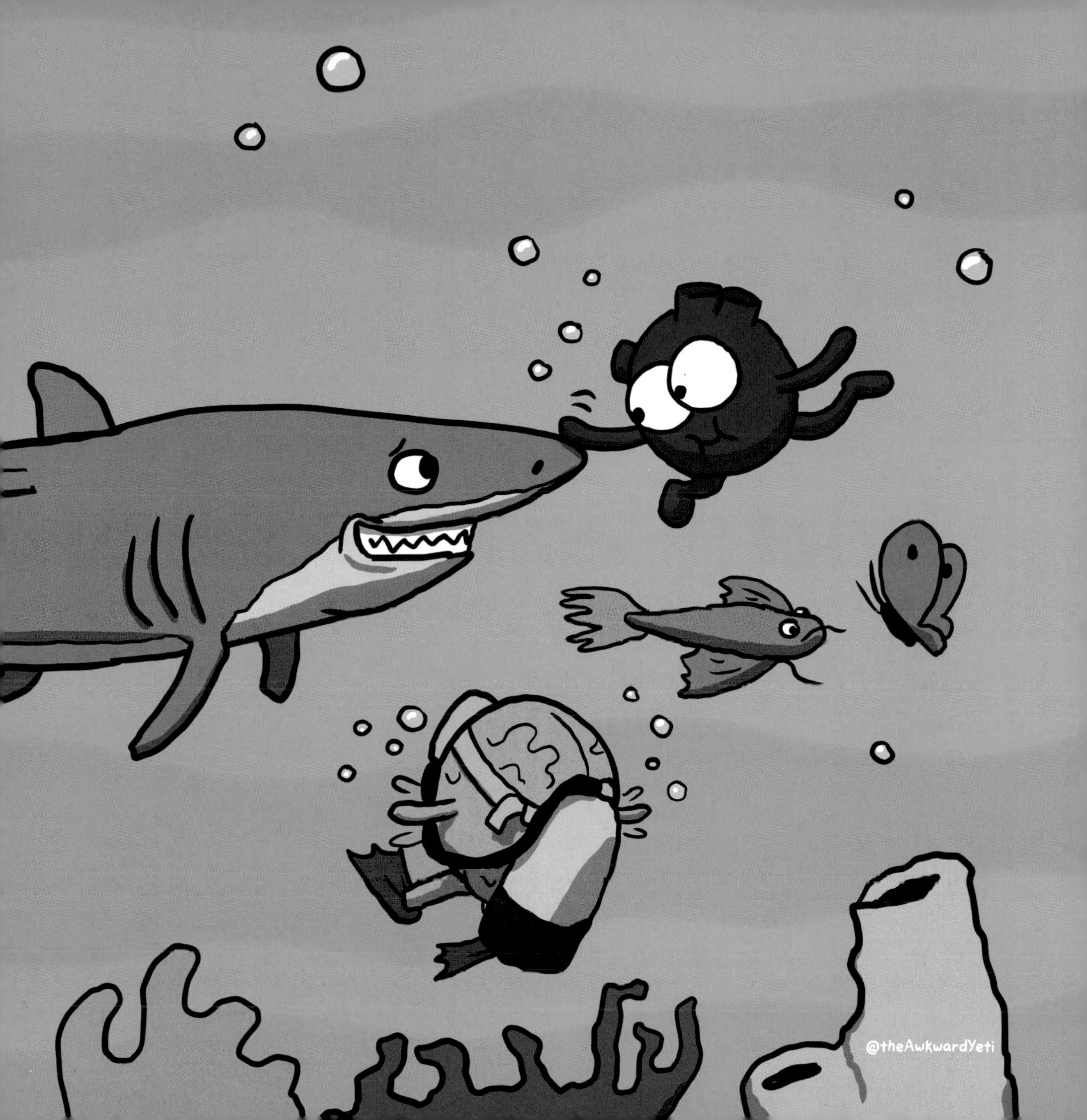
@theAwkwardYeti

Andrews McMeel Publishing
a division of Andrews McMeel Universal
1130 Walnut Street, Kansas City, Missouri 64106

www.andrewsmcmeel.com

23 24 25 26 27 TEN 10 9 8 7 6 5 4 3 2 1

ISBN: 978-1-5248-8222-8

Library of Congress Control Number: 2022949440

Editor: Lucas Wetzel
Art Director/Designer: Diane Marsh
Production Editor: Jasmine Lim
Production Manager: Chadd Keim

ATTENTION: SCHOOLS AND BUSINESSES
Andrews McMeel books are available at quantity discounts with bulk purchase for educational, business, or sales promotional use. For information, please e-mail the Andrews McMeel Publishing Special Sales Department: sales@amuniversal.com.

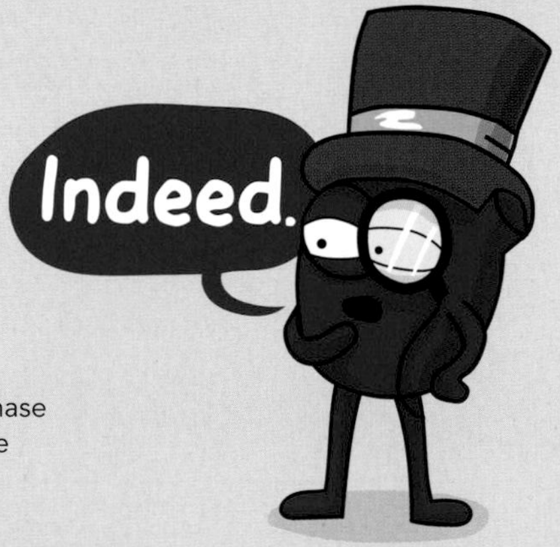
Indeed.

Contents

INTRODUCTION

Have you ever woken up in the middle of a life that didn't feel like your own? A life built around the expectations of others, hardly reflecting your inner truth? I certainly have. My whole life was spent trying to squeeze into a mold I was told to fit into. It wasn't until I finally had the audacity to believe in myself that I began the most harrowing life transition imaginable: leaving the safety of a mid-range salaried corporate graphic design job at a promotional products company.

Perhaps it's not so harrowing if you have any other skills, but I did not. Besides, after seeing my company nonchalantly lay off thirty percent of the entire workforce multiple times, my day job didn't look any safer than going it alone. So I started doing what I always wanted to do anyway: drawing comics. The process required finding the time that most of us claim not to have (we always do, it's really just a matter of HOW we want to spend it). I worked incredibly hard, sacrificing my free time and headspace to build something of my own. Initially, it was an escape, then it got really serious, then my life burned to the ground just in time for a pandemic, and finally, it has become a source of peace for me.

In the midst of finding myself and my place in the world, I made a lot of mistakes. I became narrowly focused and blind to people I loved. My dog died. I had a nasty business partnership fallout. I went through a divorce. And I entered the pandemic completely pre-broken.

Oh, how sad for me, right? Well, yes, actually it was, thanks for noticing!

But just like many people, I was being forced into an awakening. Forcing myself into one, perhaps subconsciously. Forcing myself into finding a path to self-awareness of my own flaws and, just as importantly, my strengths. This was a period of push and pull with my own heart and brain, as I had to take a really hard look at who I truly was, what I truly wanted, and how I wanted to treat the people in my life.

It turns out I'm not perfect (GASP!). It also turns out that no matter how much self-awareness I get, there is always room for improvement. Being the best version of myself, adding to the world in a positive way, and letting go of trauma that only poisons emotions is a lifelong process. This book is a glance at that journey in the form of the best therapy I've ever done for myself: comic strips about disembodied organs. These comics are never meant to tell people what to do. I don't have any answers. What I do have is the way I see myself and the world, which is absurd, imperfect, hilarious, and beautiful. I am an anxiety machine who has been through major growing pains, and I'm looking onward to good things.

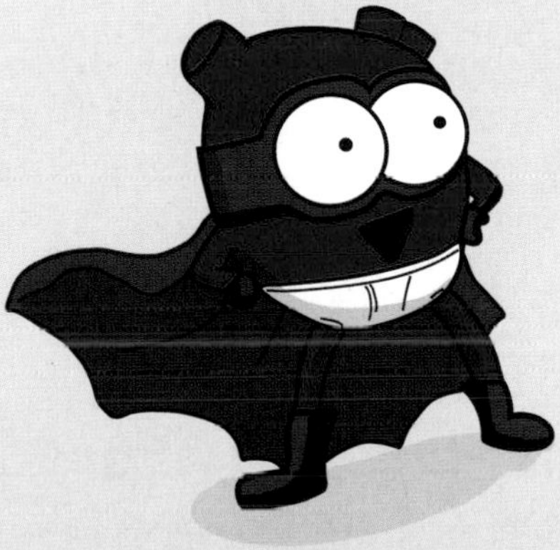

I hope you enjoy this long overdue collection as much as I have enjoyed creating it.

NICK SELUK

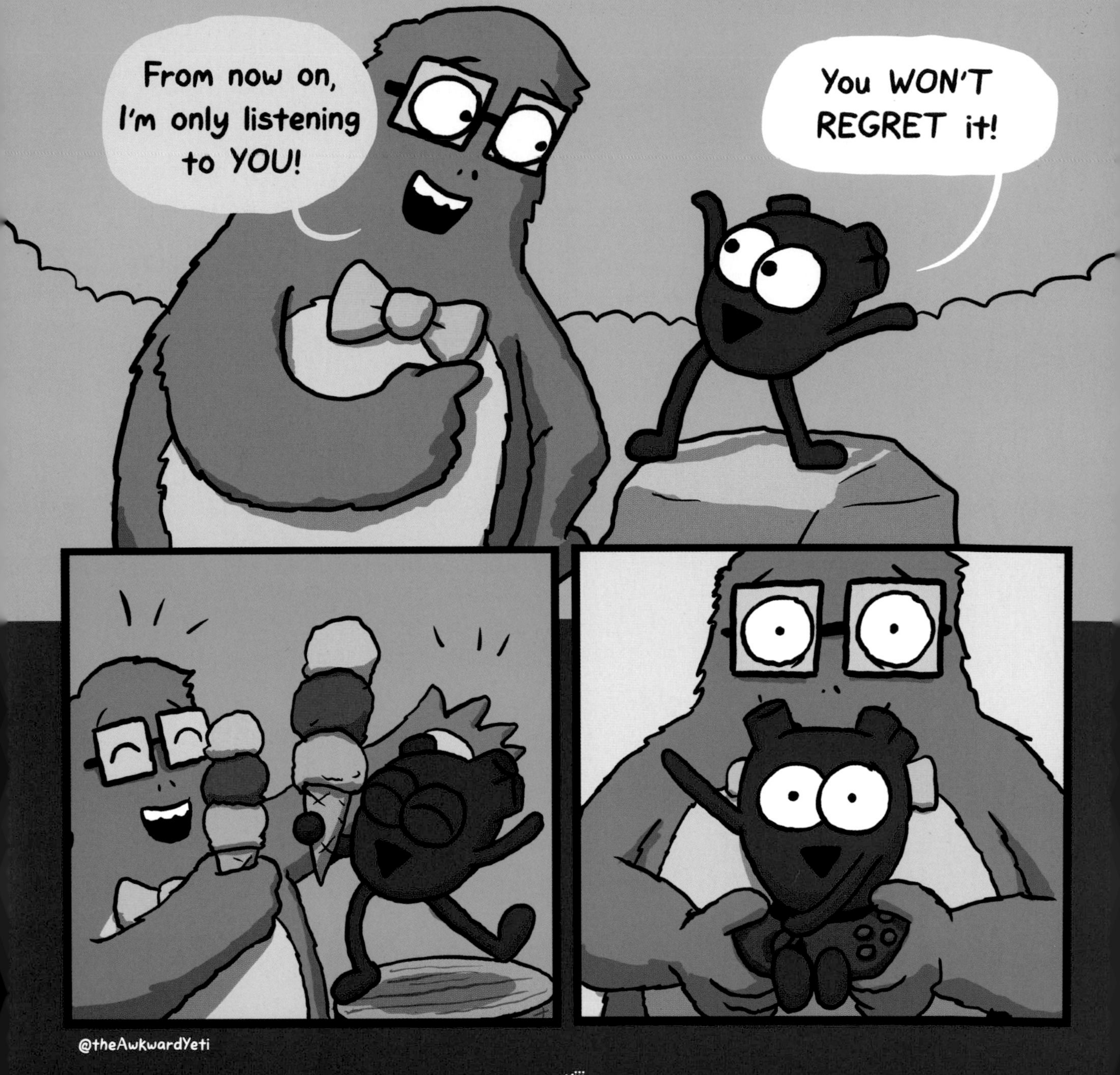
From now on, I'm only listening to YOU!
You WON'T REGRET it!
@theAwkwardYeti

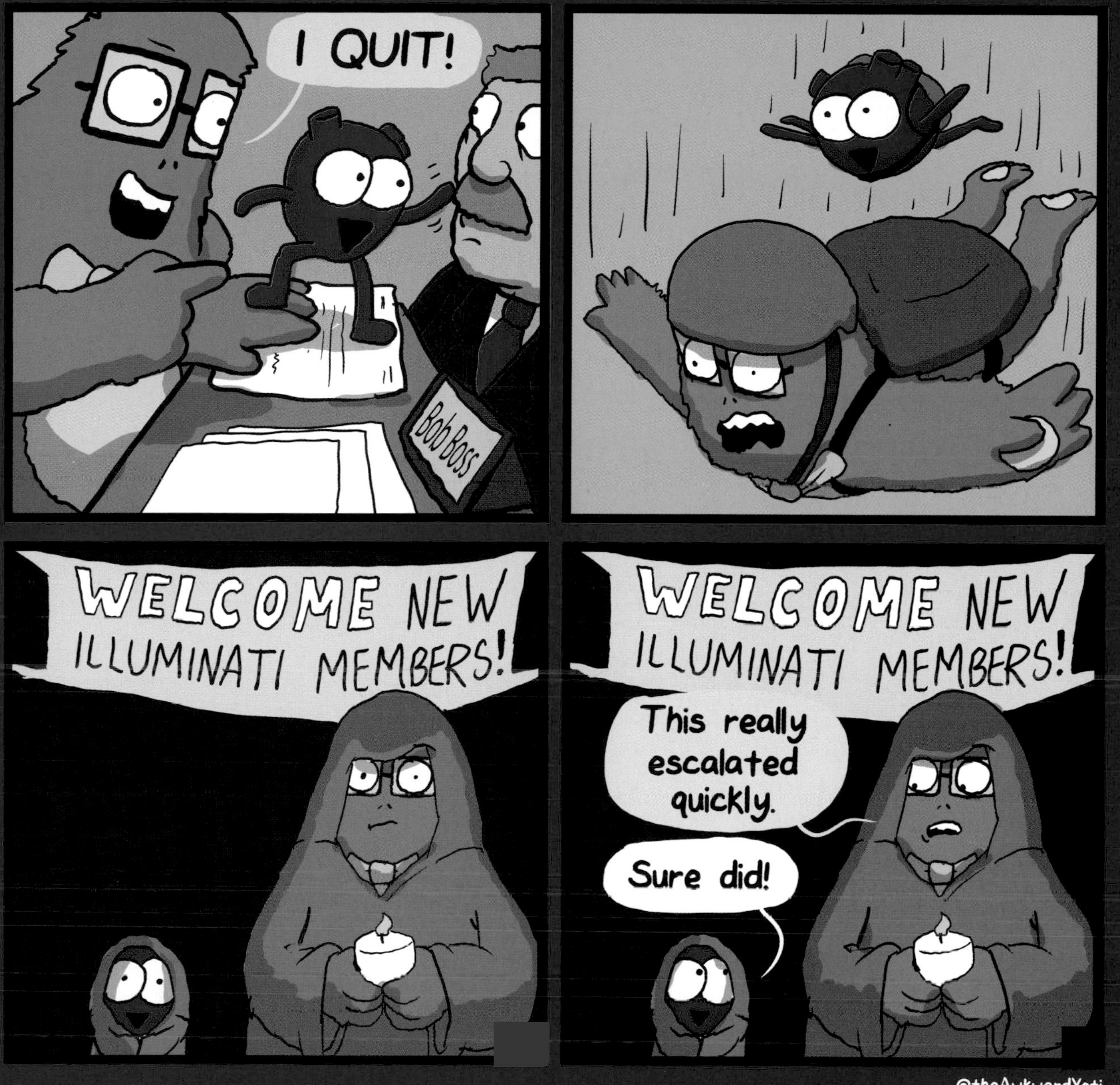
I QUIT!
Bob Boss
WELCOME NEW ILLUMINATI MEMBERS!
WELCOME NEW ILLUMINATI MEMBERS!
This really escalated quickly.
Sure did!

@theAwkwardYeti

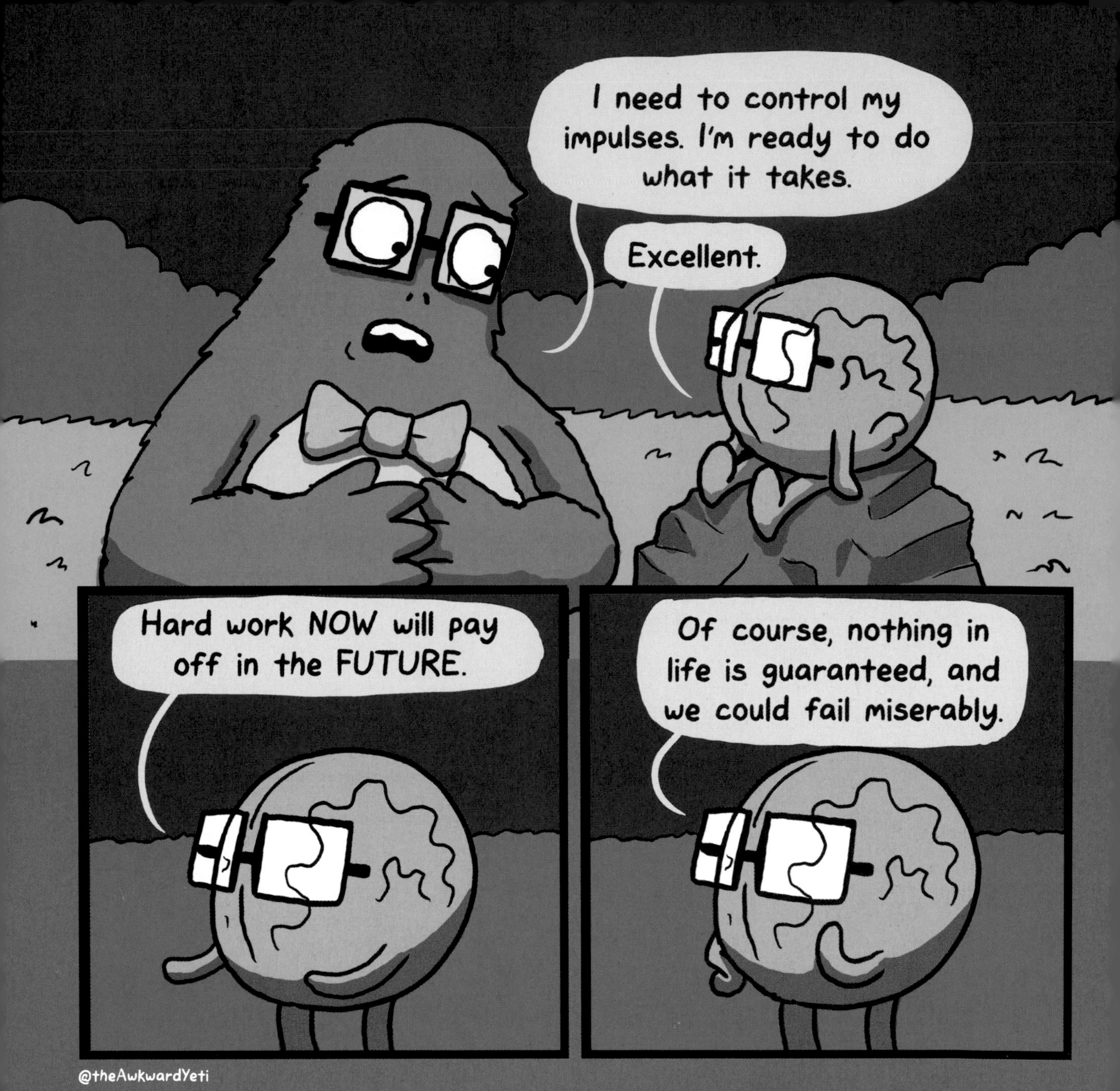
I need to control my impulses. I'm ready to do what it takes.
Excellent.
Hard work NOW will pay off in the FUTURE.
Of course, nothing in life is guaranteed, and we could fail miserably.
@theAwkwardYeti

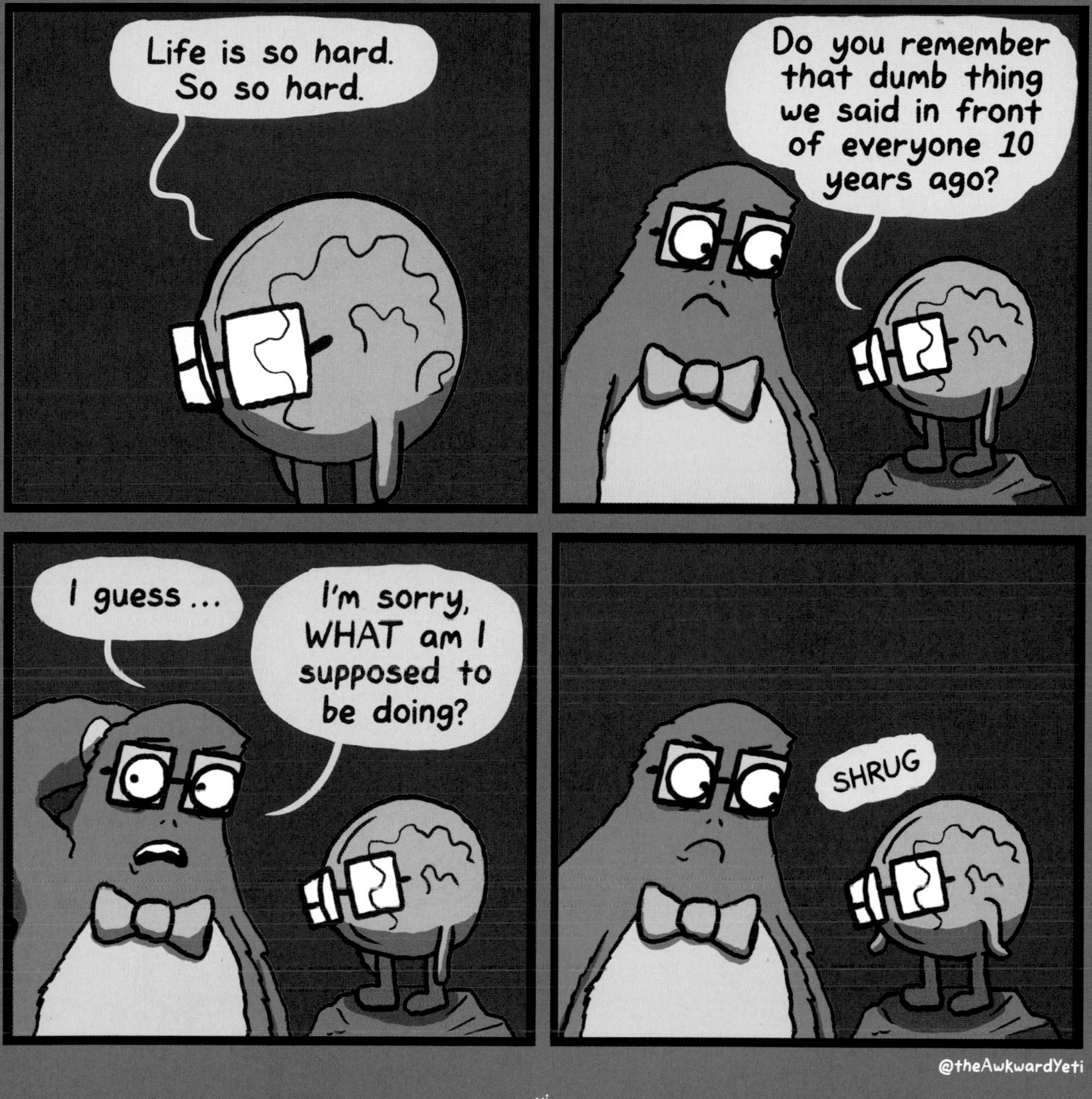

Life is so hard. So so hard.
Do you remember that dumb thing we said in front of everyone 10 years ago?
I guess ...
I'm sorry, WHAT am I supposed to be doing?
SHRUG
@theAwkwardYeti

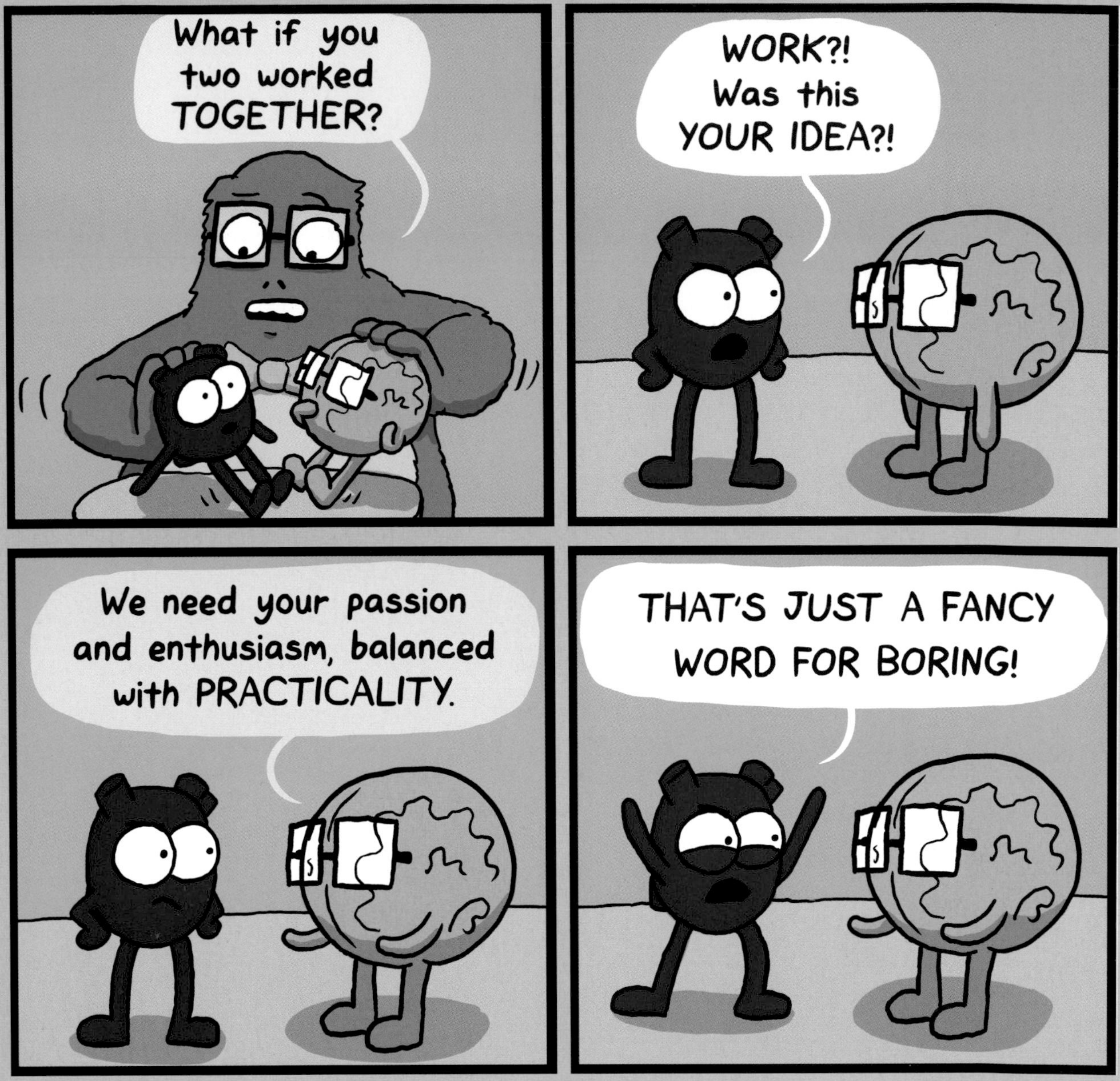
What if you two worked TOGETHER?
WORK?! Was this YOUR IDEA?!
We need your passion and enthusiasm, balanced with PRACTICALITY.
THAT'S JUST A FANCY WORD FOR BORING!

@theAwkwardYeti

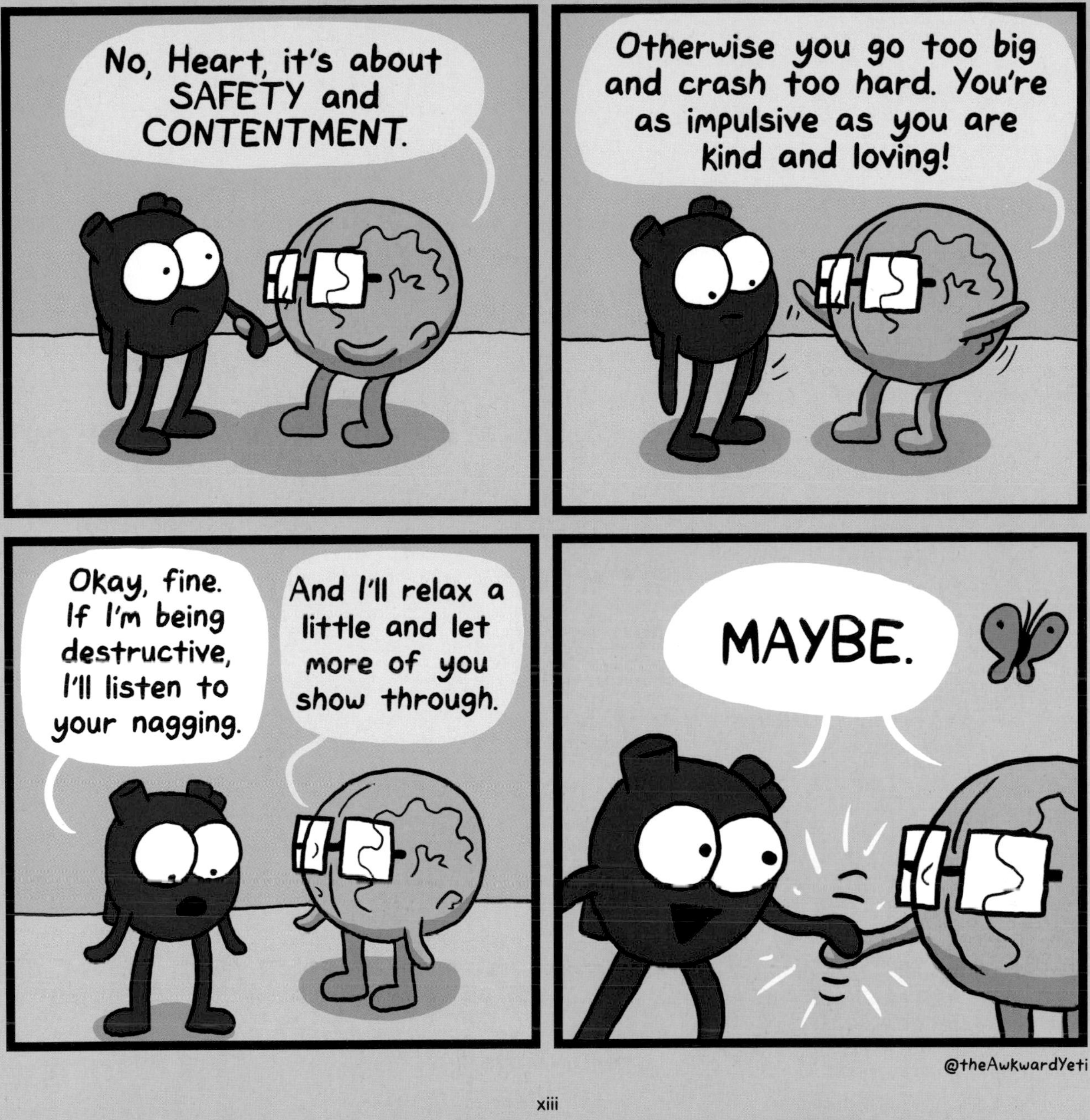
No, Heart, it's about SAFETY and CONTENTMENT.
Otherwise you go too big and crash too hard. You're as impulsive as you are kind and loving!
Okay, fine. If I'm being destructive, I'll listen to your nagging.
And I'll relax a little and let more of you show through.
MAYBE.
@theAwkwardYeti

Dedicated to Calan, Emmett, and Nola

Your imperfect dad loves you just the way you are.

And to all those who helped me along the way and believed in me even when I didn't believe in myself, thank you.

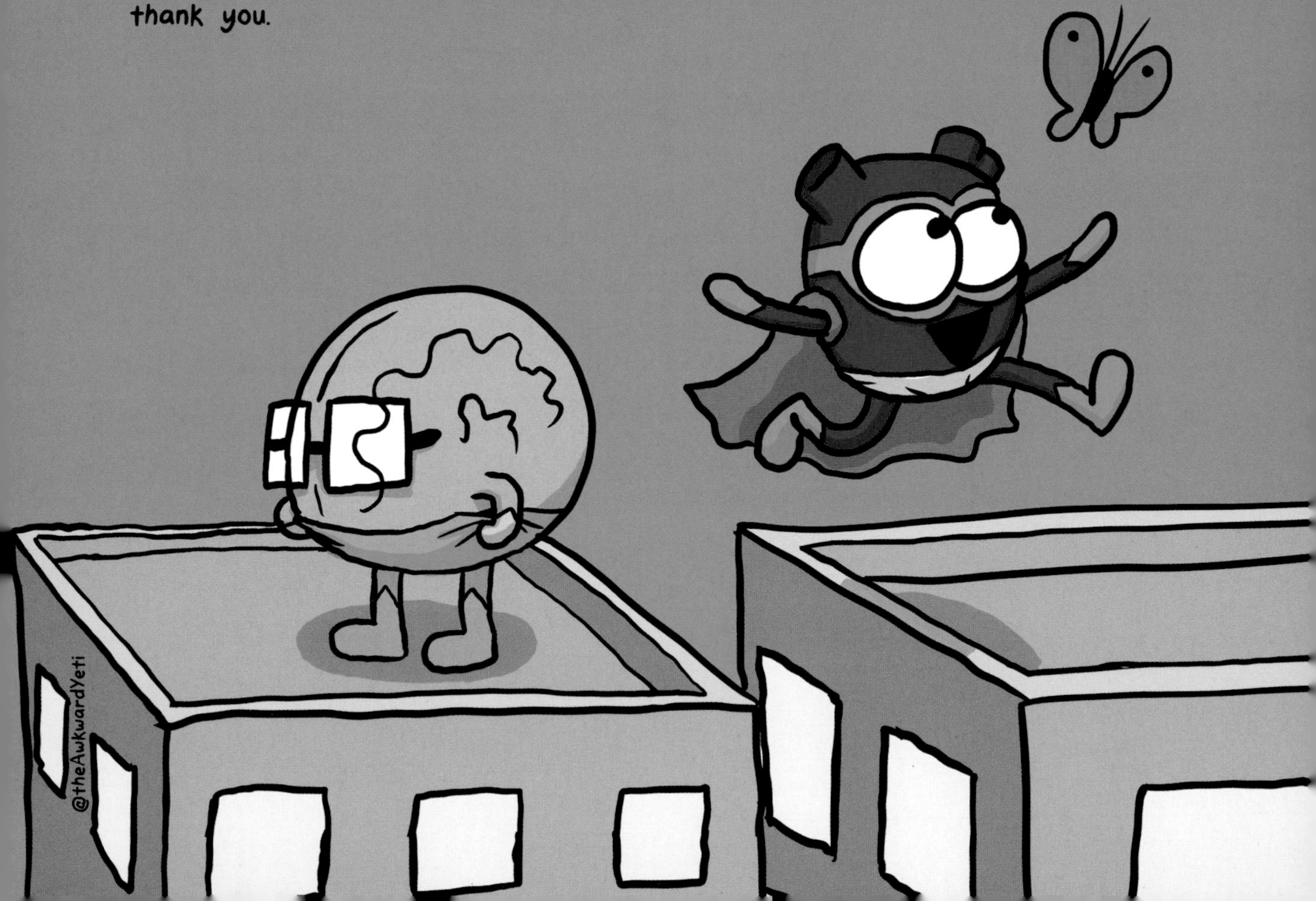

@theAwkwardYeti

PART 1

anxiety machine

"Full of broken thoughts,
I cannot repair"
—Nine Inch Nails

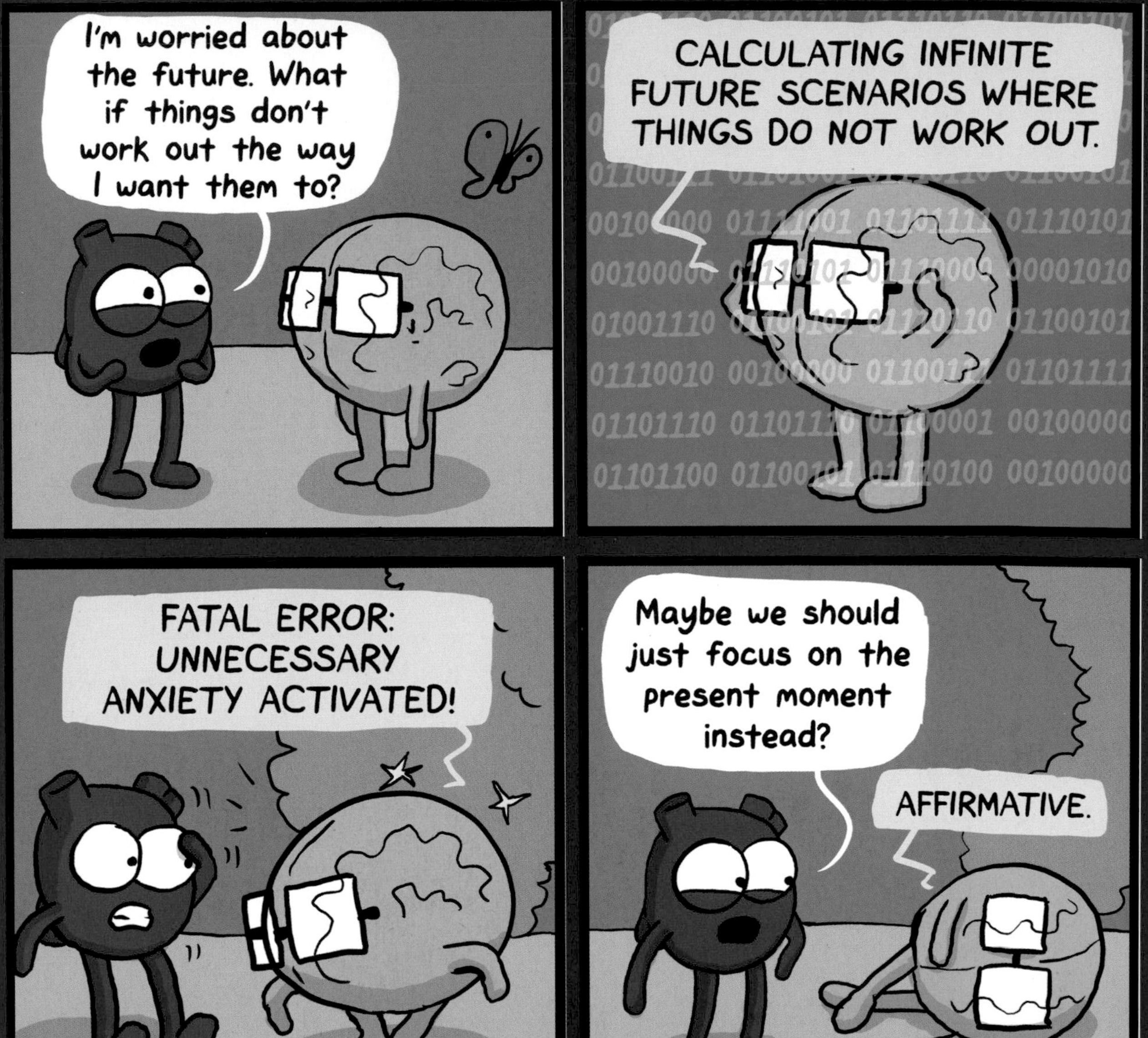
I'm worried about the future. What if things don't work out the way I want them to?
CALCULATING INFINITE FUTURE SCENARIOS WHERE THINGS DO NOT WORK OUT.
FATAL ERROR: UNNECESSARY ANXIETY ACTIVATED!
Maybe we should just focus on the present moment instead?
AFFIRMATIVE.

@theAwkwardYeti

I am a meat machine running on outdated software.

You know what's funny about overthinking? Nothing. Wait, actually everything.

An overthinker like myself can easily talk himself into ruining just about any situation. It's like the opposite of a superpower. I can hardly get through a menu without trying to go to the depth of my soul to find out if my higher self wants the tacos or the burrito. Same ingredients, but at what angle am I willing to hold my head as I eat?

Overthinking causes great anxiety as my brain gets obsessed with resolving a problem that hasn't even come into existence yet, or even better, I might be trying to resolve something that already resolved itself years ago. It doesn't work that way, brain! And yet, that wrinkled mess tries.

Deep down, there is something really wonderful and genuine inside of me, and I'm stuck in this meat machine that's running on outdated software. Time to upgrade the operating system so I can install some better programs.

If I have learned anything throughout all of this, it's that making fun of myself for my little nuanced shortcomings is fantastic short-term therapy. Acknowledging something I'm not particularly happy with, then putting it right out there in front of a million people isn't exactly easy, but it's kind of liberating. Let's not be so hard on ourselves, okay?

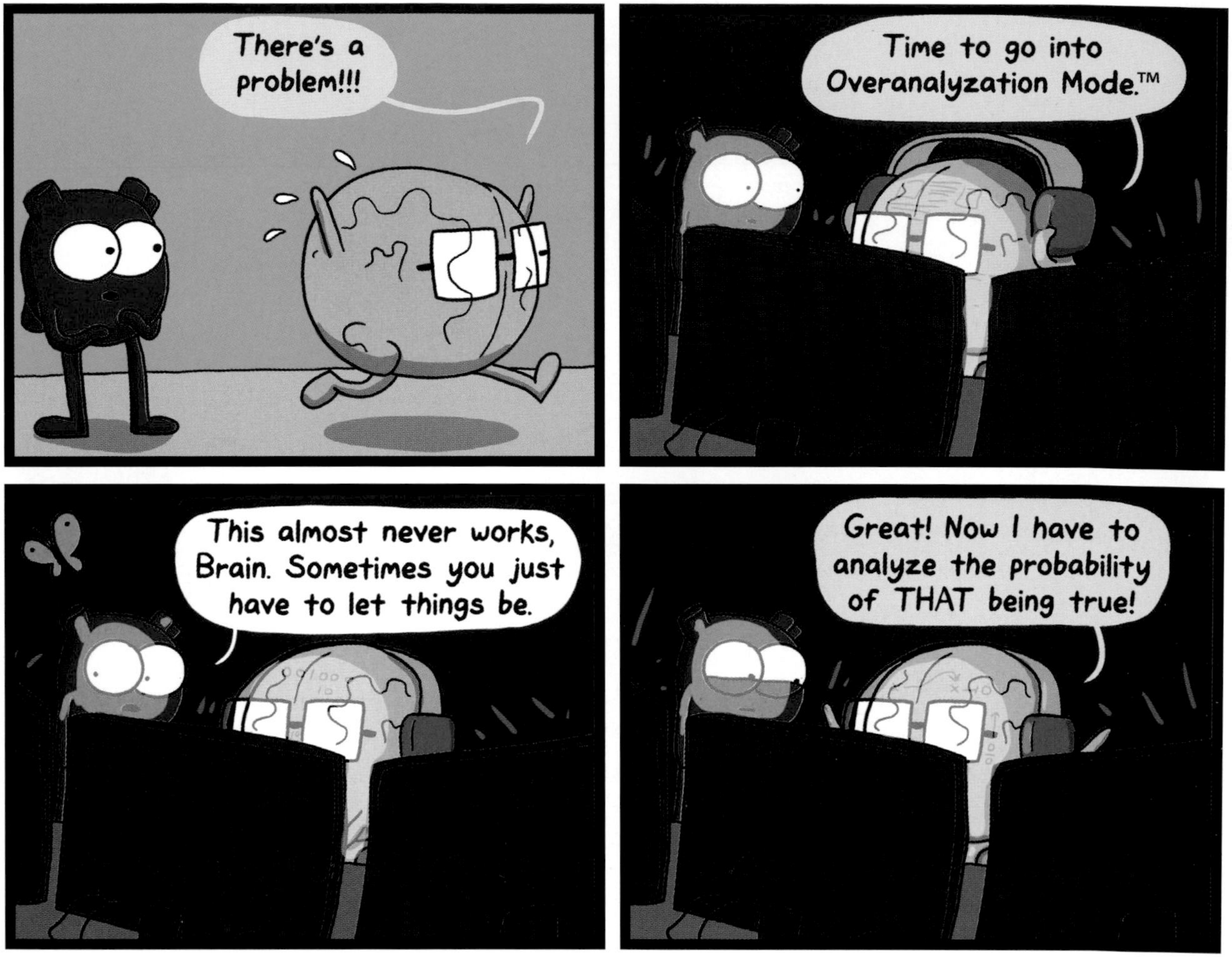
There's a problem!!!
Time to go into Overanalyzation Mode.™
This almost never works, Brain. Sometimes you just have to let things be.
Great! Now I have to analyze the probability of THAT being true!

@theAwkwardYeti

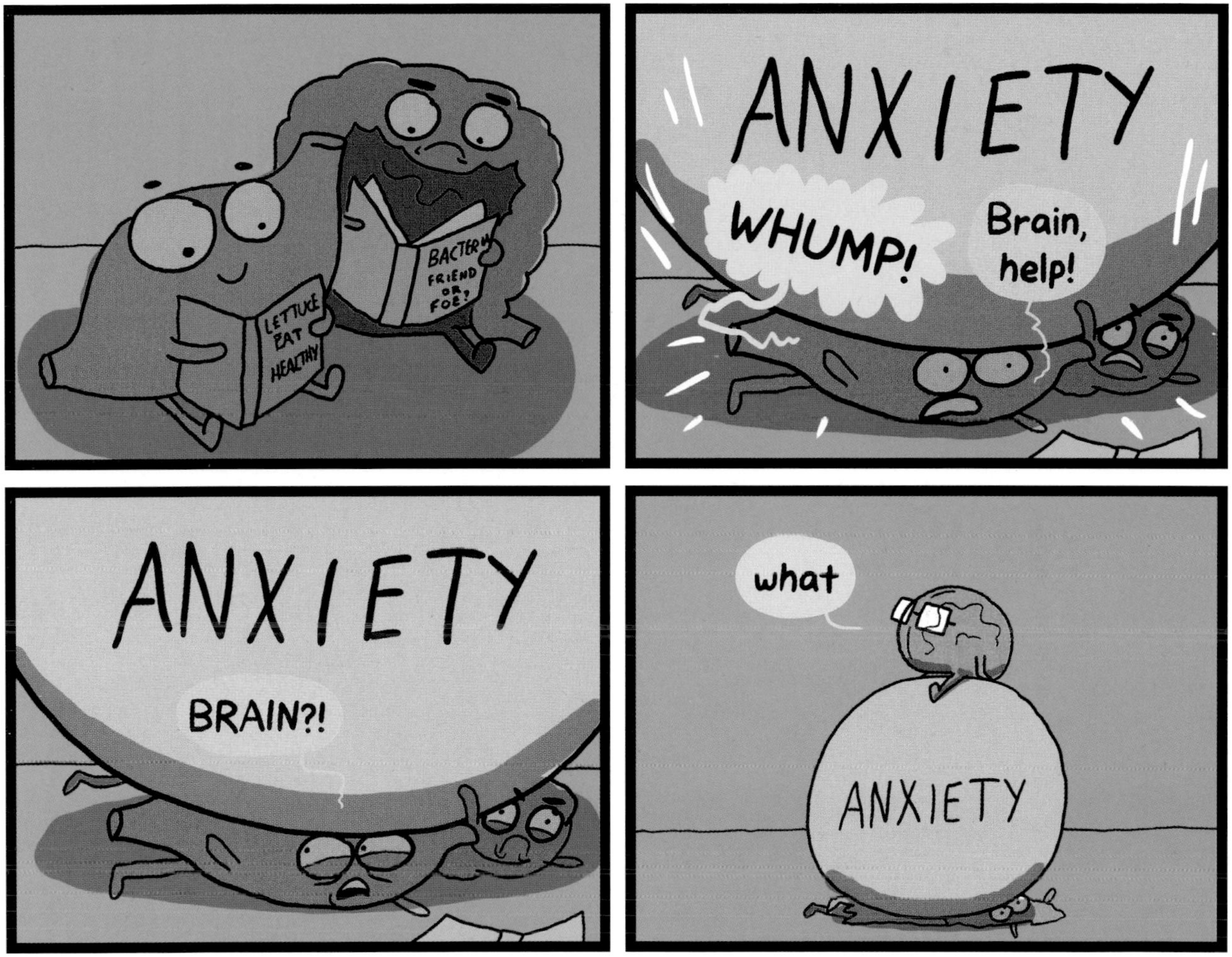
LETTUCE EAT HEALTHY
BACTER
FRIEND OR FOE?
ANXIETY
WHUMP!
Brain, help!
ANXIETY
BRAIN?!
what
ANXIETY

@theAwkwardYeti

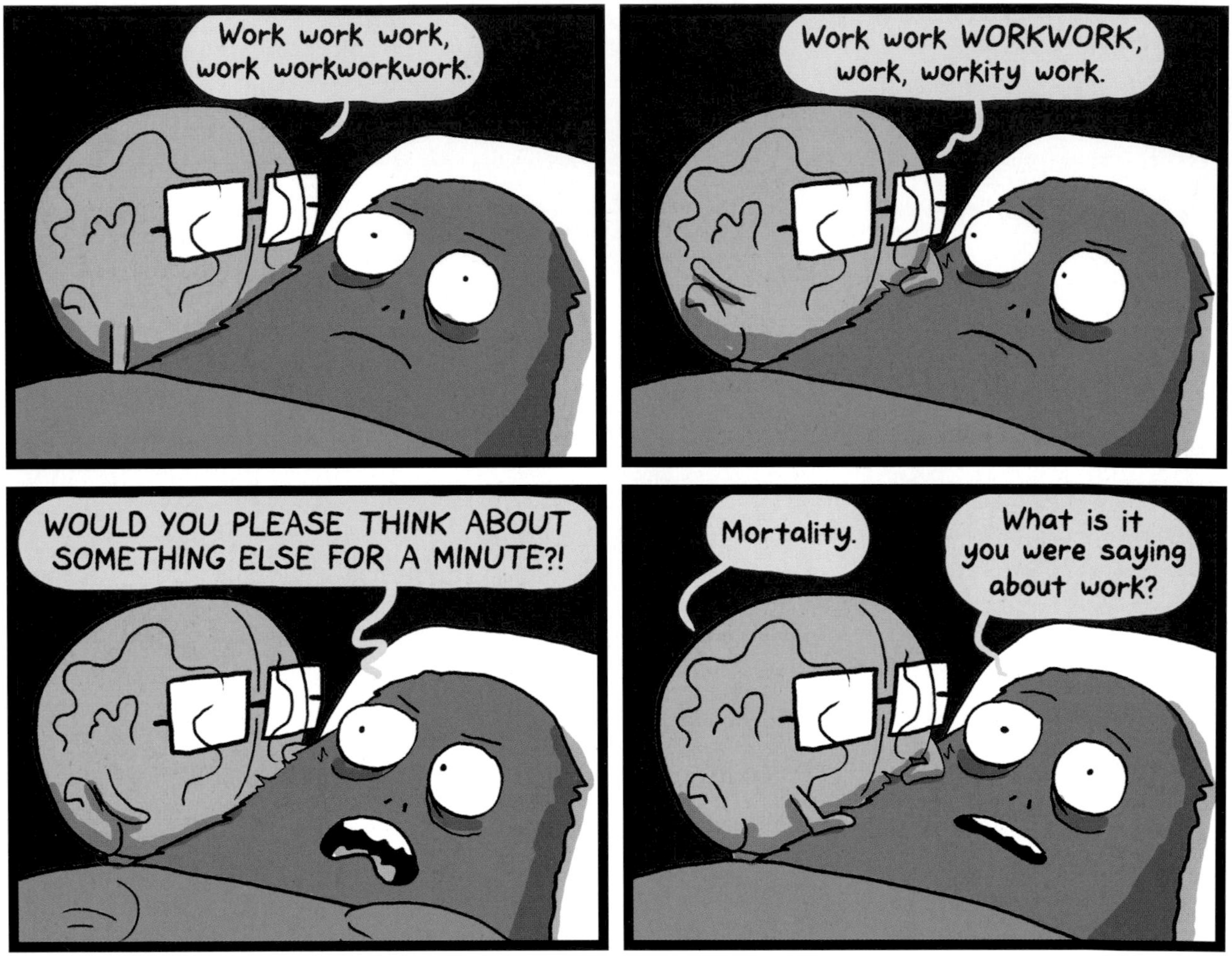
Work work work,
work workworkwork.
Work work WORKWORK,
work, workity work.
WOULD YOU PLEASE THINK ABOUT
SOMETHING ELSE FOR A MINUTE?!
Mortality.
What is it
you were saying
about work?

@theAwkwardYeti

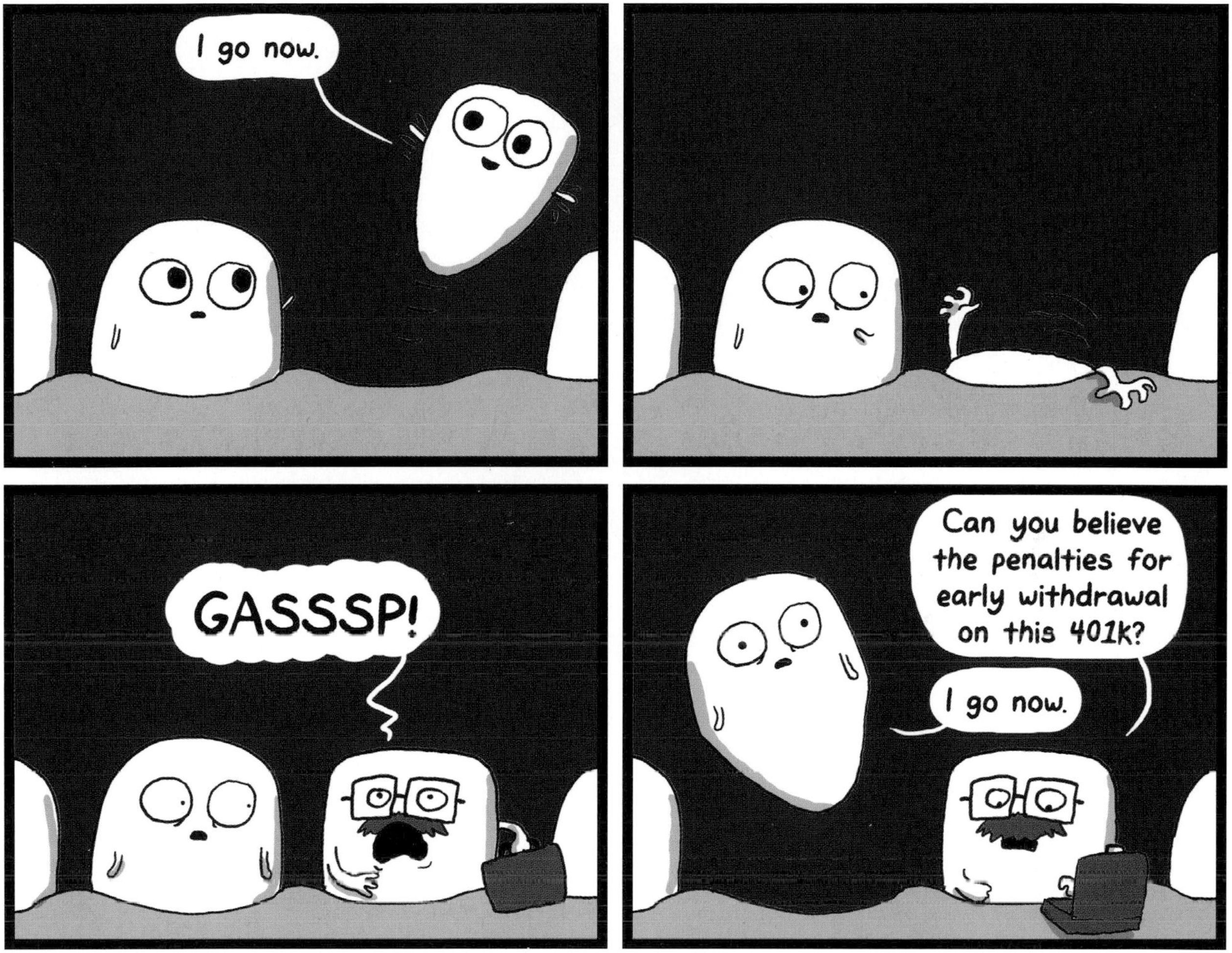
I go now.
GASSSP!
Can you believe the penalties for early withdrawal on this 401k?
I go now.

@theAwkwardYeti

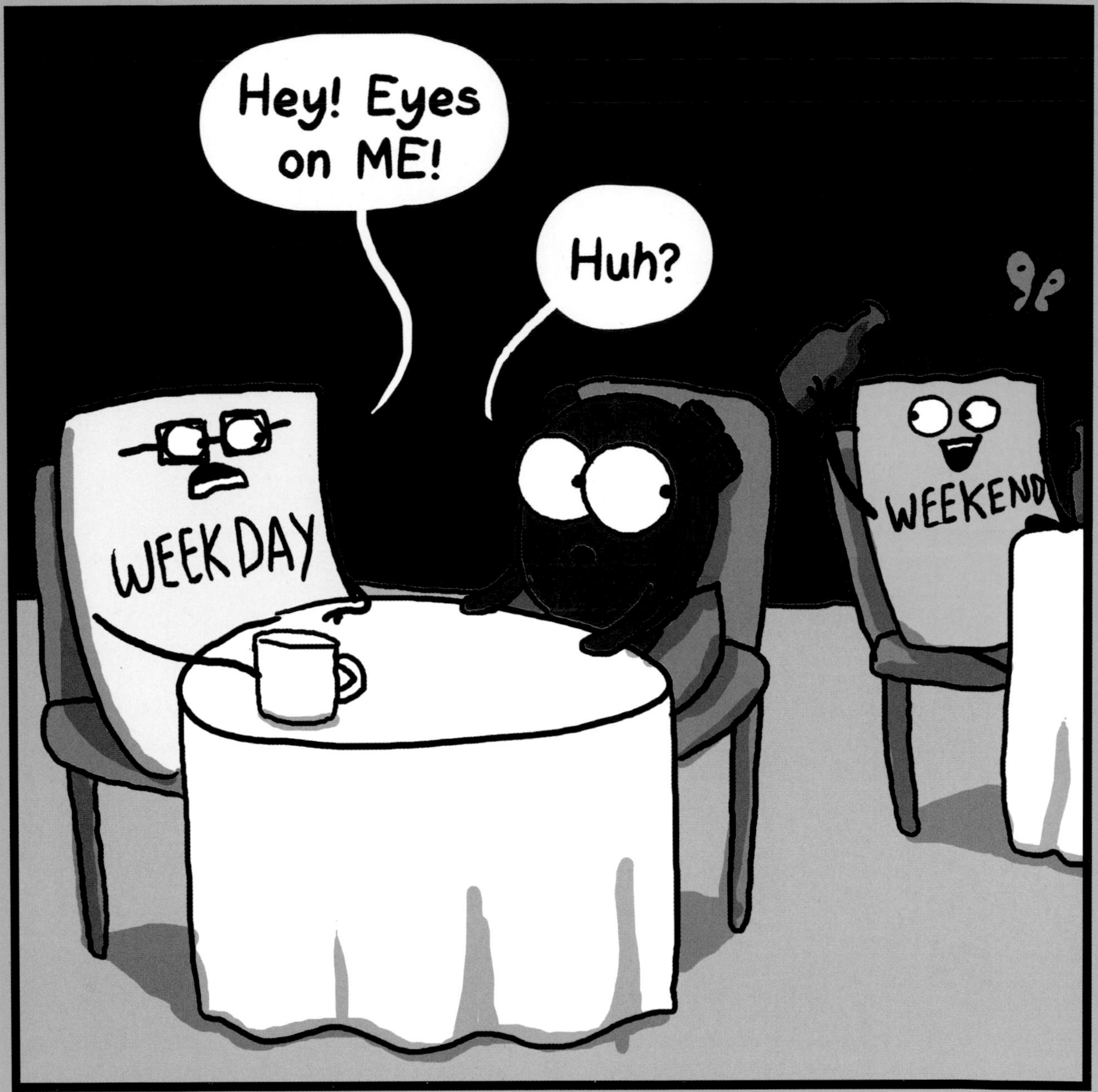
Hey! Eyes on ME!
Huh?
WEEKDAY
WEEKEND

@theAwkwardYeti

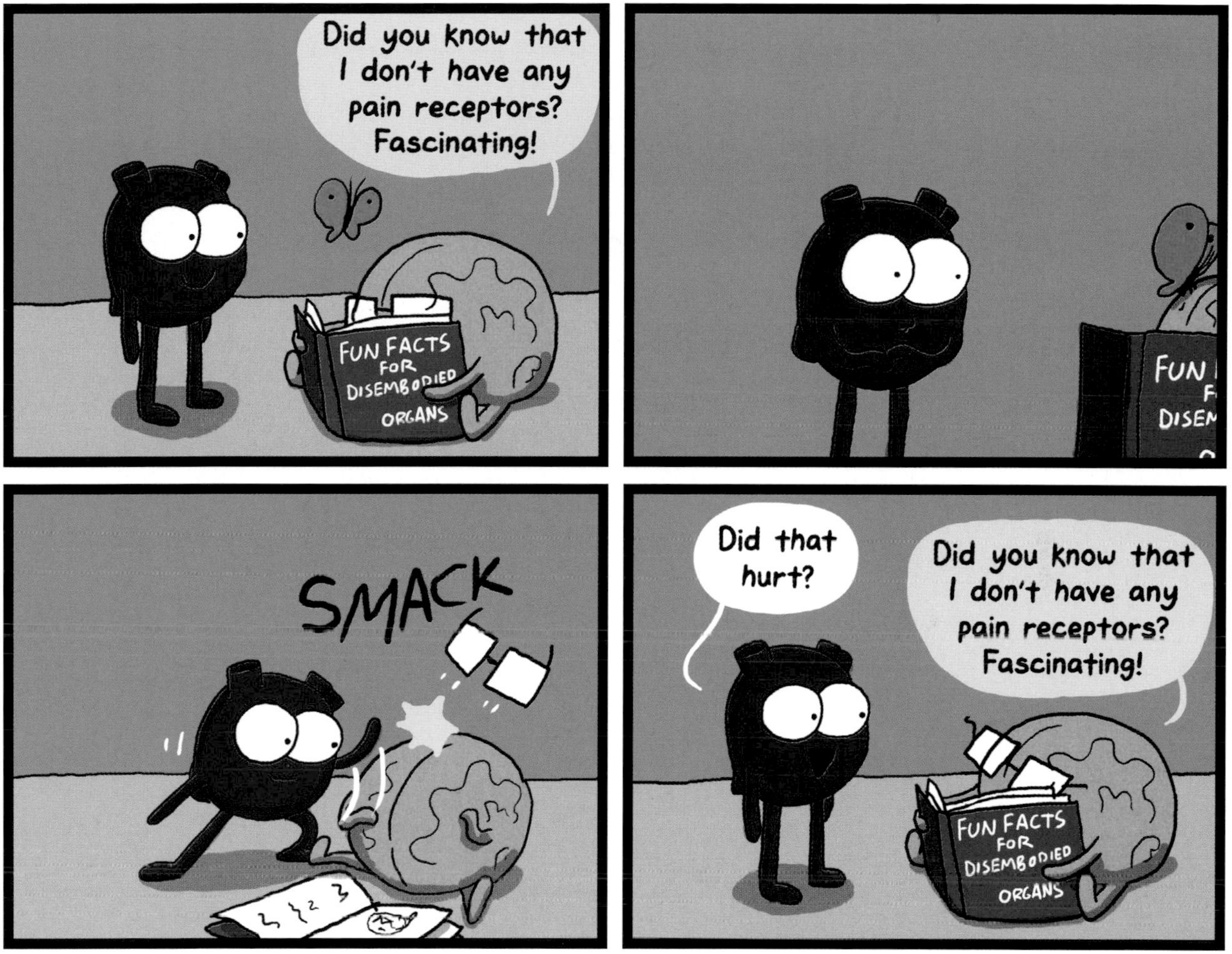
Did you know that I don't have any pain receptors? Fascinating!
FUN FACTS FOR DISEMBODIED ORGANS
FUN
DISEM
SMACK
Did that hurt?
Did you know that I don't have any pain receptors? Fascinating!
FUN FACTS FOR DISEMBODIED ORGANS

@theAwkwardYeti

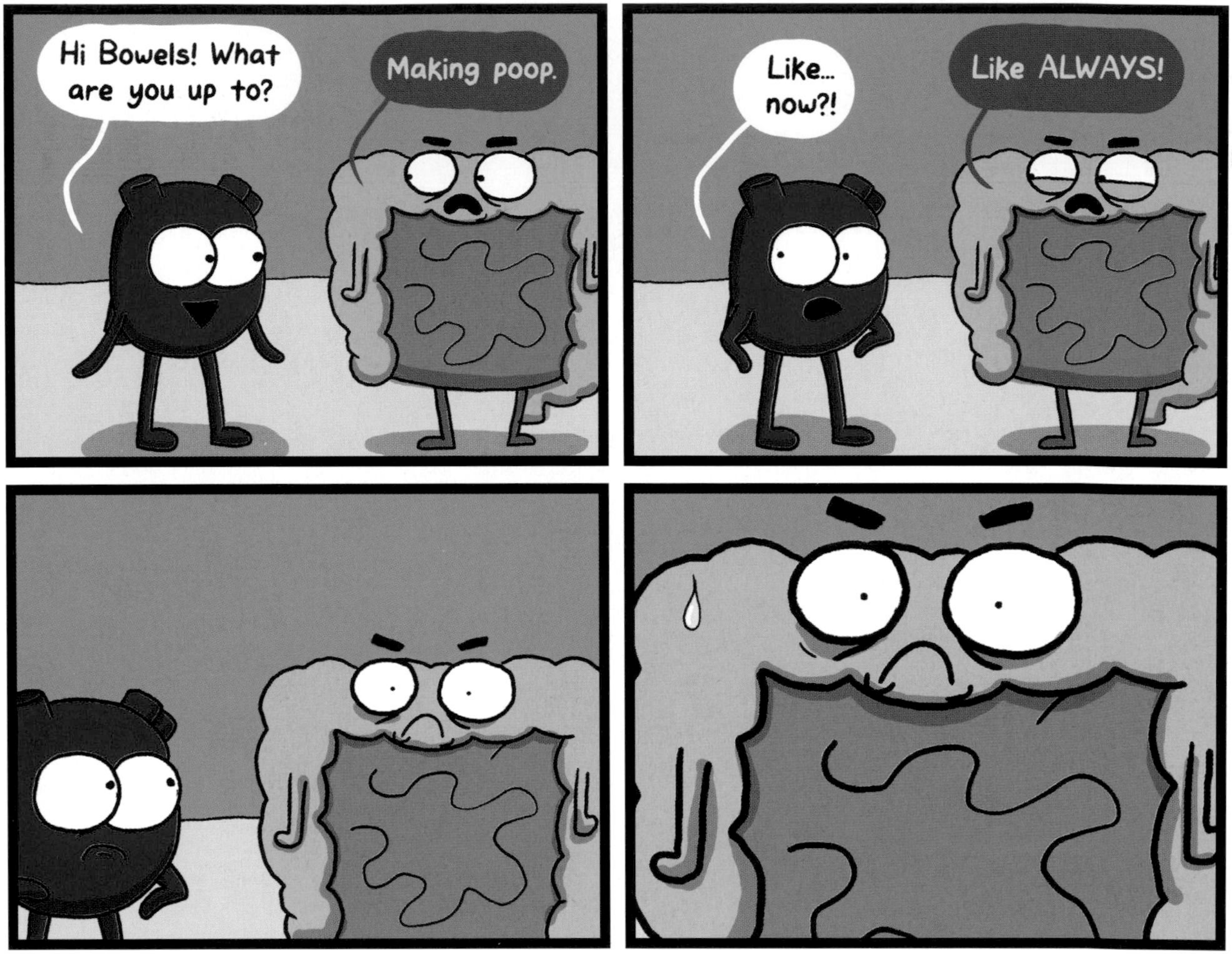
Hi Bowels! What are you up to?
Making poop.
Like... now?!
Like ALWAYS!

@theAwkwardYeti

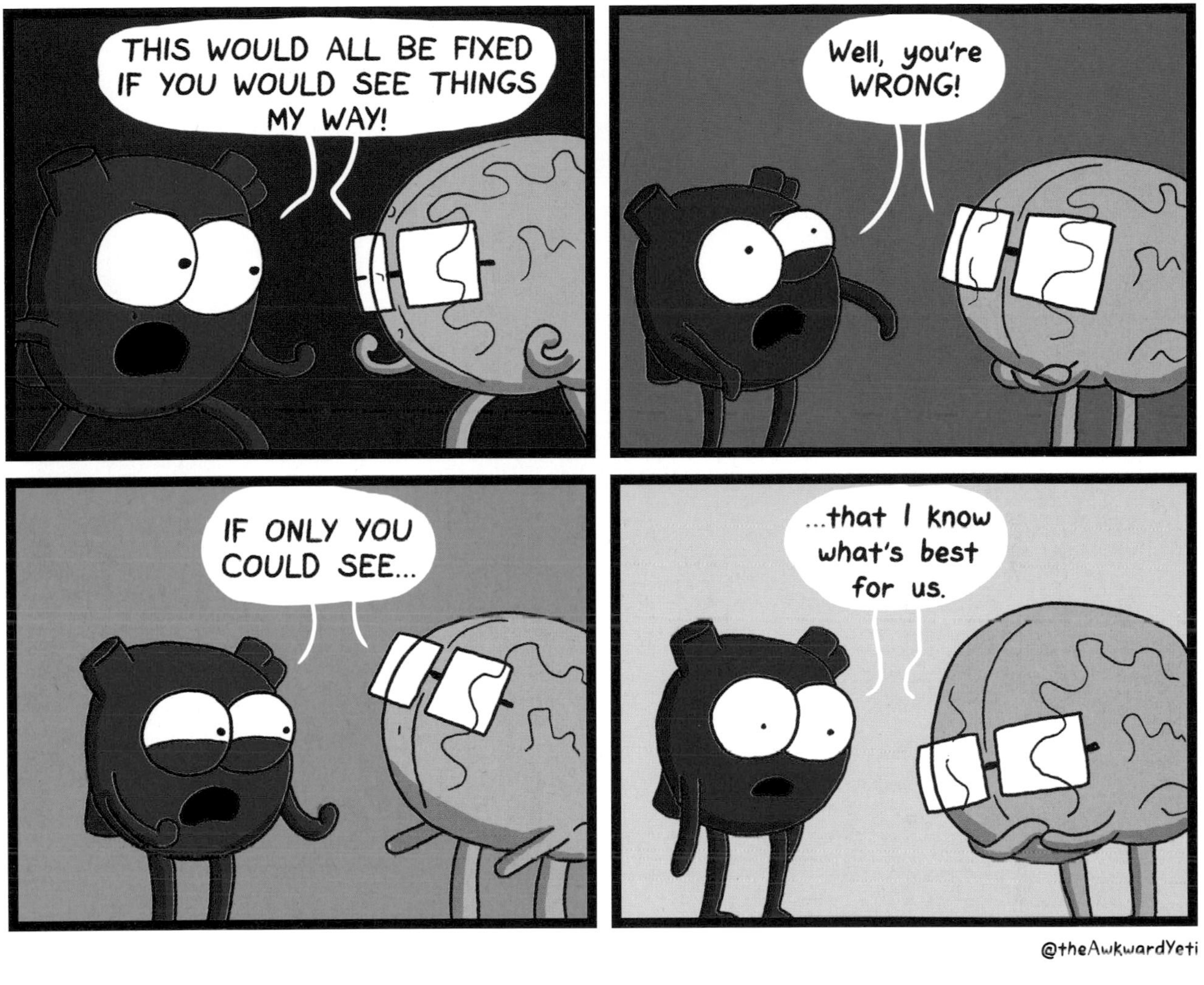
THIS WOULD ALL BE FIXED IF YOU WOULD SEE THINGS MY WAY!
Well, you're WRONG!
IF ONLY YOU COULD SEE...
...that I know what's best for us.
@theAwkwardYeti

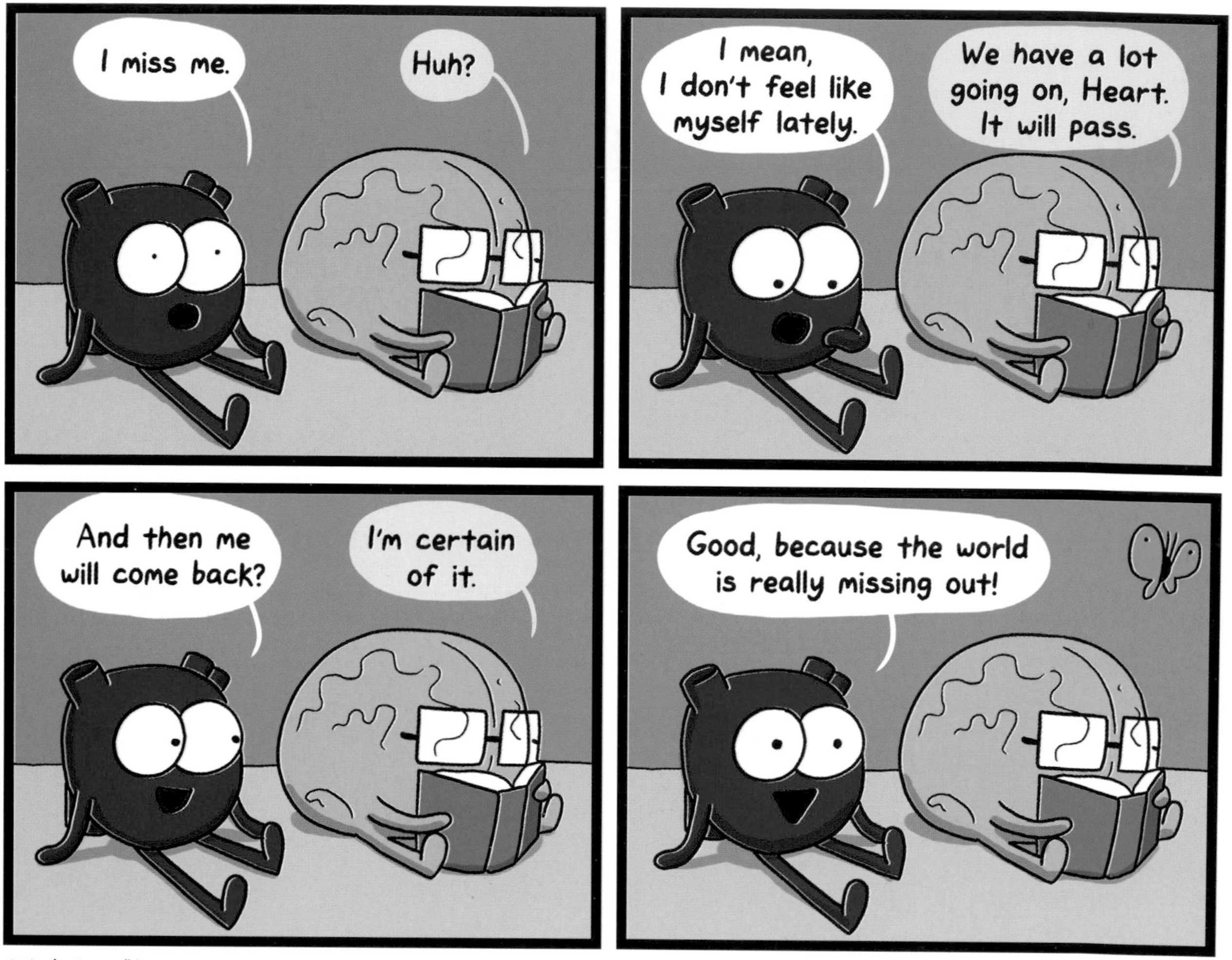
I miss me.
Huh?
I mean, I don't feel like myself lately.
We have a lot going on, Heart. It will pass.
And then me will come back?
I'm certain of it.
Good, because the world is really missing out!

@theAwkwardYeti

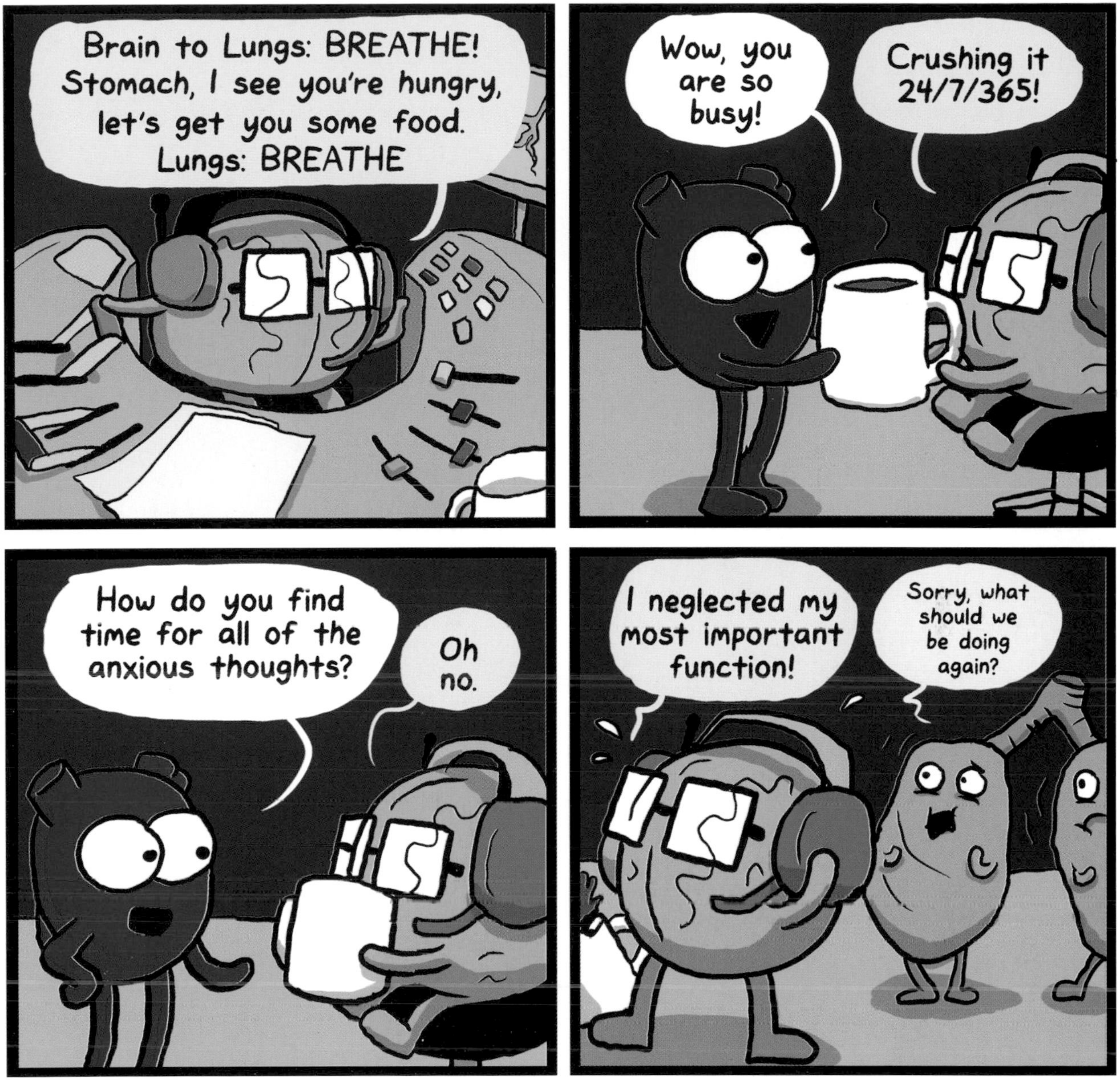
Brain to Lungs: BREATHE! Stomach, I see you're hungry, let's get you some food. Lungs: BREATHE
Wow, you are so busy!
Crushing it 24/7/365!
How do you find time for all of the anxious thoughts?
Oh no.
I neglected my most important function!
Sorry, what should we be doing again?

@theAwkwardYeti

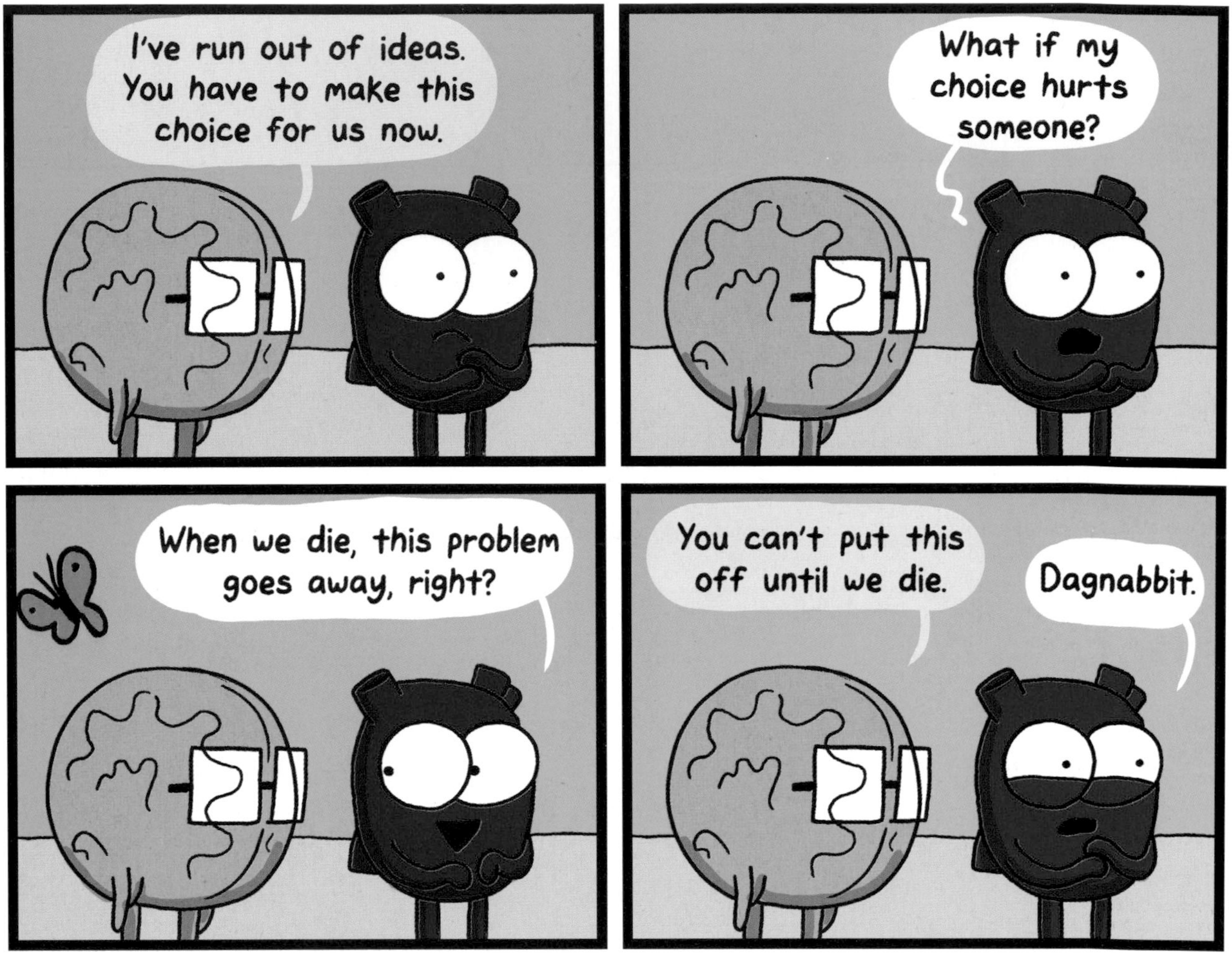
I've run out of ideas. You have to make this choice for us now.
What if my choice hurts someone?
When we die, this problem goes away, right?
You can't put this off until we die.
Dagnabbit.

@theAwkwardYeti

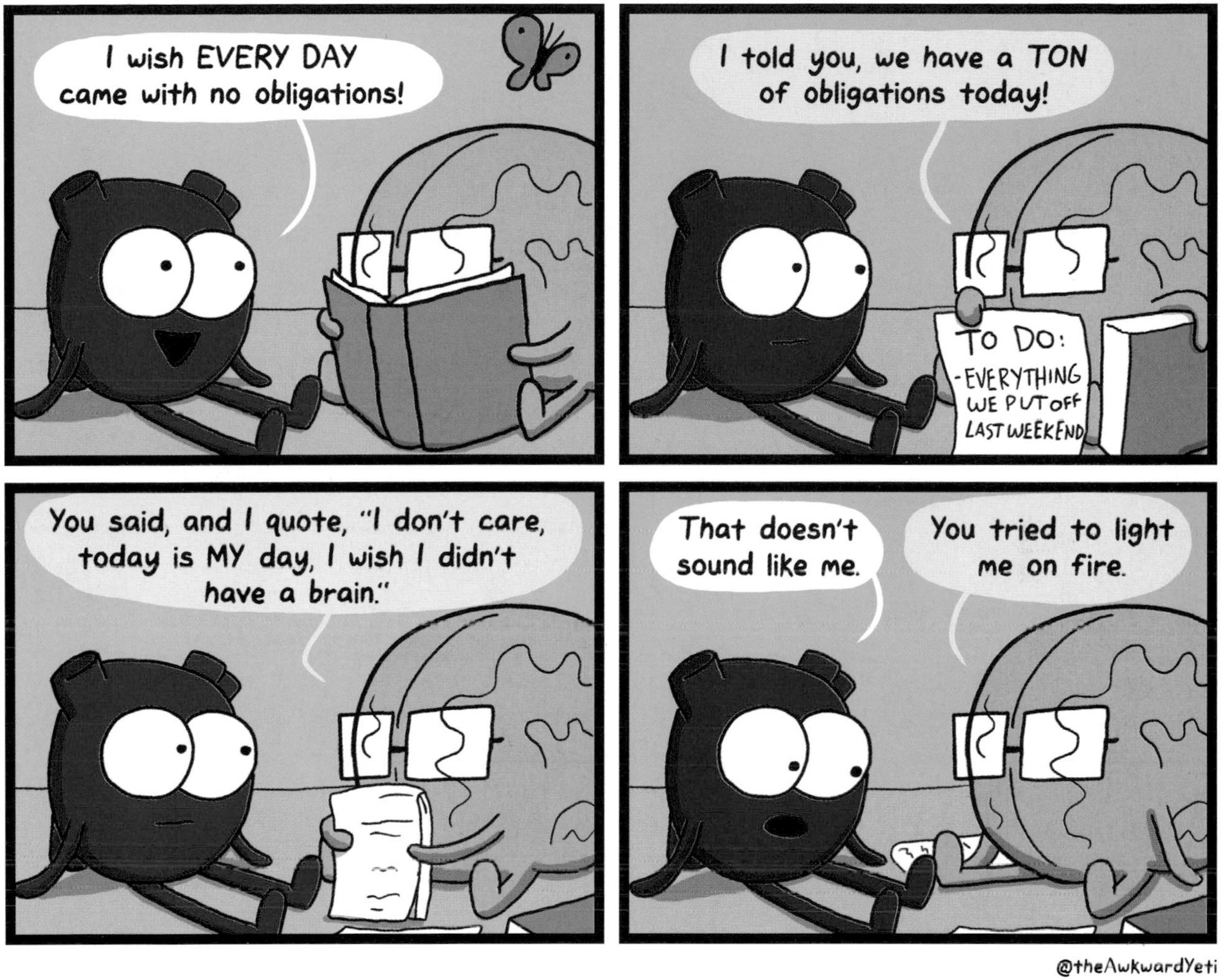
I wish EVERY DAY came with no obligations!
I told you, we have a TON of obligations today!
TO DO: -EVERYTHING WE PUT OFF LAST WEEKEND
You said, and I quote, "I don't care, today is MY day, I wish I didn't have a brain."
That doesn't sound like me.
You tried to light me on fire.
@theAwkwardYeti

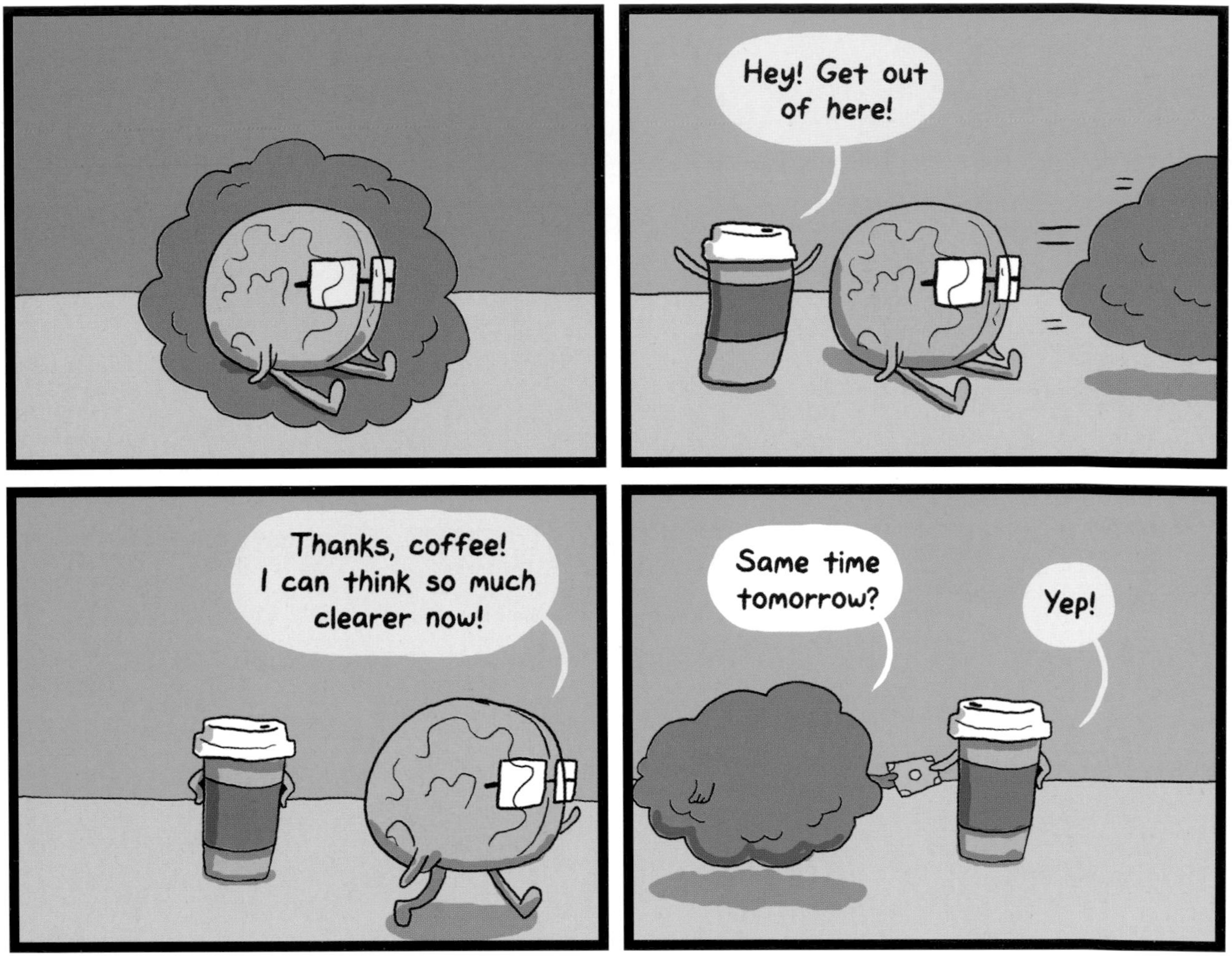
Hey! Get out of here!
Thanks, coffee! I can think so much clearer now!
Same time tomorrow?
Yep!

@theAwkwardYeti

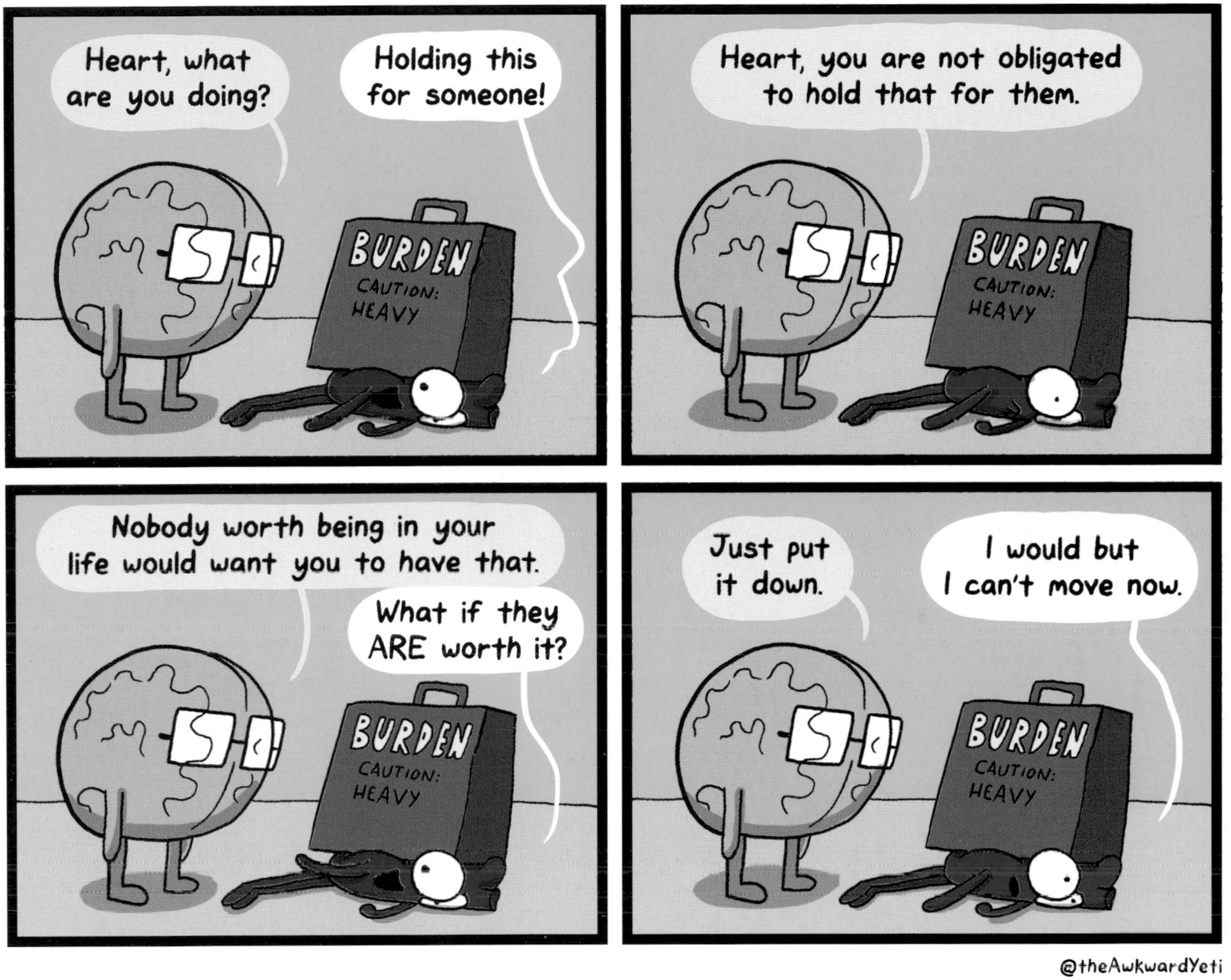
Heart, what are you doing?
Holding this for someone!
BURDEN
CAUTION: HEAVY
Heart, you are not obligated to hold that for them.
BURDEN
CAUTION: HEAVY
Nobody worth being in your life would want you to have that.
What if they ARE worth it?
BURDEN
CAUTION: HEAVY
Just put it down.
I would but I can't move now.
BURDEN
CAUTION: HEAVY
@theAwkwardYeti

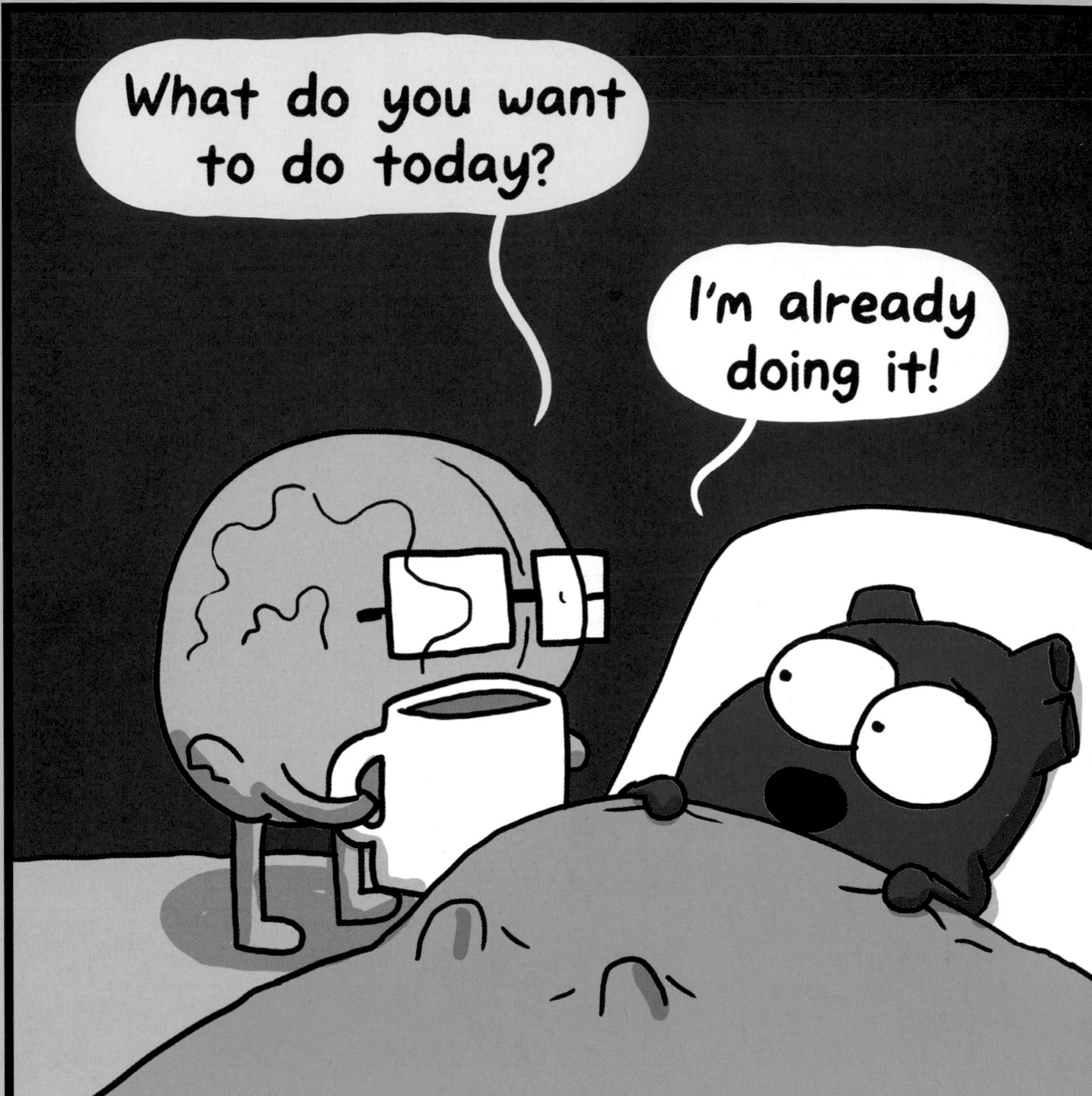

@theAwkwardYeti

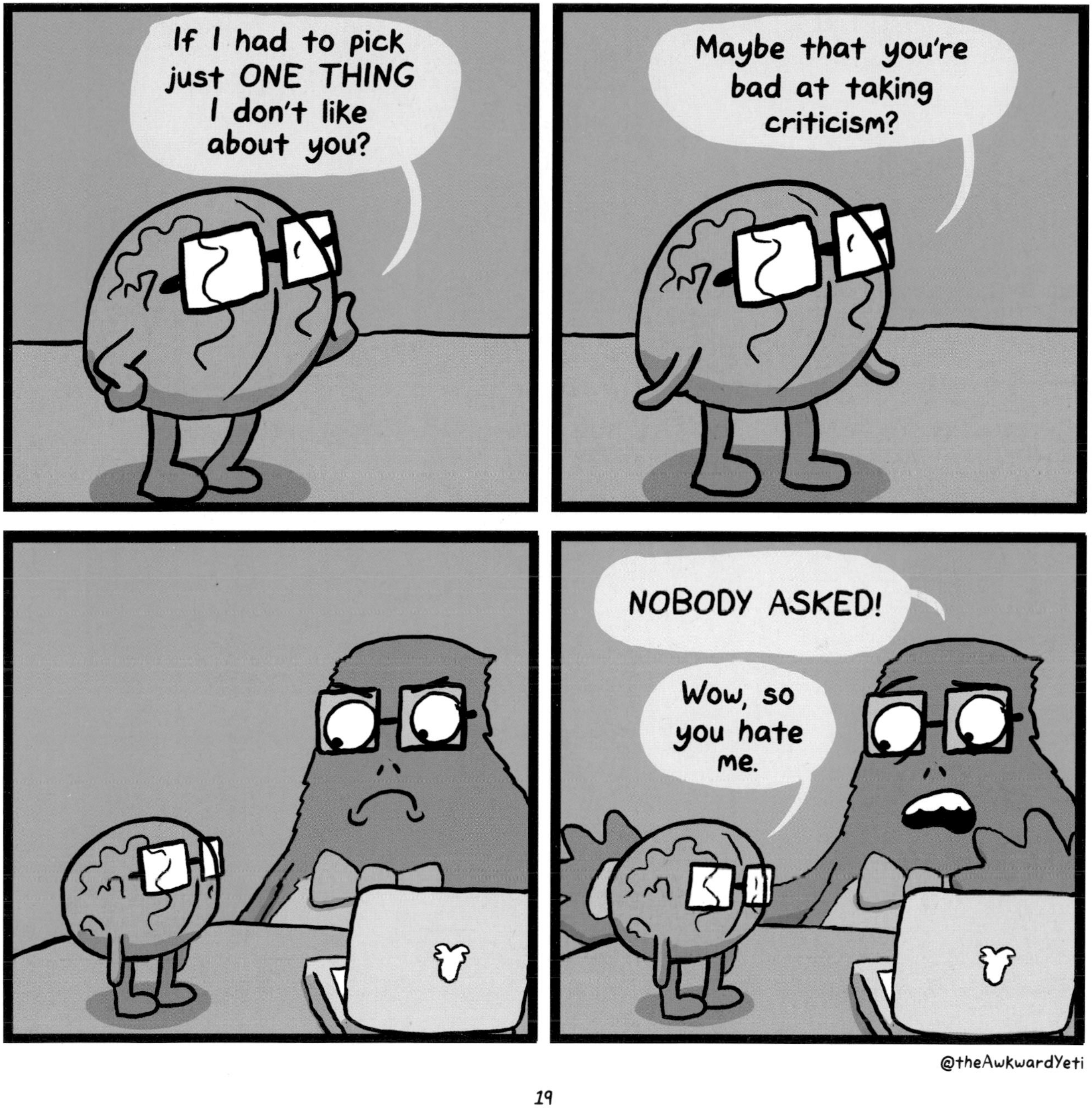
If I had to pick just ONE THING I don't like about you?
Maybe that you're bad at taking criticism?
NOBODY ASKED!
Wow, so you hate me.
@theAwkwardYeti

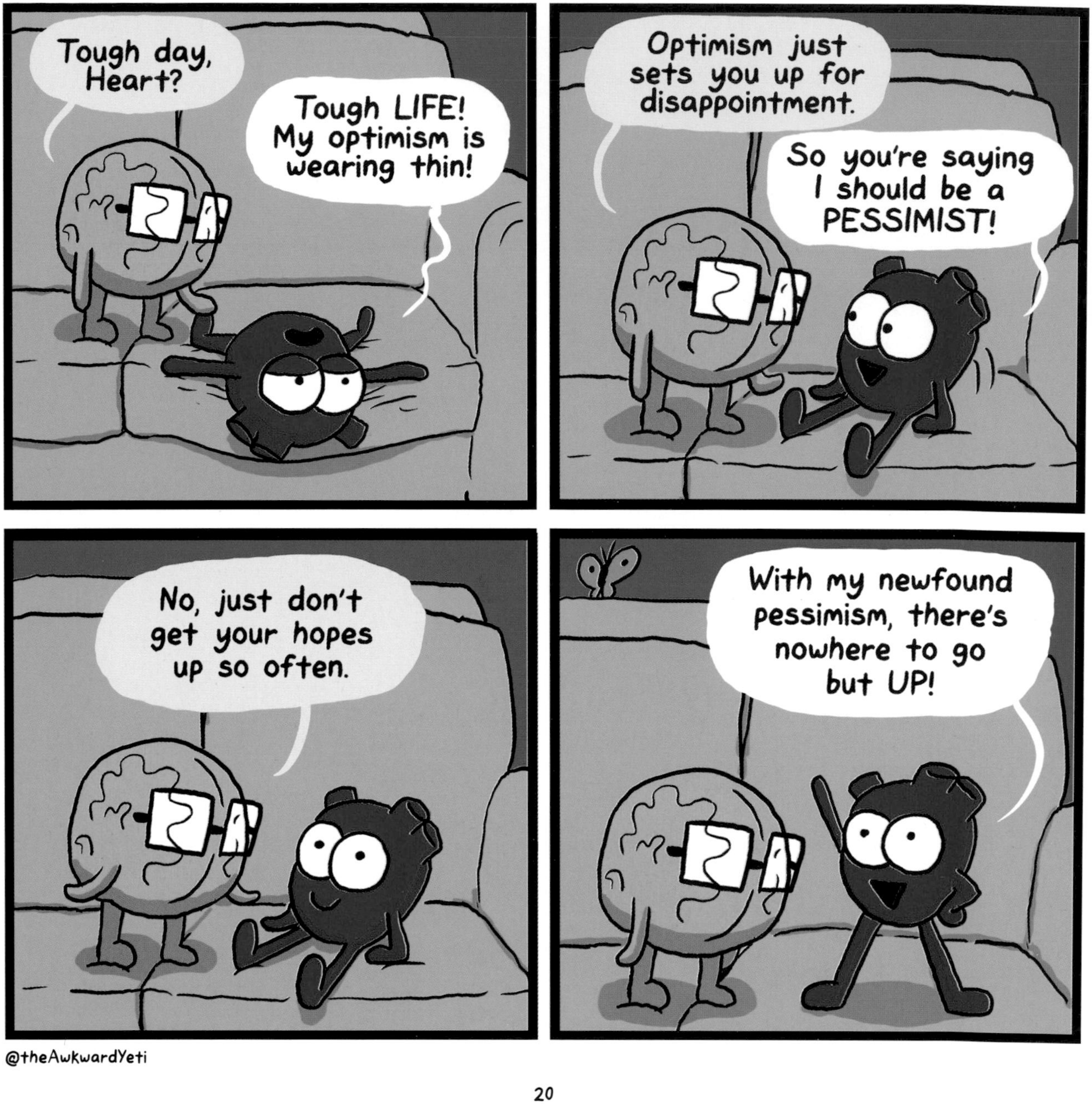
Tough day, Heart?
Tough LIFE! My optimism is wearing thin!
Optimism just sets you up for disappointment.
So you're saying I should be a PESSIMIST!
No, just don't get your hopes up so often.
With my newfound pessimism, there's nowhere to go but UP!

@theAwkwardYeti

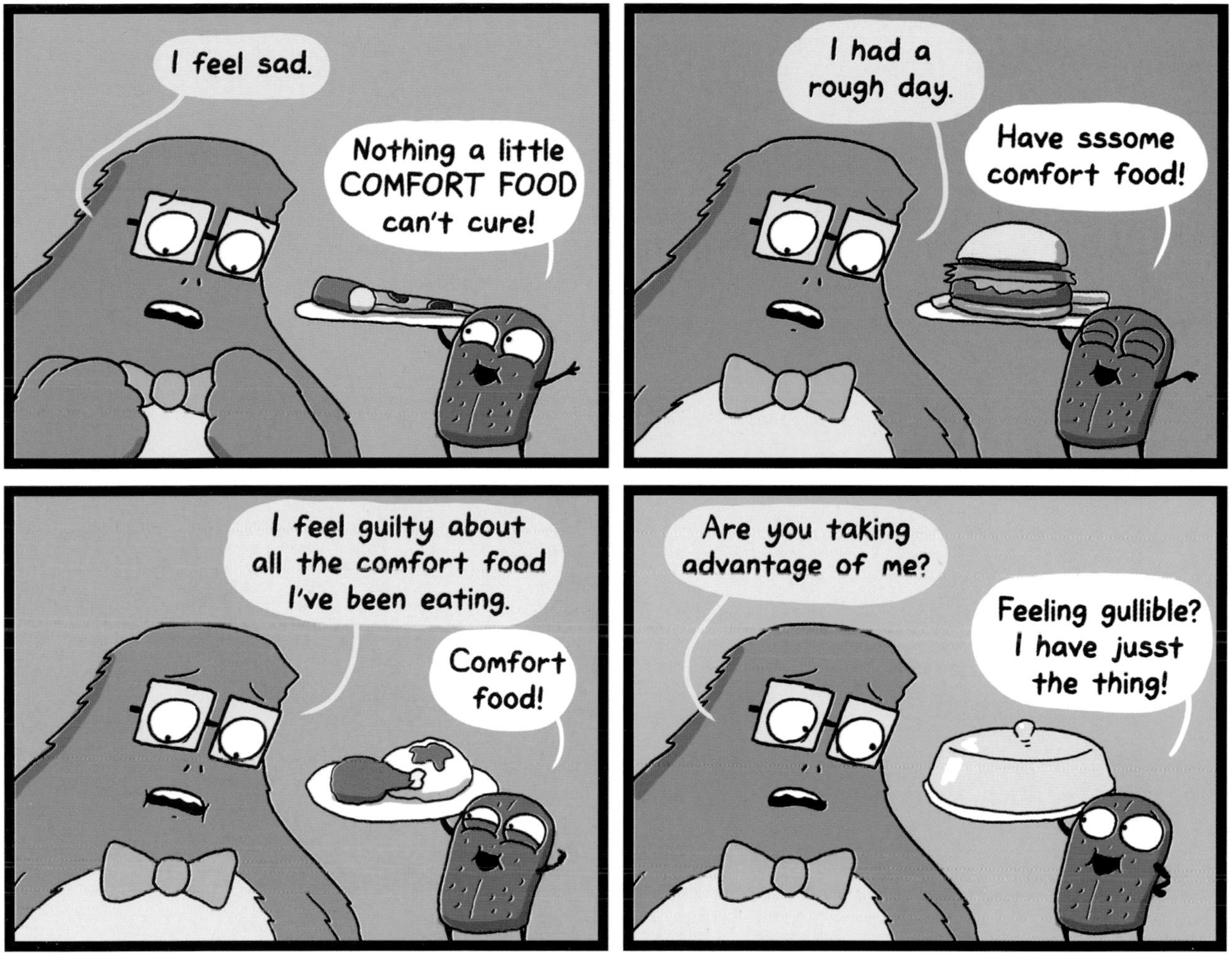
I feel sad.
Nothing a little COMFORT FOOD can't cure!
I had a rough day.
Have sssome comfort food!
I feel guilty about all the comfort food I've been eating.
Comfort food!
Are you taking advantage of me?
Feeling gullible? I have jusst the thing!

@theAwkwardYeti

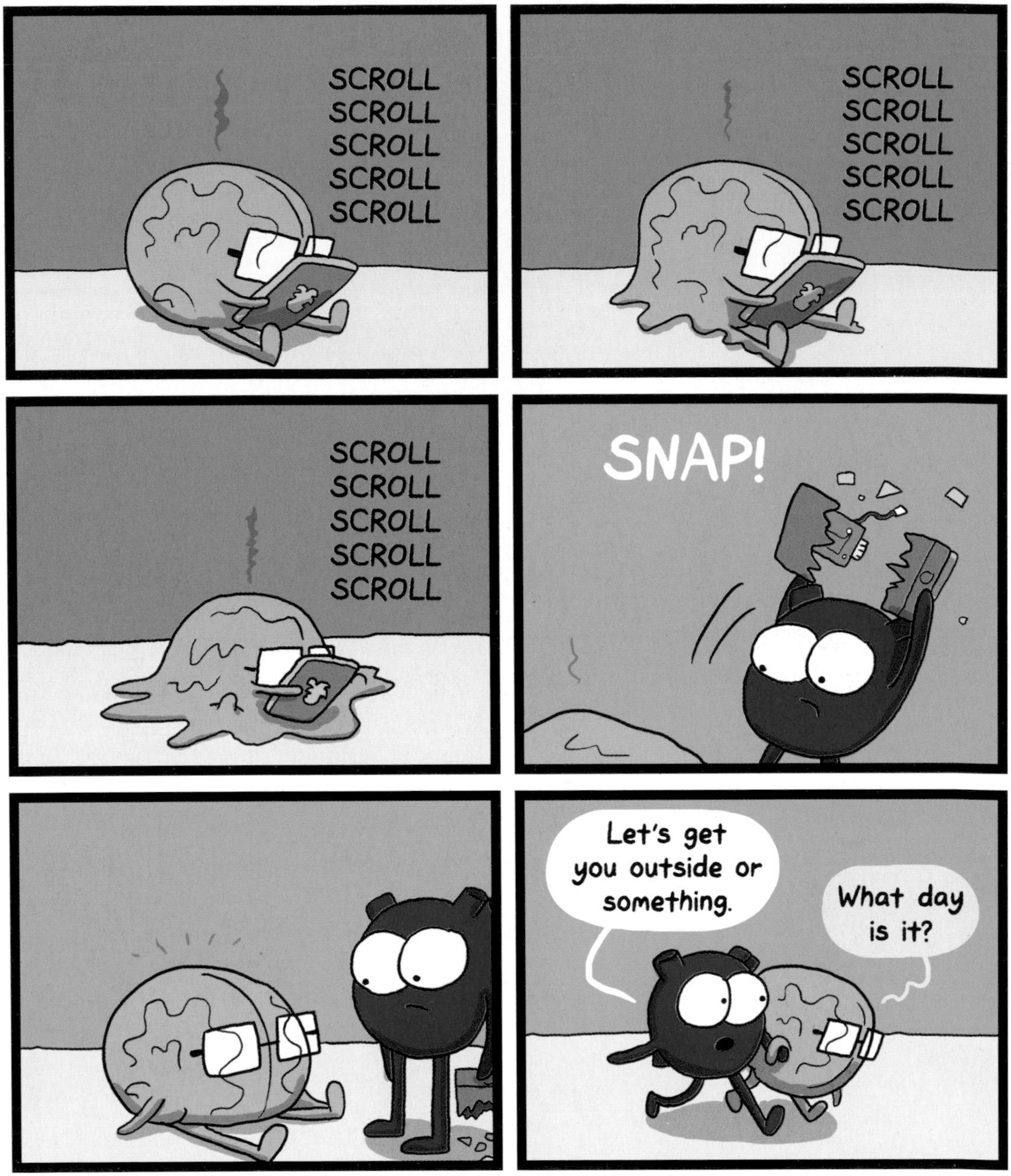
SCROLL
SCROLL
SCROLL
SCROLL
SCROLL
SCROLL
SCROLL
SCROLL
SCROLL
SCROLL
SCROLL
SCROLL
SCROLL
SCROLL
SCROLL
SNAP!
Let's get you outside or something.
What day is it?

@theAwkwardYeti

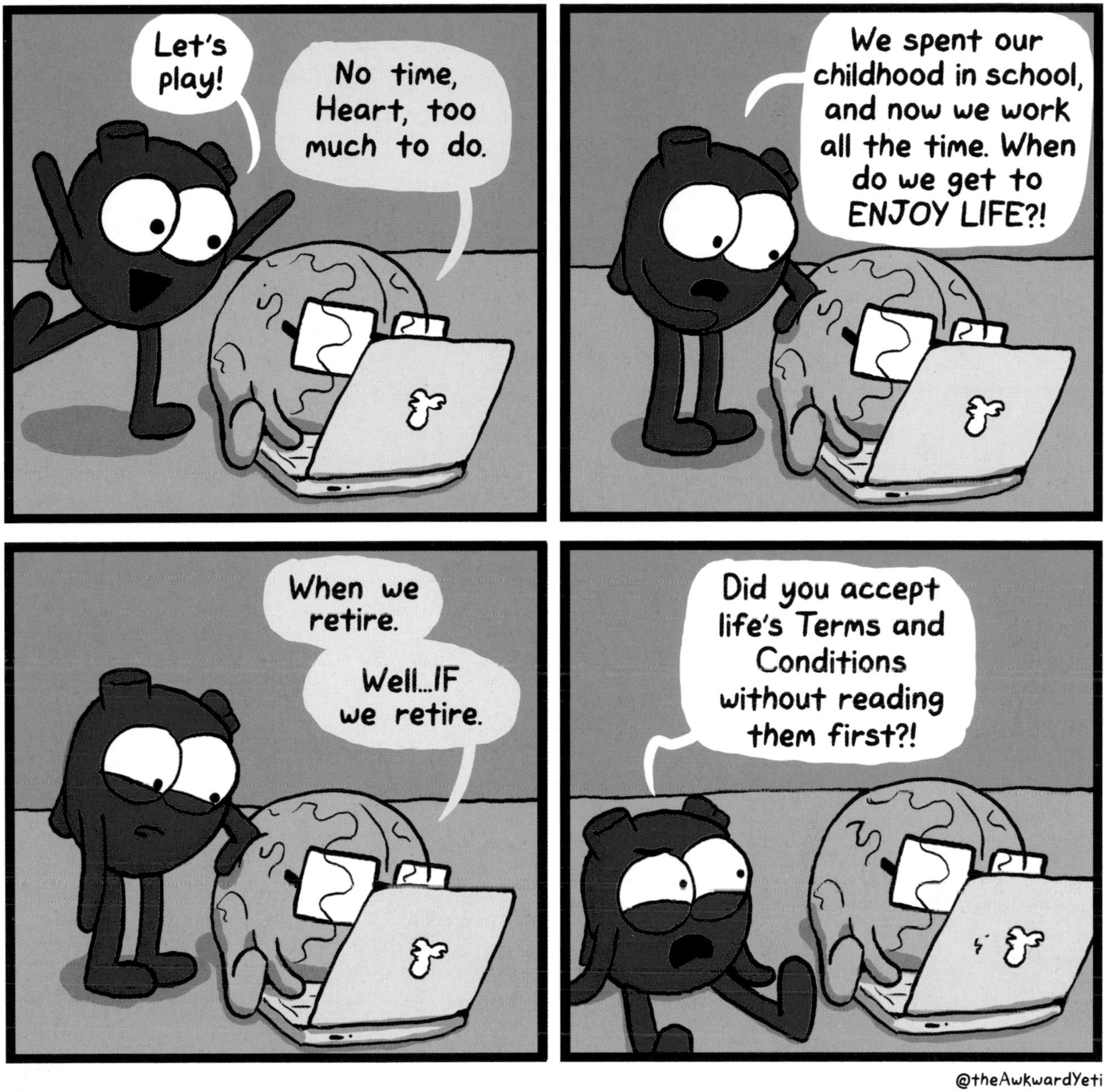
Let's play!
No time, Heart, too much to do.
We spent our childhood in school, and now we work all the time. When do we get to ENJOY LIFE?!
When we retire.
Well...IF we retire.
Did you accept life's Terms and Conditions without reading them first?!

@theAwkwardYeti

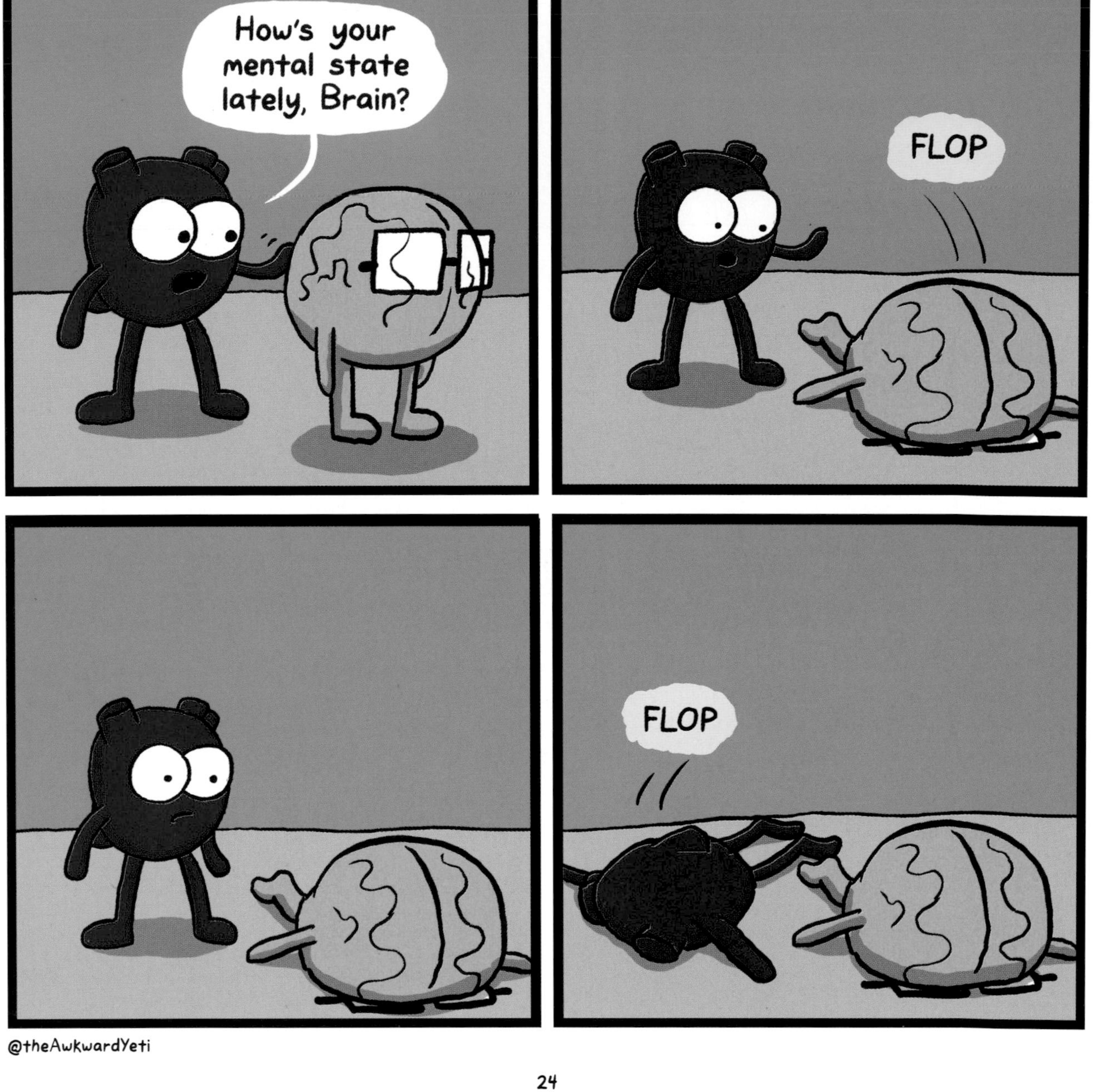
How's your mental state lately, Brain?
FLOP
FLOP
@theAwkwardYeti

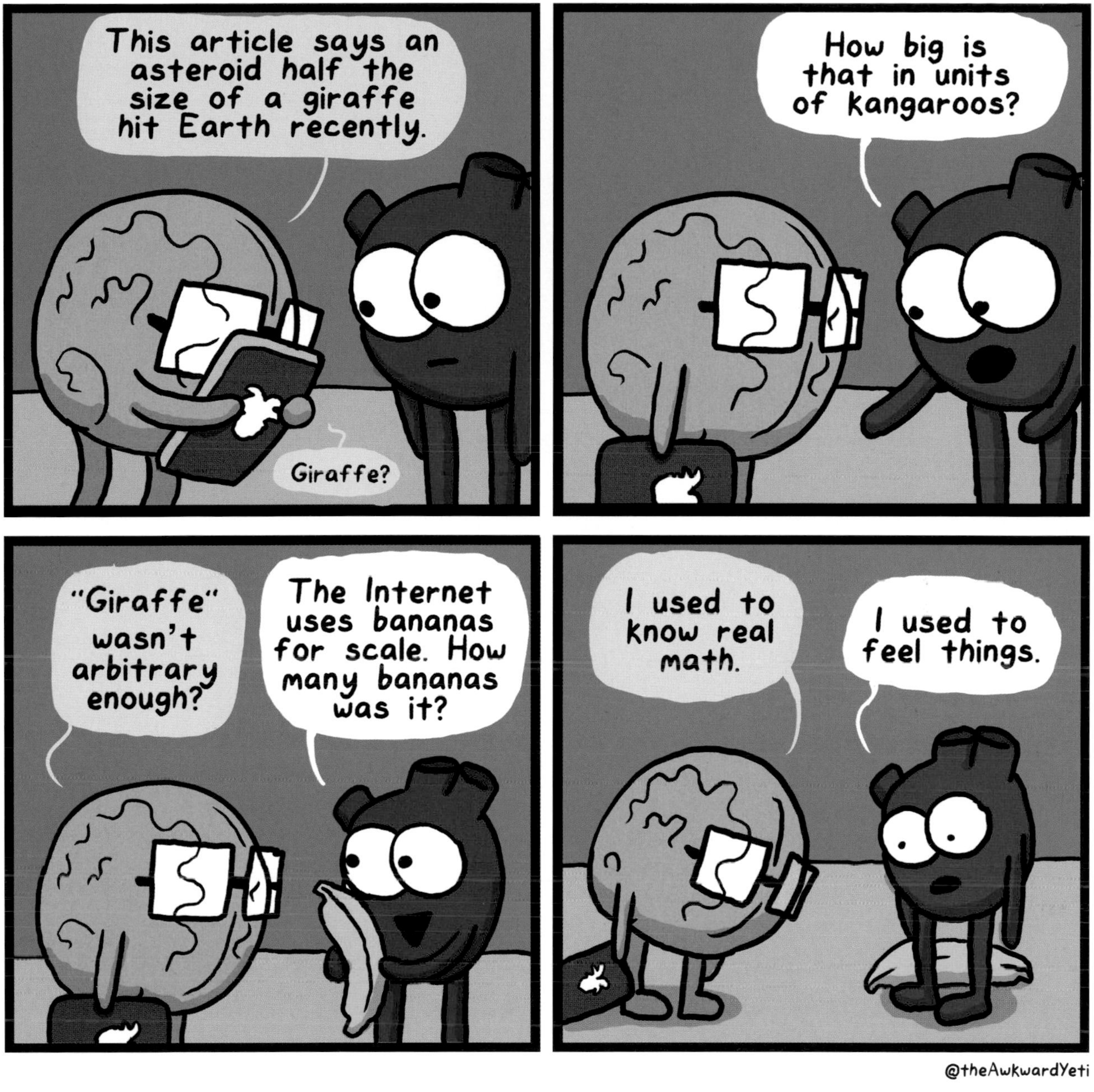
This article says an asteroid half the size of a giraffe hit Earth recently.
Giraffe?
How big is that in units of kangaroos?
"Giraffe" wasn't arbitrary enough?
The Internet uses bananas for scale. How many bananas was it?
I used to know real math.
I used to feel things.
@theAwkwardYeti

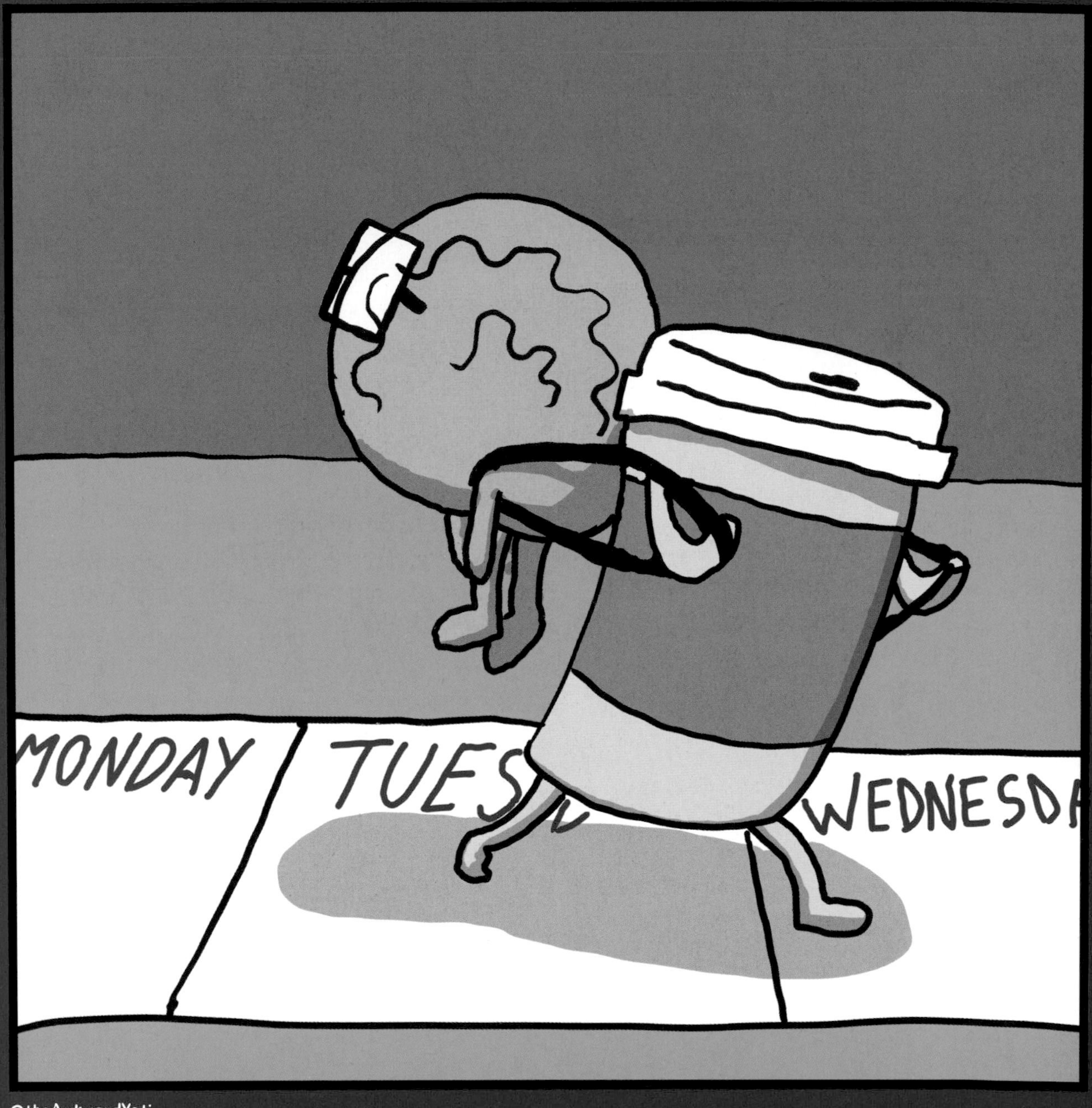
MONDAY
TUES
WEDNESDA

Brain, help! The acid reflux is getting bad!
Hmm...
Let's try cutting back on our trigger foods.
Thanks!
Tongue?! Didn't you hear BRAIN?! Why are you doing this?
I like the tassste.
@theAwkwardYeti

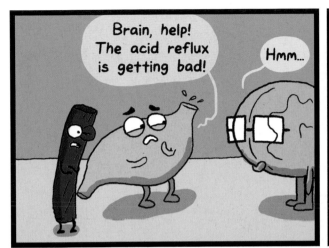

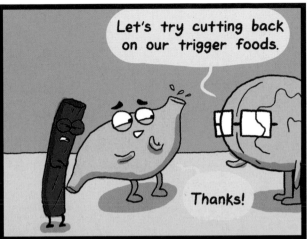

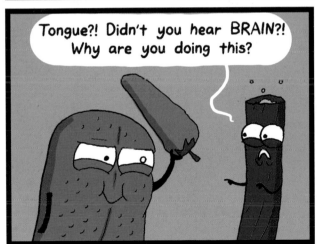

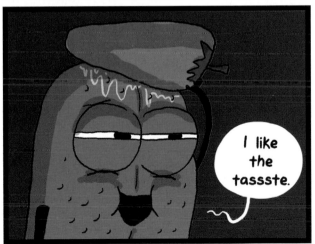

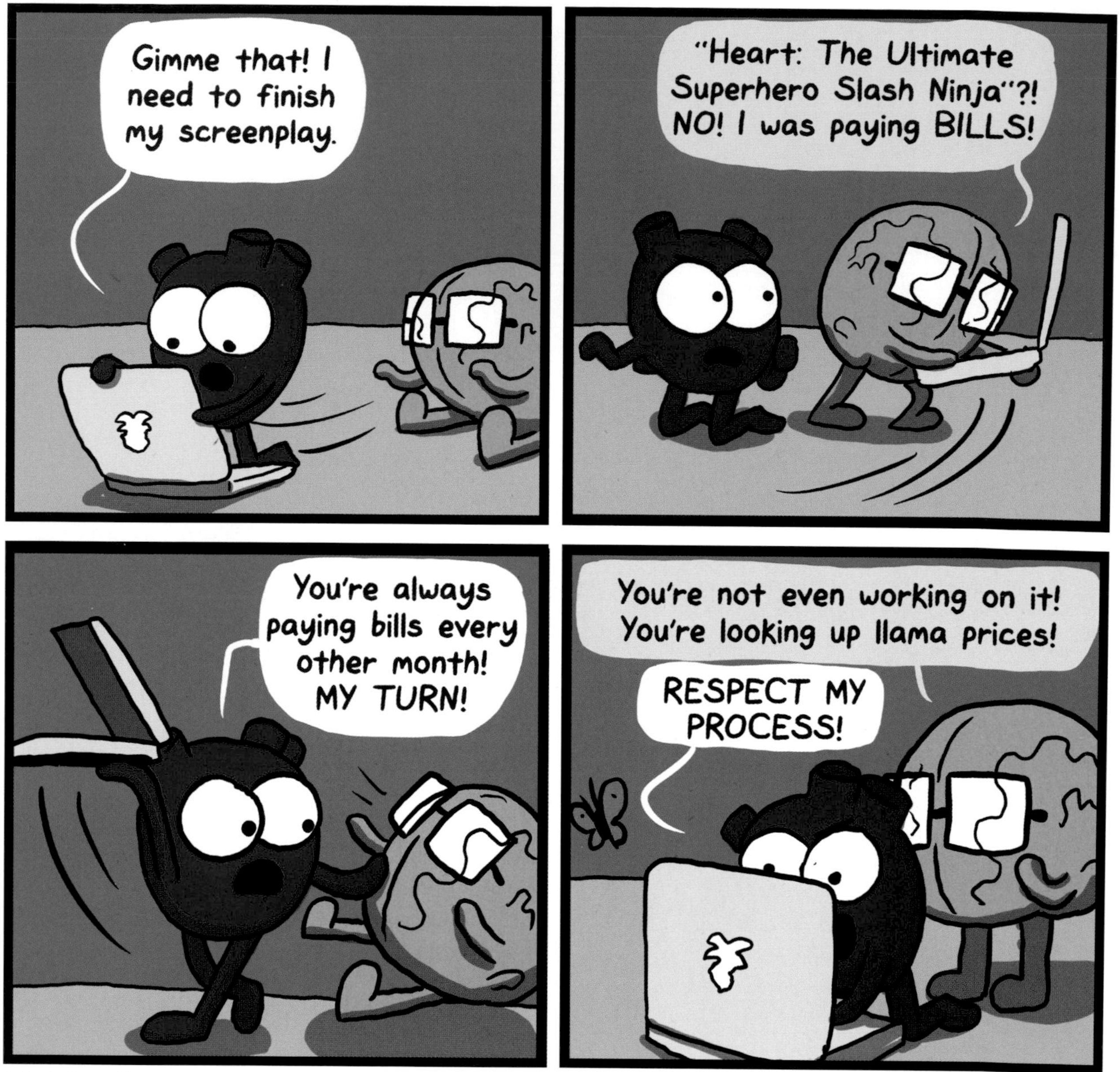
Gimme that! I need to finish my screenplay.
"Heart: The Ultimate Superhero Slash Ninja"?! NO! I was paying BILLS!
You're always paying bills every other month! MY TURN!
You're not even working on it! You're looking up llama prices!
RESPECT MY PROCESS!

@theAwkwardYeti

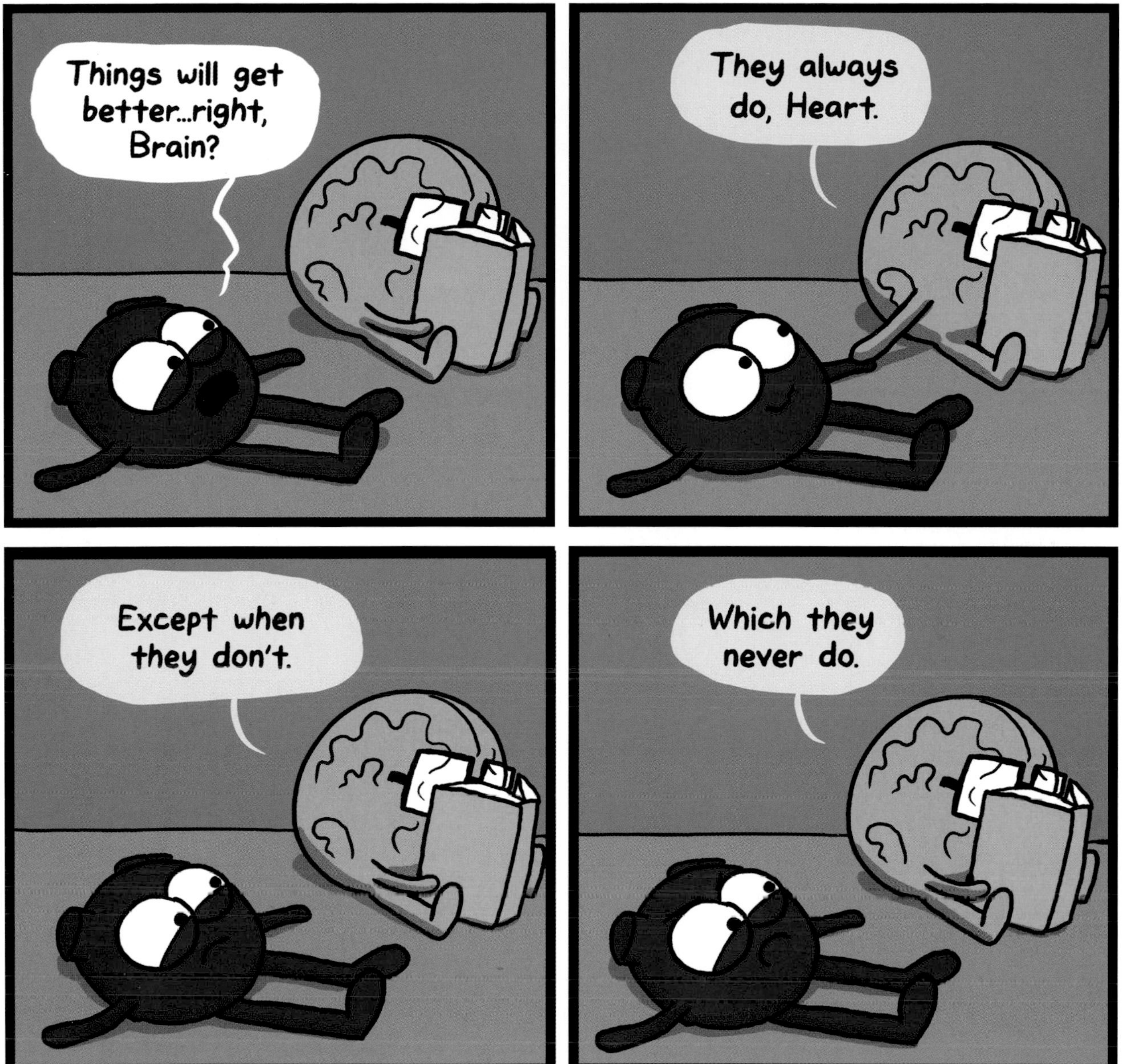
Things will get better...right, Brain?
They always do, Heart.
Except when they don't.
Which they never do.
@theAwkwardYeti

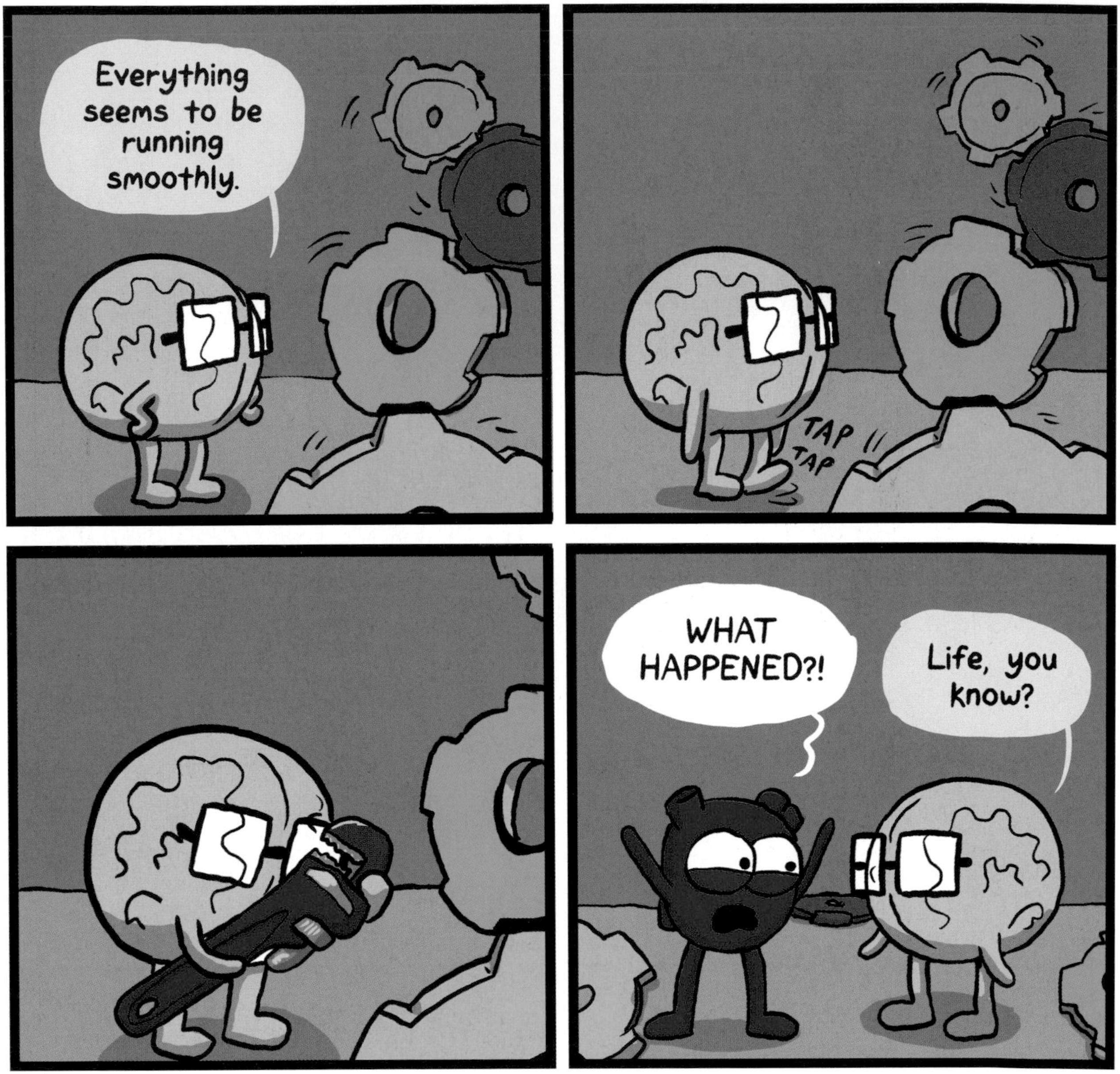
Everything seems to be running smoothly.
TAP TAP
WHAT HAPPENED?!
Life, you know?

@theAwkwardYeti

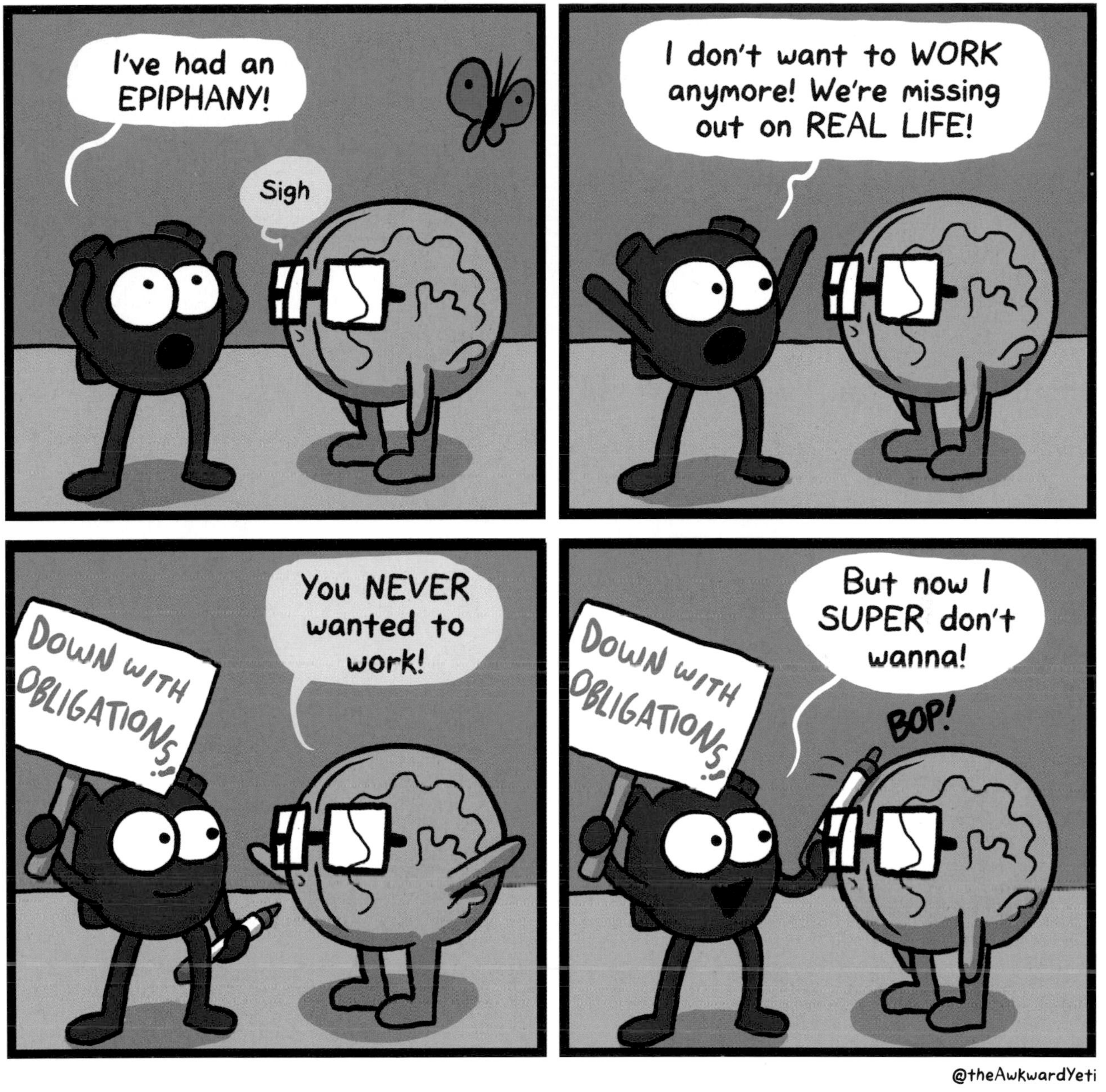
I've had an EPIPHANY!
Sigh
I don't want to WORK anymore! We're missing out on REAL LIFE!
DOWN WITH OBLIGATIONS!
You NEVER wanted to work!
DOWN WITH OBLIGATIONS!
But now I SUPER don't wanna!
BOP!
@theAwkwardYeti

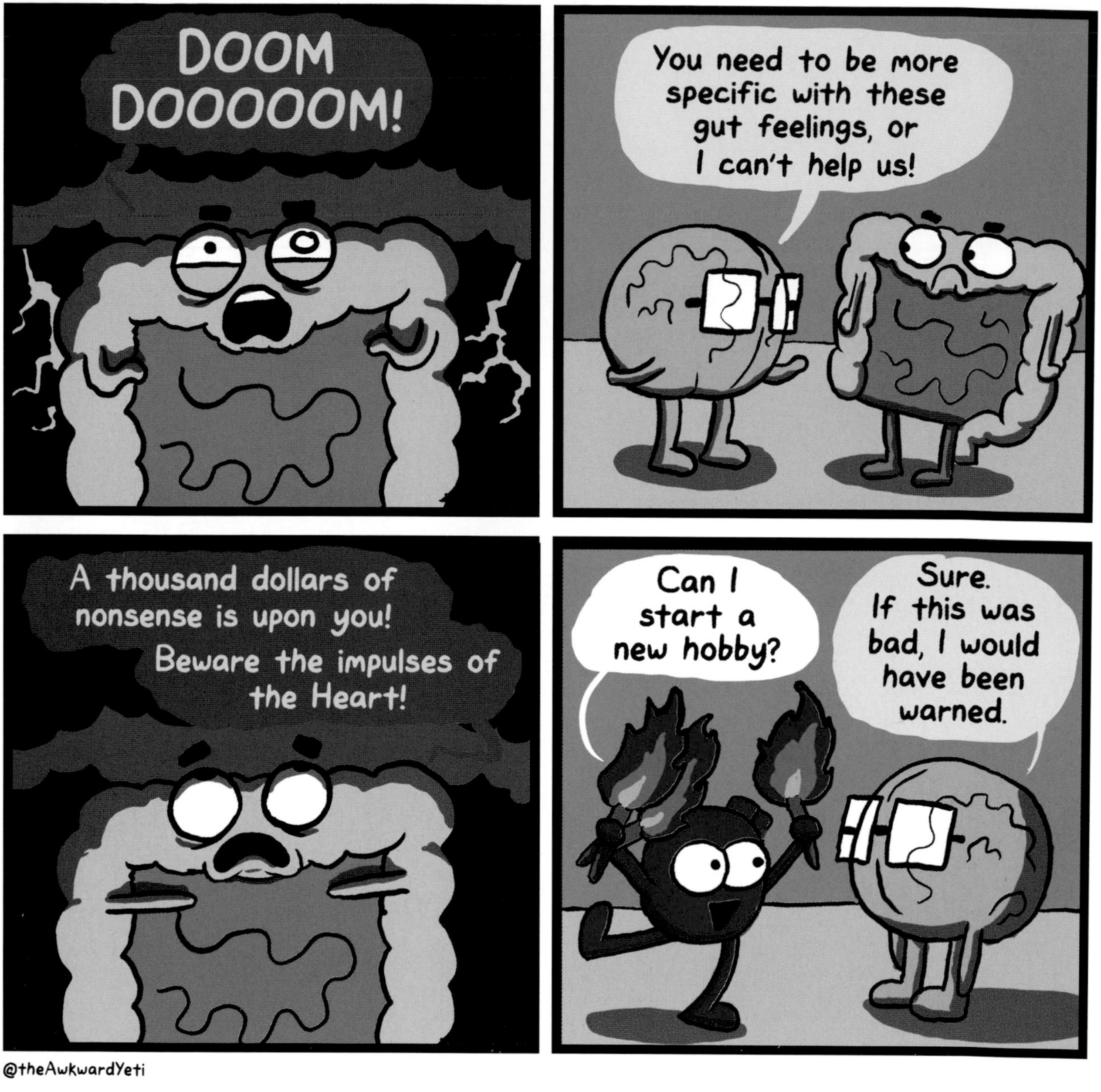
DOOM DOOOOOM!
You need to be more specific with these gut feelings, or I can't help us!
A thousand dollars of nonsense is upon you!
Beware the impulses of the Heart!
Can I start a new hobby?
Sure. If this was bad, I would have been warned.

@theAwkwardYeti

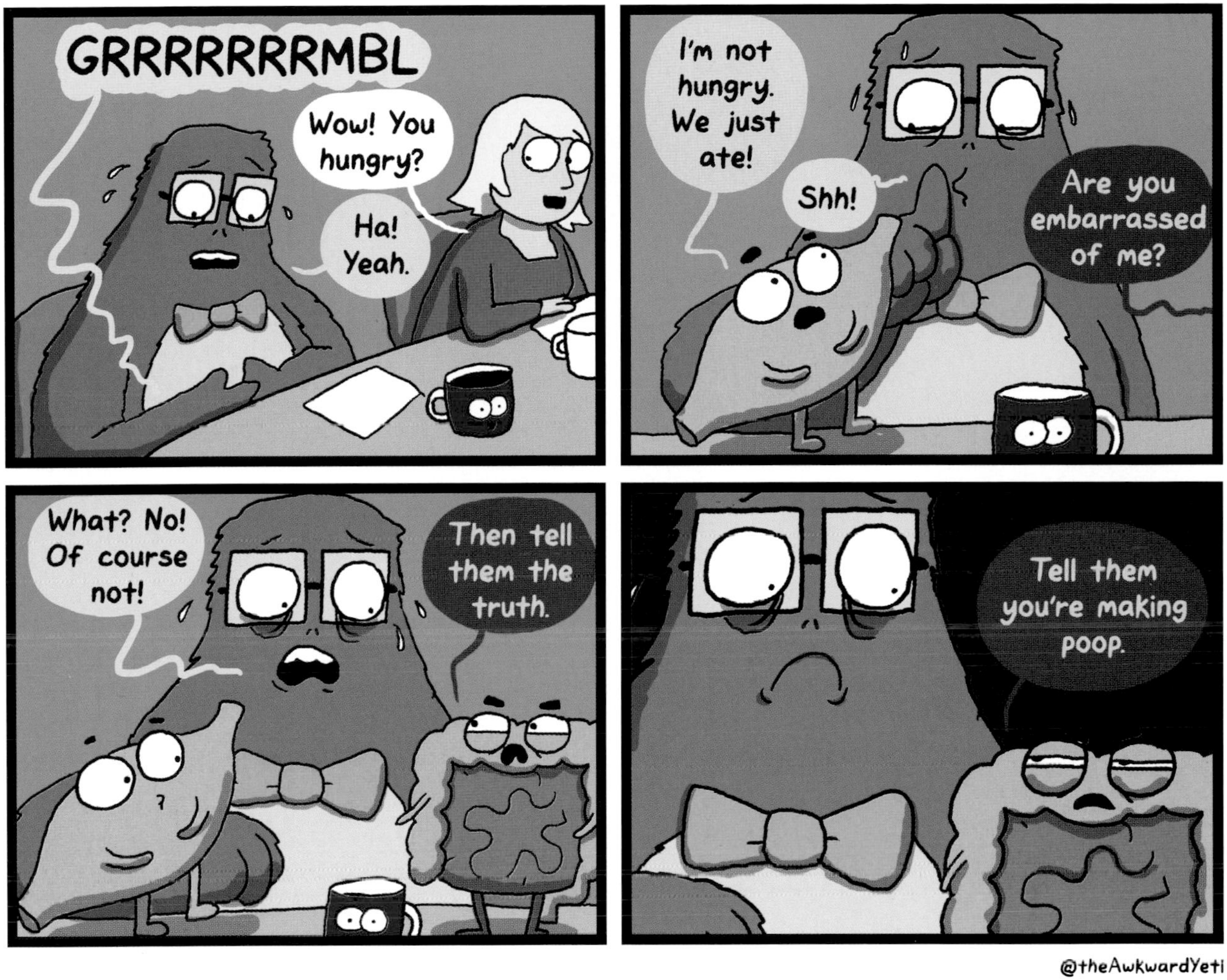
GRRRRRRRMBL
Wow! You hungry?
Ha! Yeah.
I'm not hungry. We just ate!
Shh!
Are you embarrassed of me?
What? No! Of course not!
Then tell them the truth.
Tell them you're making poop.
@theAwkwardYeti

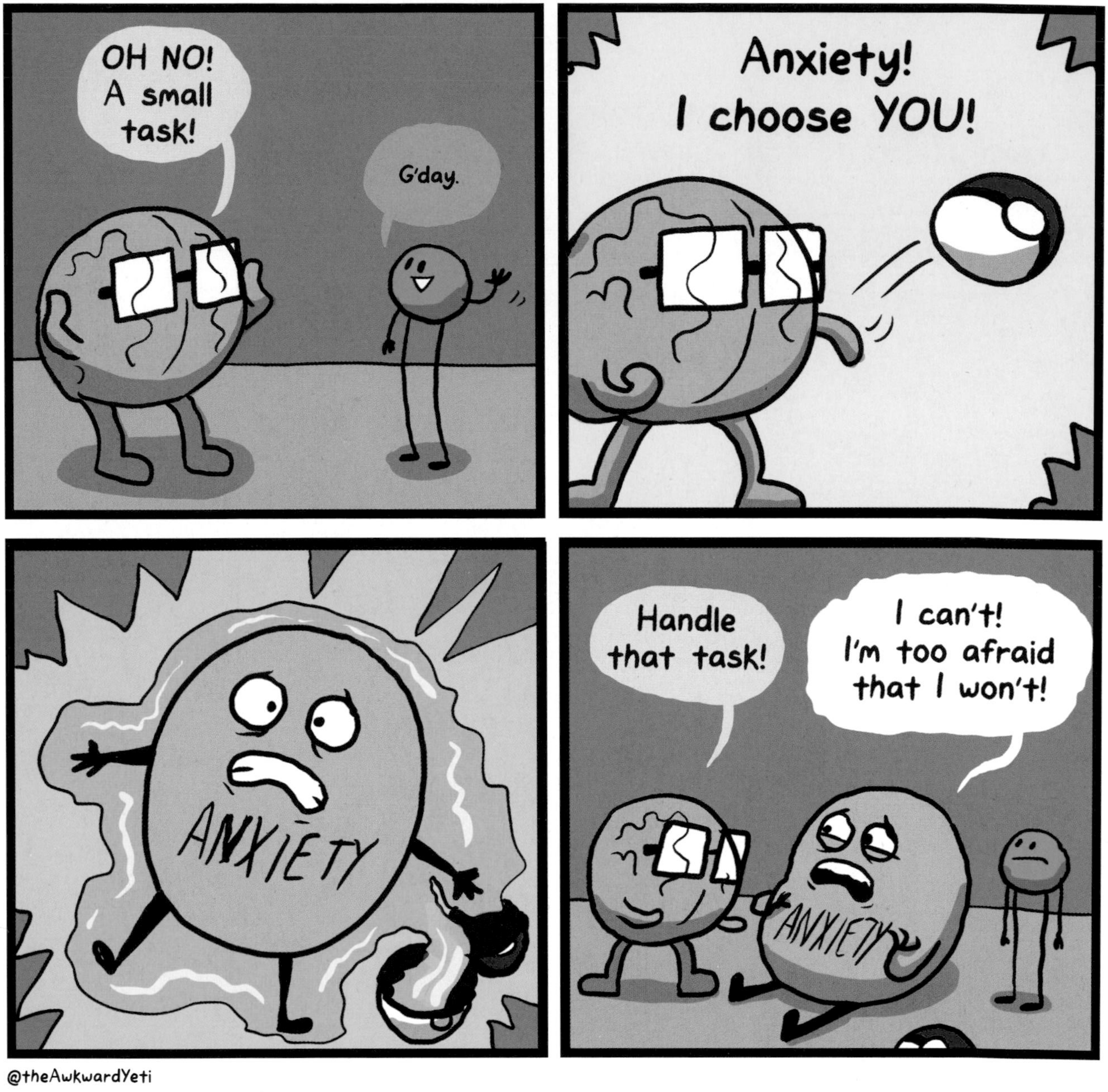
OH NO! A small task!
G'day.
Anxiety! I choose YOU!
ANXIETY
Handle that task!
I can't! I'm too afraid that I won't!
ANXIETY

@theAwkwardYeti

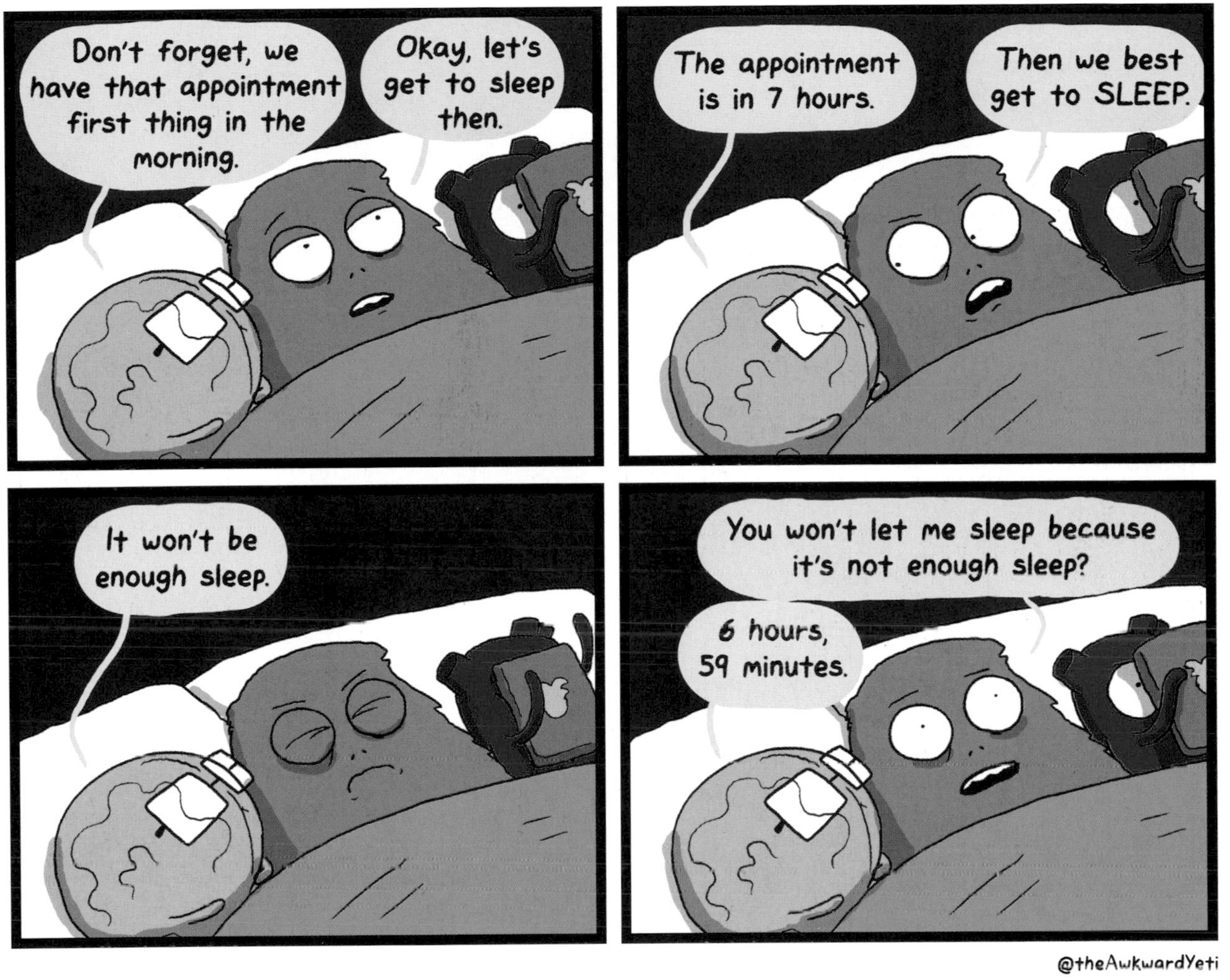
Don't forget, we have that appointment first thing in the morning.
Okay, let's get to sleep then.
The appointment is in 7 hours.
Then we best get to SLEEP.
It won't be enough sleep.
You won't let me sleep because it's not enough sleep?
6 hours, 59 minutes.
@theAwkwardYeti

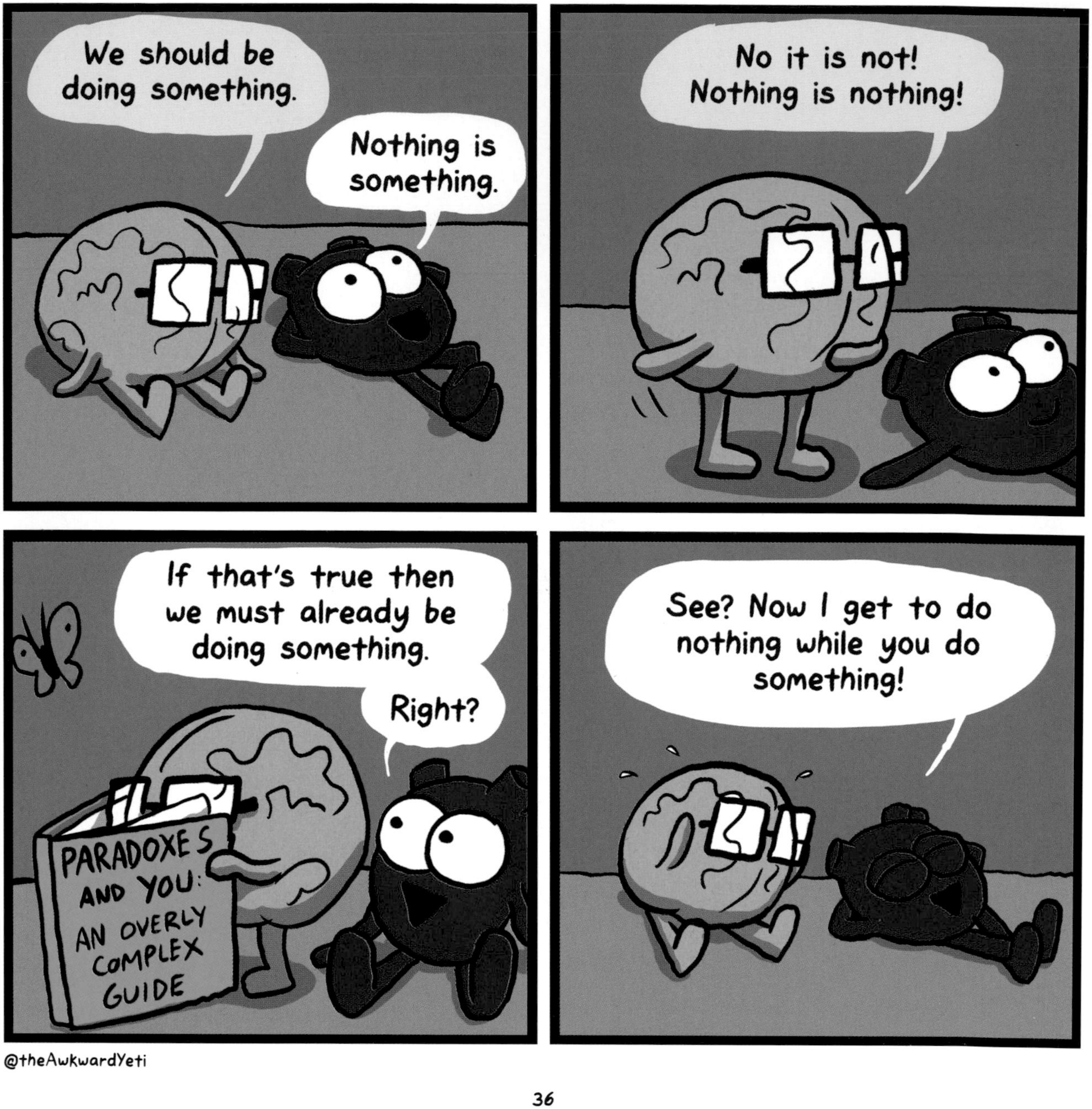
We should be doing something.
Nothing is something.
No it is not! Nothing is nothing!
If that's true then we must already be doing something.
Right?
PARADOXES AND YOU: AN OVERLY COMPLEX GUIDE
See? Now I get to do nothing while you do something!

@theAwkwardYeti

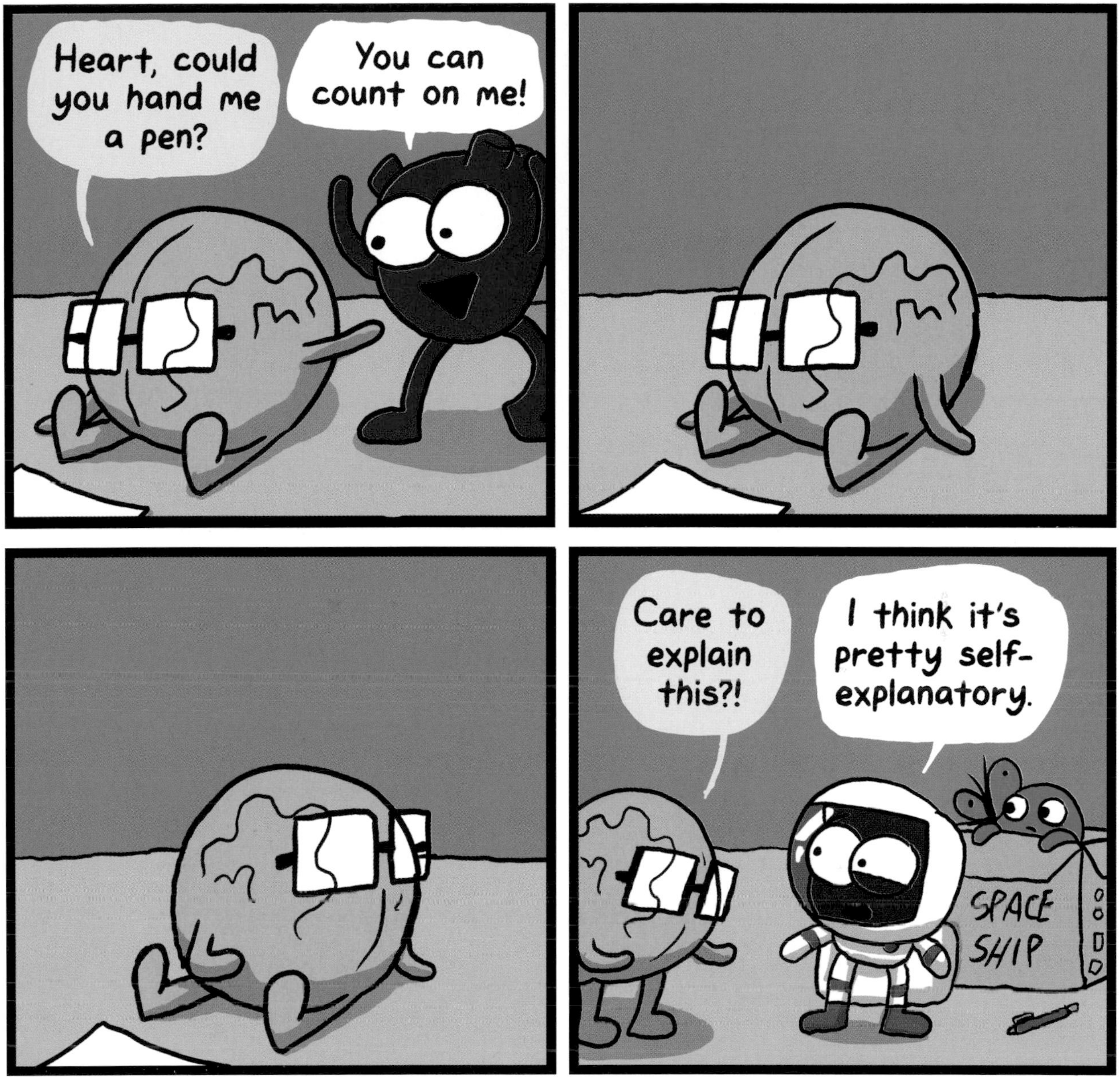
Heart, could you hand me a pen?
You can count on me!
Care to explain this?!
I think it's pretty self-explanatory.
SPACE SHIP

@theAwkwardYeti

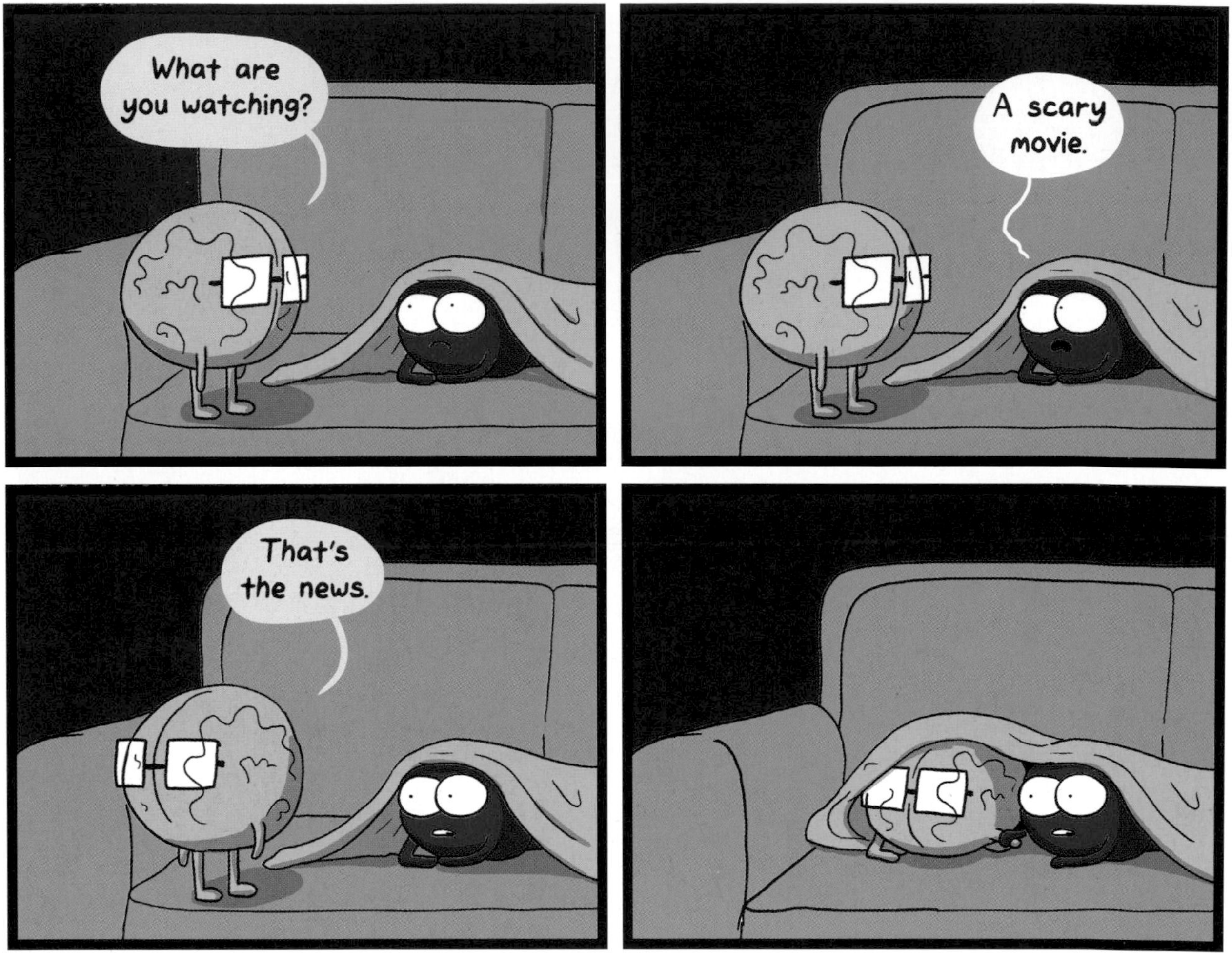
What are you watching?
A scary movie.
That's the news.

@theAwkwardYeti

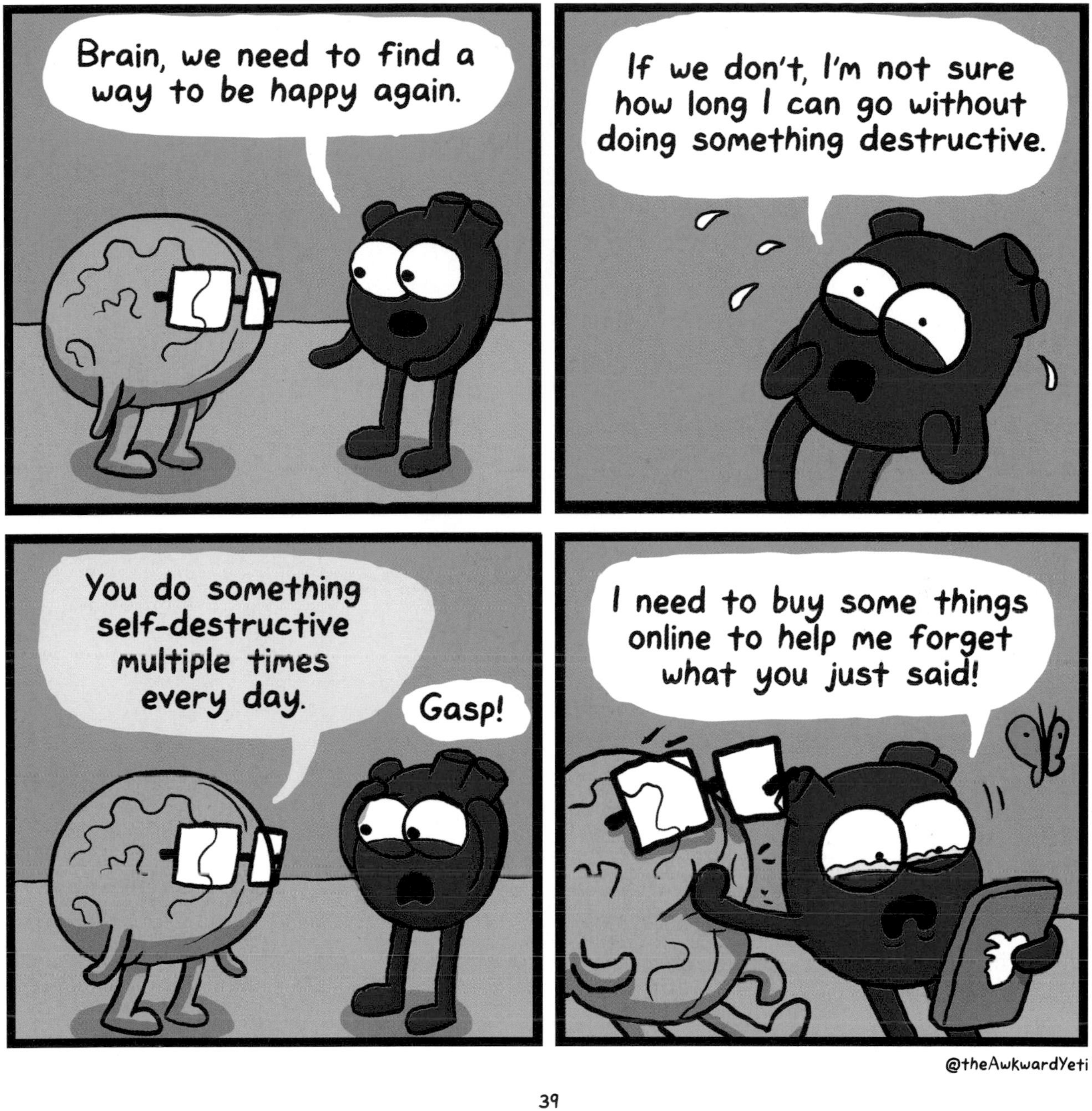
Brain, we need to find a way to be happy again.
If we don't, I'm not sure how long I can go without doing something destructive.
You do something self-destructive multiple times every day.
Gasp!
I need to buy some things online to help me forget what you just said!
@theAwkwardYeti

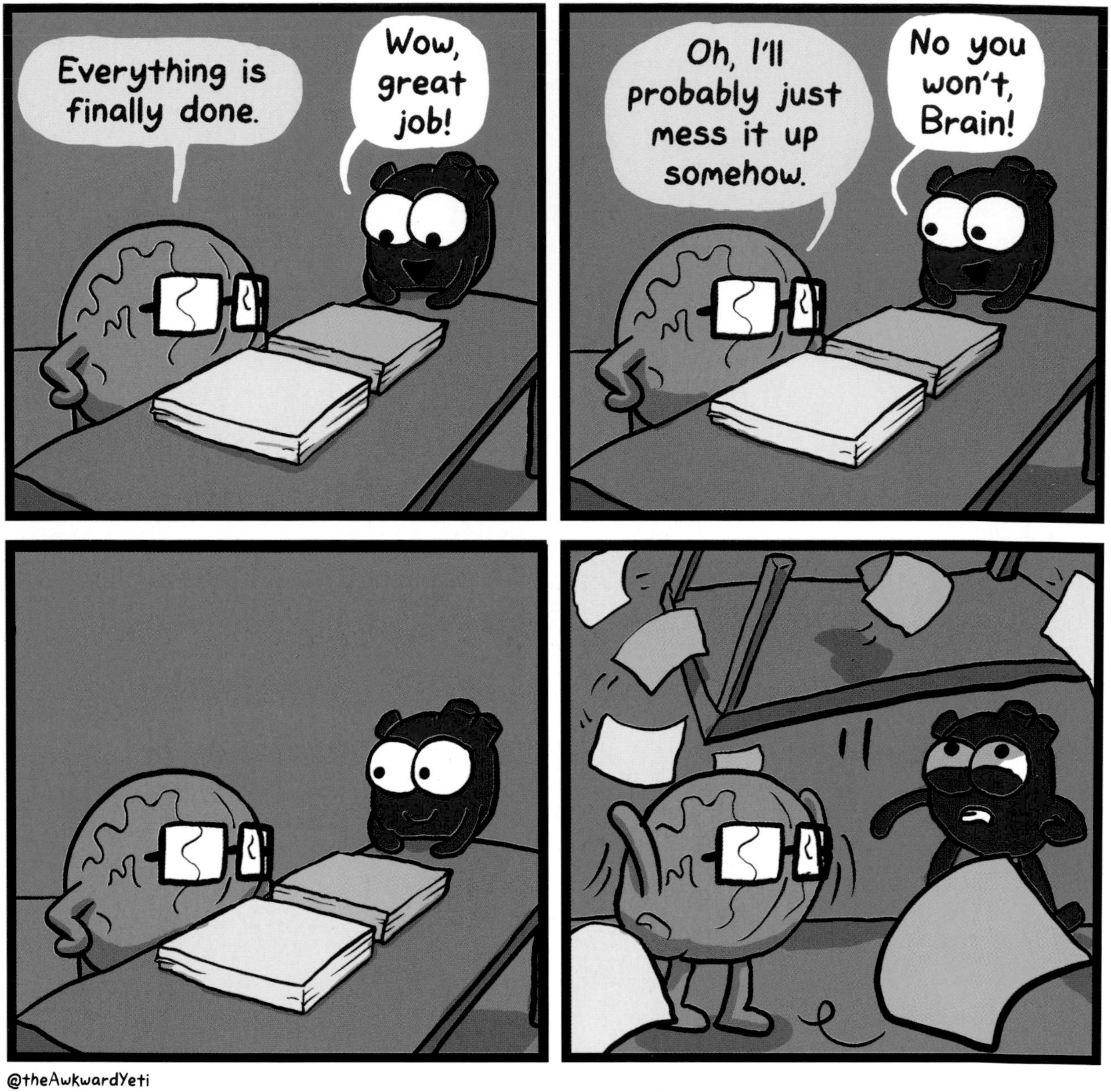
Everything is finally done.
Wow, great job!
Oh, I'll probably just mess it up somehow.
No you won't, Brain!

@theAwkwardYeti

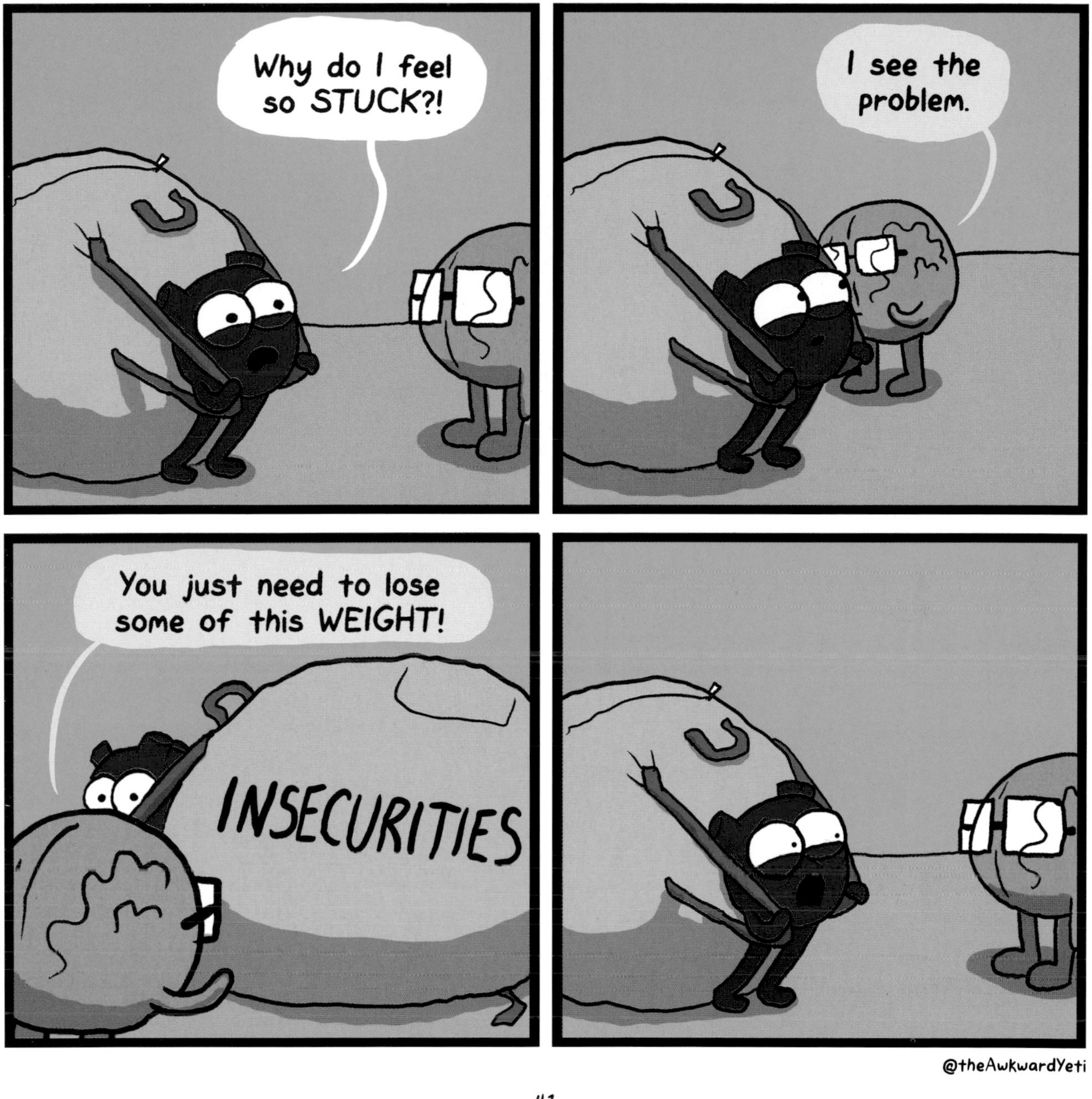
Why do I feel so STUCK?!
I see the problem.
You just need to lose some of this WEIGHT!
INSECURITIES

@theAwkwardYeti

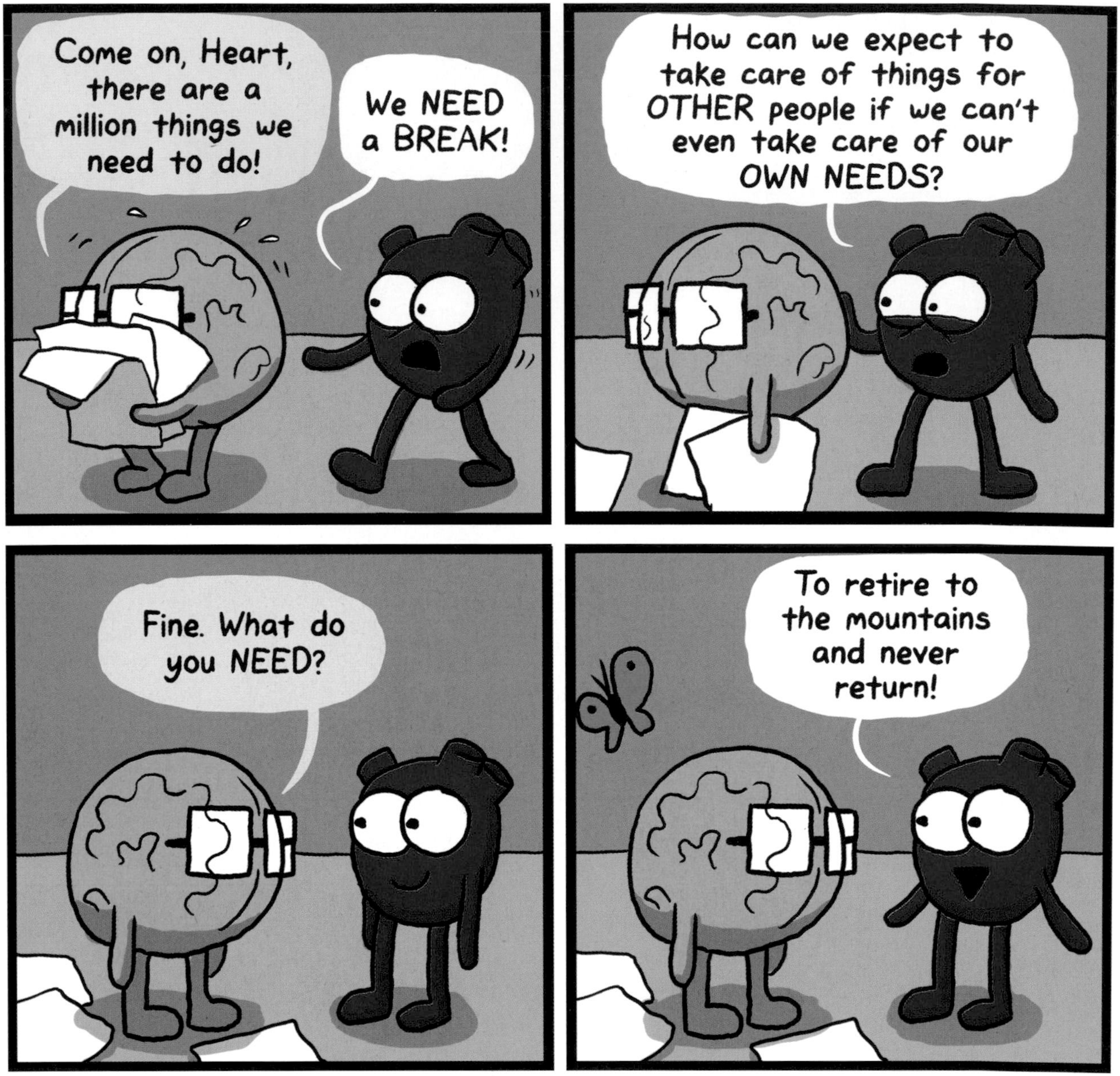
Come on, Heart, there are a million things we need to do!
We NEED a BREAK!
How can we expect to take care of things for OTHER people if we can't even take care of our OWN NEEDS?
Fine. What do you NEED?
To retire to the mountains and never return!

@theAwkwardYeti

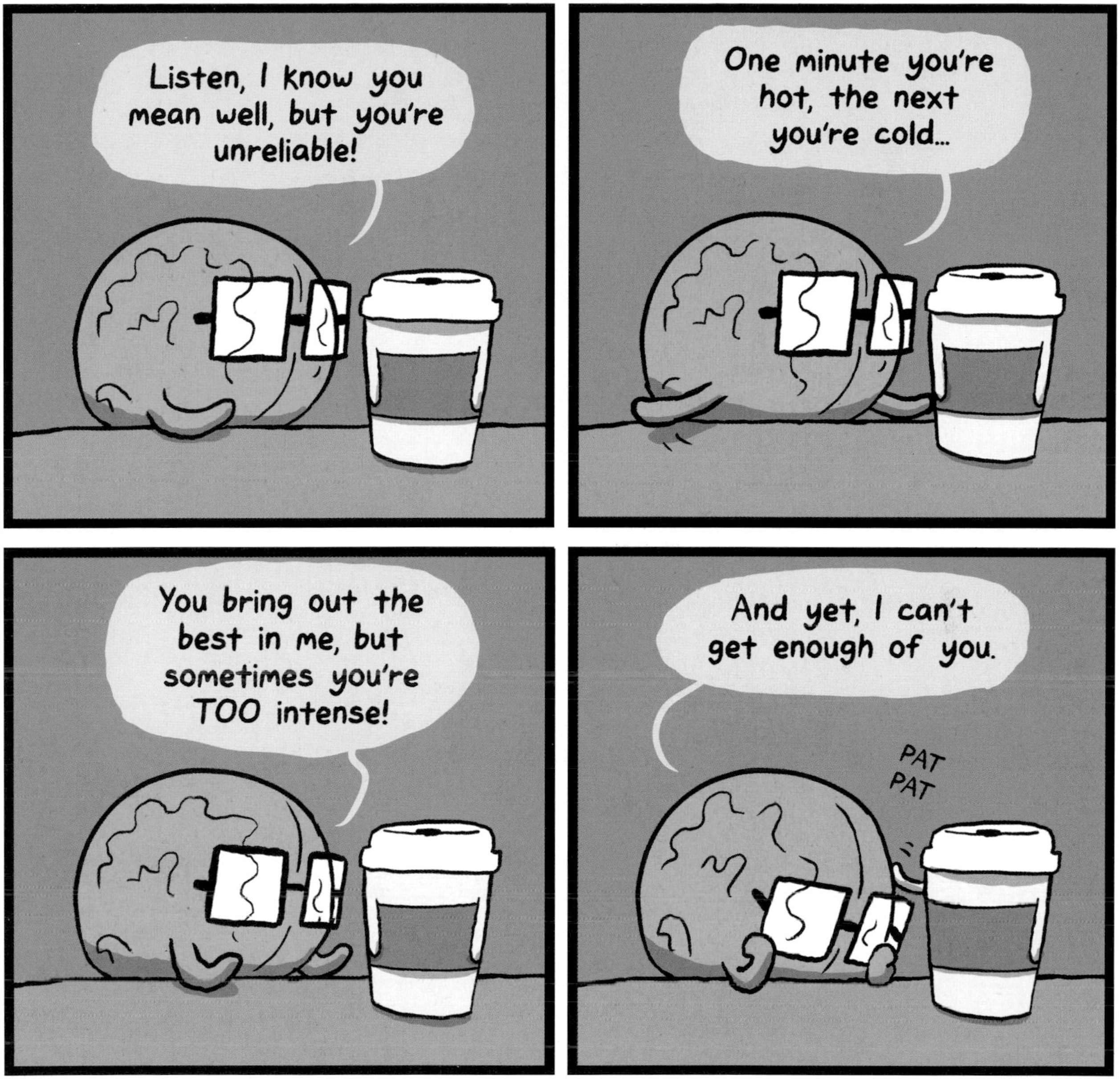
Listen, I know you mean well, but you're unreliable!
One minute you're hot, the next you're cold...
You bring out the best in me, but sometimes you're TOO intense!
And yet, I can't get enough of you.
PAT PAT

@theAwkwardYeti

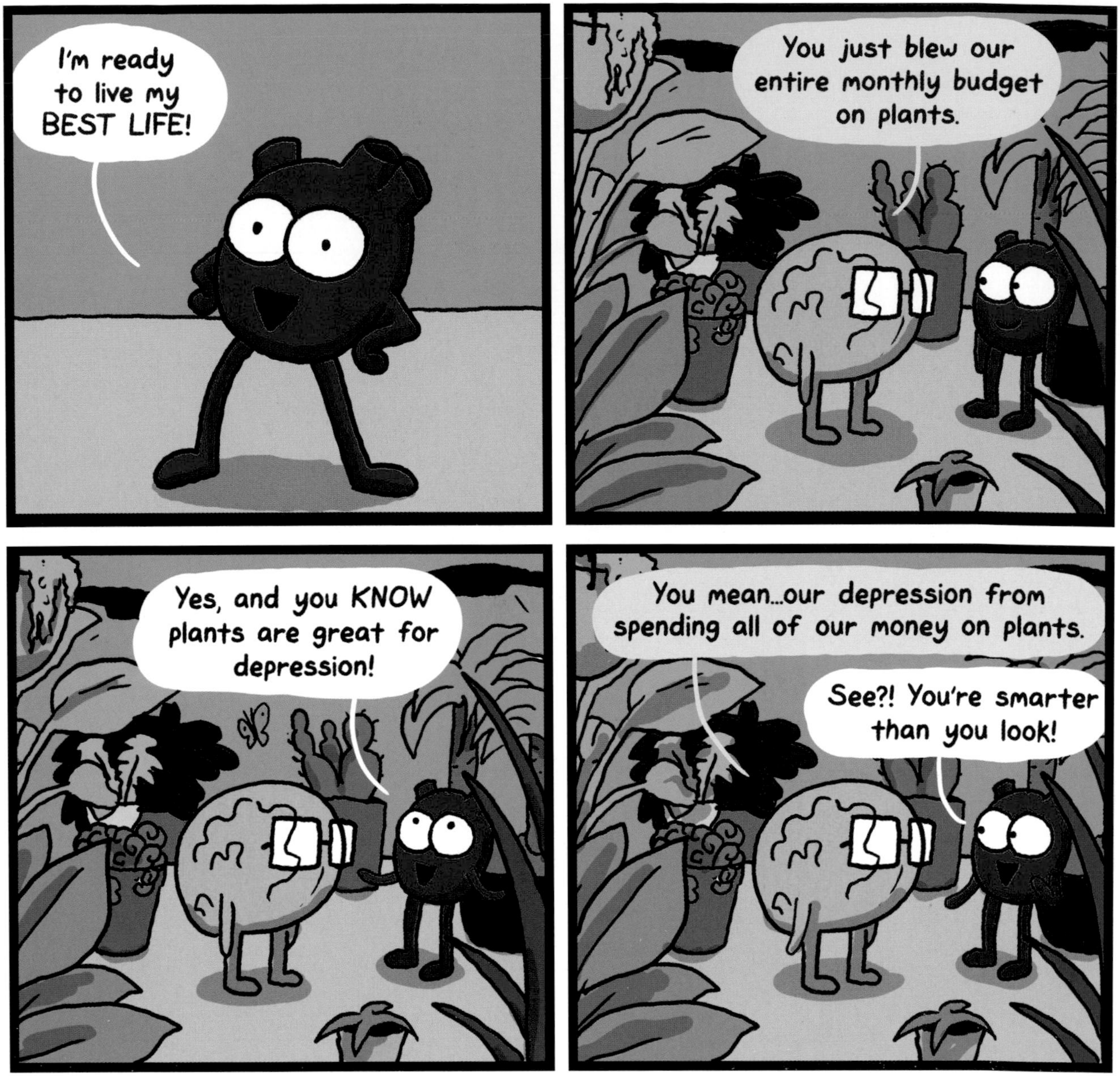
I'm ready to live my BEST LIFE!
You just blew our entire monthly budget on plants.
Yes, and you KNOW plants are great for depression!
You mean...our depression from spending all of our money on plants.
See?! You're smarter than you look!

@theAwkwardYeti

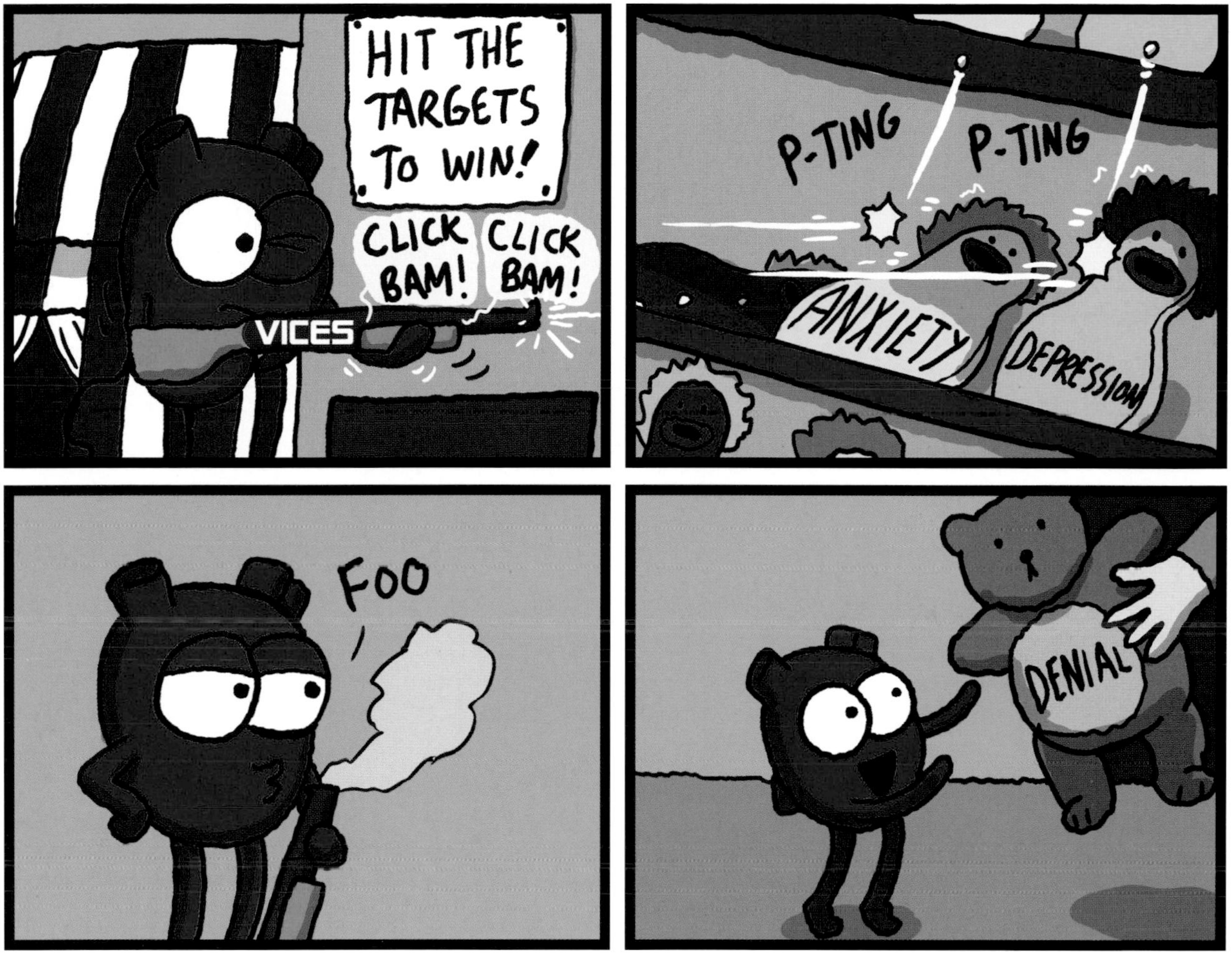
HIT THE TARGETS TO WIN!
VICES
CLICK BAM!
CLICK BAM!
P-TING
P-TING
ANXIETY
DEPRESSION
FOO
DENIAL

@theAwkwardYeti

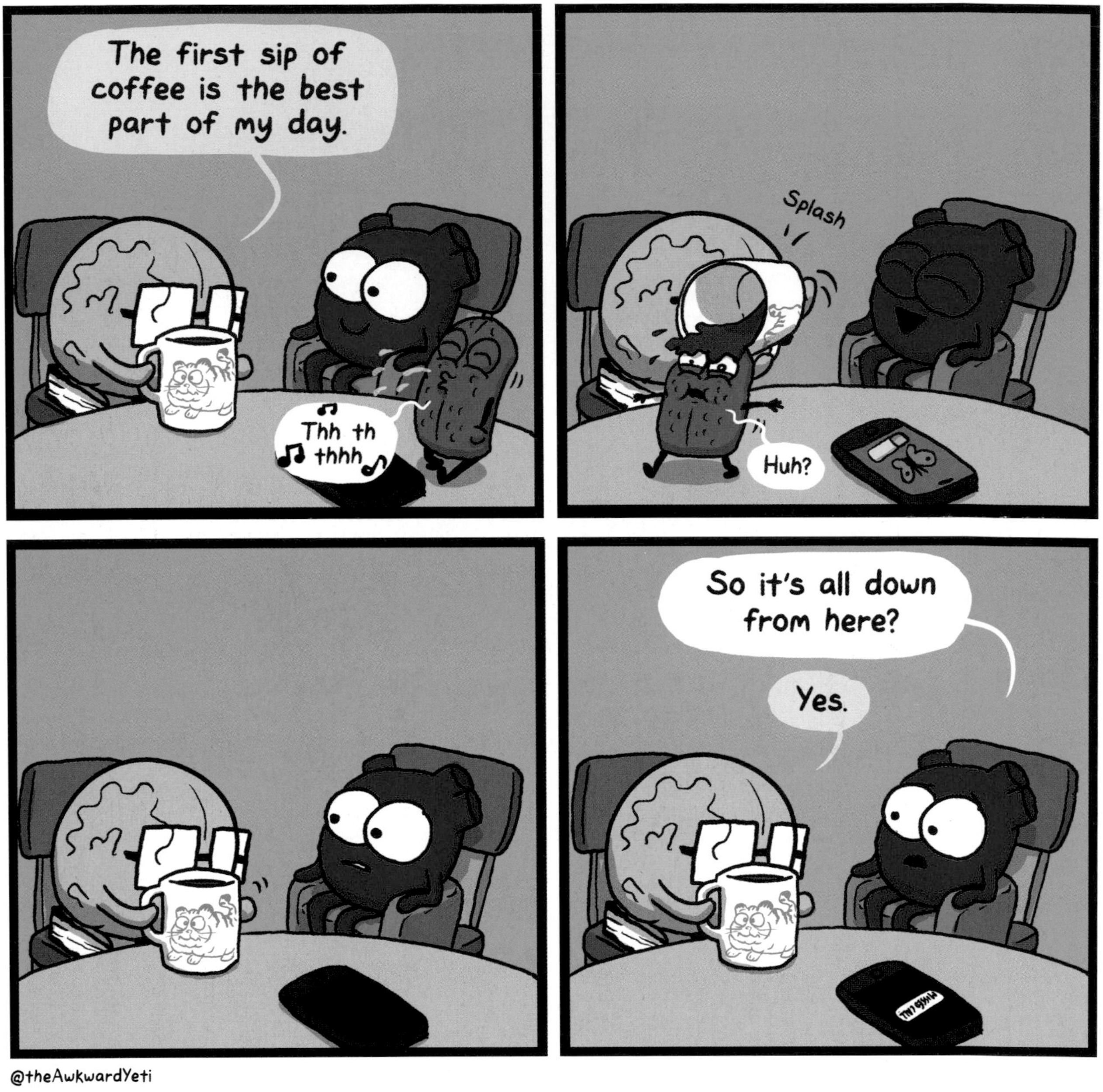
The first sip of coffee is the best part of my day.
Thh th thhh
Splash
Huh?
So it's all down from here?
Yes.

@theAwkwardYeti

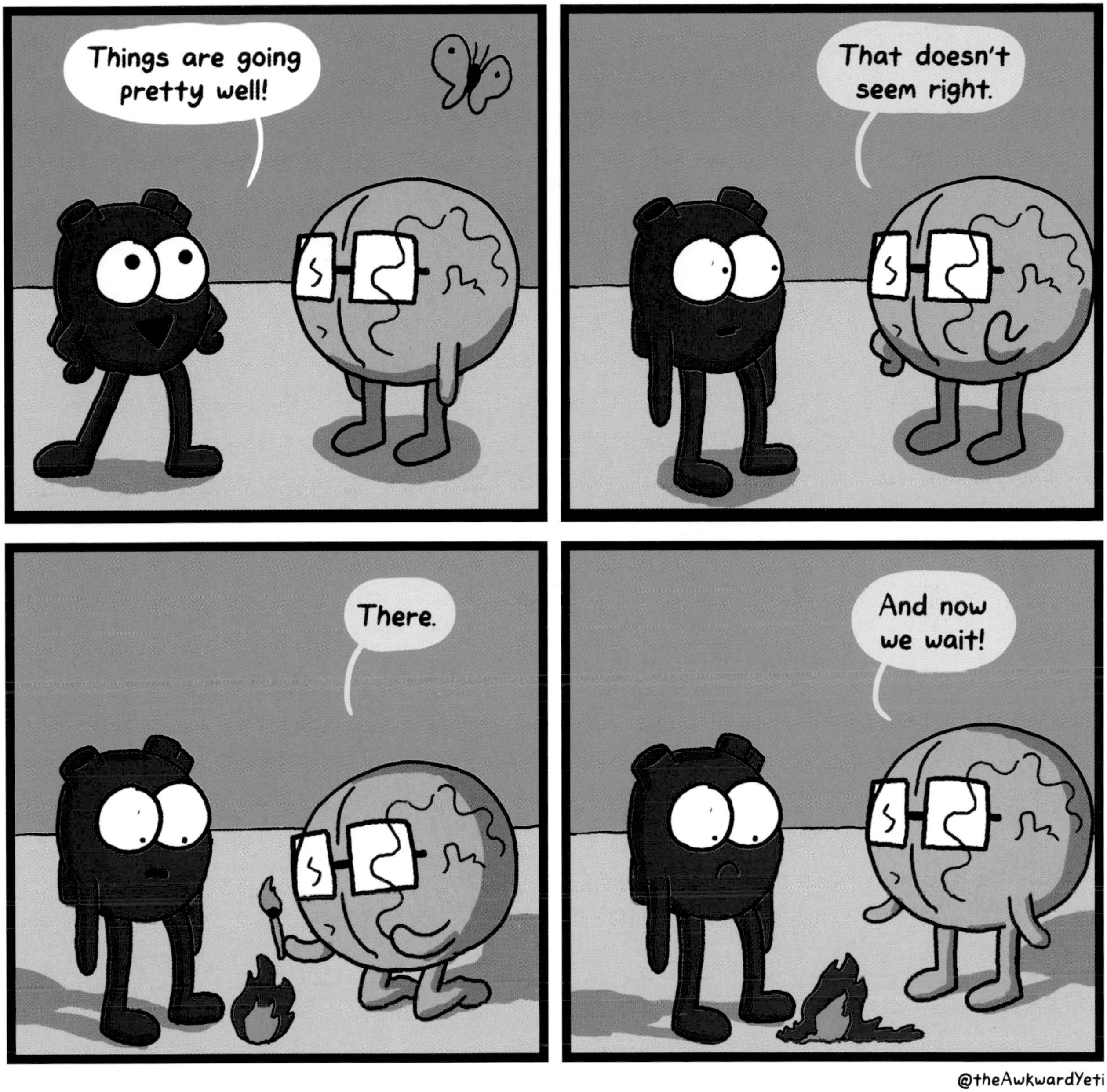
Things are going pretty well!
That doesn't seem right.
There.
And now we wait!
@theAwkwardYeti

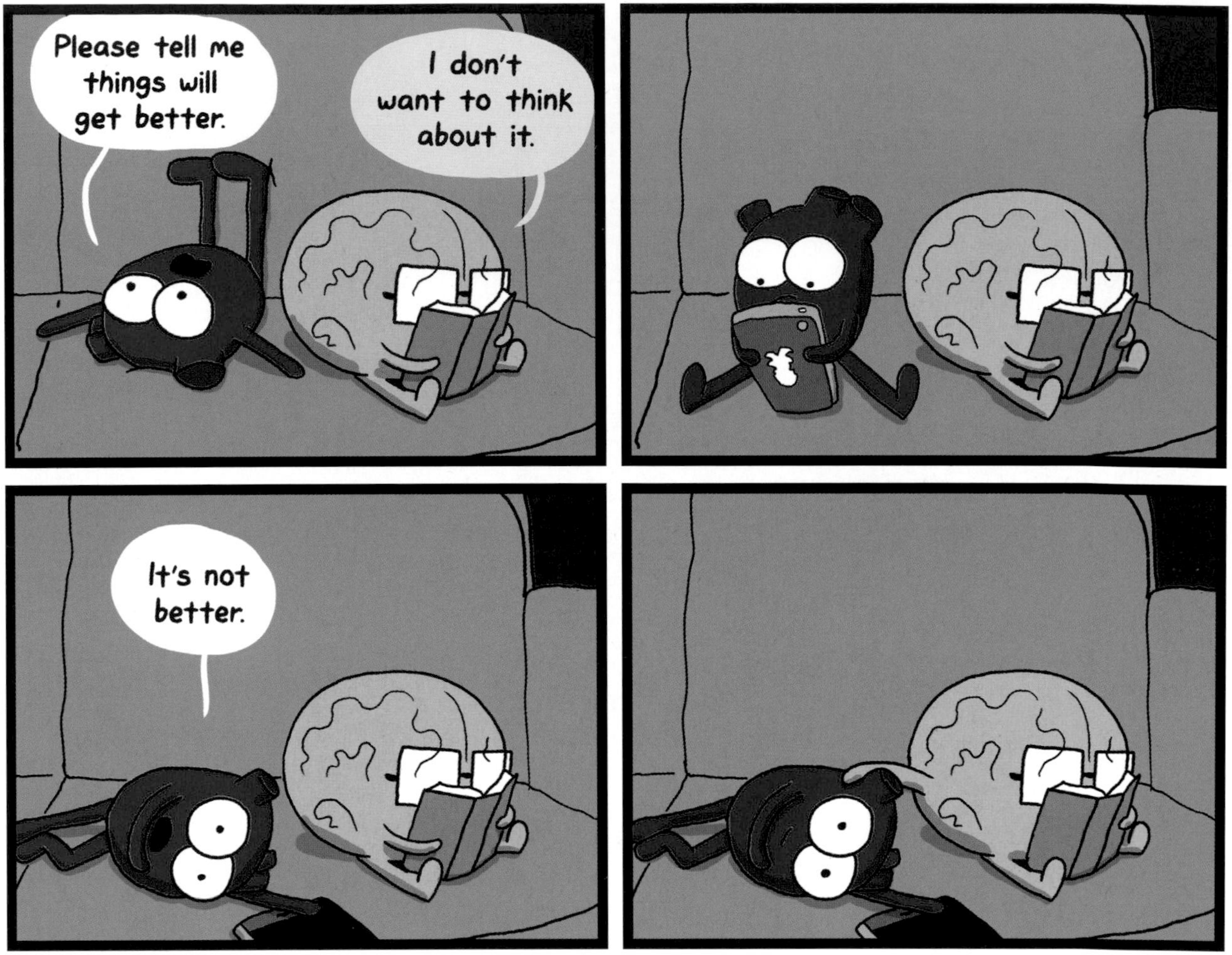
Please tell me things will get better.
I don't want to think about it.
It's not better.

@theAwkwardYeti

PART 2

Growing pains

"Life goes fast / It's hard to
make the good things last"

—The Flaming Lips

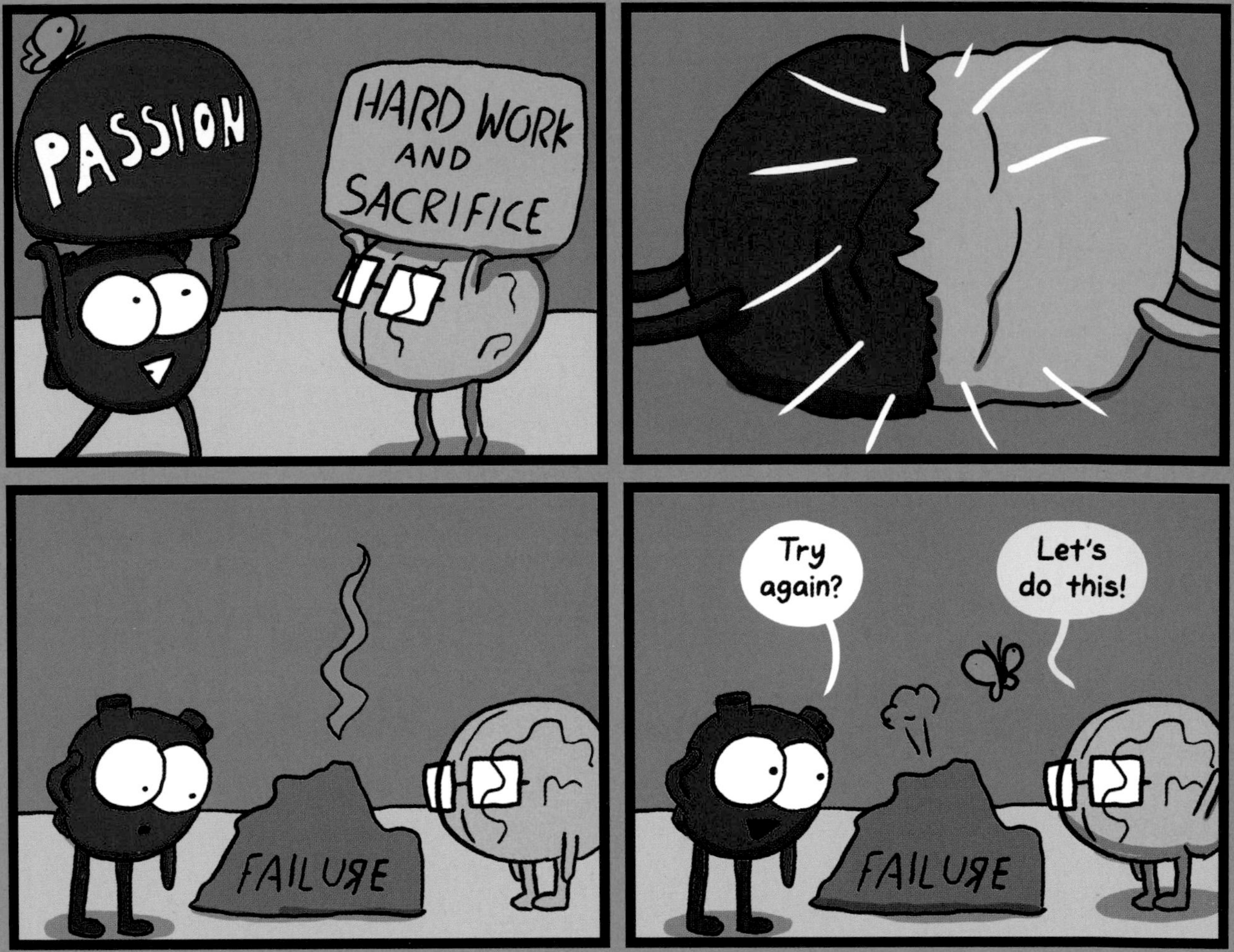
PASSION
HARD WORK AND SACRIFICE
FAILURE
FAILURE
Try again?
Let's do this!

@theAwkwardYeti

It's okay to mess up.

Growth hurts. To gain muscle, one must actively create tiny tears in the tissue by putting strain on them. Lifting heavy things, putting them down, then lifting them again seems to work well (and what could be more fun than that?). The tissue heals, and the process repeats, until one day, with enough work, the muscle is noticeably larger. Then one can flex their muscle in front of people, pretending they are just reaching for something. Emotional growth works similarly—we have to purposely tear ourselves bit by bit to heal and grow. Then one can talk about how enlightened they are (but don't do that).

As a seasoned lazy person, I have spent most of my life doing neither of these very well. I will do the work for a few weeks, then get distracted by literally anything. I don't discriminate when it comes to reasons not to exercise or work on emotional growth. However, if you're anything like me and your lack of growth is causing real problems in your life, it's time to take it more seriously.

Health problems might motivate someone to take care of their body. Relationship problems or destructive coping skills might motivate someone to take care of their trauma and emotional health. My motivation of choice is to wait for everything to fall apart completely in order to seek help. It works wonders. Much like drowning, it is a very good motivation to find air.

My heart and brain are always at odds, pushing and pulling. It's really frustrating and kind of hilarious. Really, life is kind of an absurd thing to begin with; what's the point in taking it so seriously all the time?

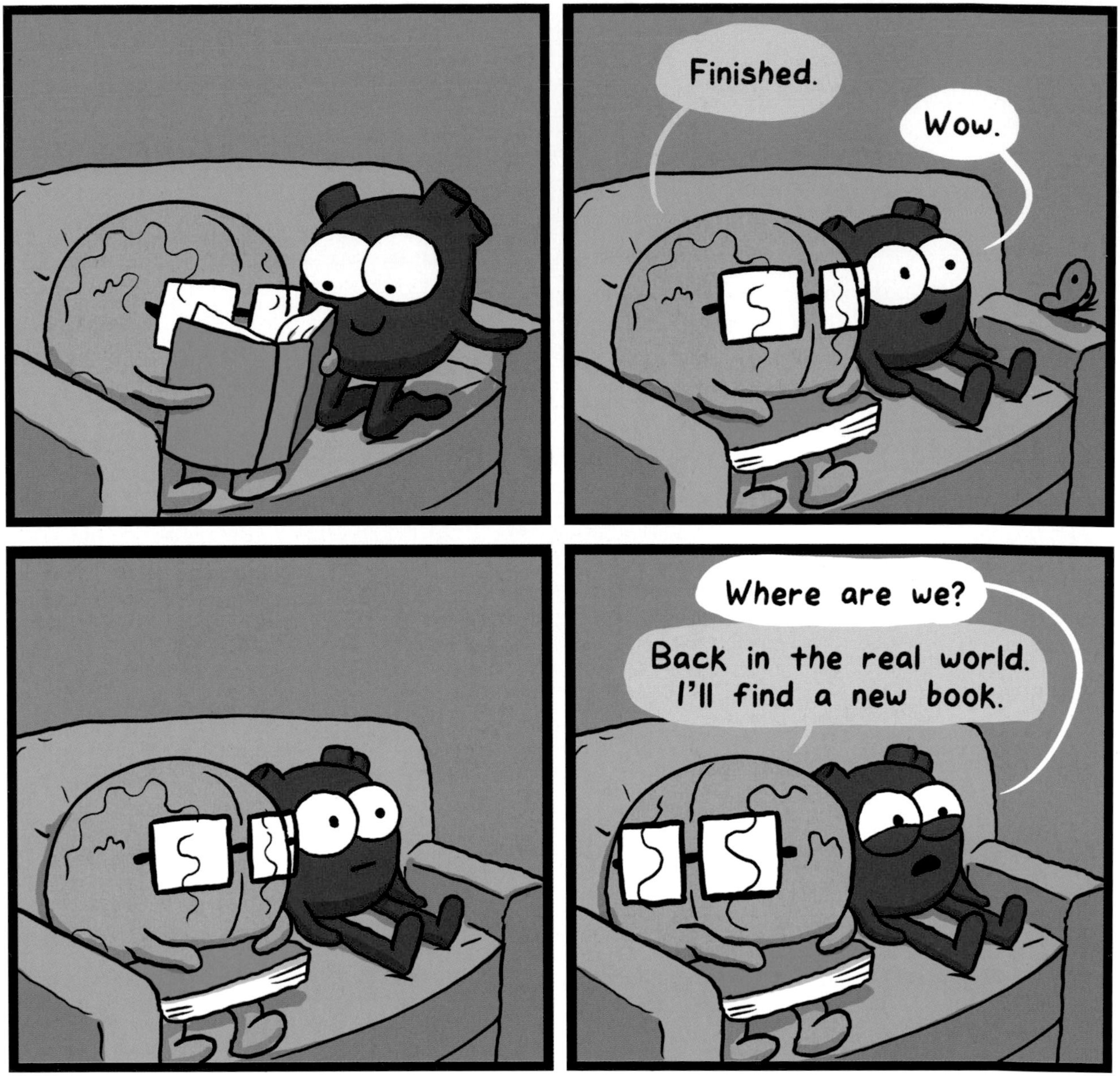
Finished.
Wow.
Where are we?
Back in the real world.
I'll find a new book.

@theAwkwardYeti

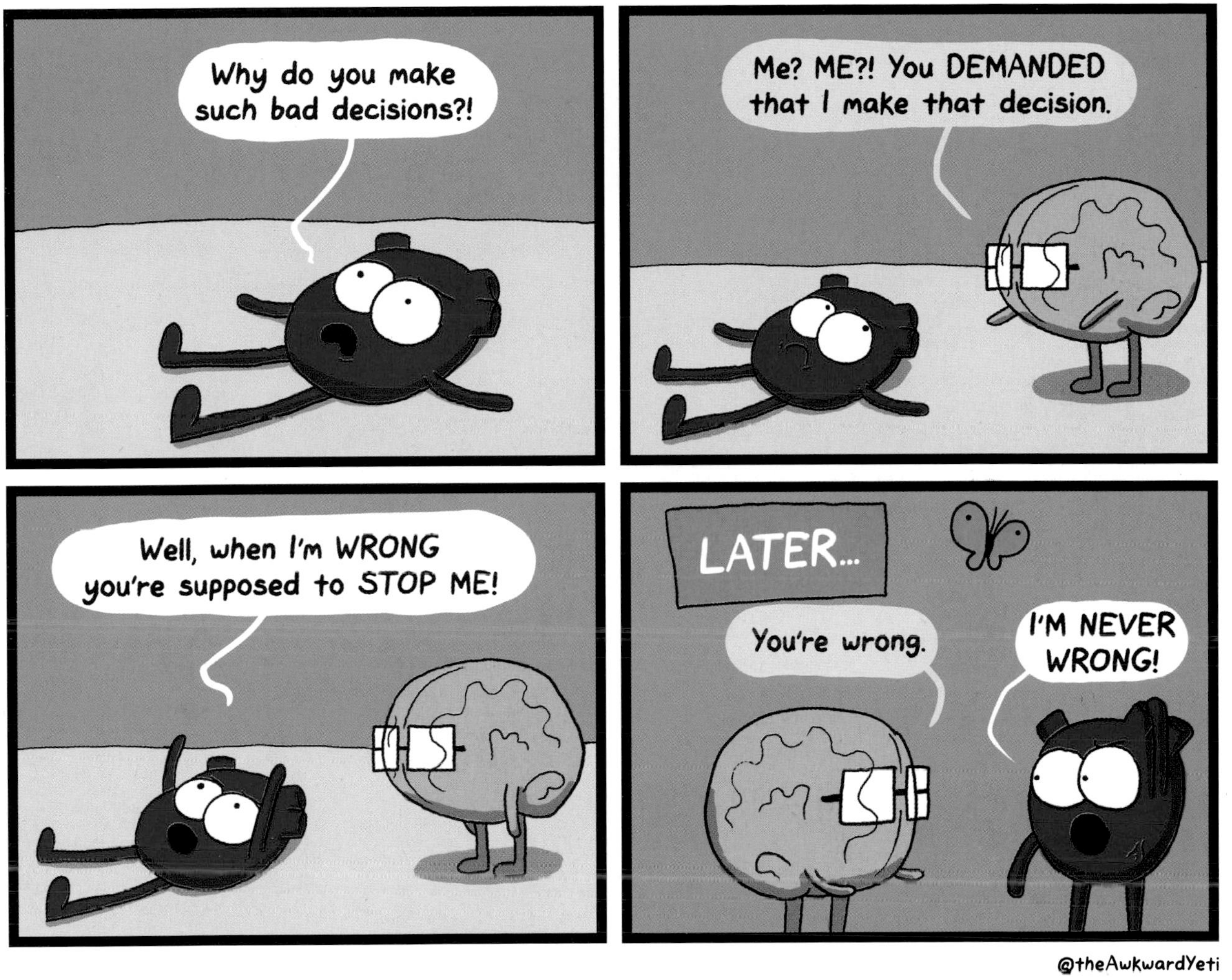
Why do you make such bad decisions?!
Me? ME?! You DEMANDED that I make that decision.
Well, when I'm WRONG you're supposed to STOP ME!
LATER...
You're wrong.
I'M NEVER WRONG!
@theAwkwardYeti

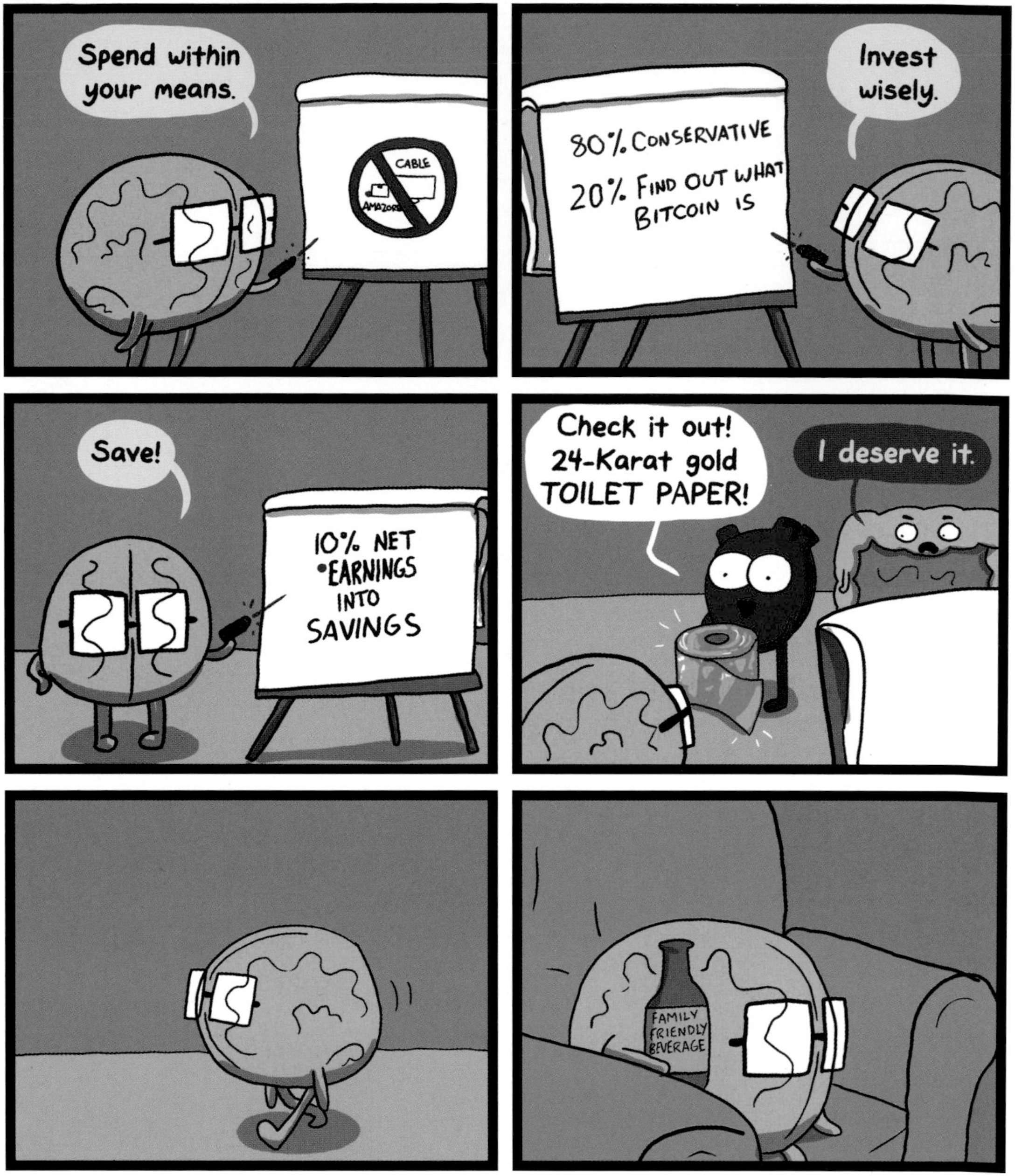
Spend within your means.
CABLE
AMAZON
Invest wisely.
80% CONSERVATIVE
20% FIND OUT WHAT BITCOIN IS
Save!
10% NET •EARNINGS INTO SAVINGS
Check it out! 24-Karat gold TOILET PAPER!
I deserve it.
FAMILY FRIENDLY BEVERAGE

@theAwkwardYeti

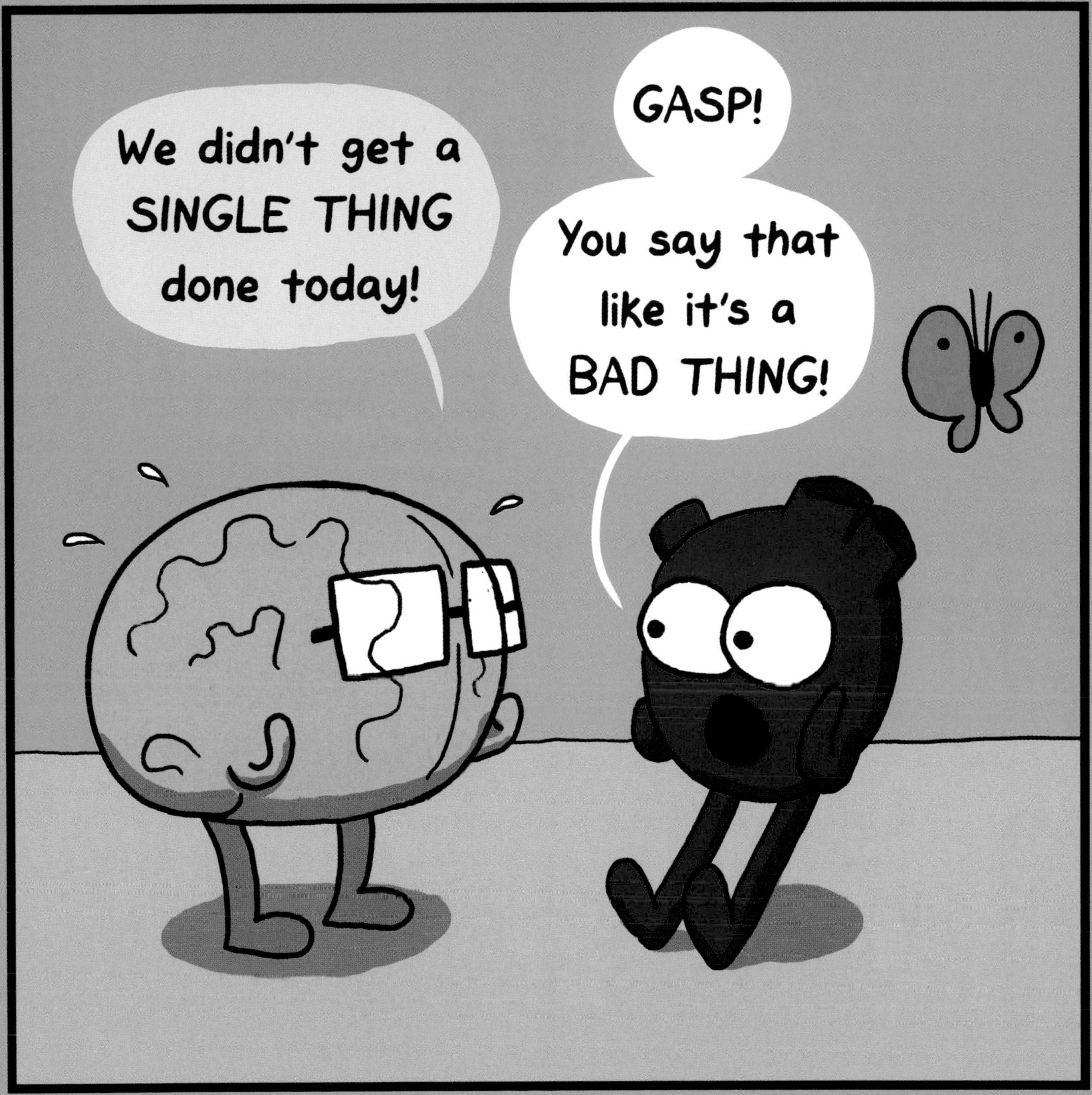
We didn't get a SINGLE THING done today!
GASP!
You say that like it's a BAD THING!

@theAwkwardYeti

I LOVE that song!
Okay! That's enough!
Brain? I don't think I like that song anymore...
I...can't stop!
Brain?
SOB PLEASE!
Help... me...

@theAwkwardYeti

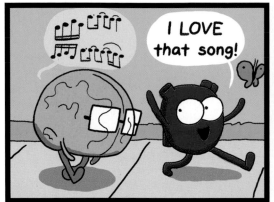

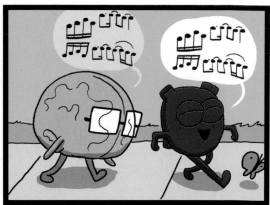

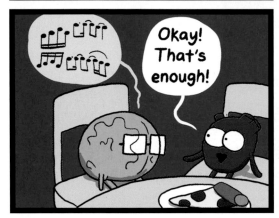

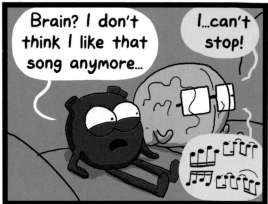

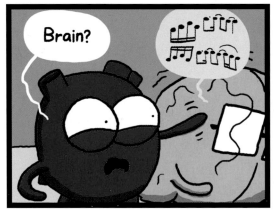

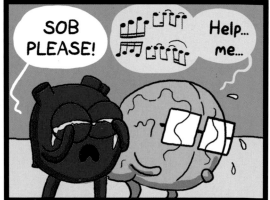

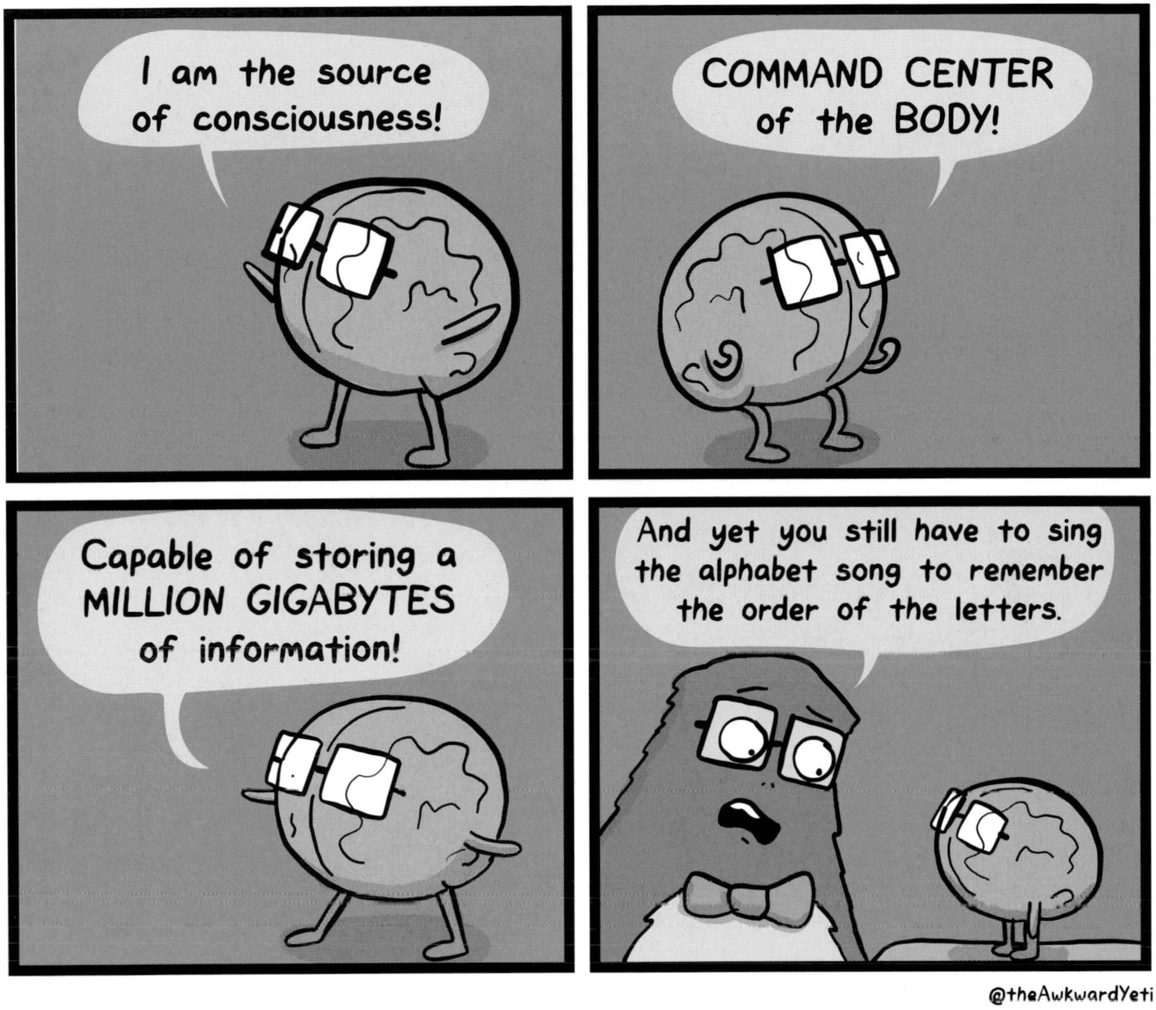
I am the source of consciousness!
COMMAND CENTER of the BODY!
Capable of storing a MILLION GIGABYTES of information!
And yet you still have to sing the alphabet song to remember the order of the letters.
@theAwkwardYeti

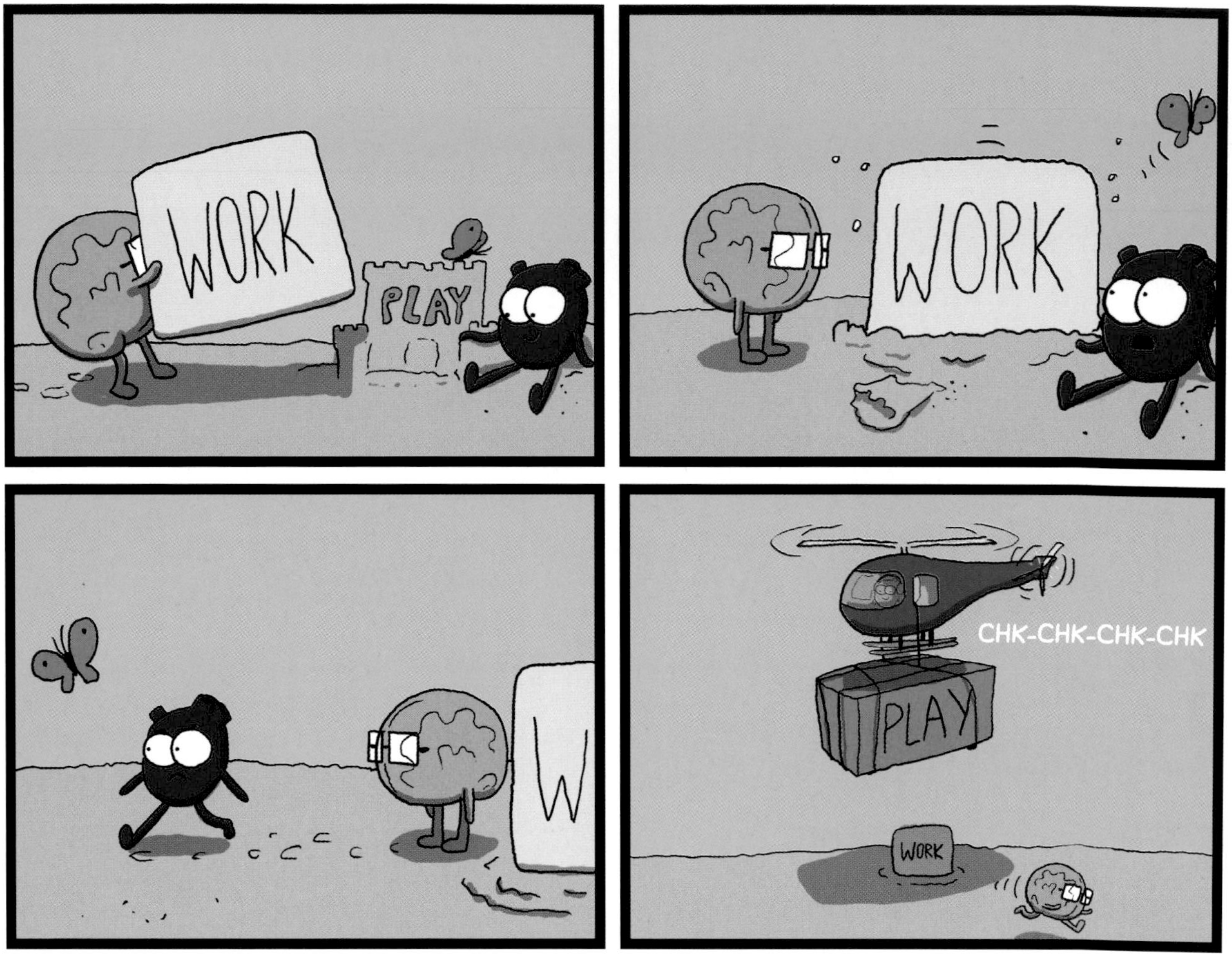
WORK
PLAY
WORK
W
CHK-CHK-CHK-CHK
PLAY
WORK

@theAwkwardYeti

Hey Brain, care for a tasste?!
Too many calories, Tongue.
Oh no! DOPAMINE hassk too many CALORIESSK?!
Dopamine?
Guessk I'll dissposse of thissk.
Wait.
You're nothing but a two-bit drug dealer!
Open up, acid breath!
@theAwkwardYeti

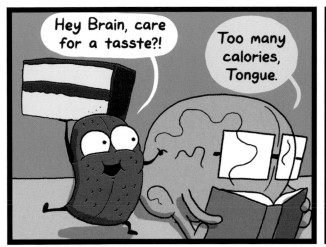

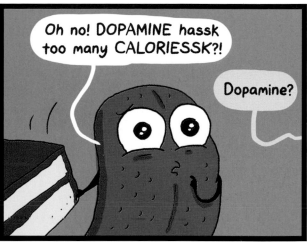

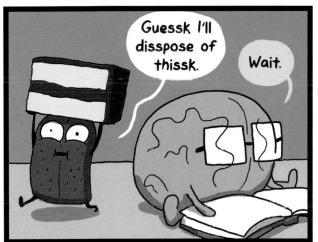

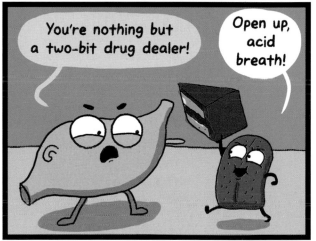

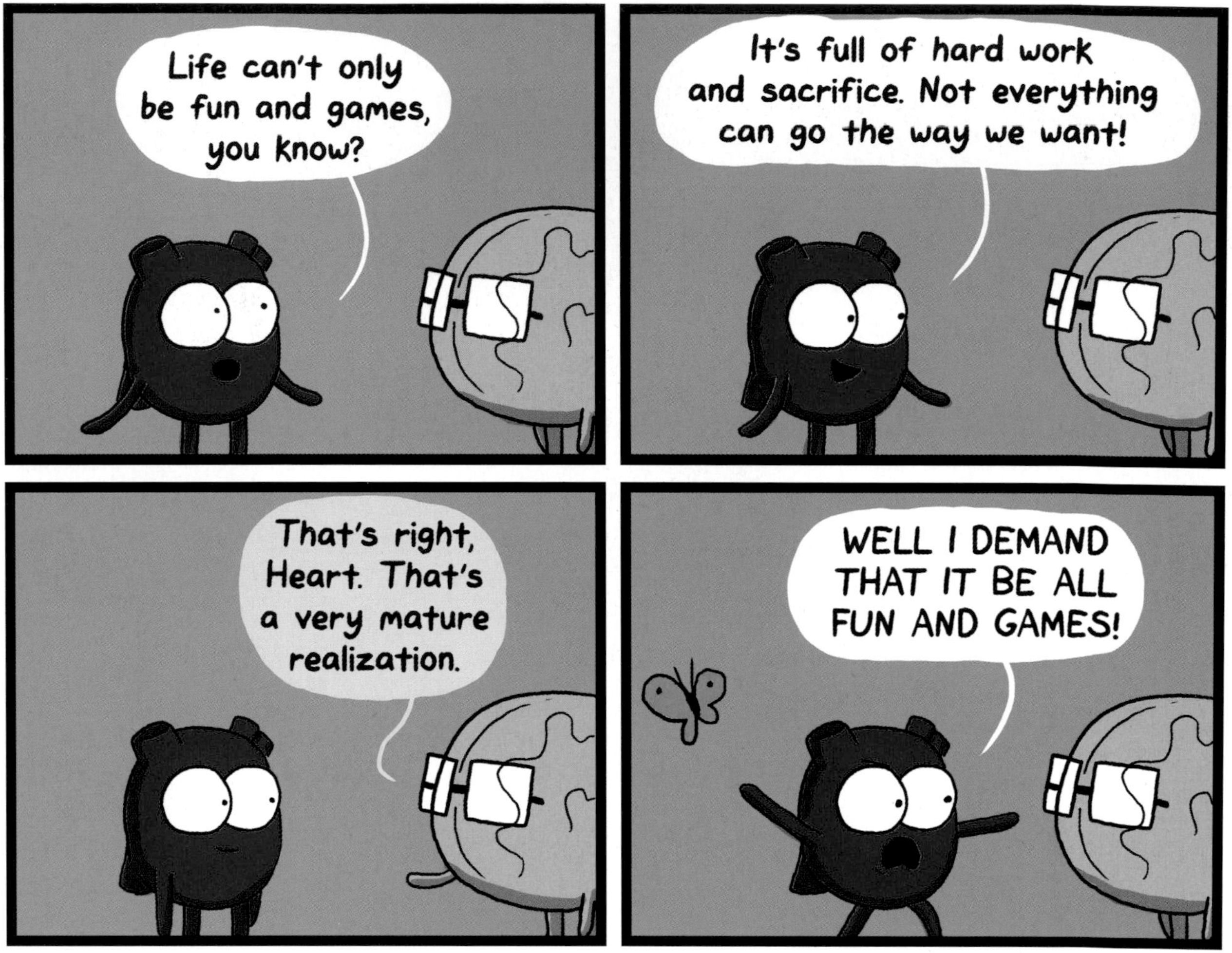
Life can't only be fun and games, you know?
It's full of hard work and sacrifice. Not everything can go the way we want!
That's right, Heart. That's a very mature realization.
WELL I DEMAND THAT IT BE ALL FUN AND GAMES!

@theAwkwardYeti

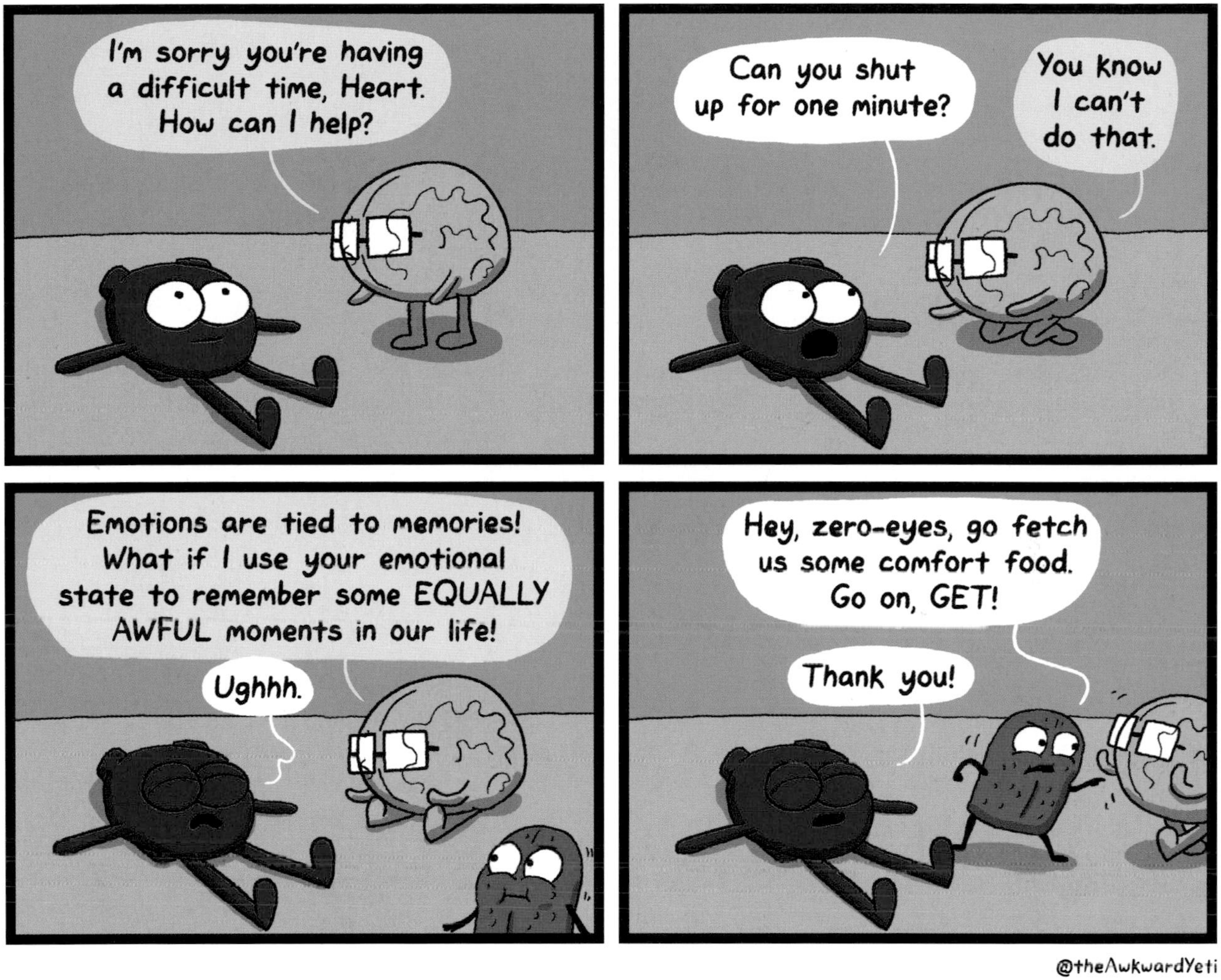
I'm sorry you're having a difficult time, Heart. How can I help?
Can you shut up for one minute?
You know I can't do that.
Emotions are tied to memories! What if I use your emotional state to remember some EQUALLY AWFUL moments in our life!
Ughhh.
Hey, zero-eyes, go fetch us some comfort food. Go on, GET!
Thank you!
@theAwkwardYeti

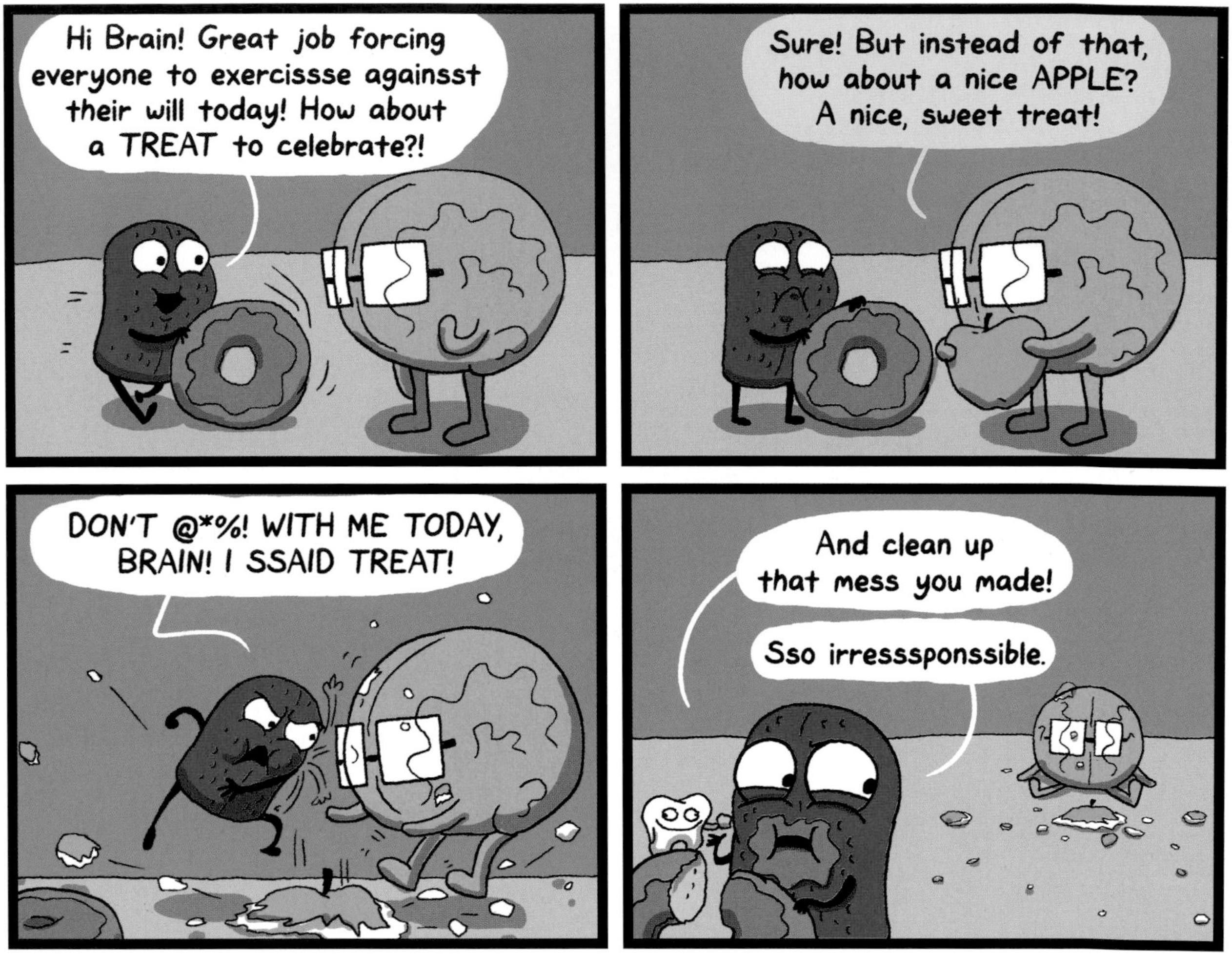

Hi Brain! Great job forcing everyone to exercissse againsst their will today! How about a TREAT to celebrate?!
Sure! But instead of that, how about a nice APPLE? A nice, sweet treat!
DON'T @*%! WITH ME TODAY, BRAIN! I SSAID TREAT!
And clean up that mess you made!
Sso irressspsonssible.

@theAwkwardYeti

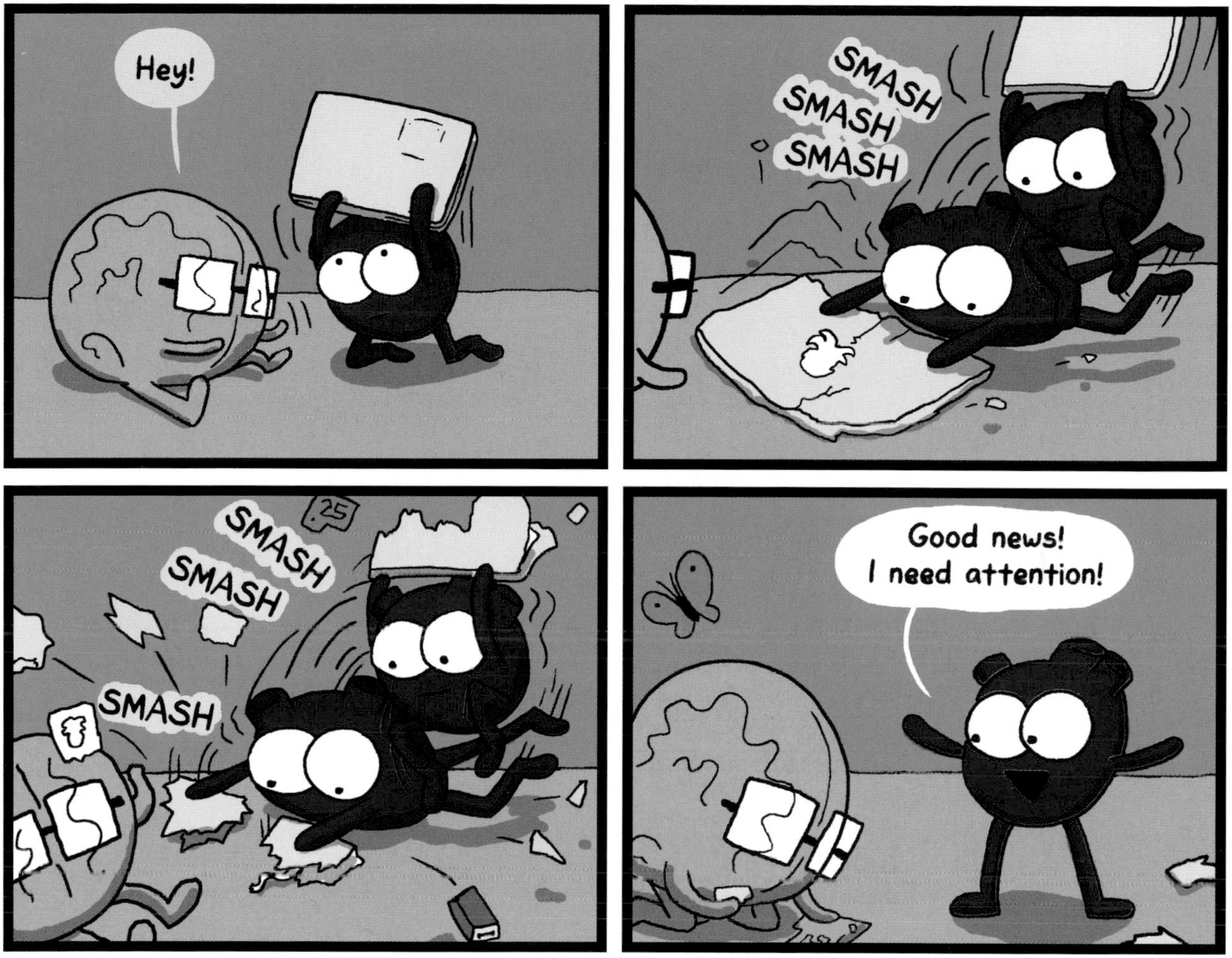
Hey!
SMASH
SMASH
SMASH
SMASH
SMASH
SMASH
Good news!
I need attention!

@theAwkwardYeti

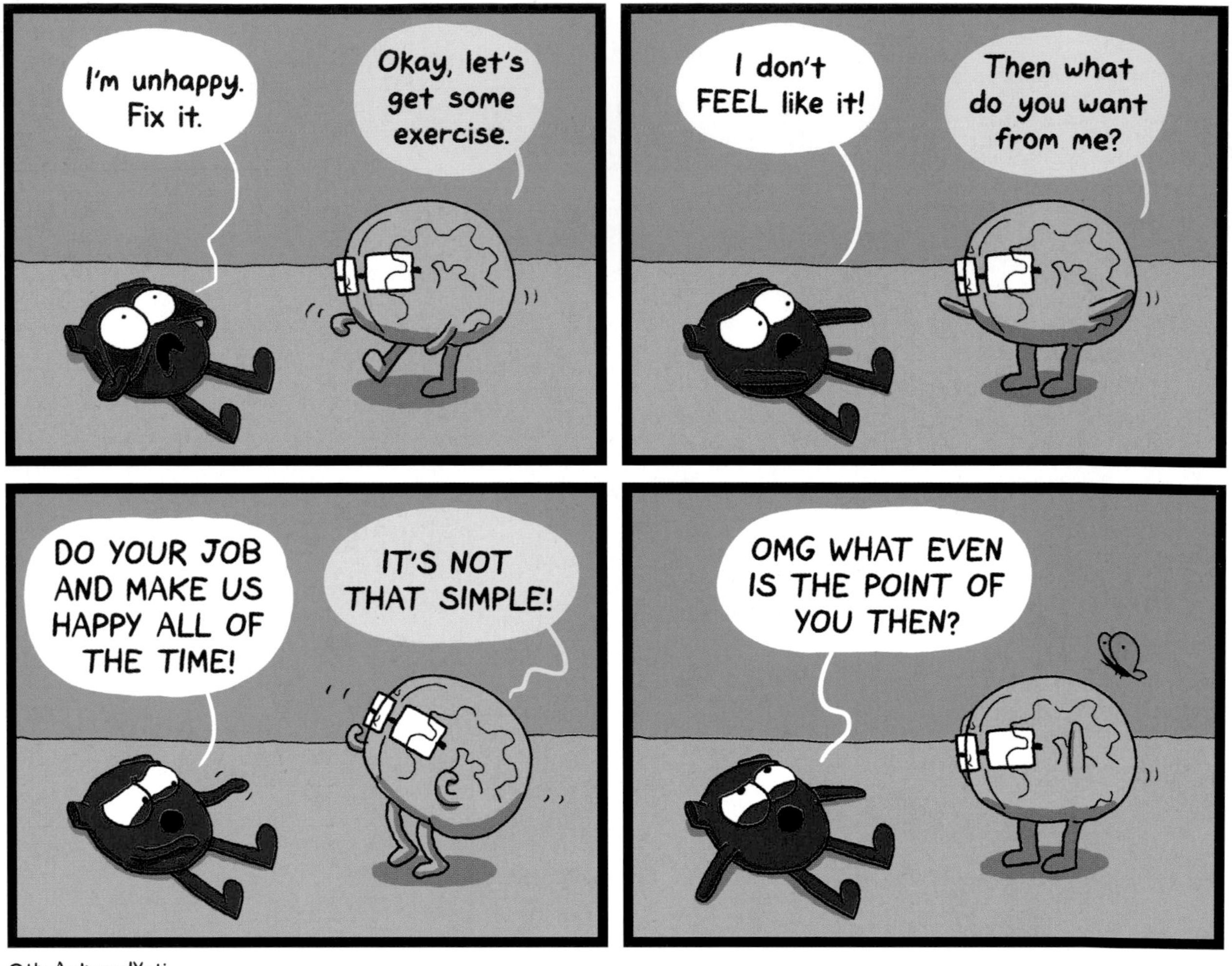
I'm unhappy. Fix it.
Okay, let's get some exercise.
I don't FEEL like it!
Then what do you want from me?
DO YOUR JOB AND MAKE US HAPPY ALL OF THE TIME!
IT'S NOT THAT SIMPLE!
OMG WHAT EVEN IS THE POINT OF YOU THEN?

@theAwkwardYeti

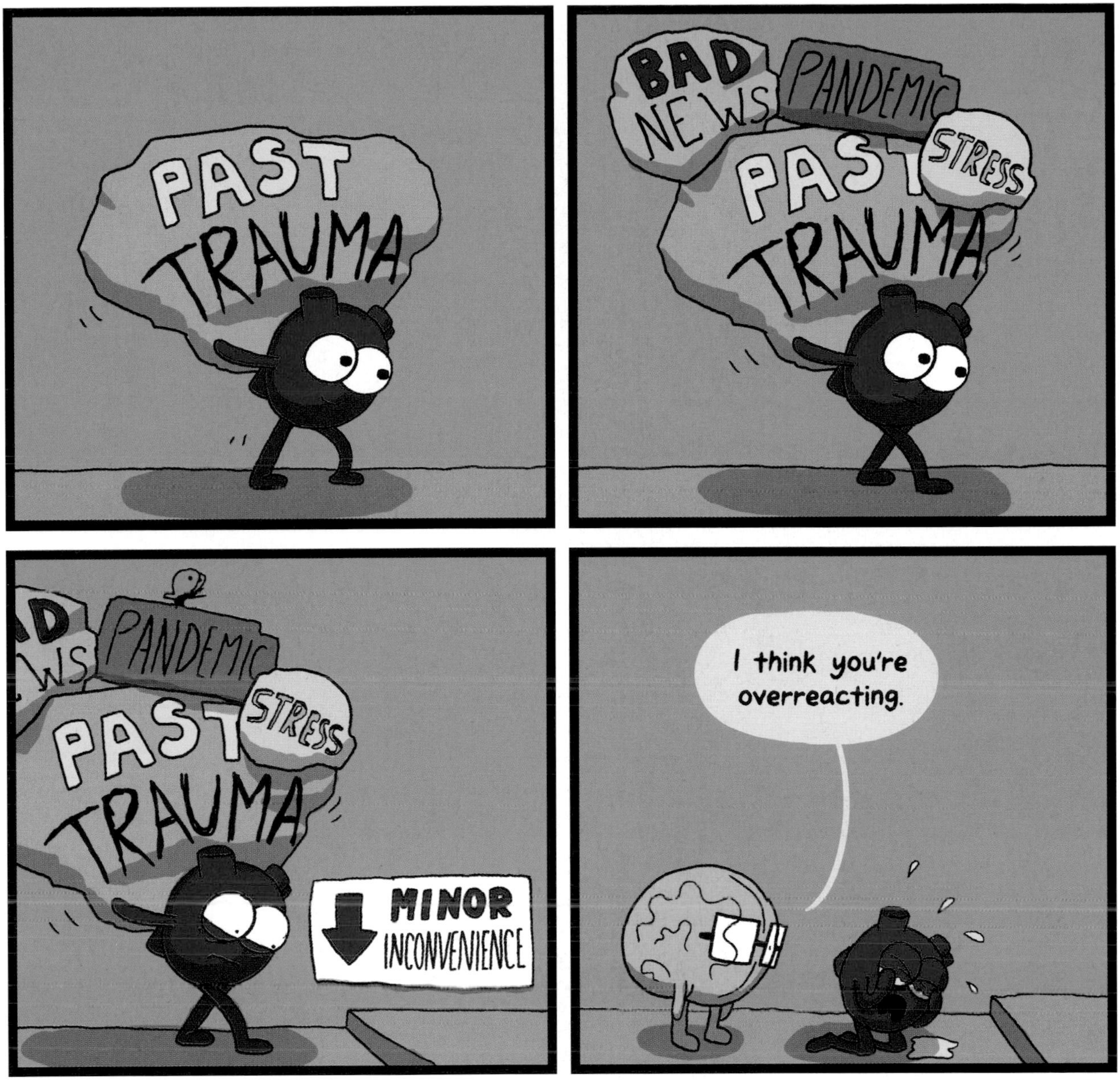
PAST
TRAUMA
BAD
NEWS
PANDEMIC
PAST
STRESS
TRAUMA
PANDEMIC
PAST
STRESS
TRAUMA
MINOR
INCONVENIENCE
I think you're overreacting.
@theAwkwardYeti

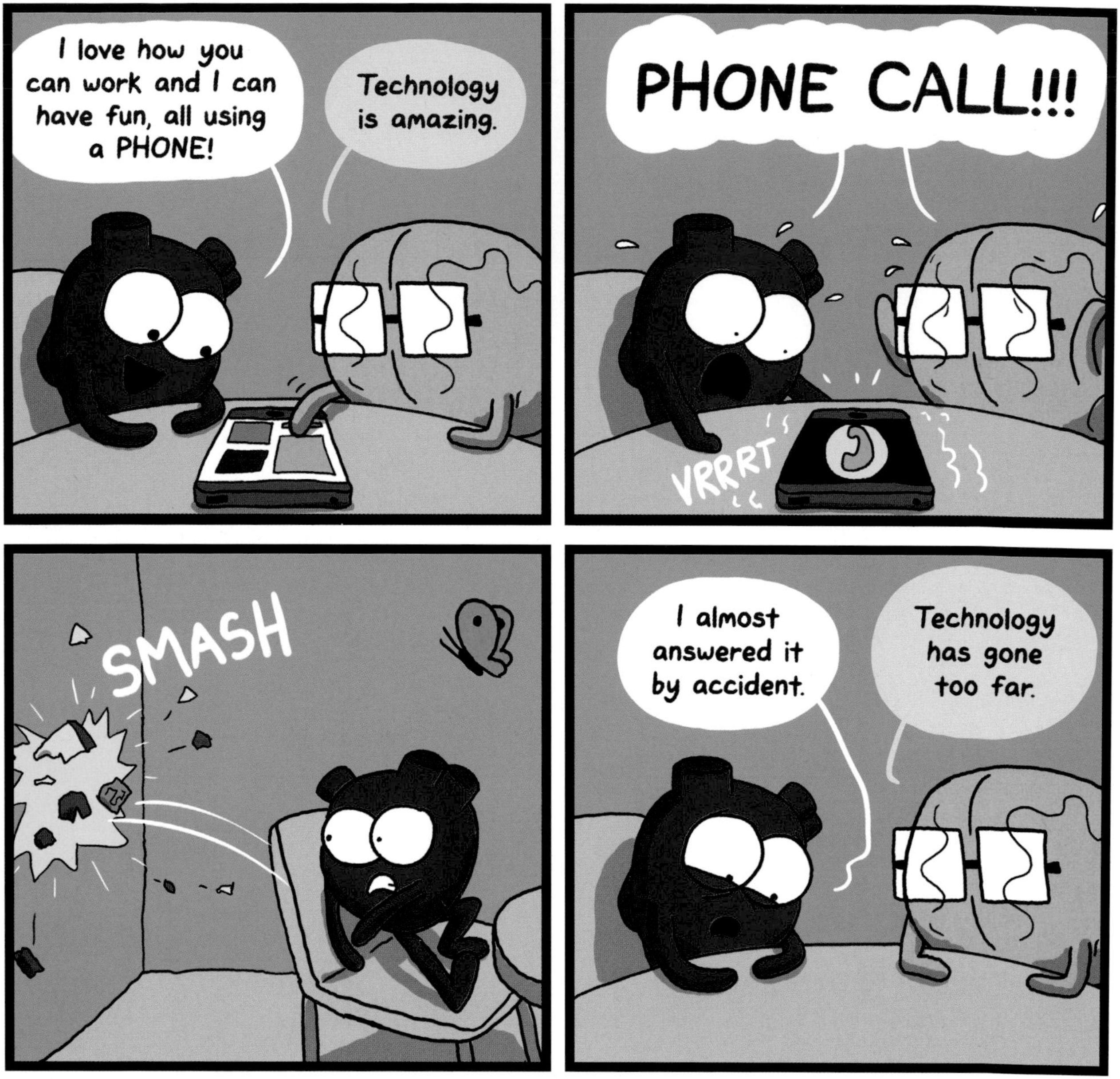
I love how you can work and I can have fun, all using a PHONE!
Technology is amazing.
PHONE CALL!!!
VRRRT
SMASH
I almost answered it by accident.
Technology has gone too far.

@theAwkwardYeti

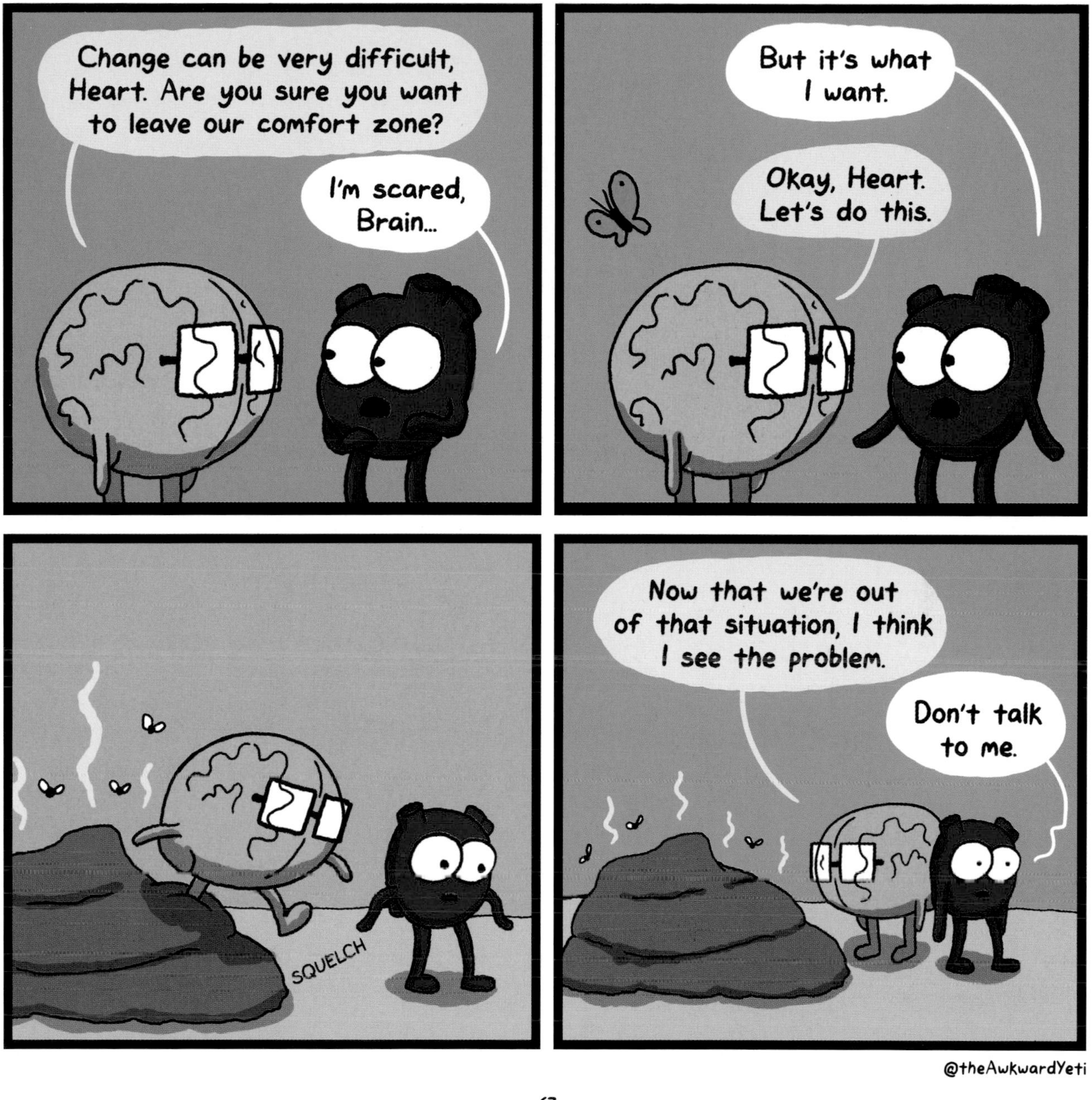
Change can be very difficult, Heart. Are you sure you want to leave our comfort zone?
I'm scared, Brain...
But it's what I want.
Okay, Heart. Let's do this.
SQUELCH
Now that we're out of that situation, I think I see the problem.
Don't talk to me.

@theAwkwardYeti

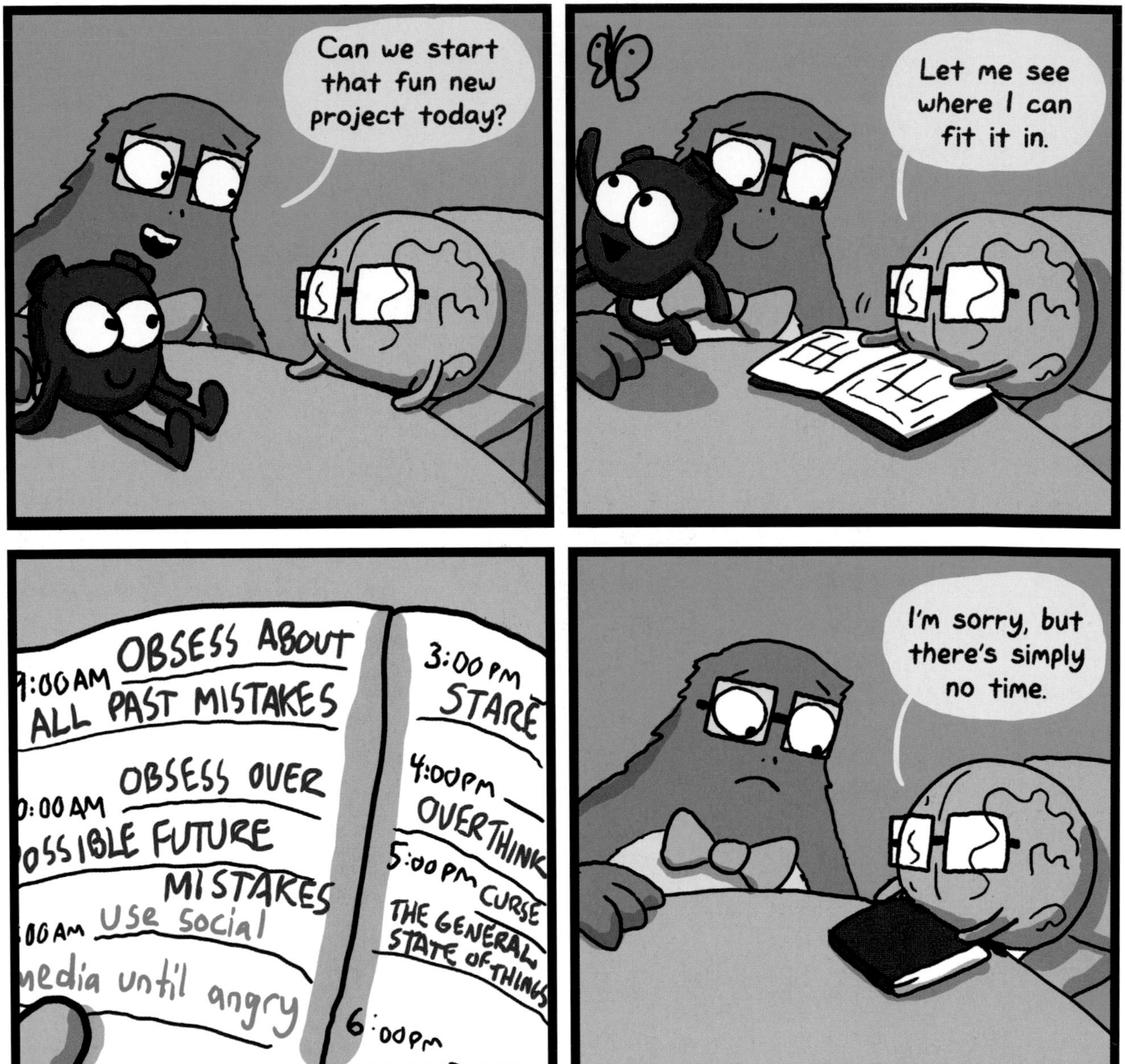
Can we start that fun new project today?
Let me see where I can fit it in.
:00AM OBSESS ABOUT ALL PAST MISTAKES
:00 AM OBSESS OVER
OSSIBLE FUTURE MISTAKES
00 AM Use social
edia until angry
3:00 PM STARE
4:00PM OVERTHINK
5:00 PM CURSE THE GENERAL STATE OF THINGS
6:00PM
I'm sorry, but there's simply no time.

@theAwkwardYeti

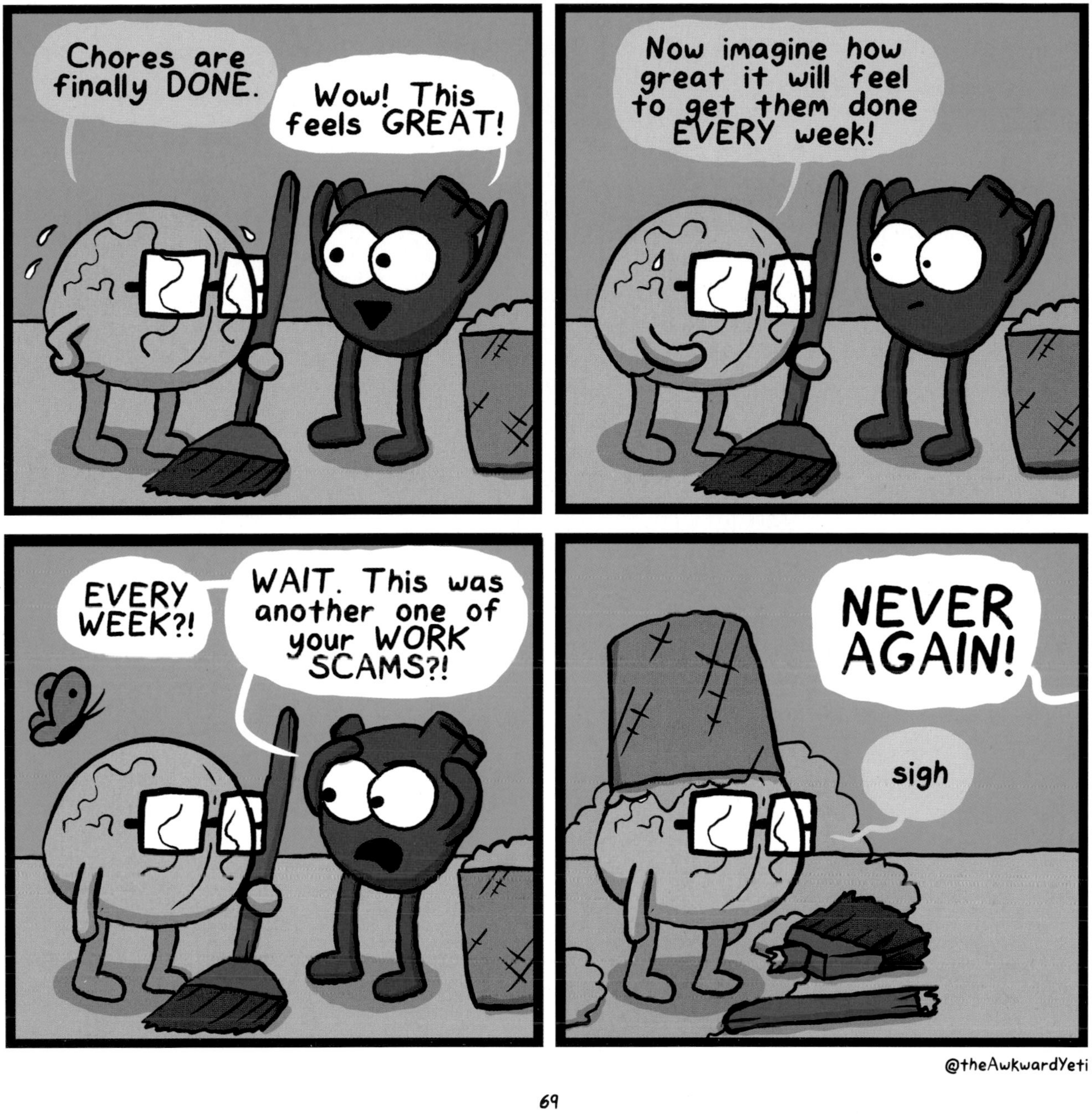
Chores are finally DONE.
Wow! This feels GREAT!
Now imagine how great it will feel to get them done EVERY week!
EVERY WEEK?!
WAIT. This was another one of your WORK SCAMS?!
NEVER AGAIN!
sigh

@theAwkwardYeti

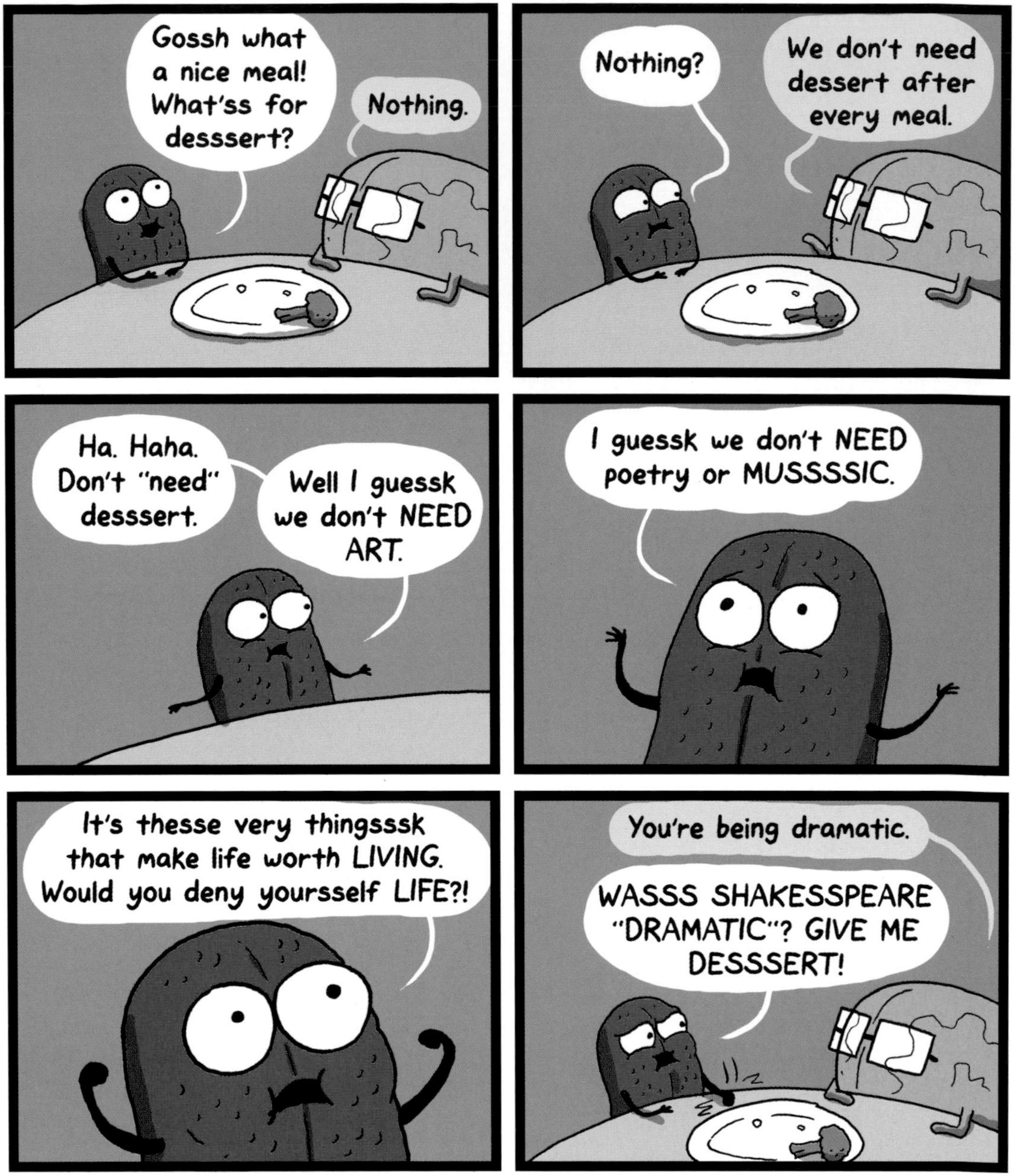
Gossh what a nice meal! What'ss for desssert?
Nothing.
Nothing?
We don't need dessert after every meal.
Ha. Haha. Don't "need" desssert.
Well I guessk we don't NEED ART.
I guessk we don't NEED poetry or MUSSSSIC.
It's thesse very thingsssk that make life worth LIVING. Would you deny yoursself LIFE?!
You're being dramatic.
WASSS SHAKESSPEARE "DRAMATIC"? GIVE ME DESSSERT!

@theAwkwardYeti

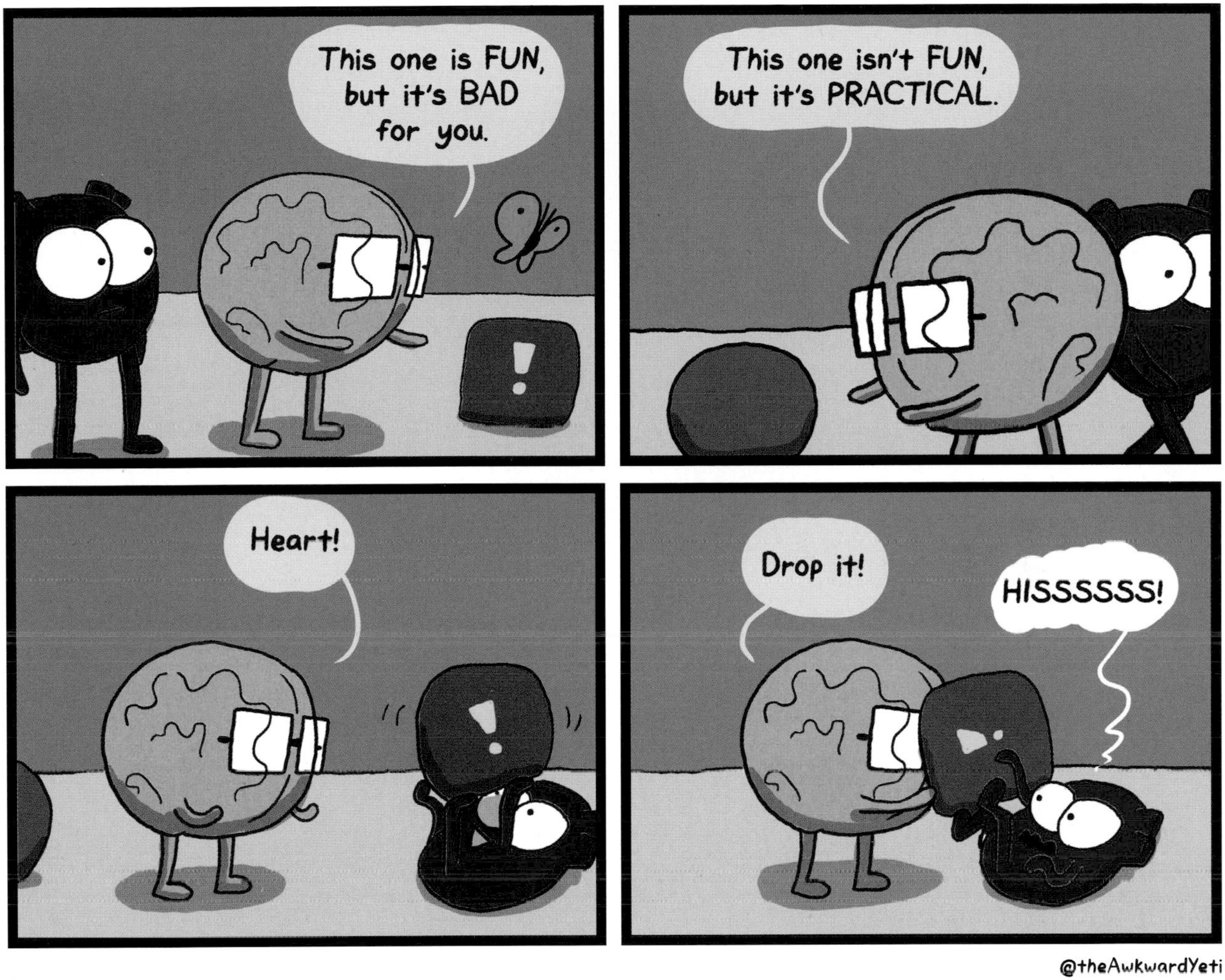
This one is FUN, but it's BAD for you.
This one isn't FUN, but it's PRACTICAL.
Heart!
Drop it!
HISSSSSS!
@theAwkwardYeti

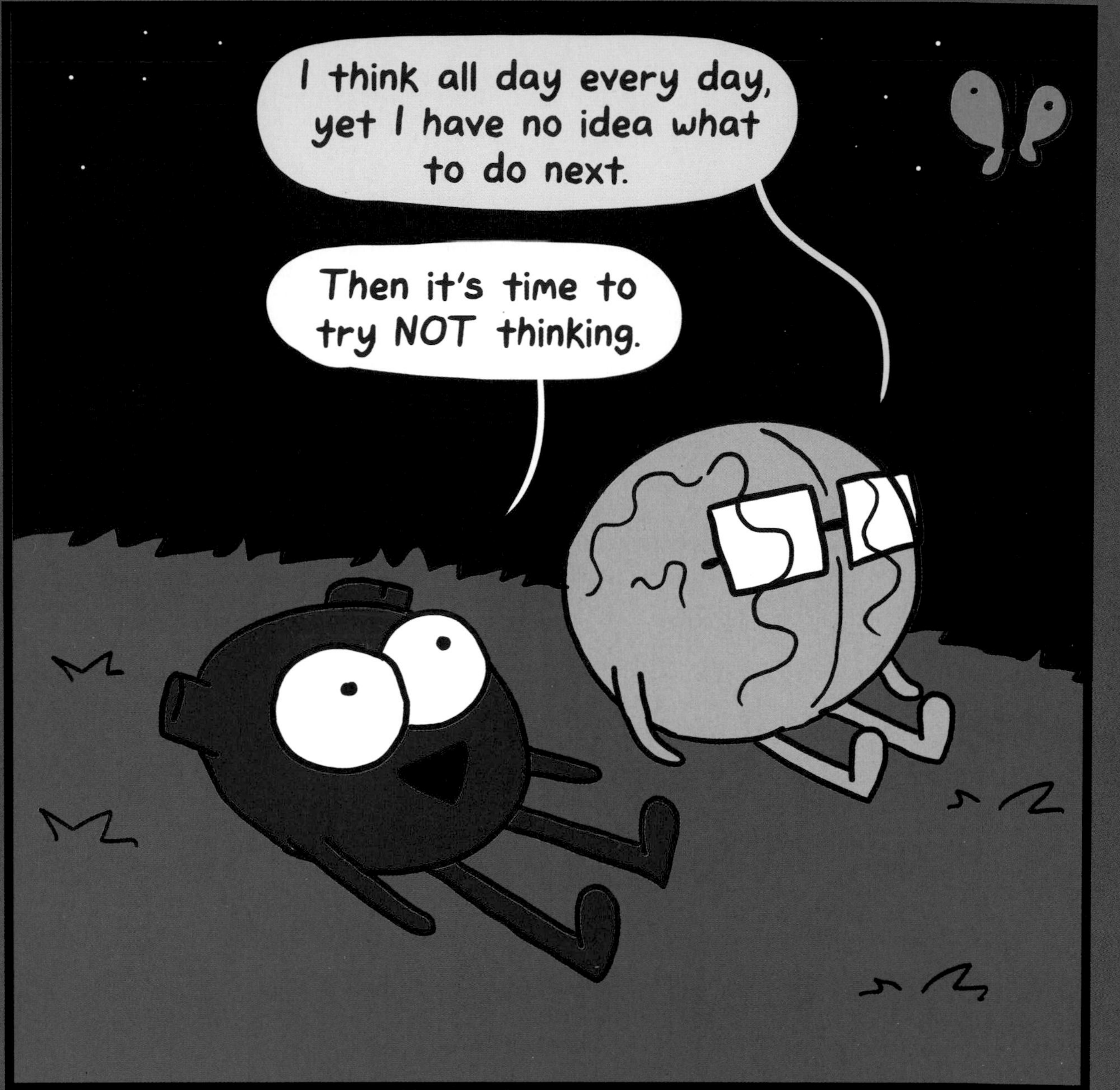
I think all day every day, yet I have no idea what to do next.
Then it's time to try NOT thinking.

@theAwkwardYeti

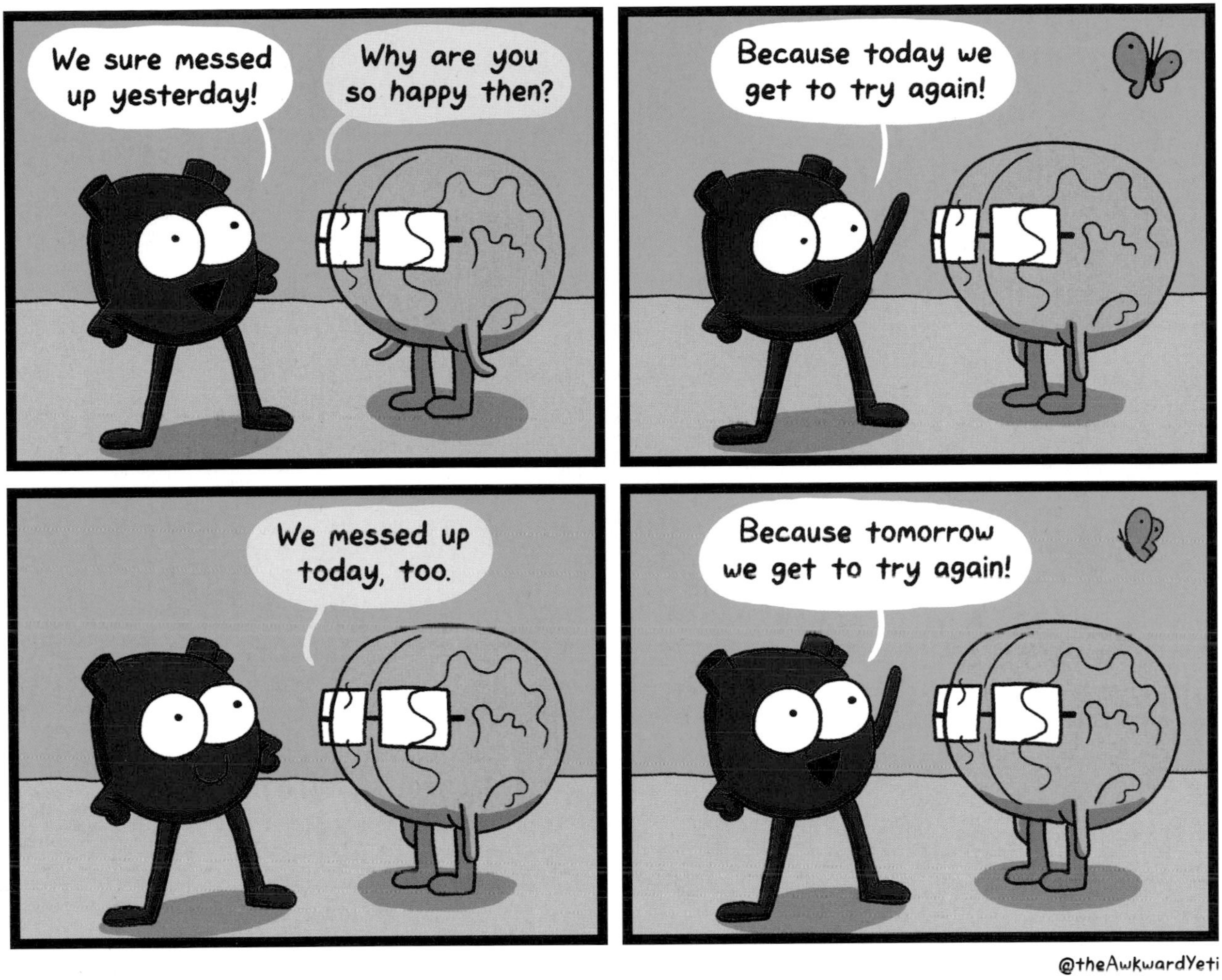
We sure messed up yesterday!
Why are you so happy then?
Because today we get to try again!
We messed up today, too.
Because tomorrow we get to try again!
@theAwkwardYeti

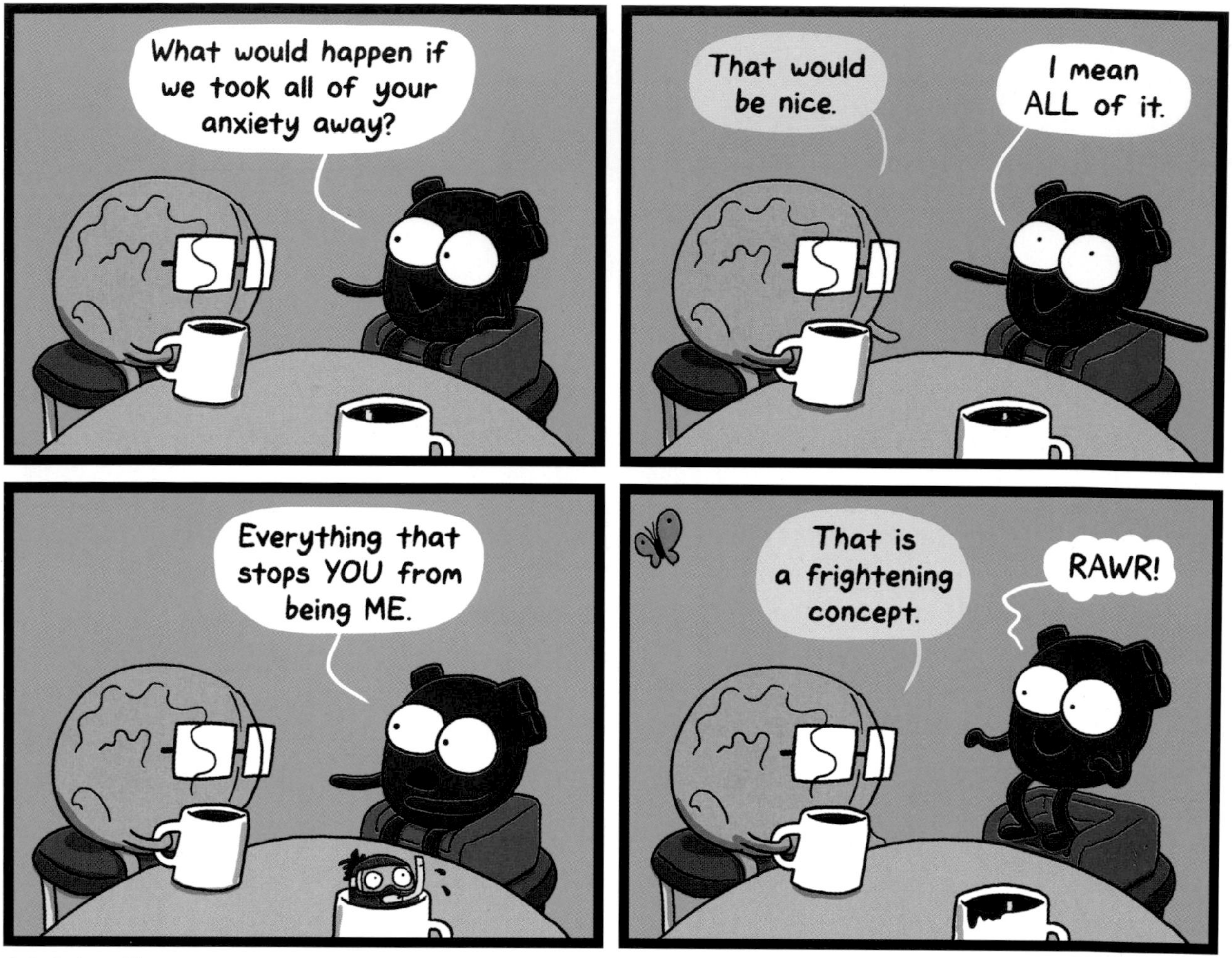
What would happen if we took all of your anxiety away?
That would be nice.
I mean ALL of it.
Everything that stops YOU from being ME.
That is a frightening concept.
RAWR!

@theAwkwardYeti

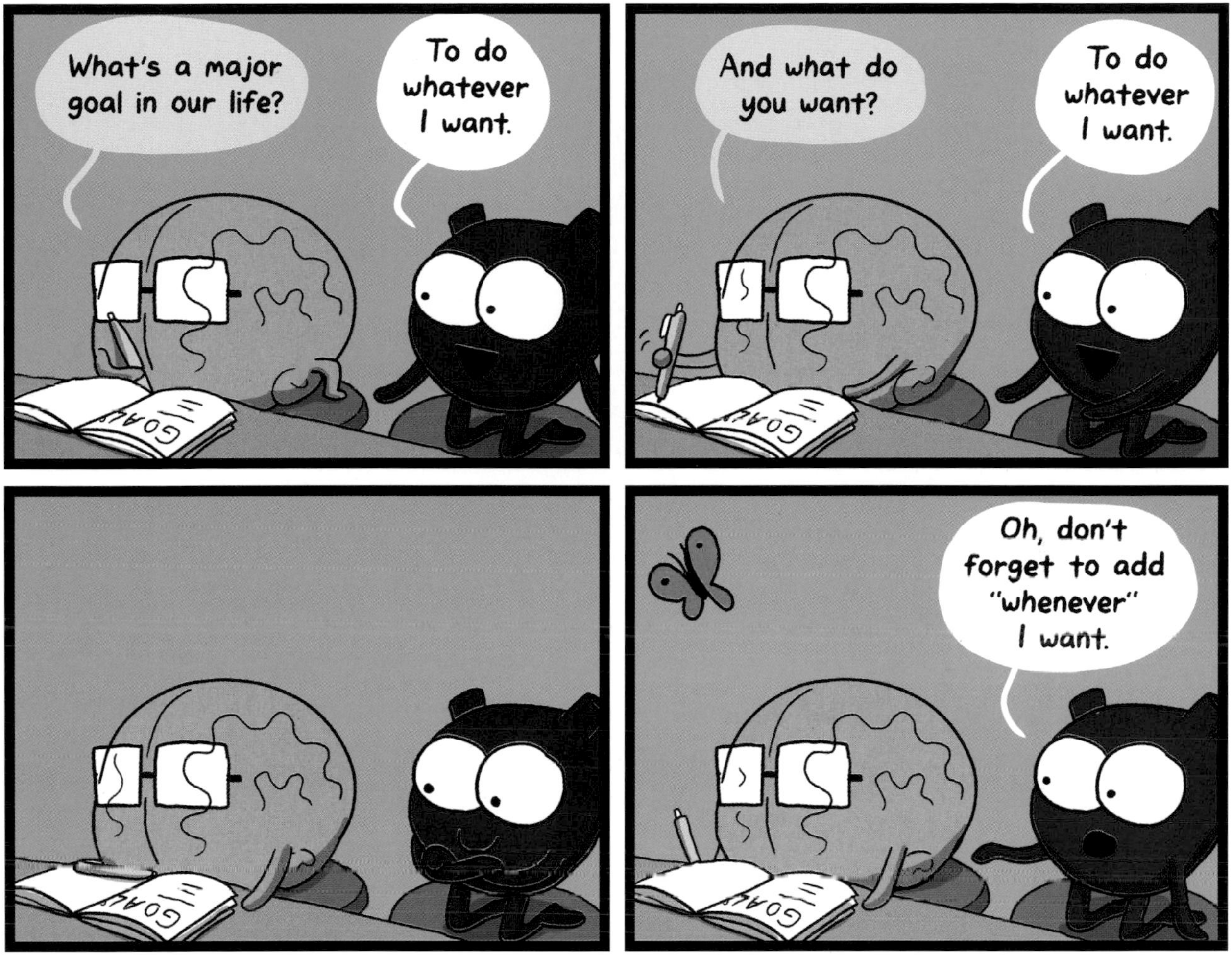
What's a major goal in our life?
To do whatever I want.
And what do you want?
To do whatever I want.
GOALS
Oh, don't forget to add "whenever" I want.

@theAwkwardYeti

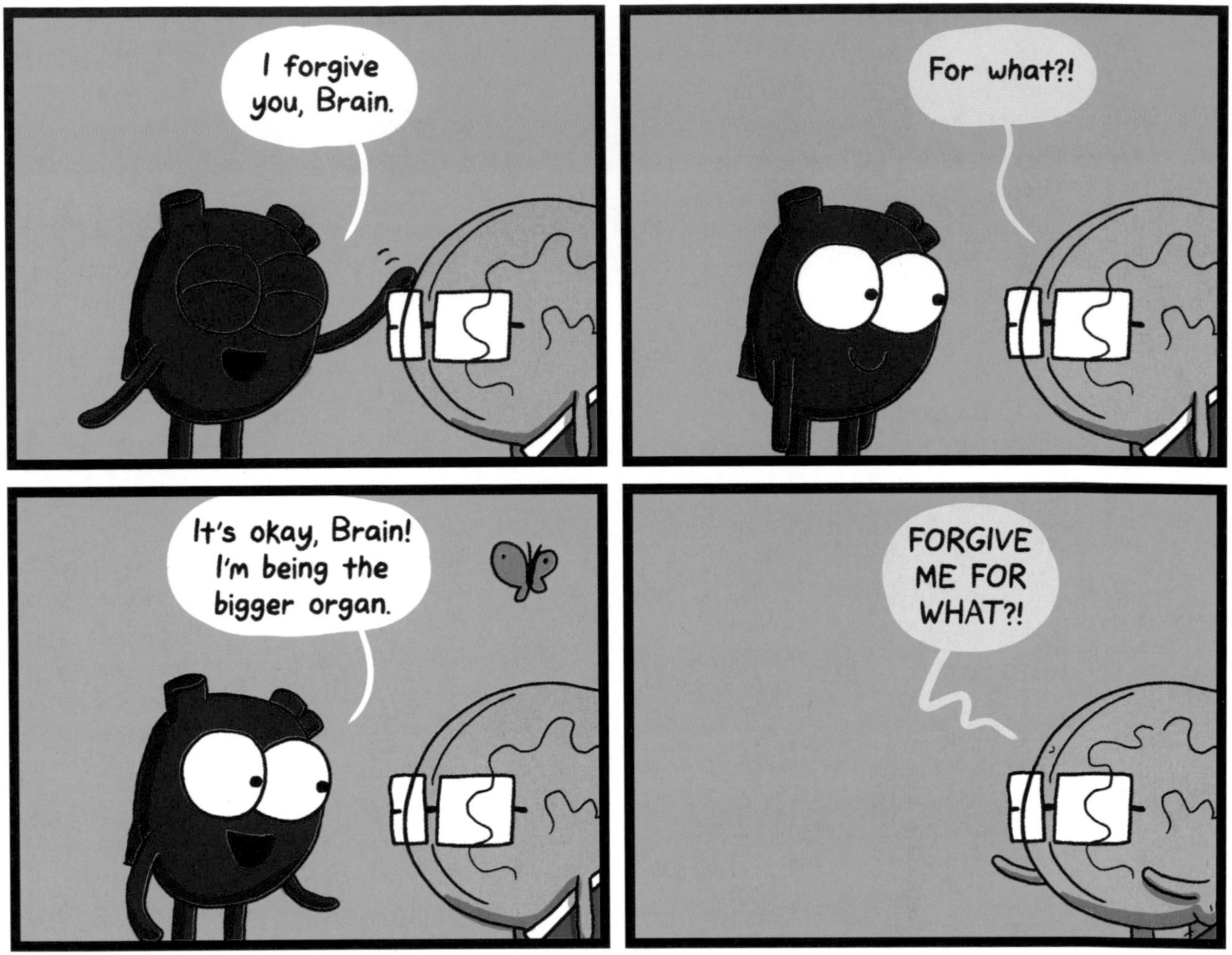
I forgive you, Brain.
For what?!
It's okay, Brain! I'm being the bigger organ.
FORGIVE ME FOR WHAT?!

@theAwkwardYeti

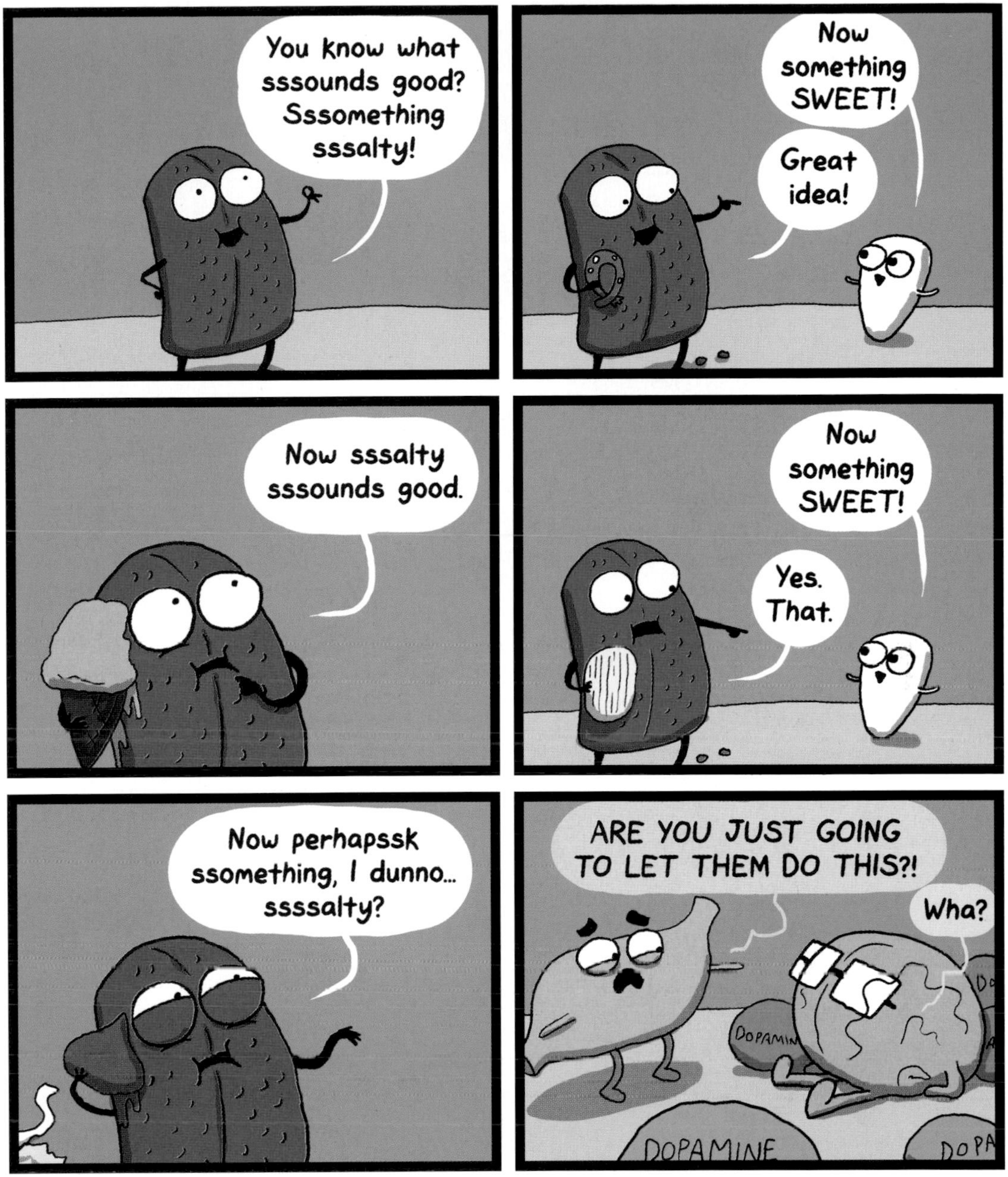
You know what sssounds good? Sssomething sssalty!
Now something SWEET!
Great idea!
Now sssalty sssounds good.
Now something SWEET!
Yes. That.
Now perhapssk ssomething, I dunno... ssssalty?
ARE YOU JUST GOING TO LET THEM DO THIS?!
Wha?
DOPAMINE

@theAwkwardYeti

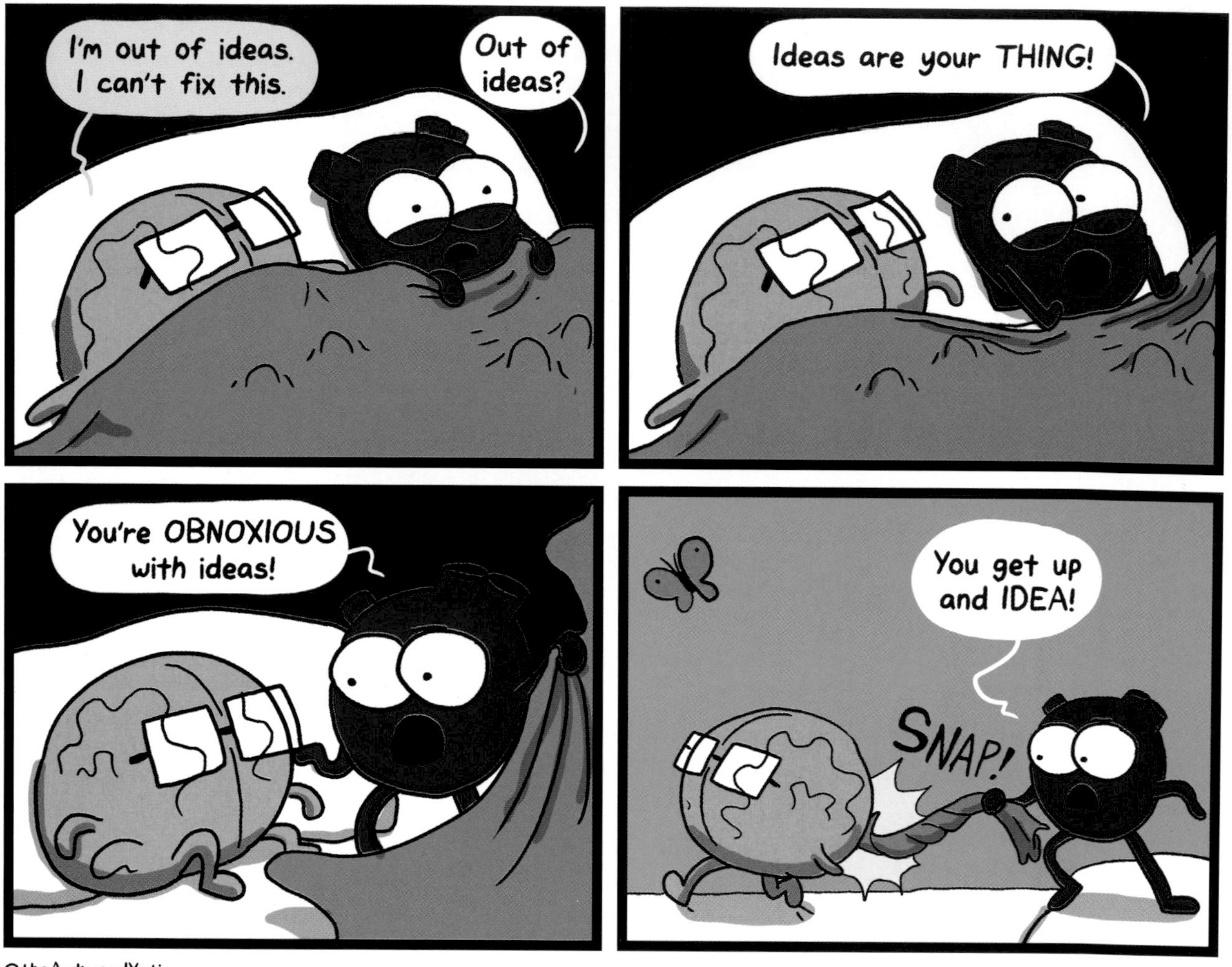

I'm out of ideas.
I can't fix this.
Out of ideas?
Ideas are your THING!
You're OBNOXIOUS with ideas!
You get up and IDEA!
SNAP!

@theAwkwardYeti

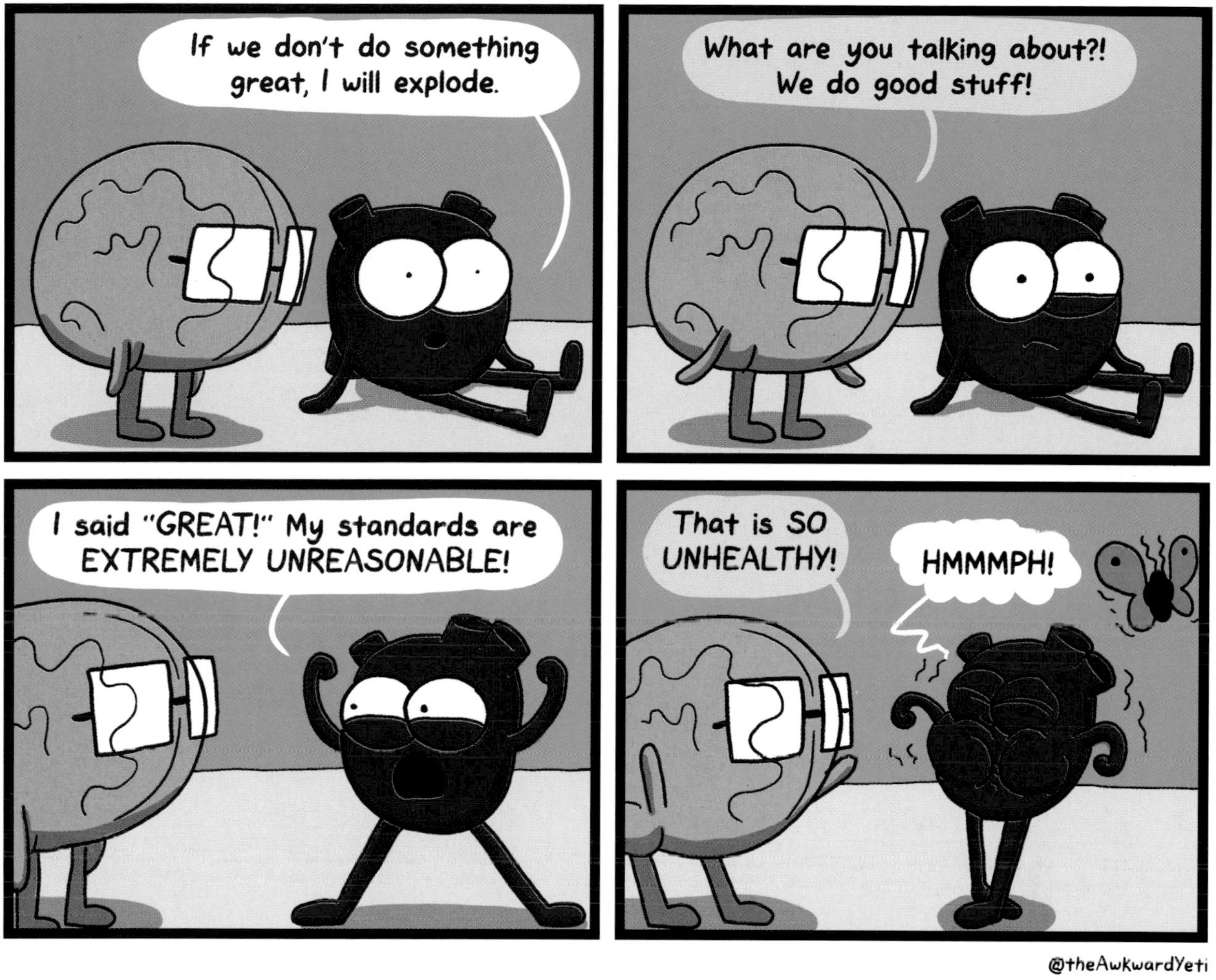
If we don't do something great, I will explode.
What are you talking about?! We do good stuff!
I said "GREAT!" My standards are EXTREMELY UNREASONABLE!
That is SO UNHEALTHY!
HMMMPH!
@theAwkwardYeti

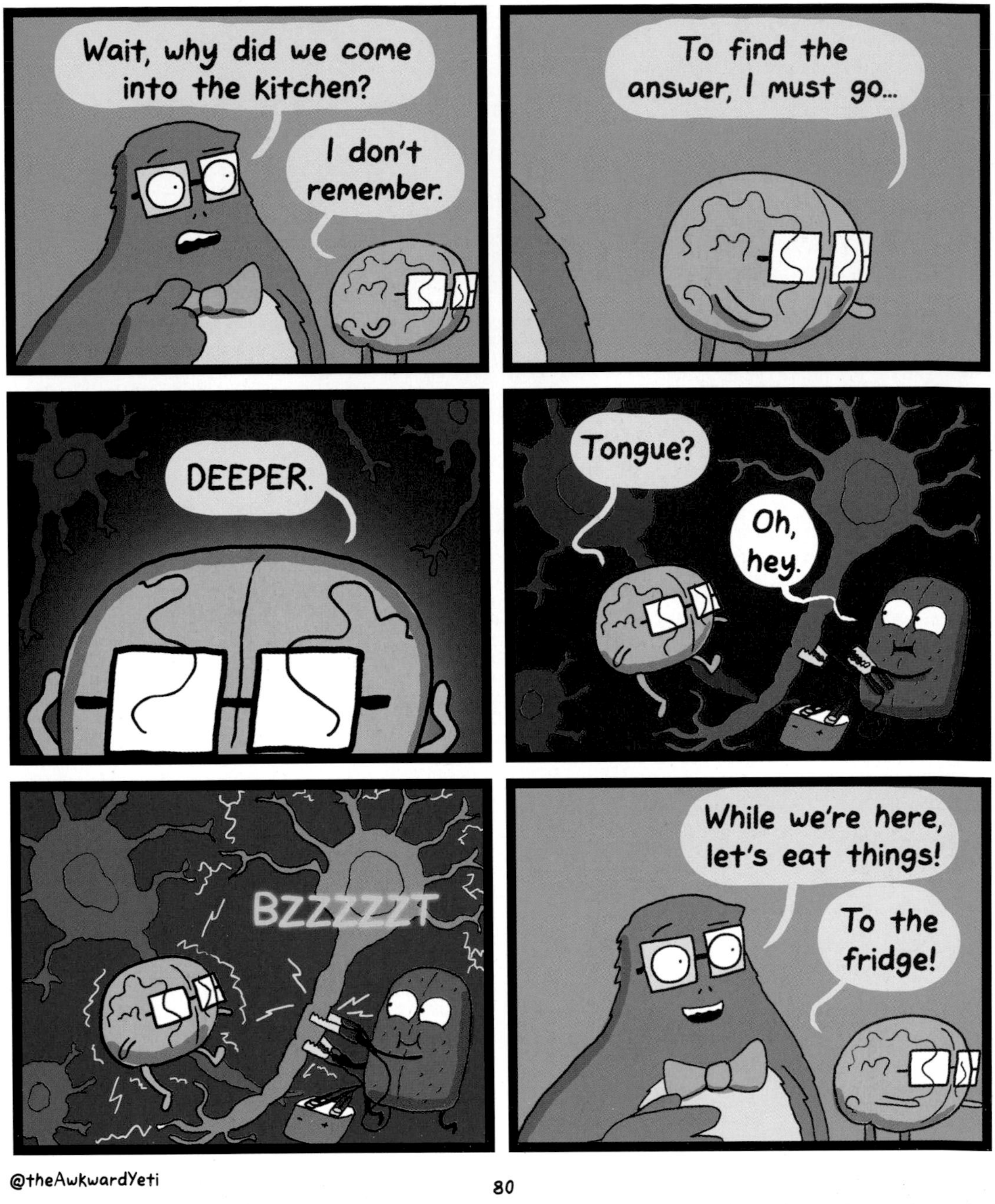
Wait, why did we come into the kitchen?
I don't remember.
To find the answer, I must go...
DEEPER.
Tongue?
Oh, hey.
BZZZZZT
While we're here, let's eat things!
To the fridge!

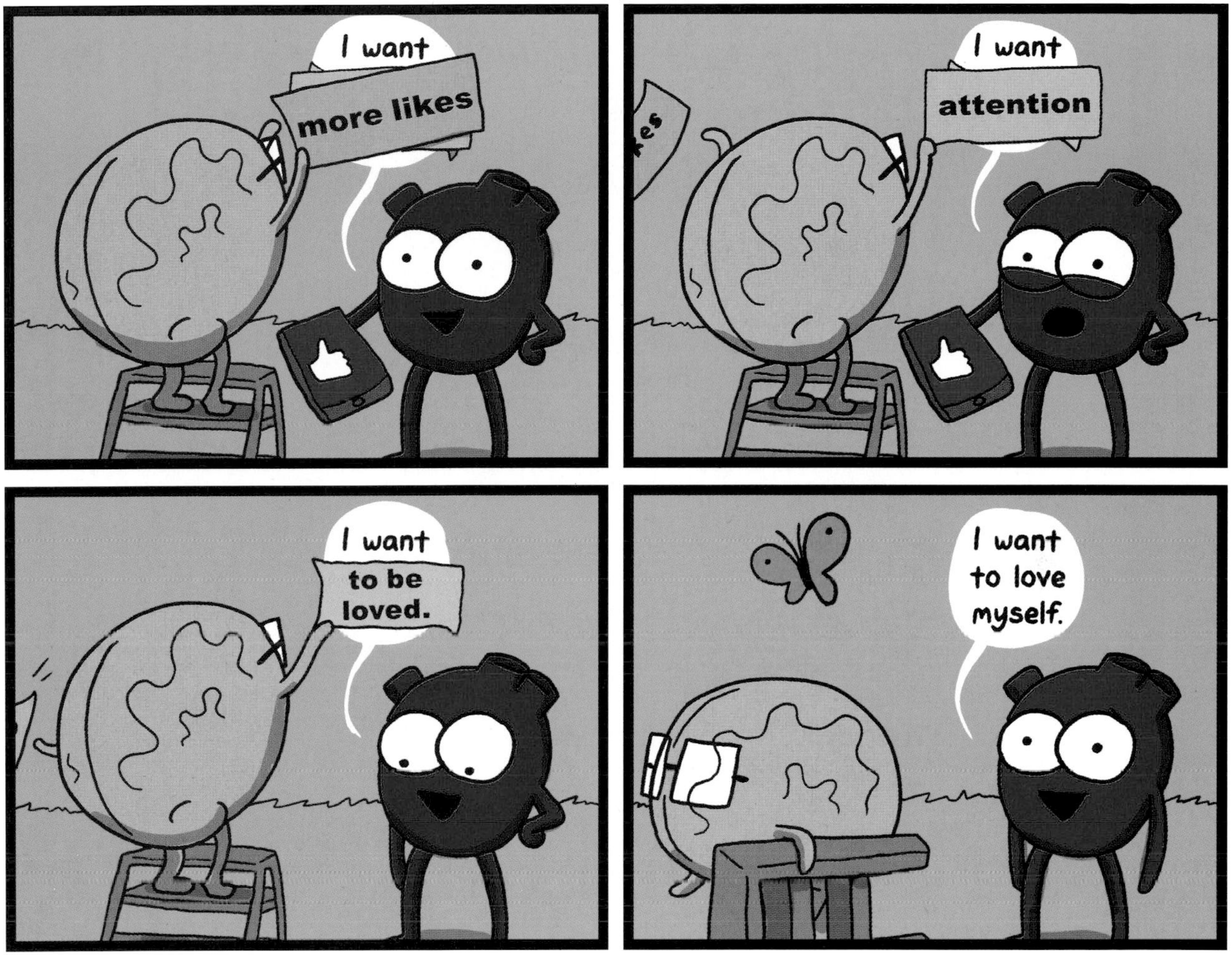
I want
more likes
I want
attention
kes
I want
to be
loved.
I want
to love
myself.

@theAwkwardYeti

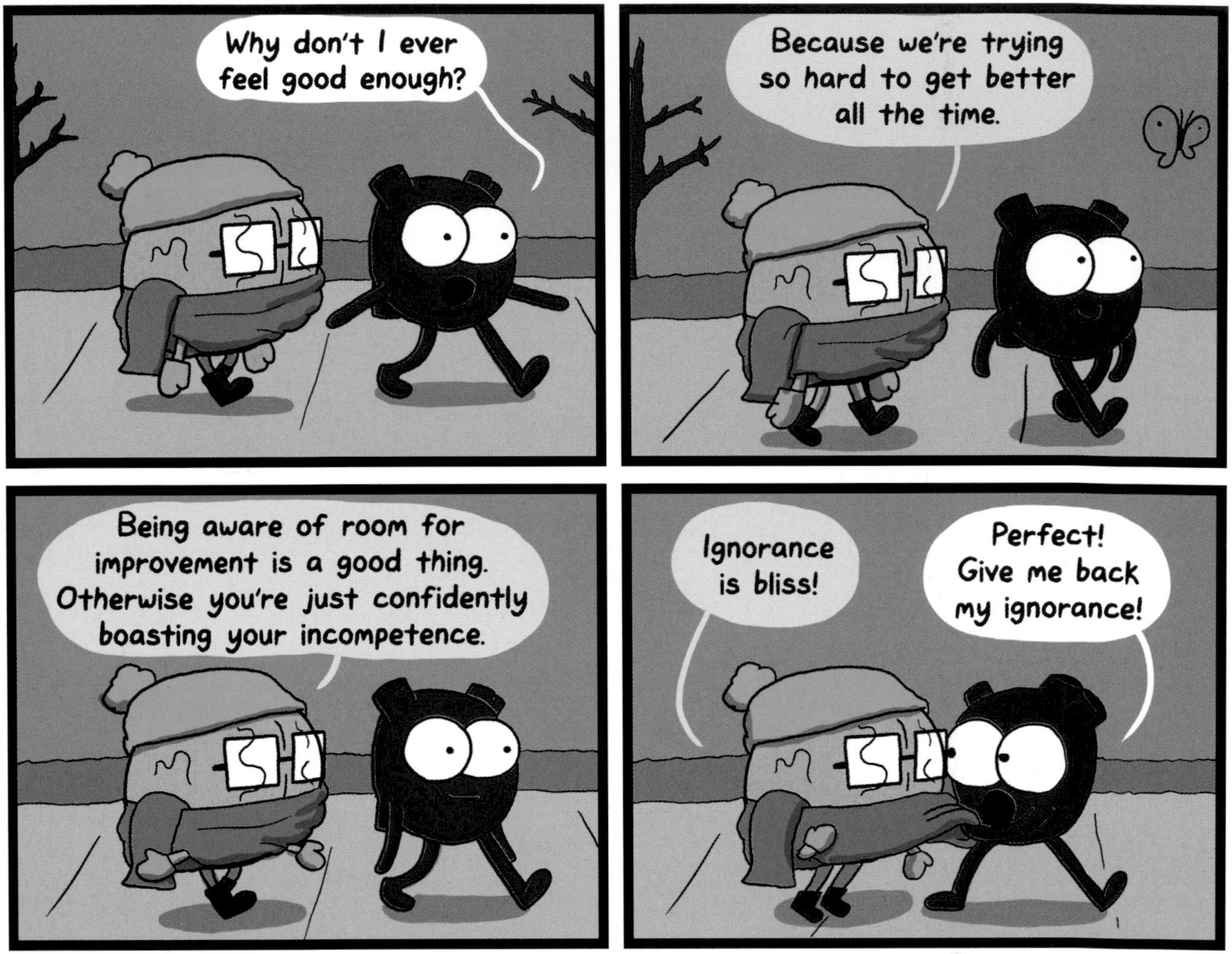
Why don't I ever feel good enough?
Because we're trying so hard to get better all the time.
Being aware of room for improvement is a good thing. Otherwise you're just confidently boasting your incompetence.
Ignorance is bliss!
Perfect! Give me back my ignorance!

@theAwkwardYeti

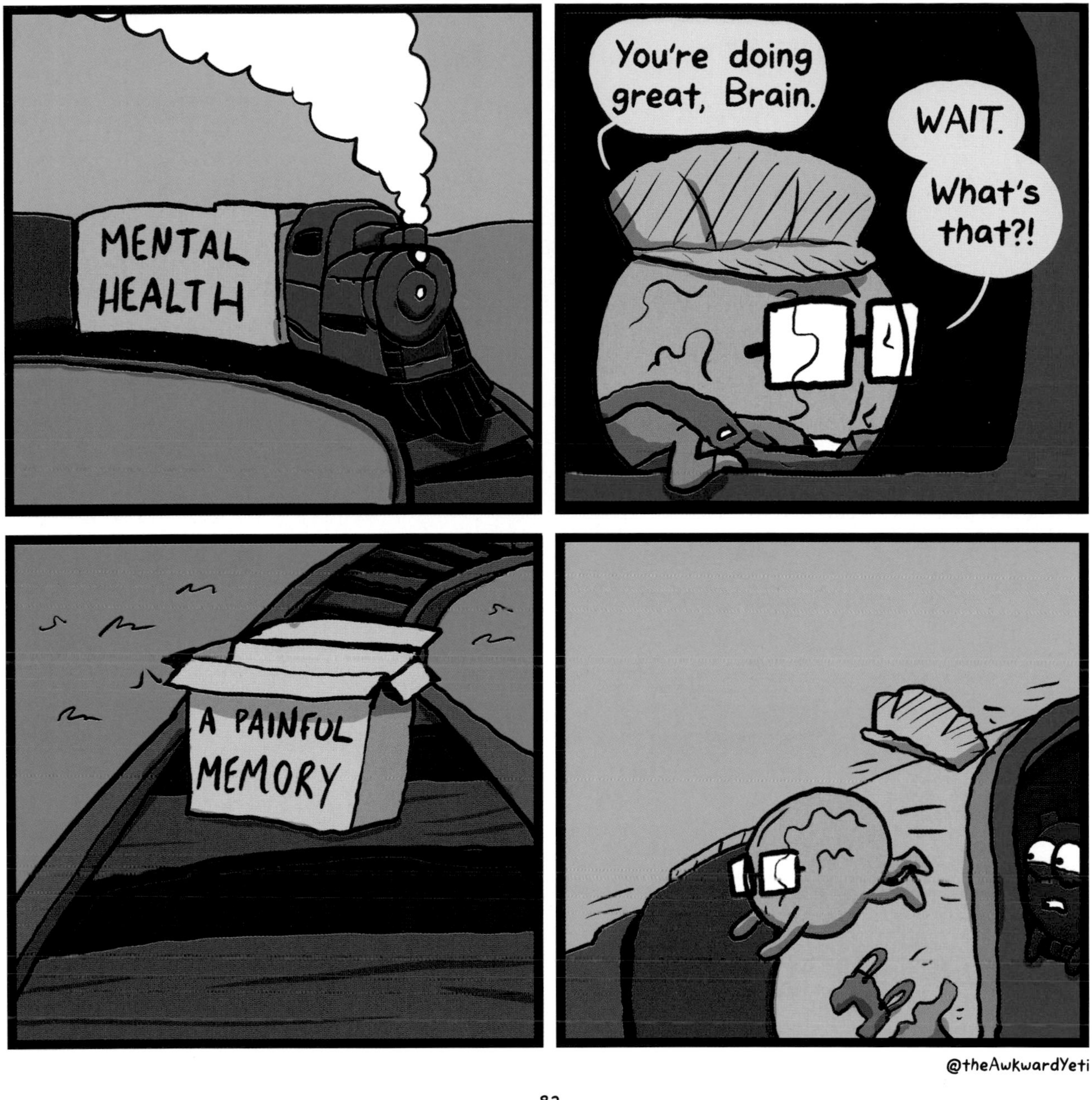
MENTAL HEALTH
You're doing great, Brain.
WAIT.
What's that?!
A PAINFUL MEMORY

@theAwkwardYeti

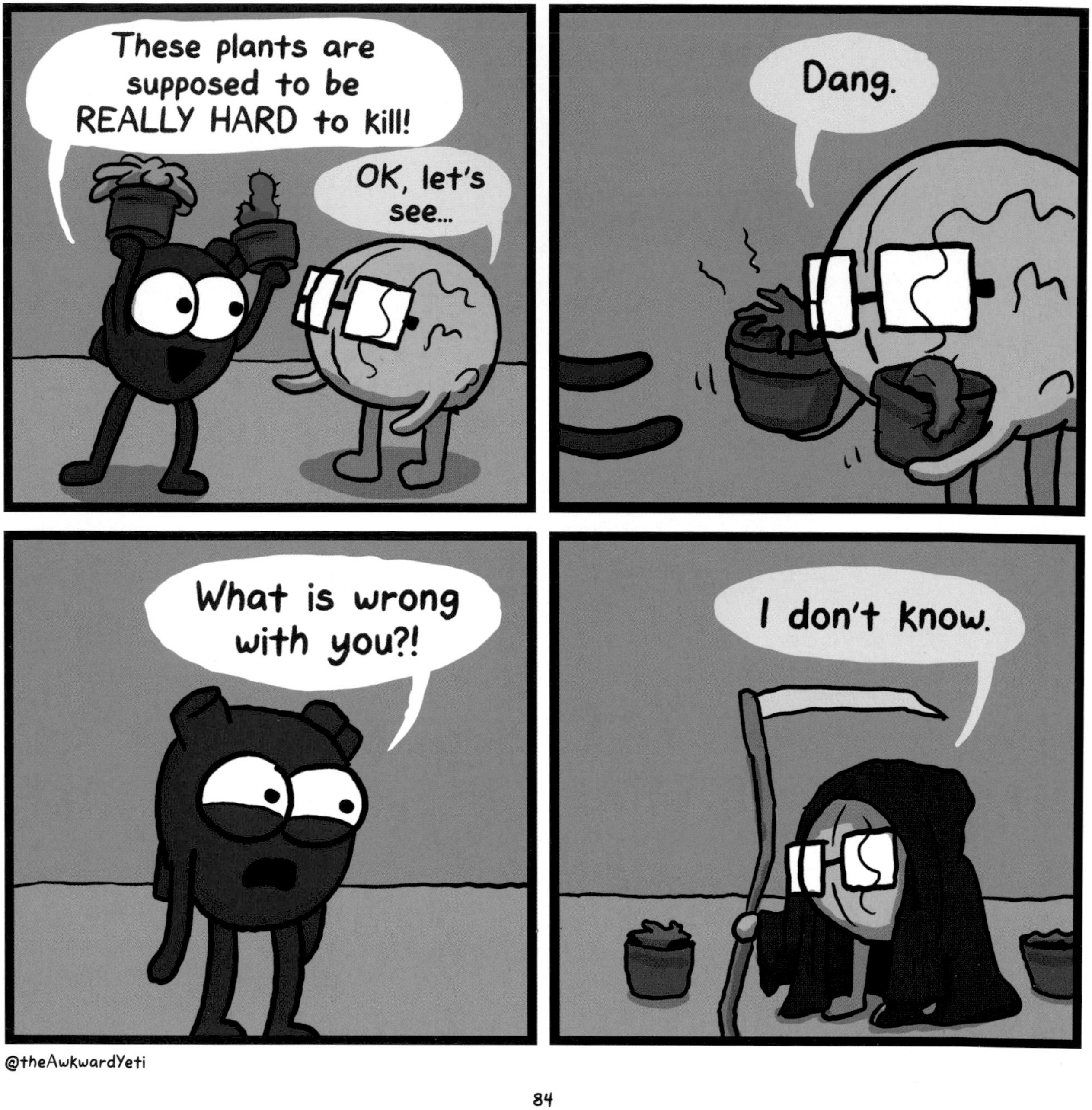
These plants are supposed to be REALLY HARD to kill!
OK, let's see...
Dang.
What is wrong with you?!
I don't know.

@theAwkwardYeti

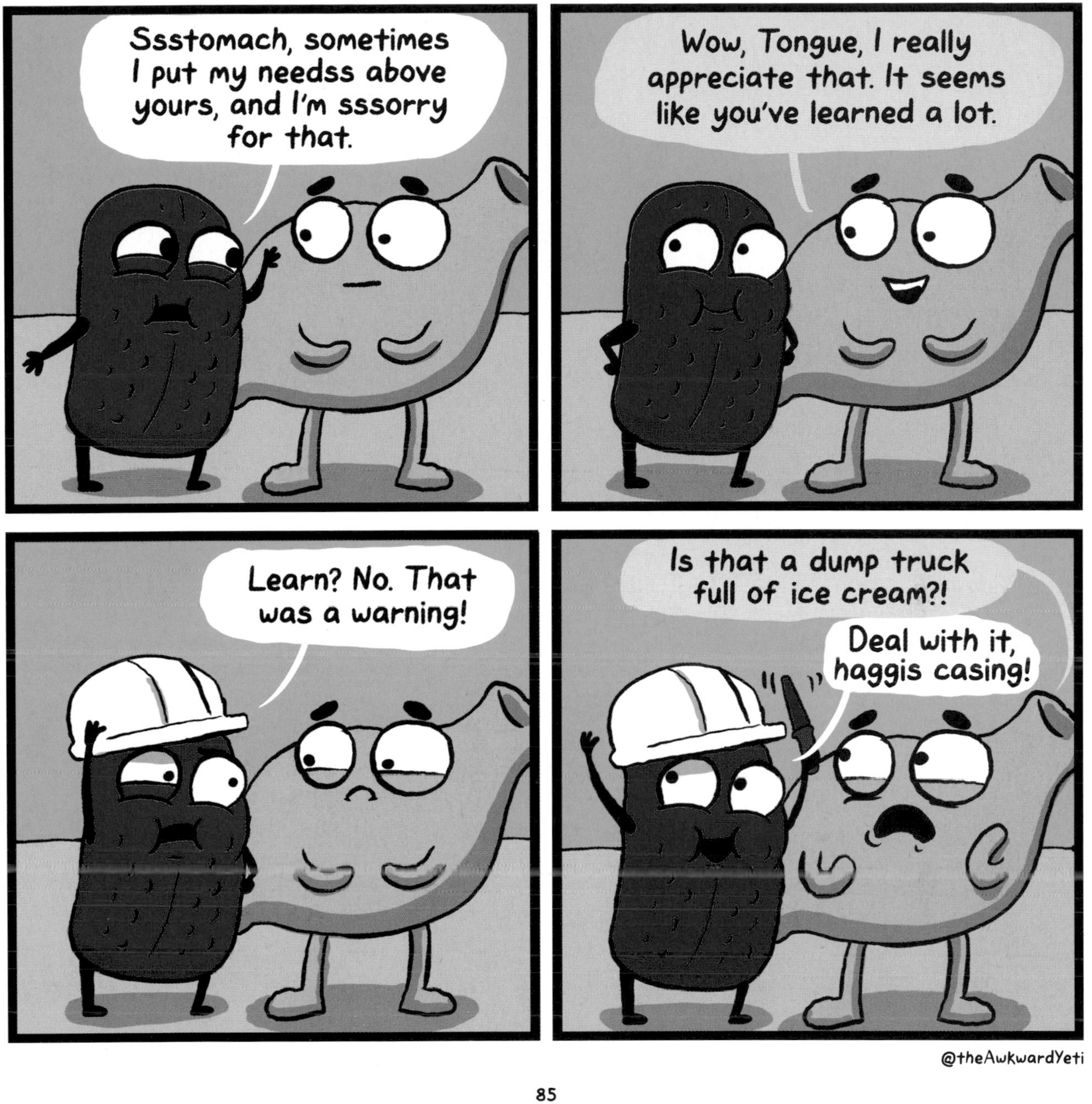
Ssstomach, sometimes I put my needss above yours, and I'm sssorry for that.
Wow, Tongue, I really appreciate that. It seems like you've learned a lot.
Learn? No. That was a warning!
Is that a dump truck full of ice cream?!
Deal with it, haggis casing!
@theAwkwardYeti

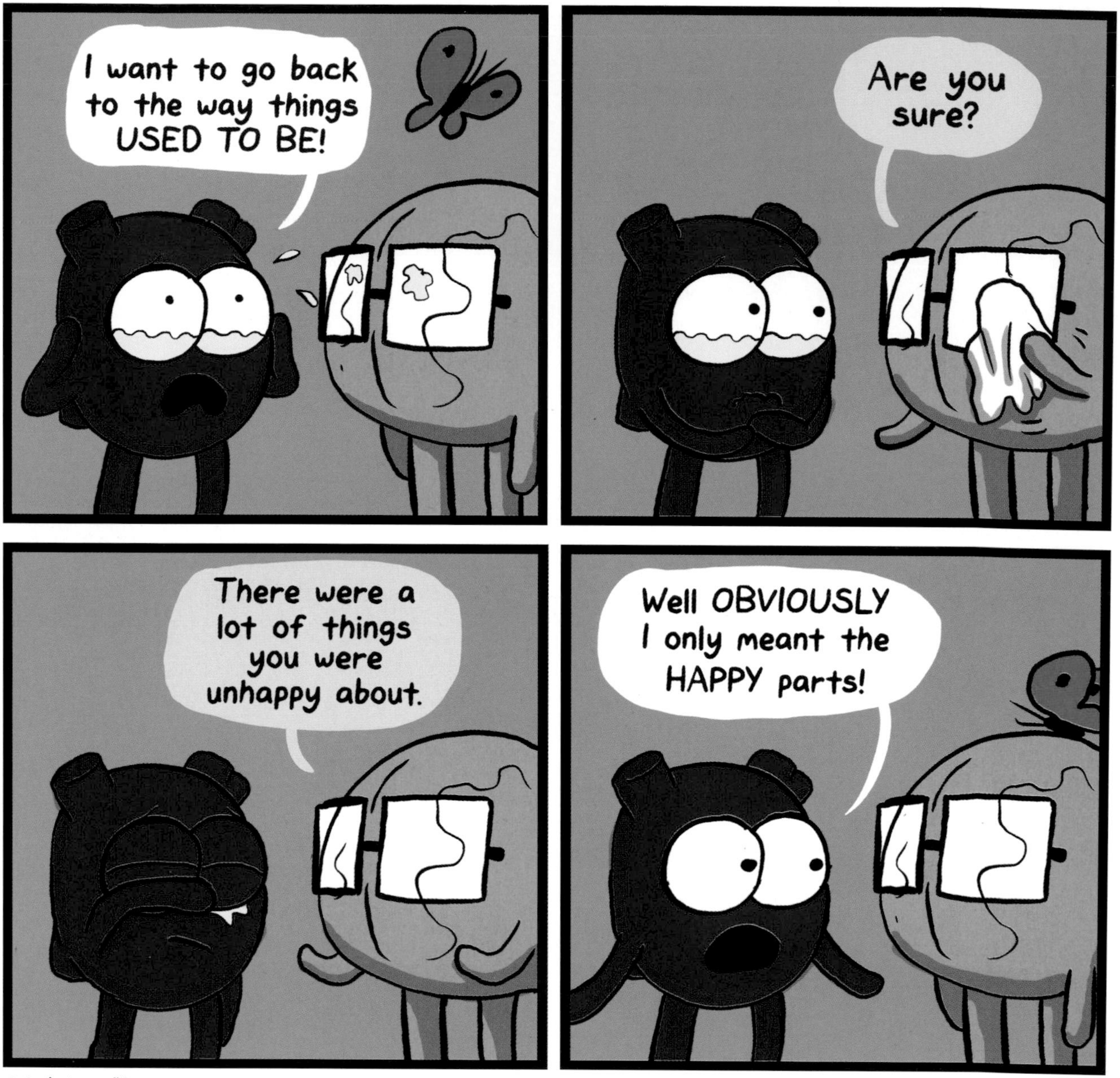
I want to go back to the way things USED TO BE!
Are you sure?
There were a lot of things you were unhappy about.
Well OBVIOUSLY I only meant the HAPPY parts!

@theAwkwardYeti

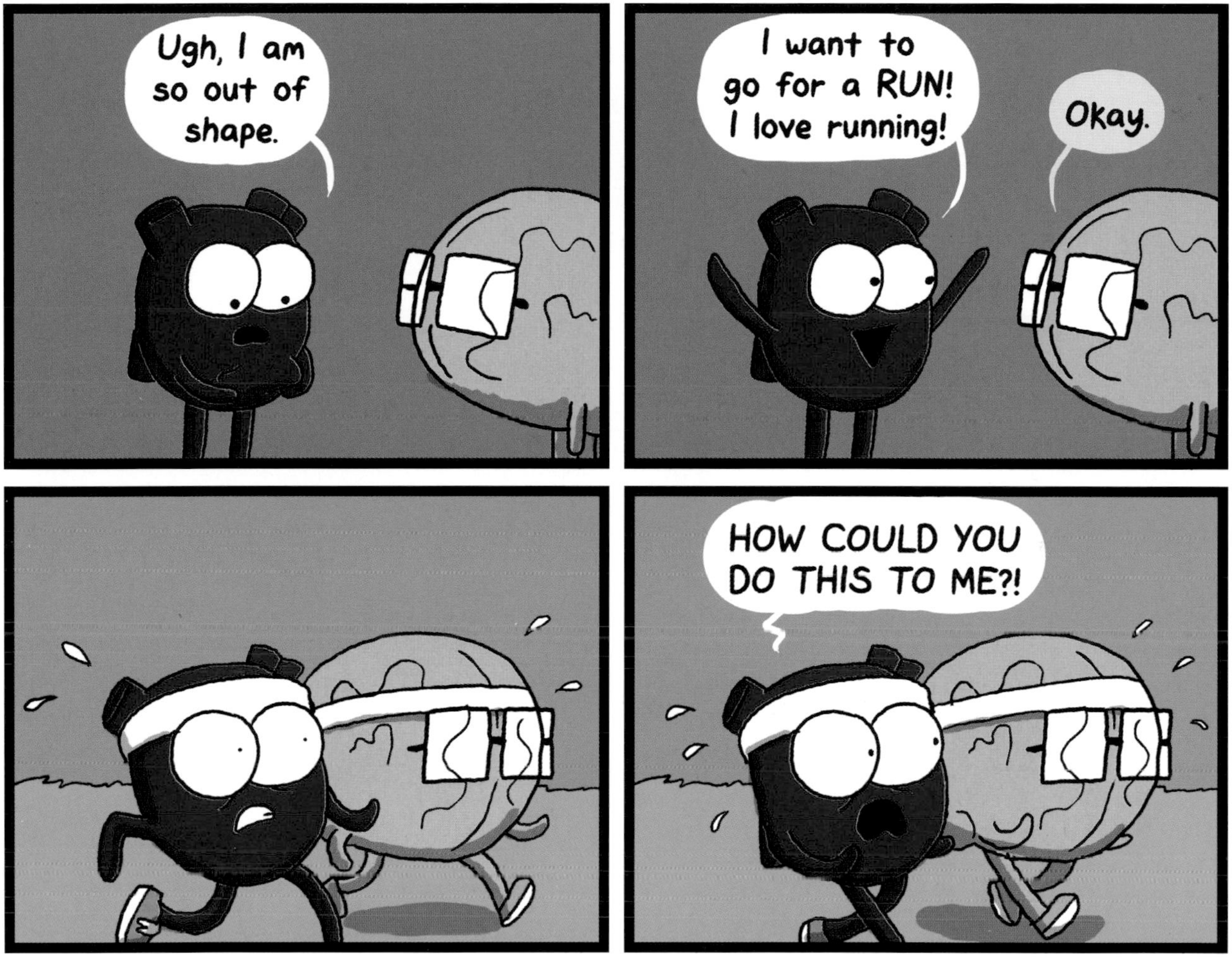
Ugh, I am so out of shape.
I want to go for a RUN! I love running!
Okay.
HOW COULD YOU DO THIS TO ME?!

@theAwkwardYeti

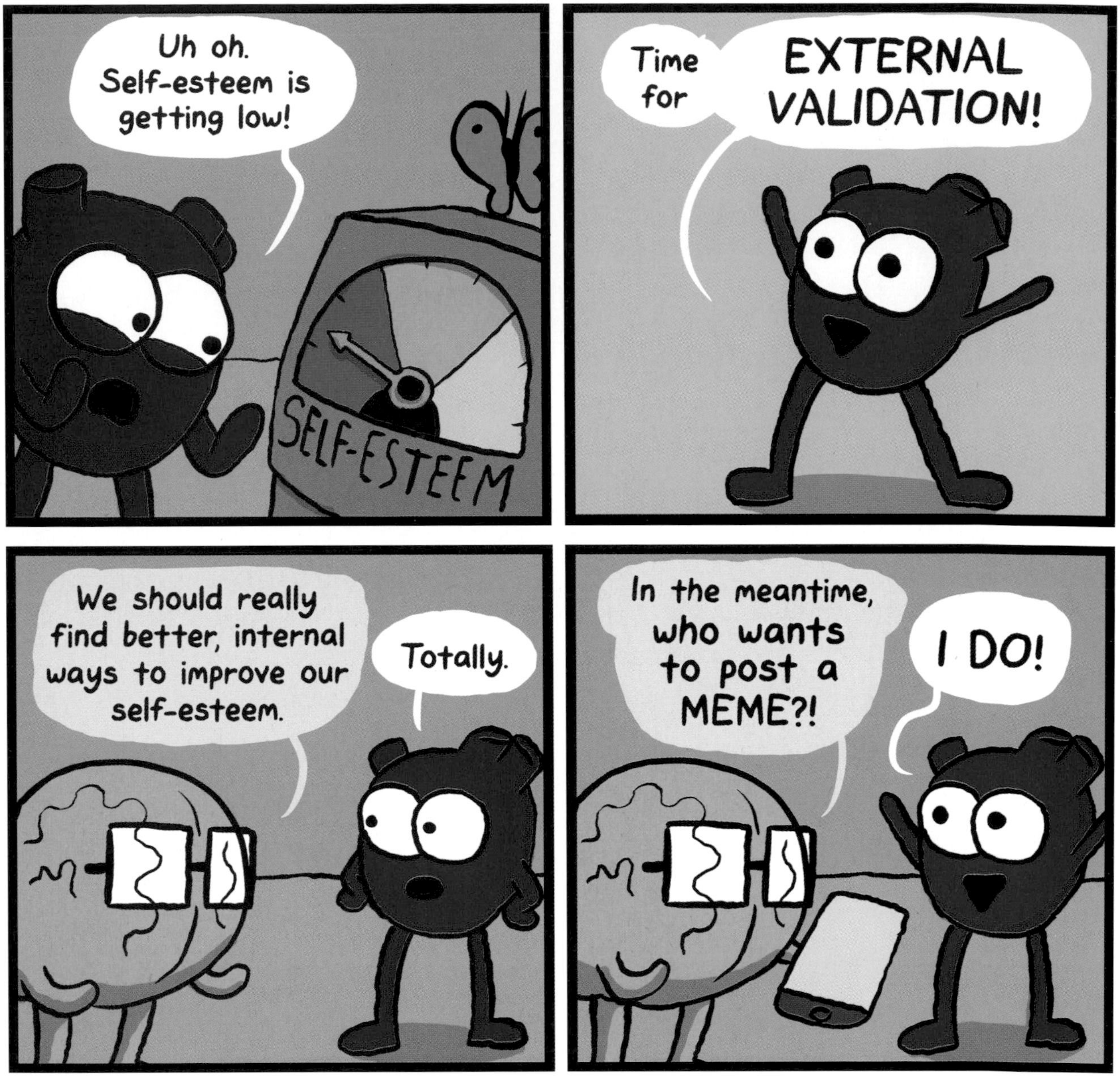
Uh oh.
Self-esteem is getting low!
SELF-ESTEEM
Time for
EXTERNAL VALIDATION!
We should really find better, internal ways to improve our self-esteem.
Totally.
In the meantime, who wants to post a MEME?!
I DO!

@theAwkwardYeti

I couldn't live without you, Brain.
That is literally true. You wouldn't last an hour without a ventilator.
Well I meant it figuratively!
Could you live without ME?
Literally or figuratively?

@theAwkwardYeti

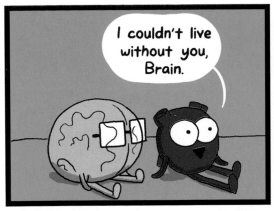

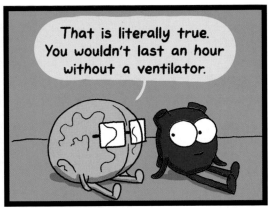

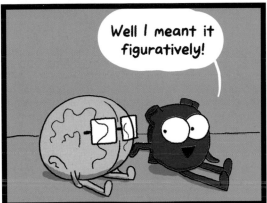

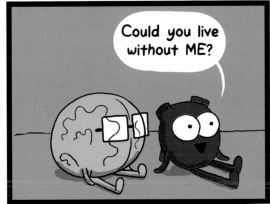

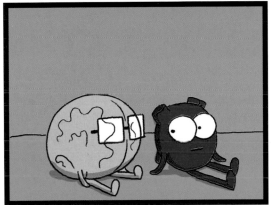

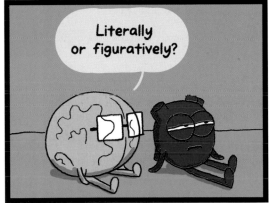

What do you want for your birthday?
GASP!
Total immunity!
Immunity from what?
Responsibilities, mean people, work, the law, Coronavirus, taxes, and death.
I can't guarantee any of that, even for one day.
Then I want to subtract a year instead of adding one.

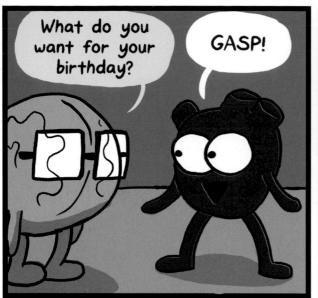

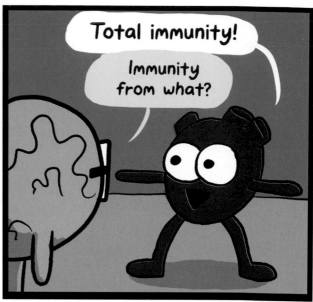

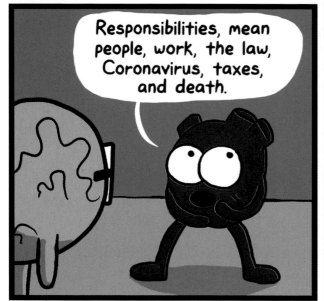

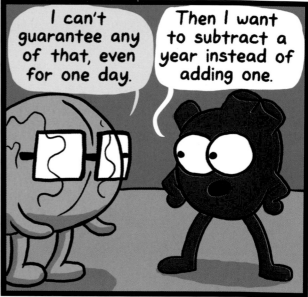

@theAwkwardYeti

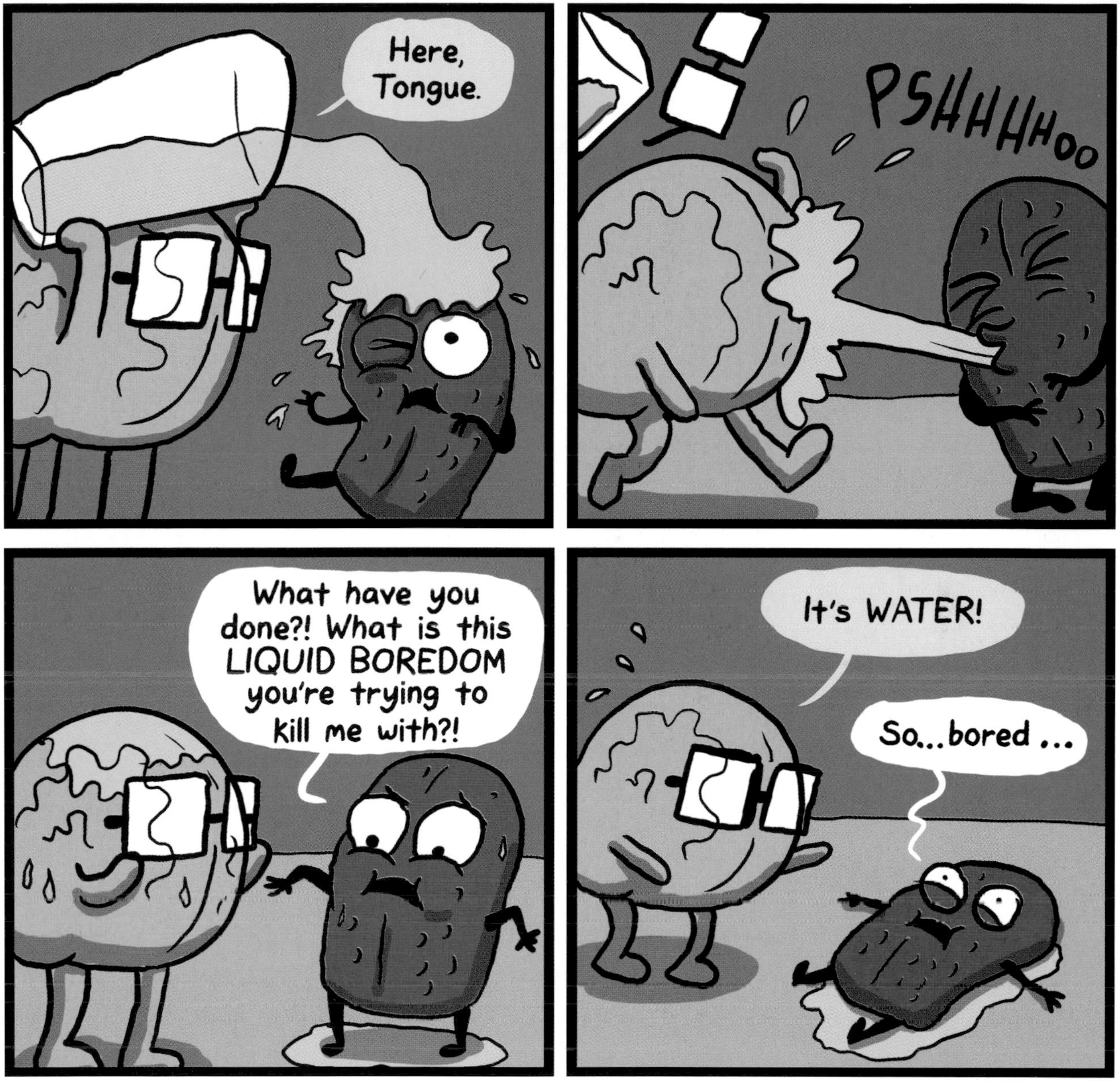
Here, Tongue.
PSHHHHHoo
What have you done?! What is this LIQUID BOREDOM you're trying to kill me with?!
It's WATER!
So...bored ...

@theAwkwardYeti

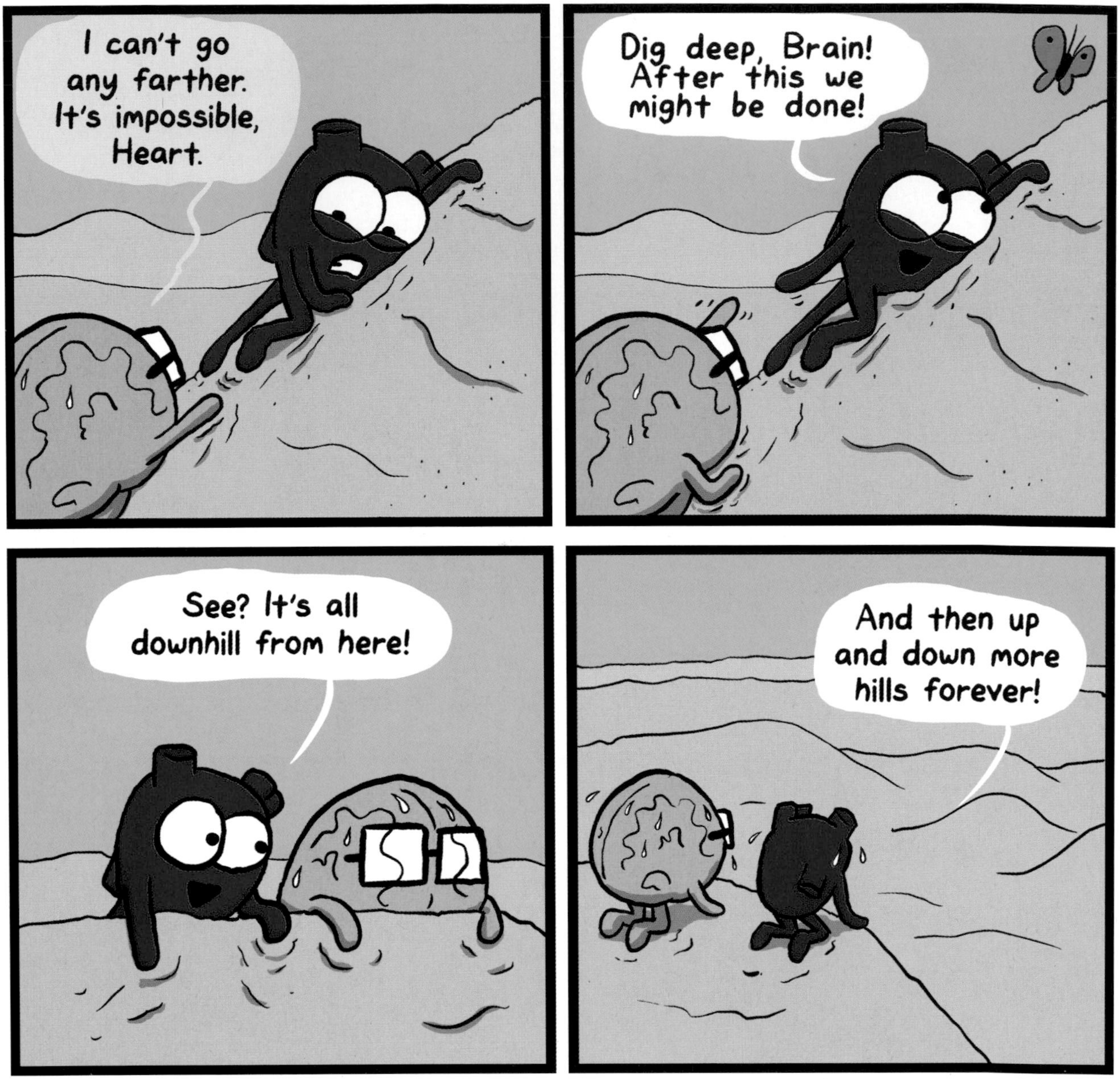
I can't go any farther. It's impossible, Heart.
Dig deep, Brain! After this we might be done!
See? It's all downhill from here!
And then up and down more hills forever!

@theAwkwardYeti

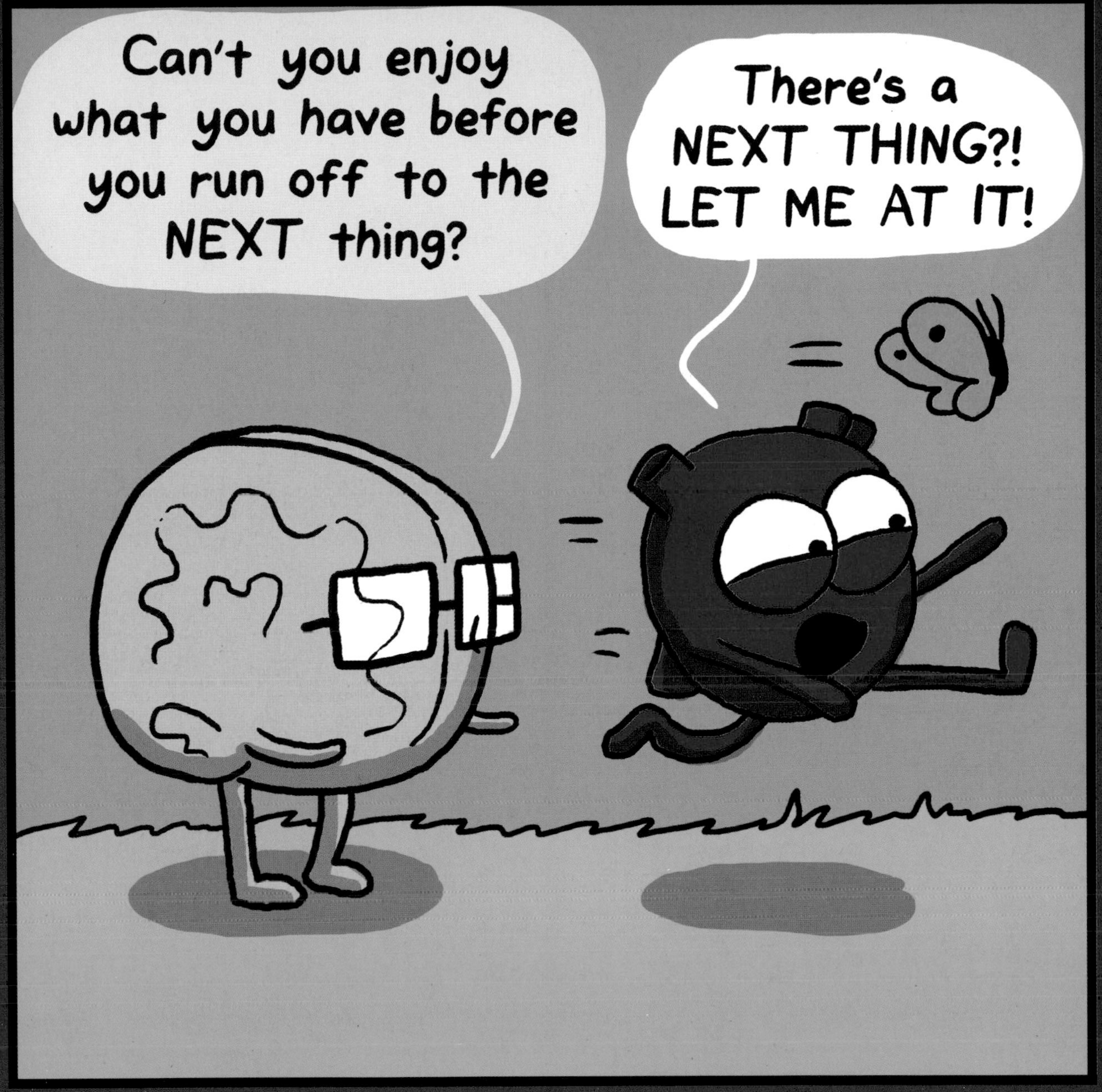
Can't you enjoy what you have before you run off to the NEXT thing?
There's a NEXT THING?! LET ME AT IT!

@theAwkwardYeti

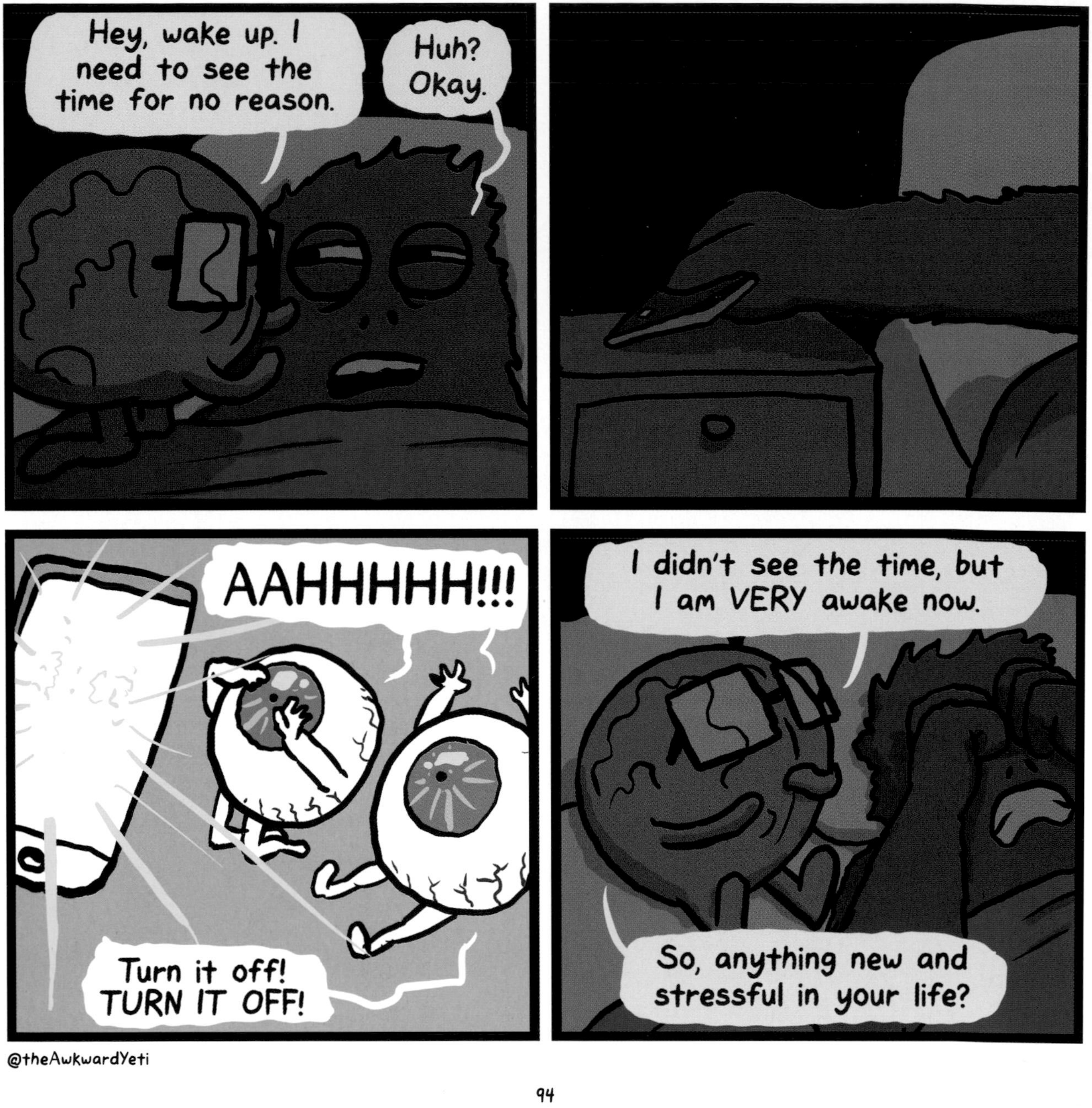
Hey, wake up. I need to see the time for no reason.
Huh? Okay.
AAHHHHH!!!
Turn it off! TURN IT OFF!
I didn't see the time, but I am VERY awake now.
So, anything new and stressful in your life?

@theAwkwardYeti

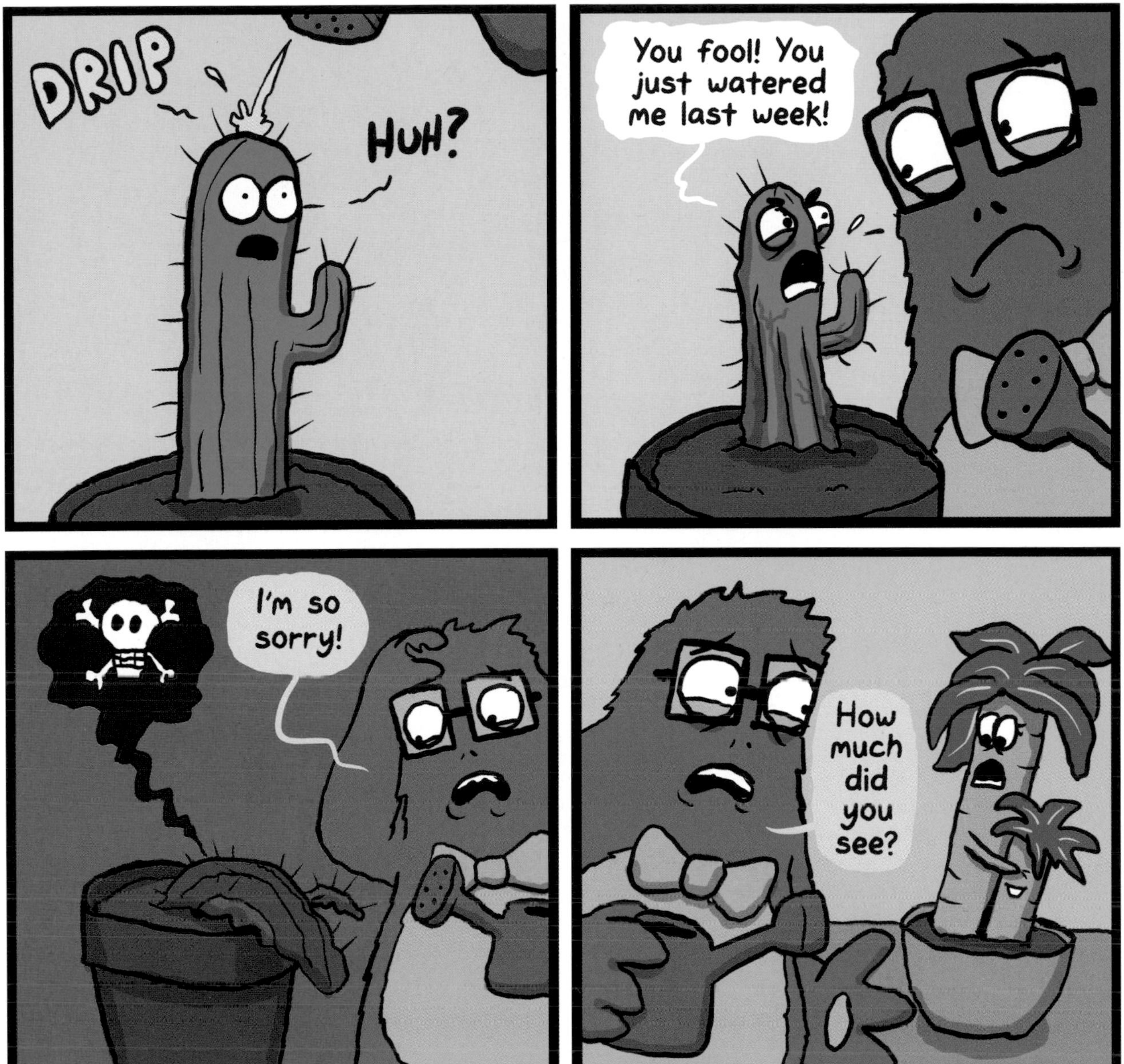
DRIP
HUH?
You fool! You just watered me last week!
I'm so sorry!
How much did you see?

@theAwkwardYeti

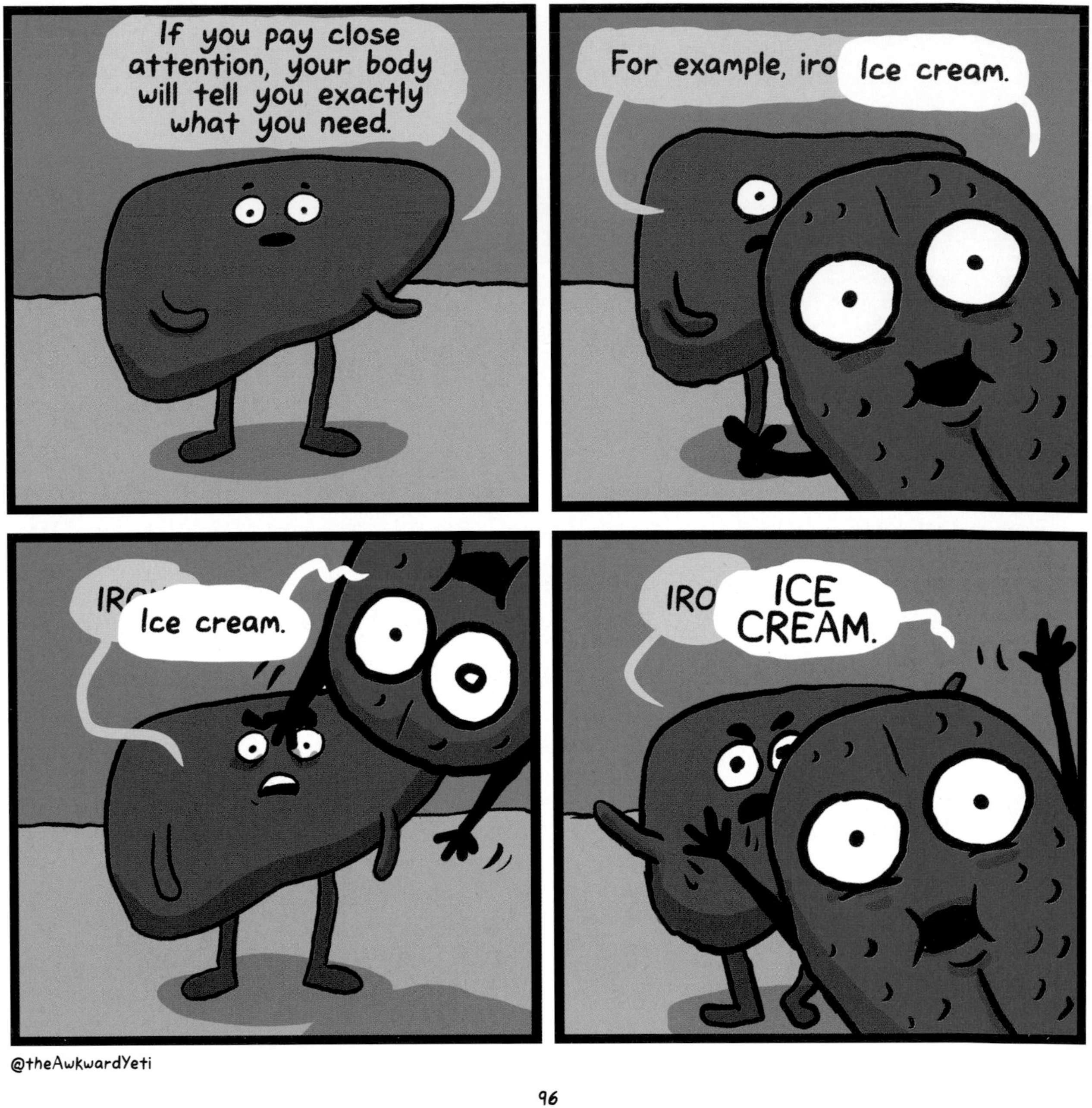
If you pay close attention, your body will tell you exactly what you need.
For example, iro
Ice cream.
IR
Ice cream.
IRO
ICE CREAM.

@theAwkwardYeti

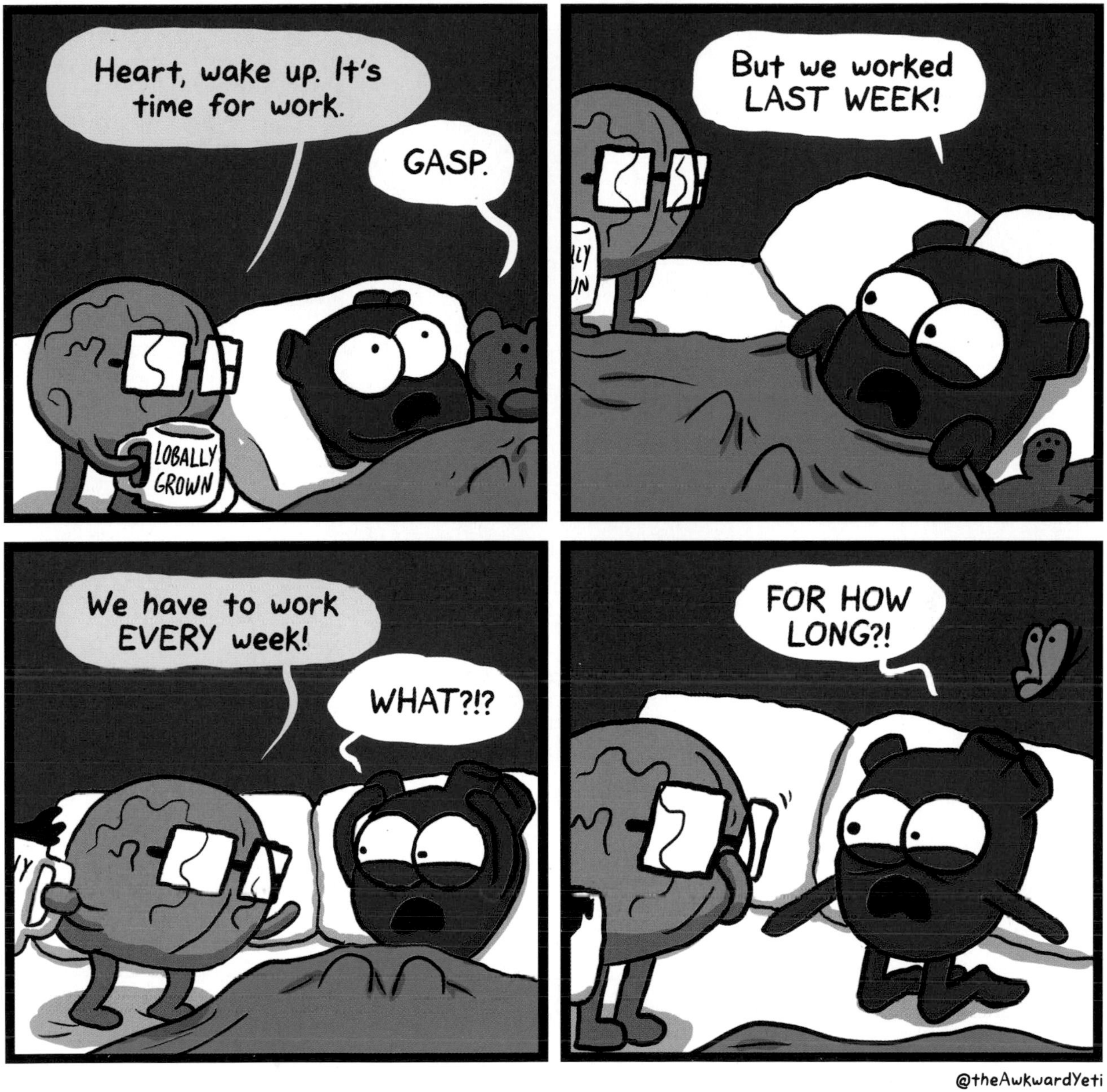
Heart, wake up. It's time for work.
GASP.
LOBALLY GROWN
But we worked LAST WEEK!
We have to work EVERY week!
WHAT?!?
FOR HOW LONG?!

@theAwkwardYeti

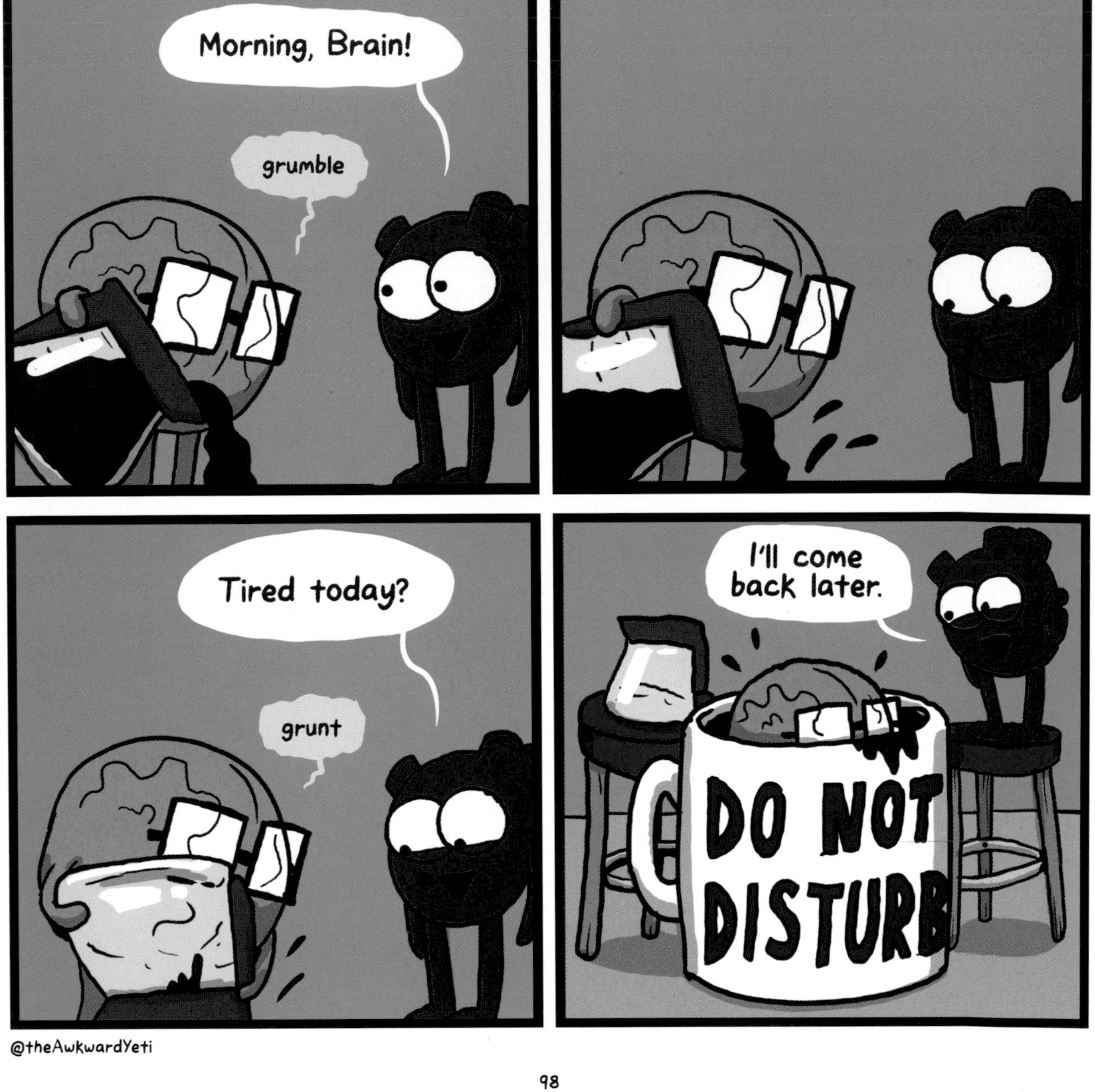
Morning, Brain!
grumble
Tired today?
grunt
I'll come back later.
DO NOT DISTURB

@theAwkwardYeti

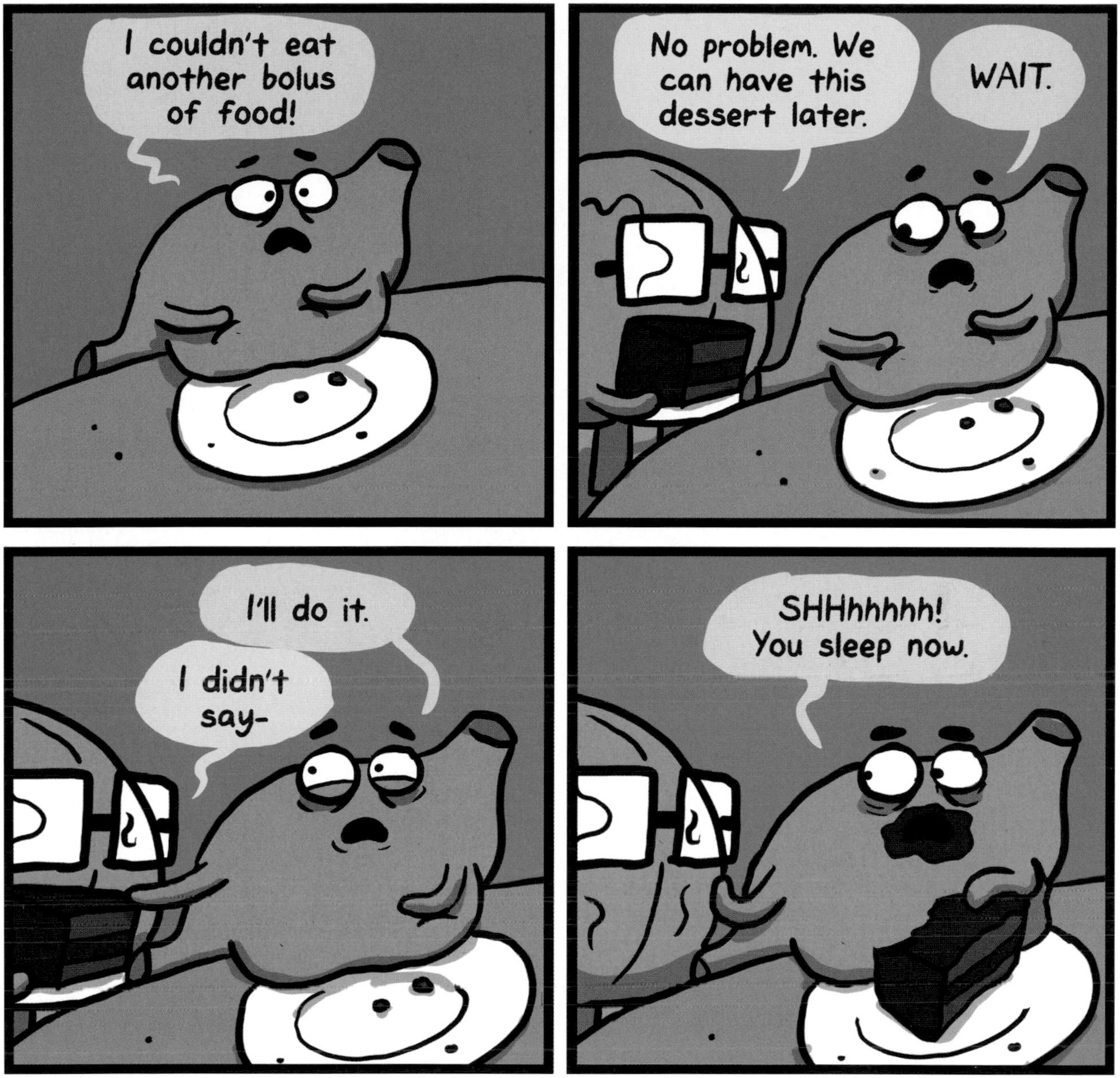
I couldn't eat another bolus of food!
No problem. We can have this dessert later.
WAIT.
I'll do it.
I didn't say-
SHHhhhhh! You sleep now.

@theAwkwardYeti

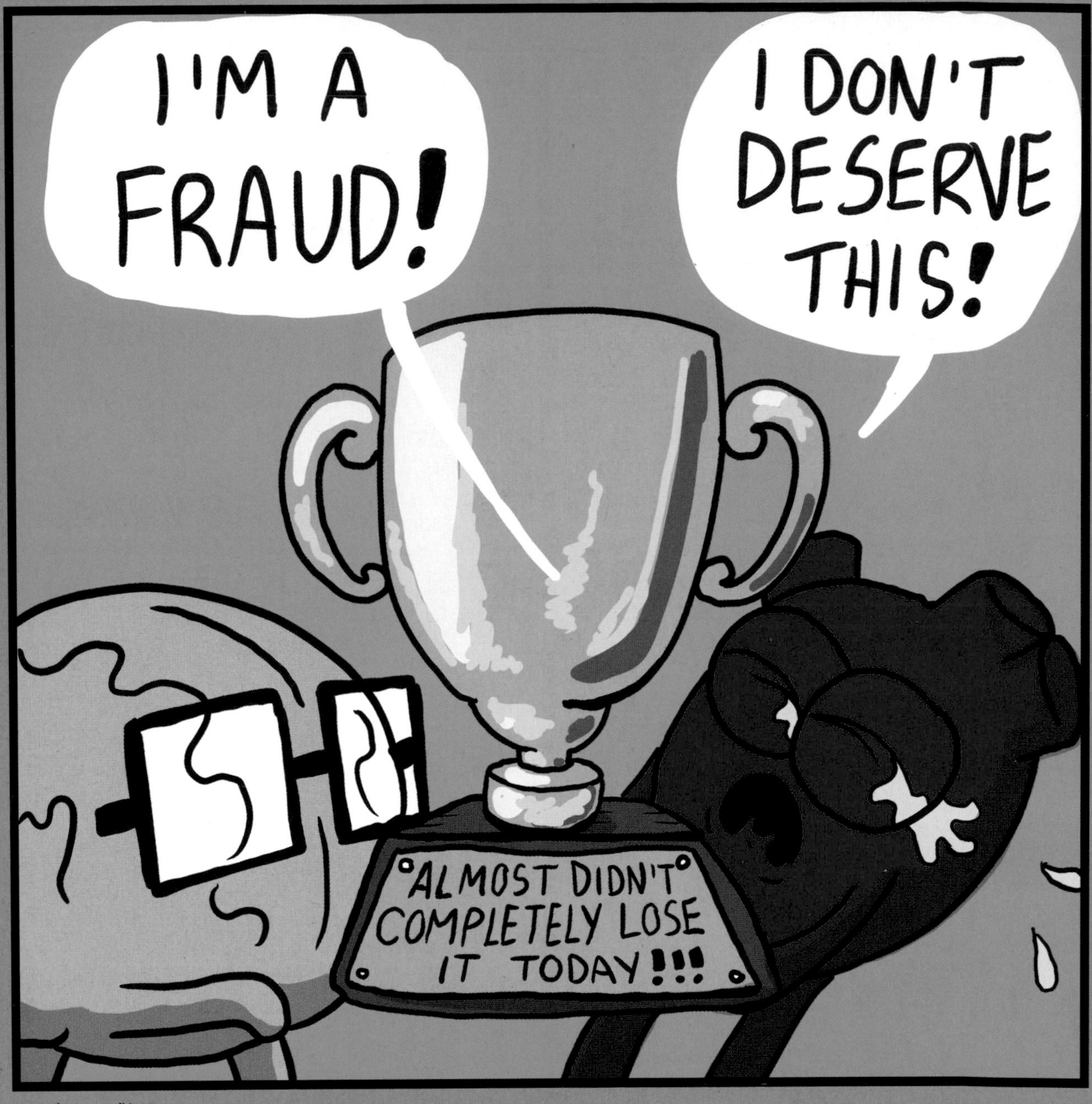
I'M A FRAUD!
I DON'T DESERVE THIS!
ALMOST DIDN'T COMPLETELY LOSE IT TODAY!!!

@theAwkwardYeti

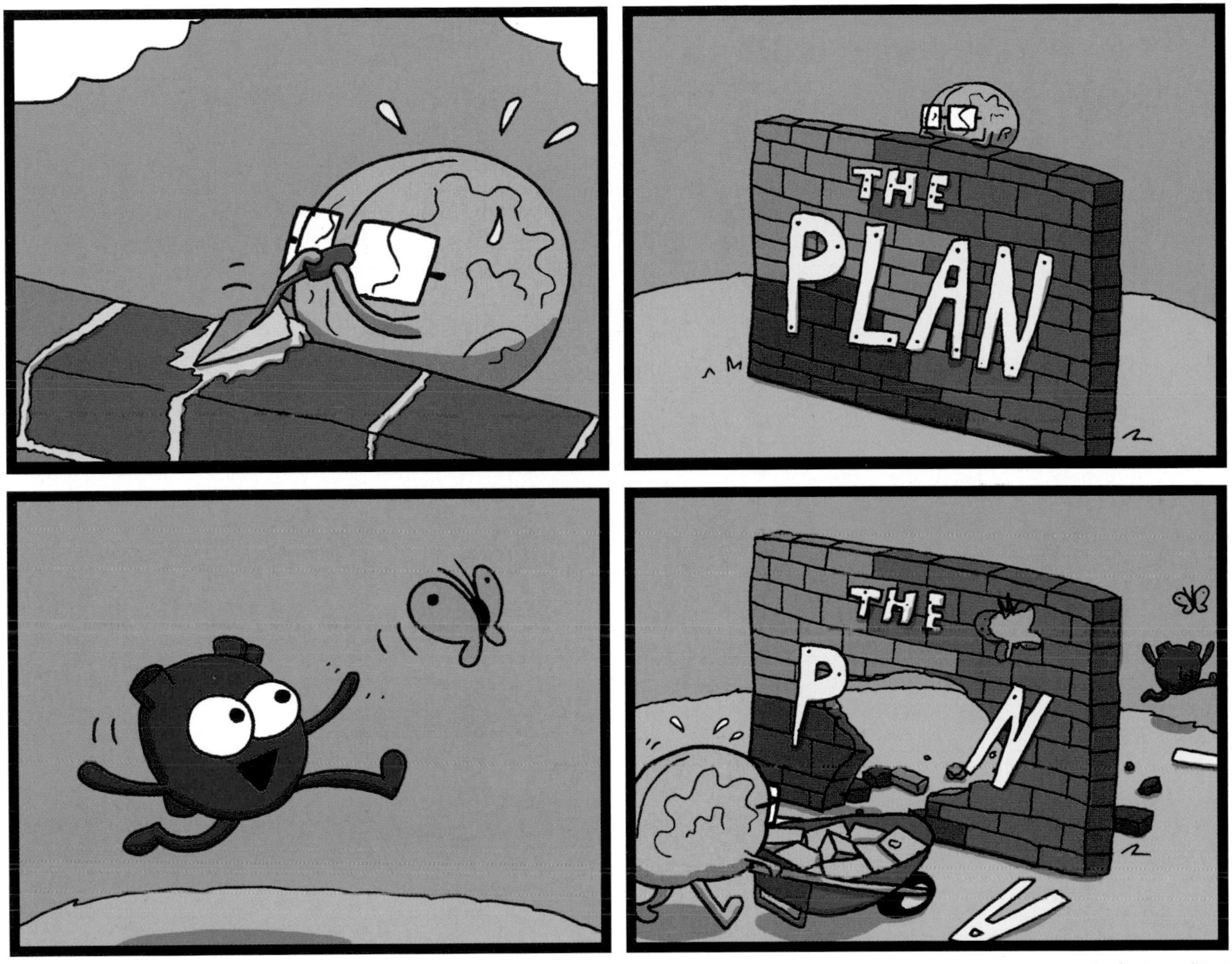
THE
PLAN
THE
P
N
@theAwkwardYeti

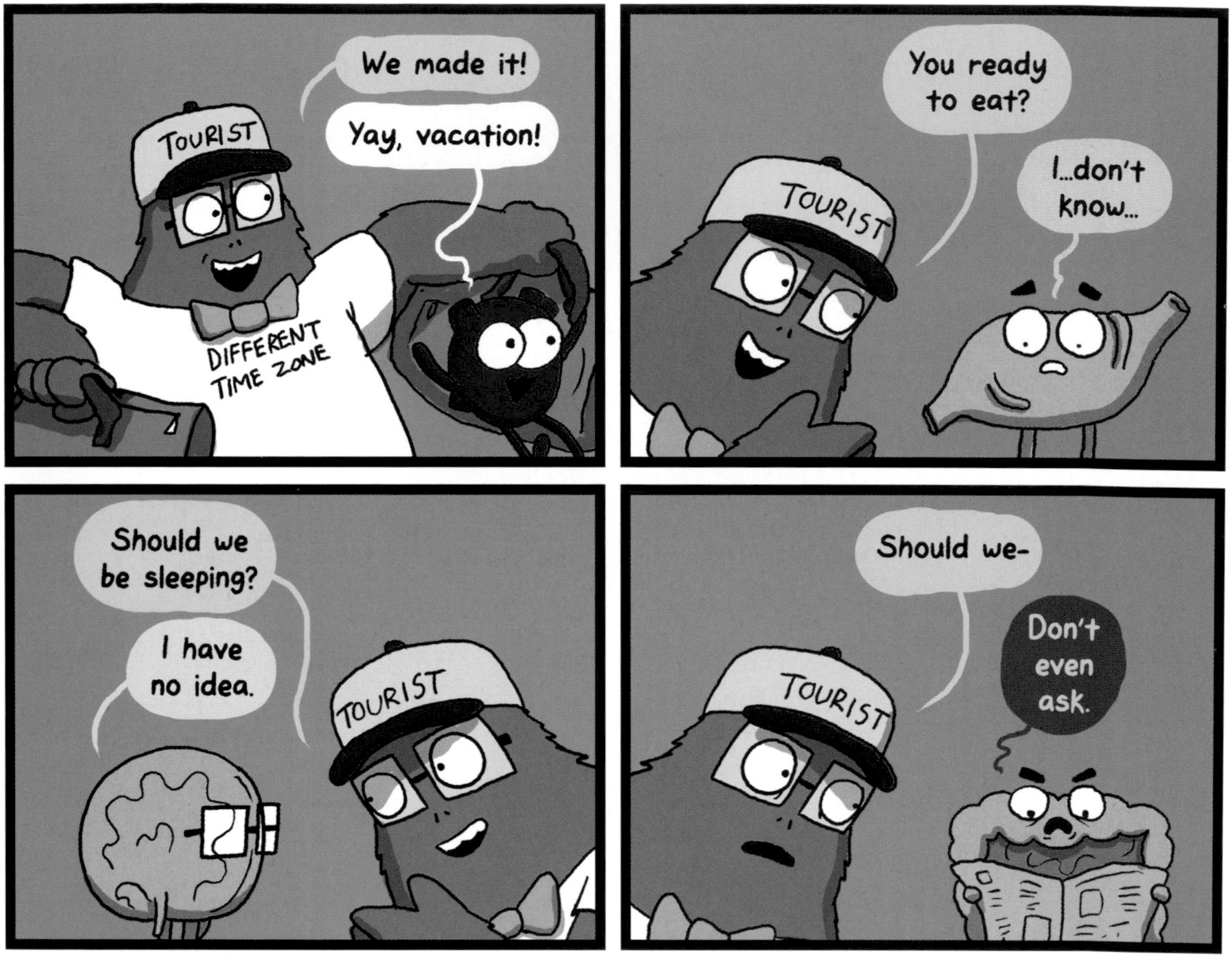
TOURIST
We made it!
Yay, vacation!
DIFFERENT TIME ZONE
TOURIST
You ready to eat?
I...don't know...
Should we be sleeping?
I have no idea.
TOURIST
Should we-
TOURIST
Don't even ask.

@theAwkwardYeti

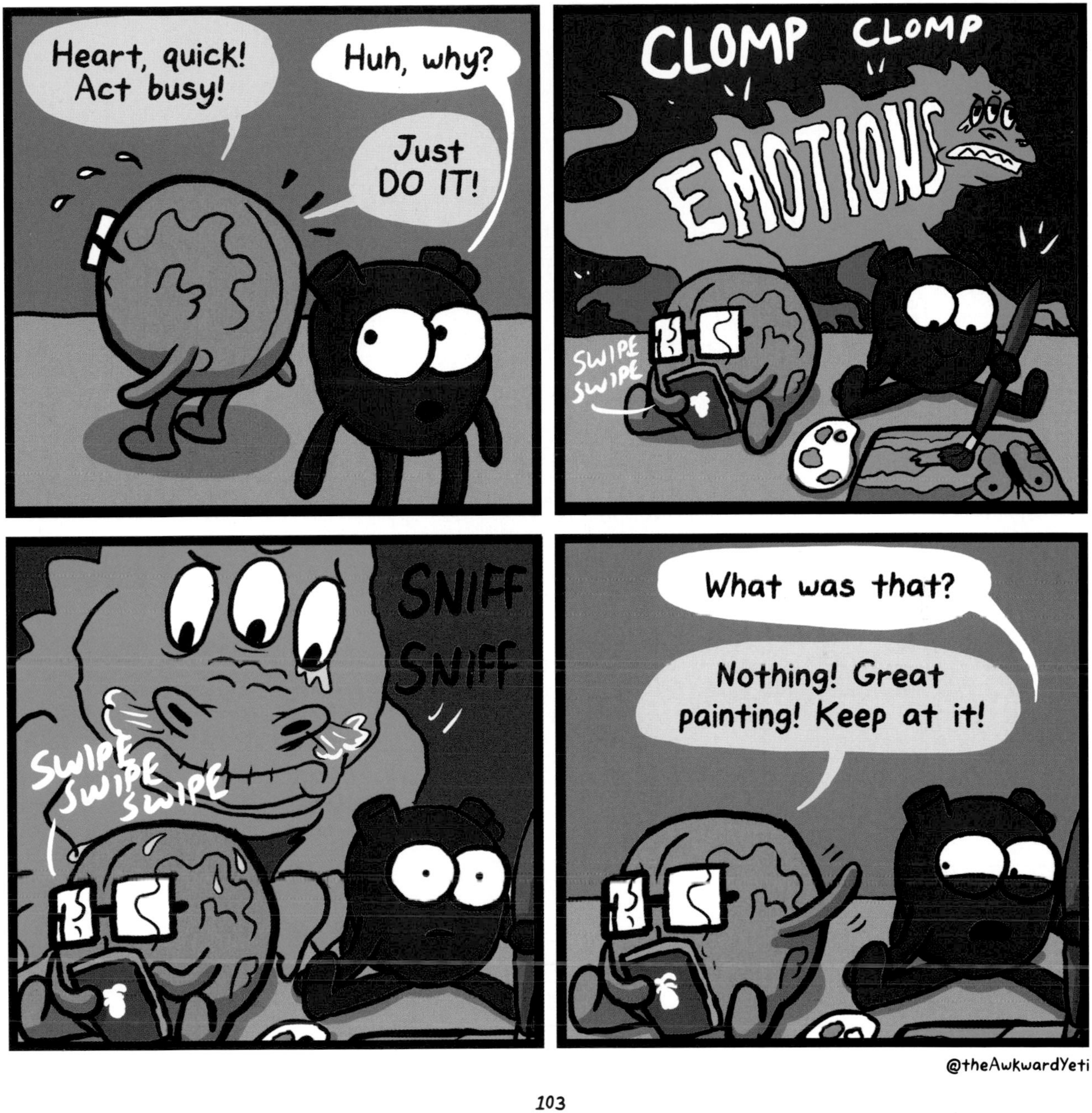
Heart, quick! Act busy!
Huh, why?
Just DO IT!
CLOMP CLOMP
EMOTIONS
SWIPE SWIPE
SNIFF SNIFF
SWIPE SWIPE SWIPE
What was that?
Nothing! Great painting! Keep at it!
@theAwkwardYeti

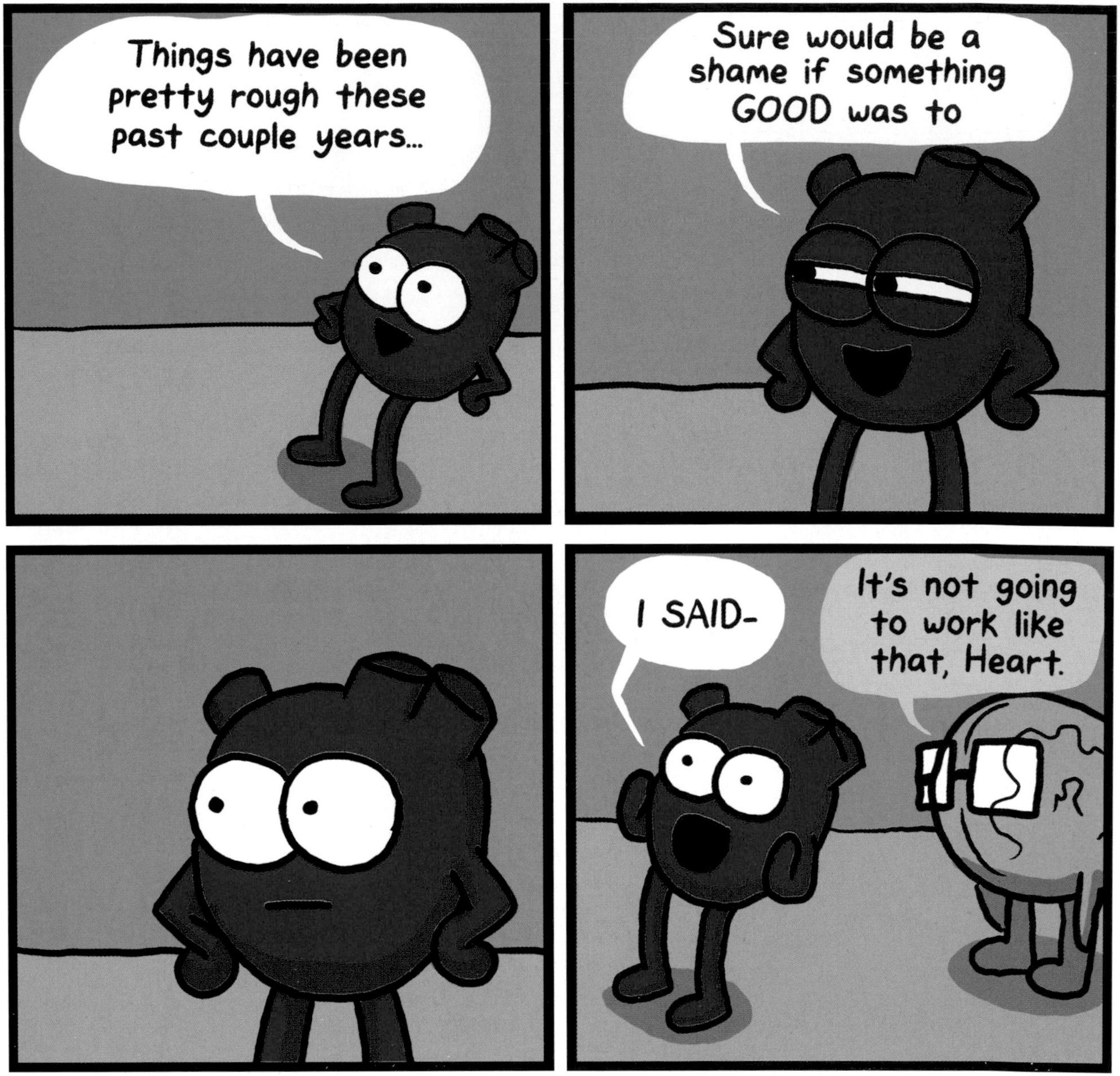
Things have been pretty rough these past couple years...
Sure would be a shame if something GOOD was to
I SAID-
It's not going to work like that, Heart.

@theAwkwardYeti

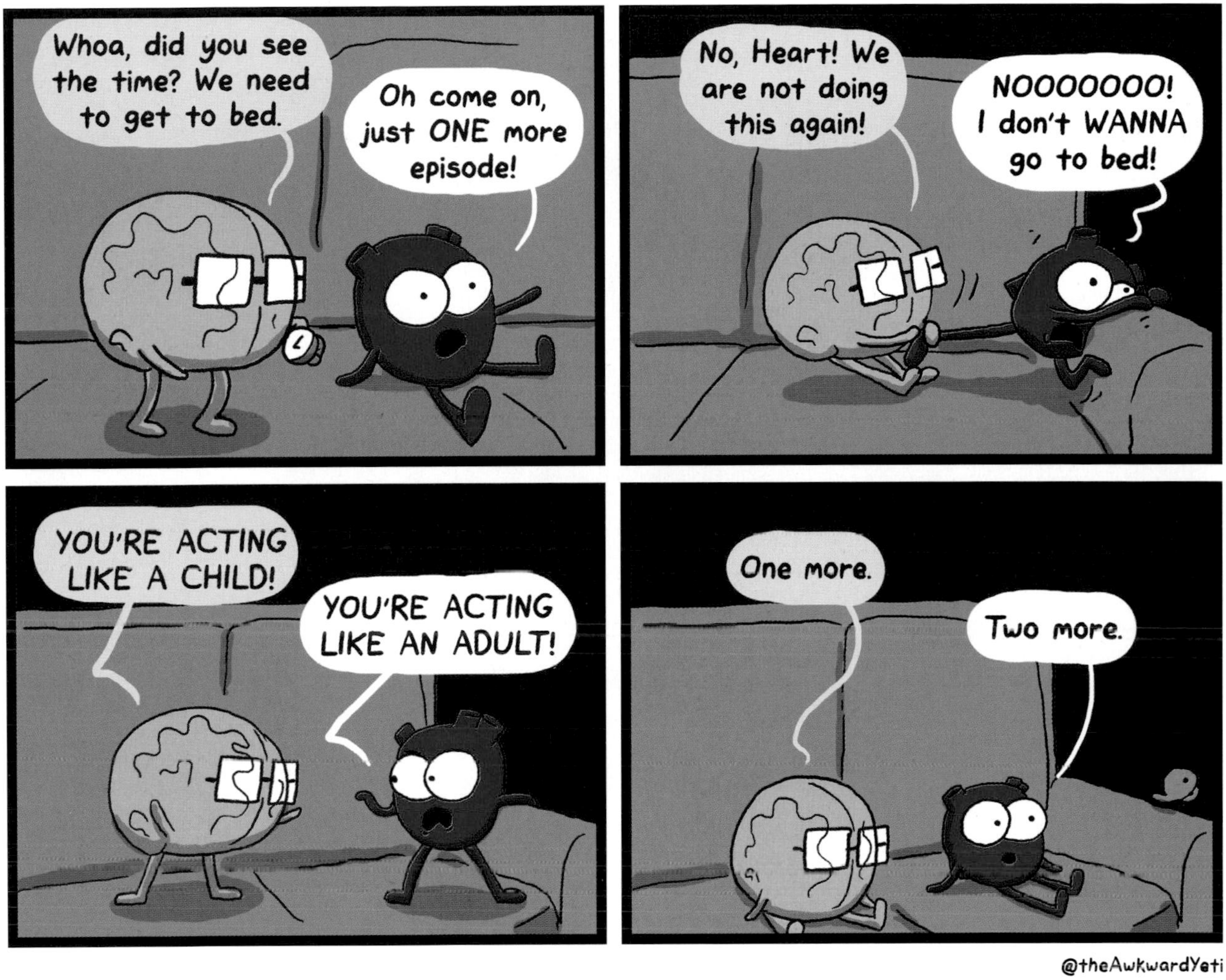
Whoa, did you see the time? We need to get to bed.
Oh come on, just ONE more episode!
No, Heart! We are not doing this again!
NOOOOOOO! I don't WANNA go to bed!
YOU'RE ACTING LIKE A CHILD!
YOU'RE ACTING LIKE AN ADULT!
One more.
Two more.
@theAwkwardYeti

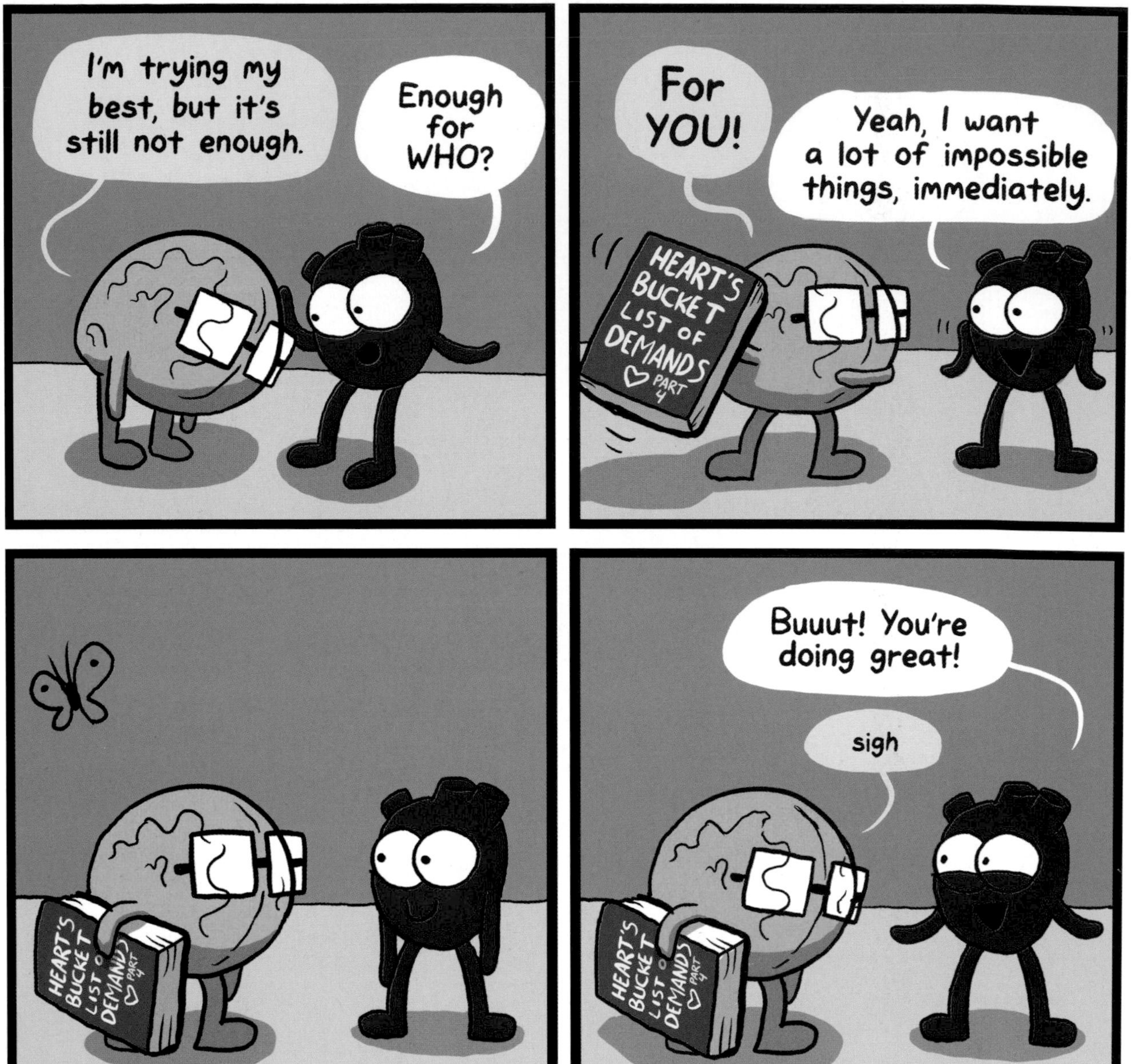
I'm trying my best, but it's still not enough.
Enough for WHO?
For YOU!
HEART'S BUCKET LIST OF DEMANDS PART 4
Yeah, I want a lot of impossible things, immediately.
Buuut! You're doing great!
sigh

@theAwkwardYeti

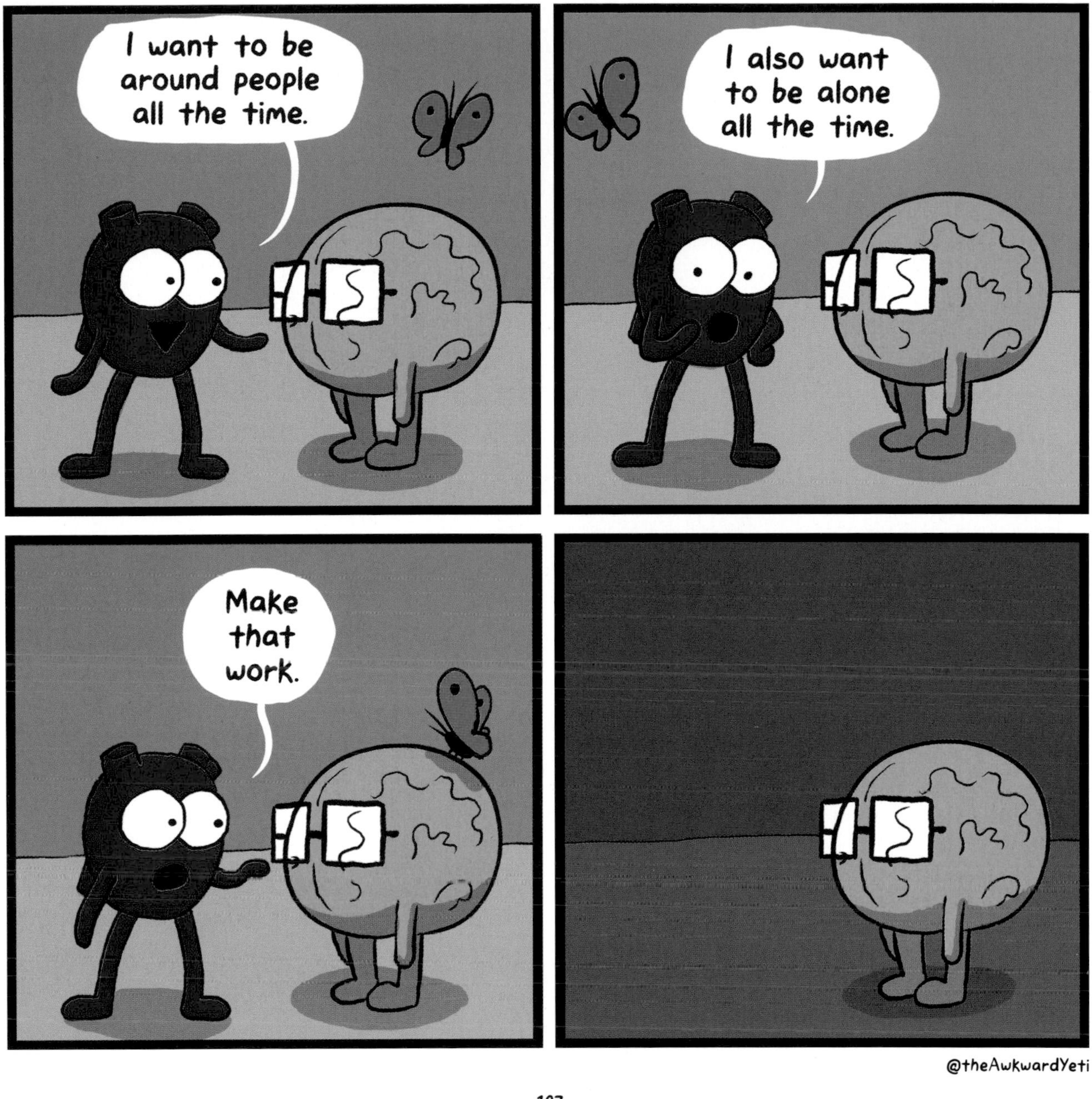
I want to be around people all the time.
I also want to be alone all the time.
Make that work.

@theAwkwardYeti

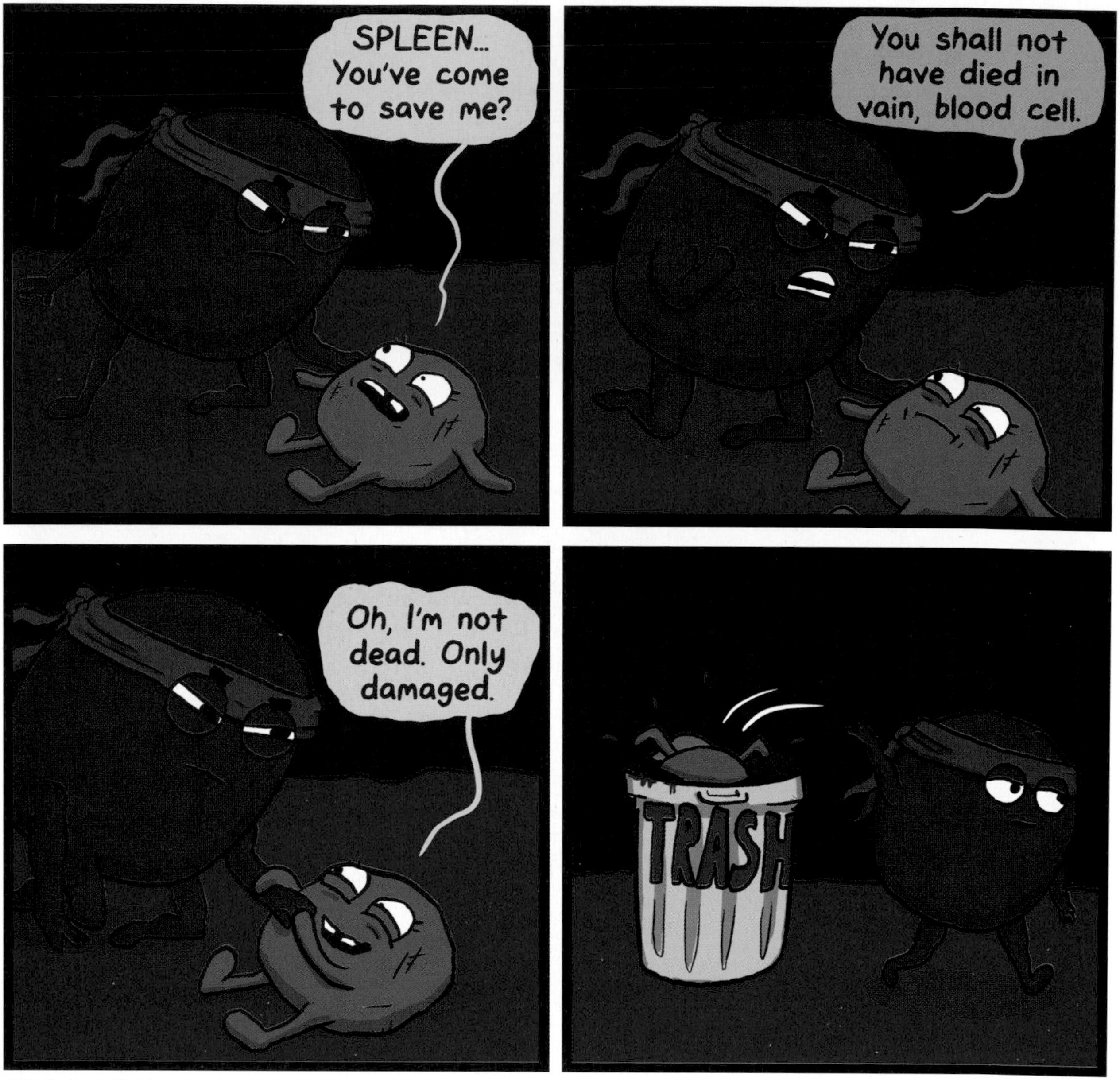
SPLEEN... You've come to save me?
You shall not have died in vain, blood cell.
Oh, I'm not dead. Only damaged.
TRASH

@theAwkwardYeti

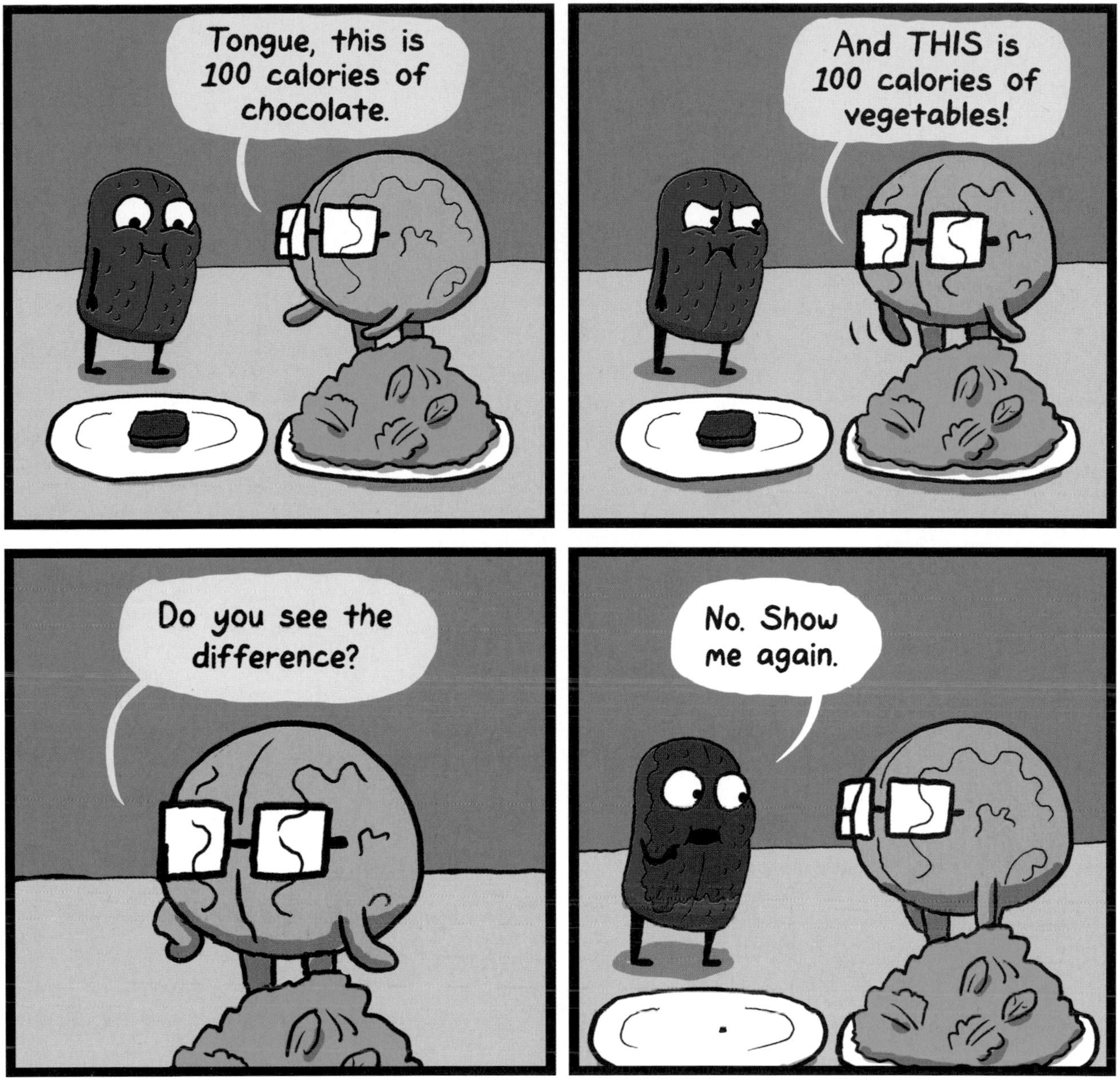
Tongue, this is 100 calories of chocolate.
And THIS is 100 calories of vegetables!
Do you see the difference?
No. Show me again.

@theAwkwardYeti

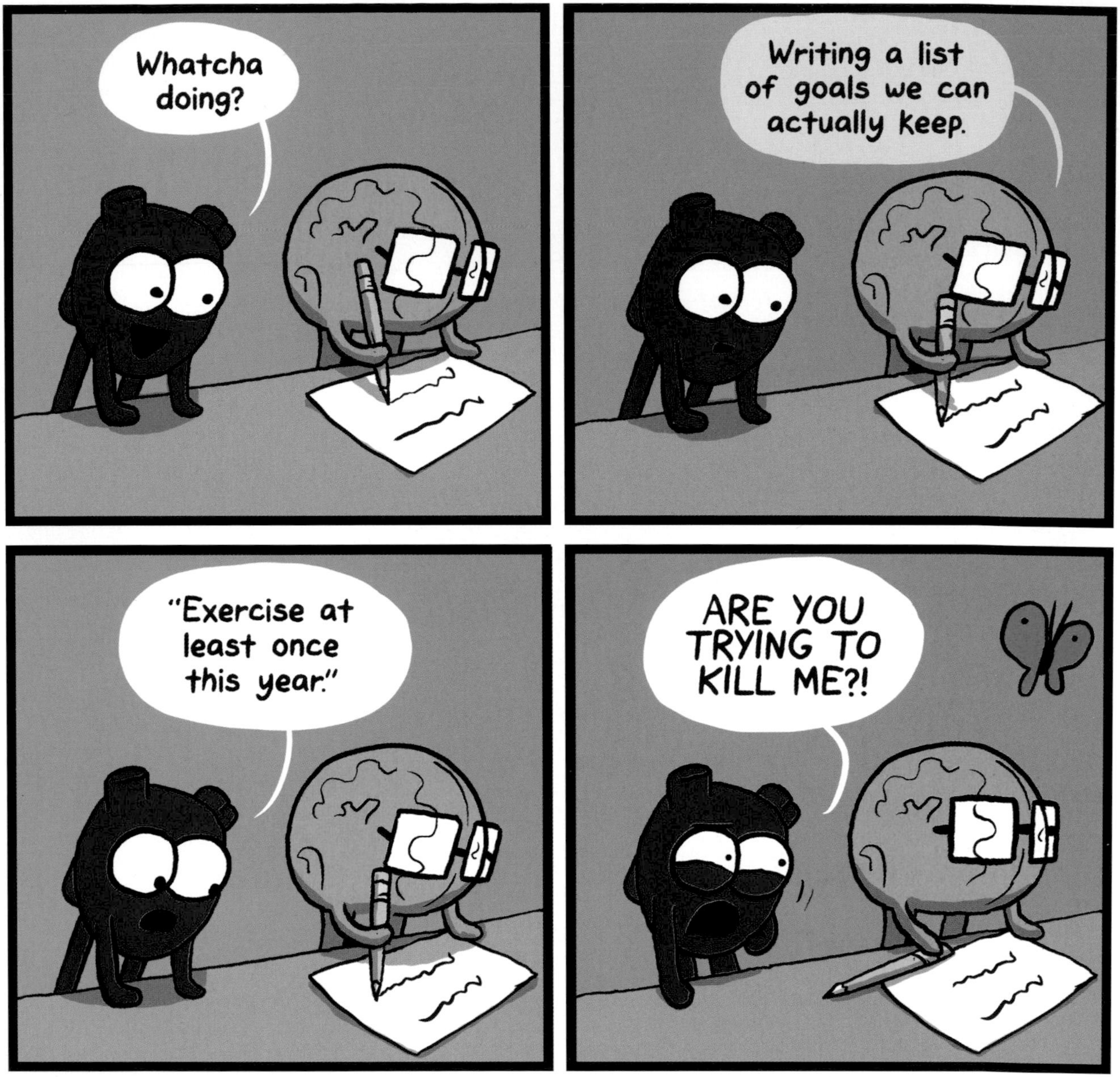
Whatcha doing?
Writing a list of goals we can actually keep.
"Exercise at least once this year."
ARE YOU TRYING TO KILL ME?!

@theAwkwardYeti

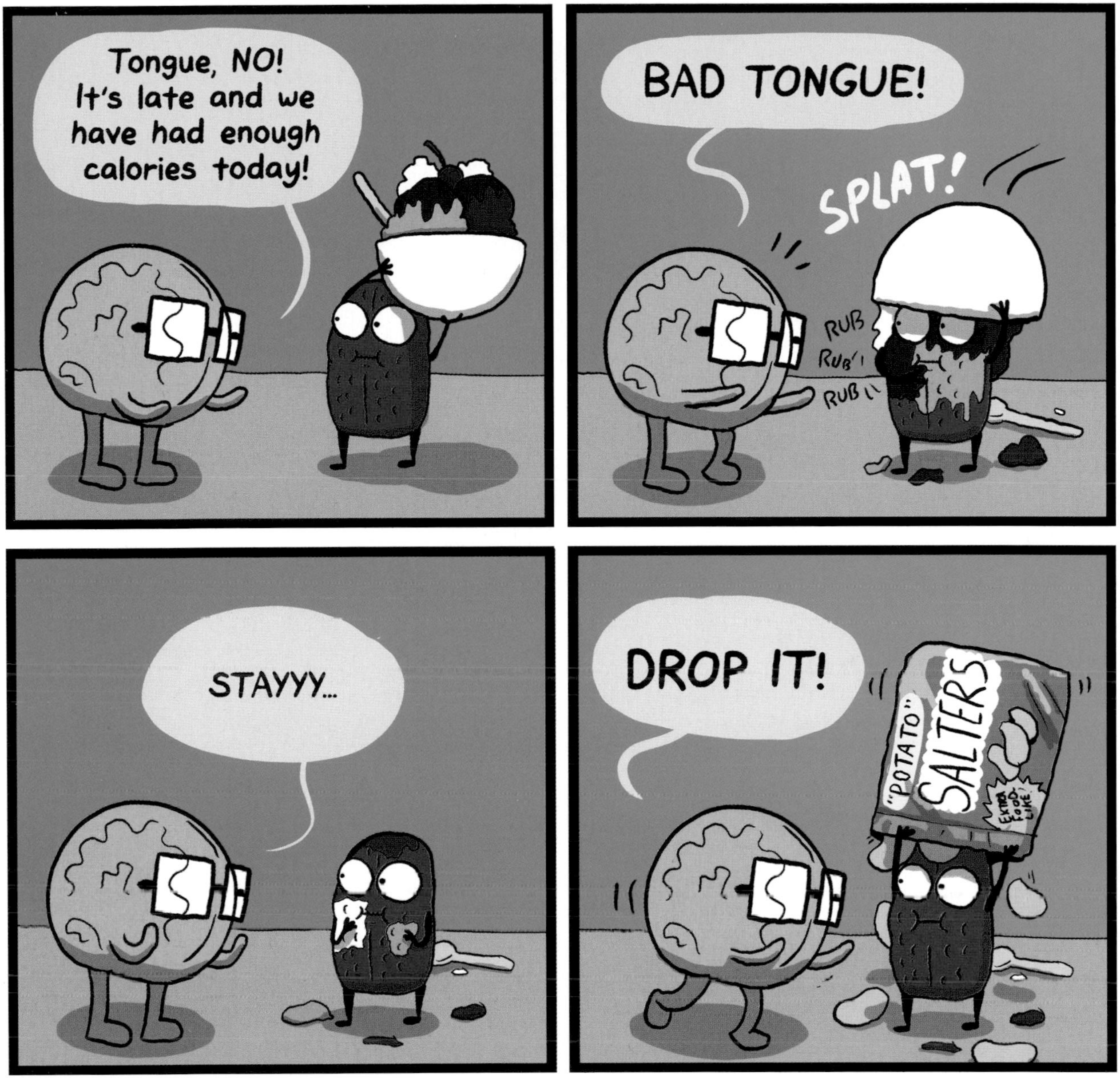
Tongue, NO!
It's late and we
have had enough
calories today!
BAD TONGUE!
SPLAT!
RUB
RUB
RUB
STAYYY...
DROP IT!
"POTATO"
SALTERS

@theAwkwardYeti

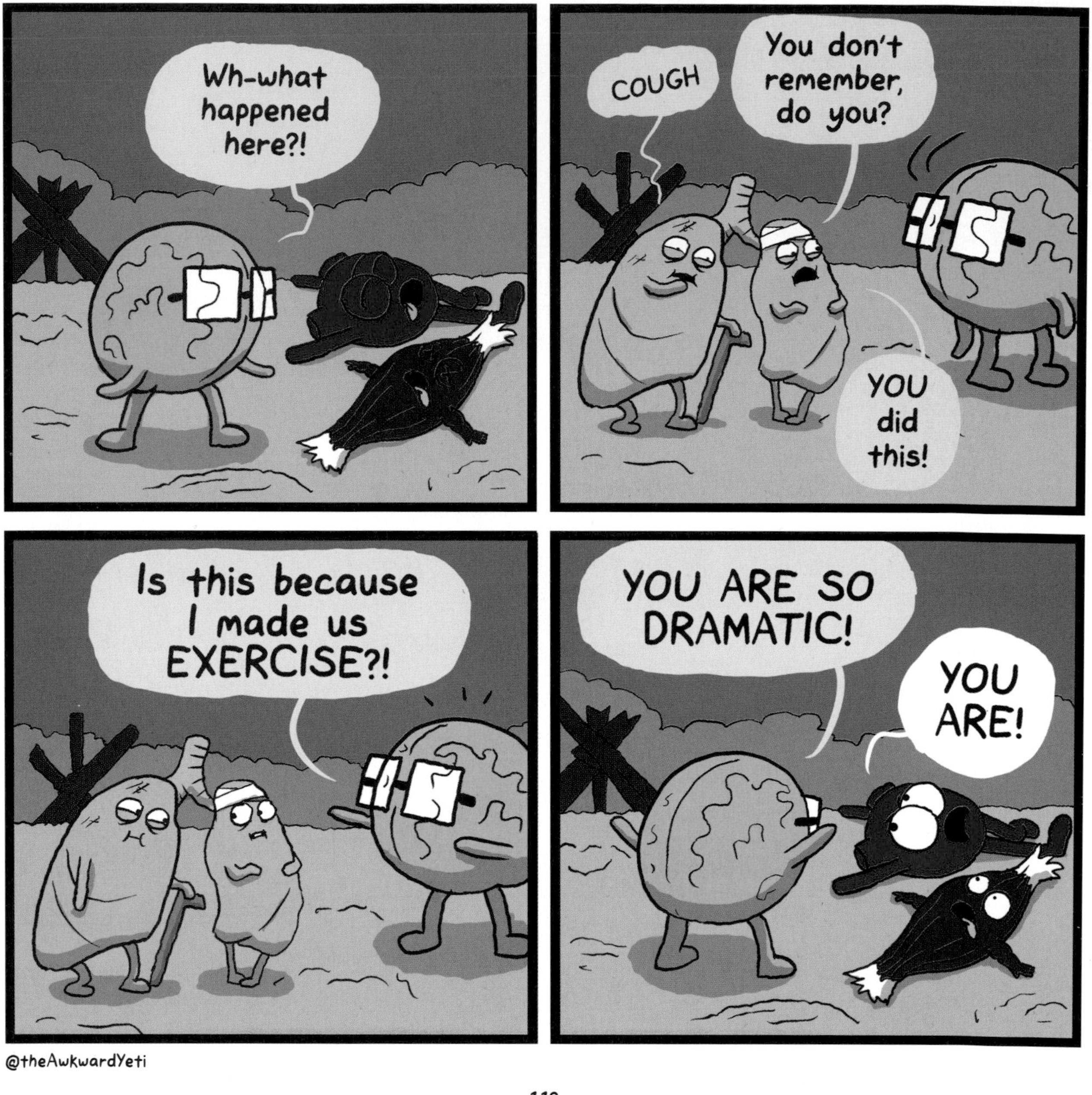

Wh-what happened here?!
COUGH
You don't remember, do you?
YOU did this!
Is this because I made us EXERCISE?!
YOU ARE SO DRAMATIC!
YOU ARE!

@theAwkwardYeti

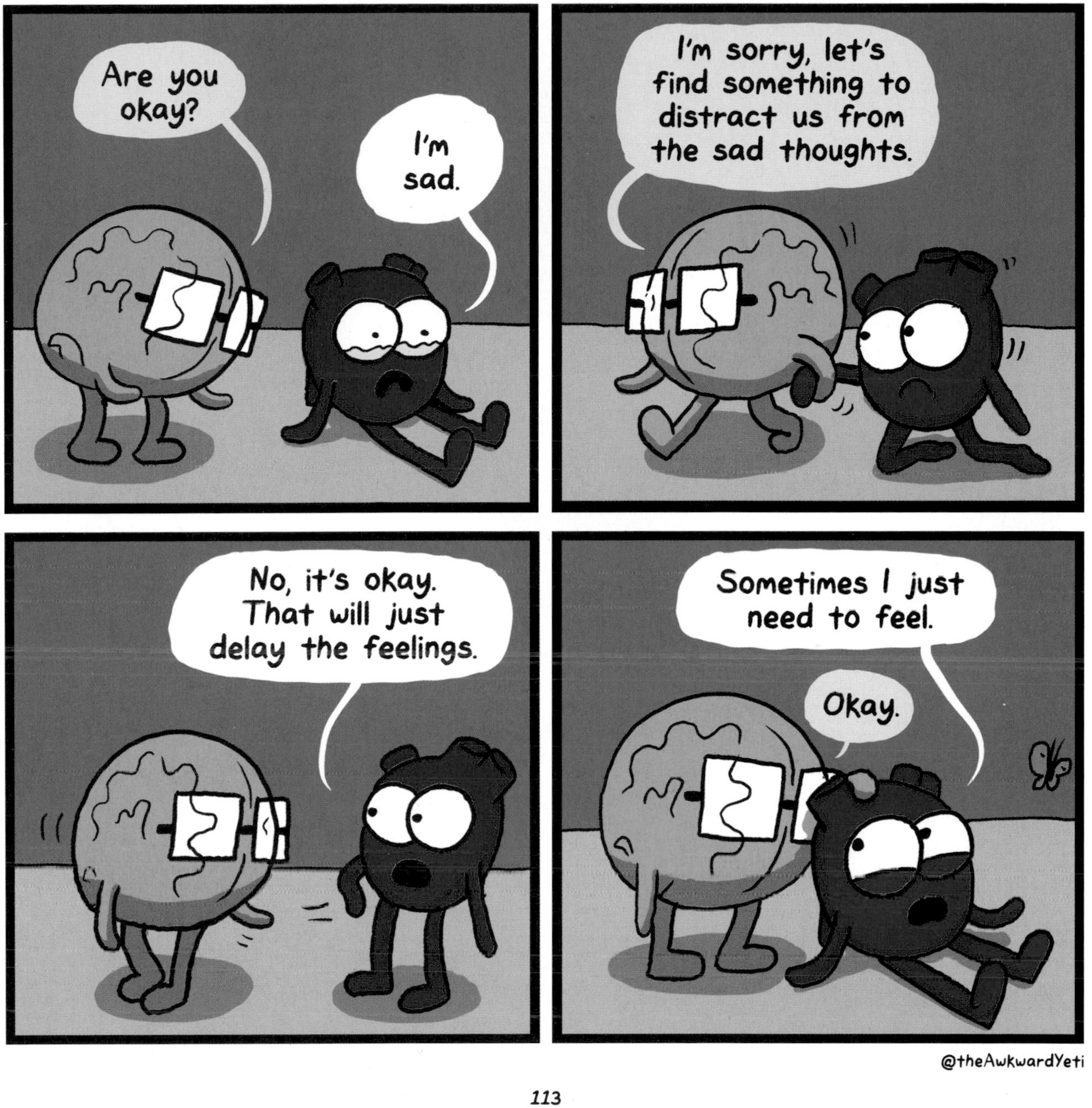
Are you okay?
I'm sad.
I'm sorry, let's find something to distract us from the sad thoughts.
No, it's okay. That will just delay the feelings.
Sometimes I just need to feel.
Okay.
@theAwkwardYeti

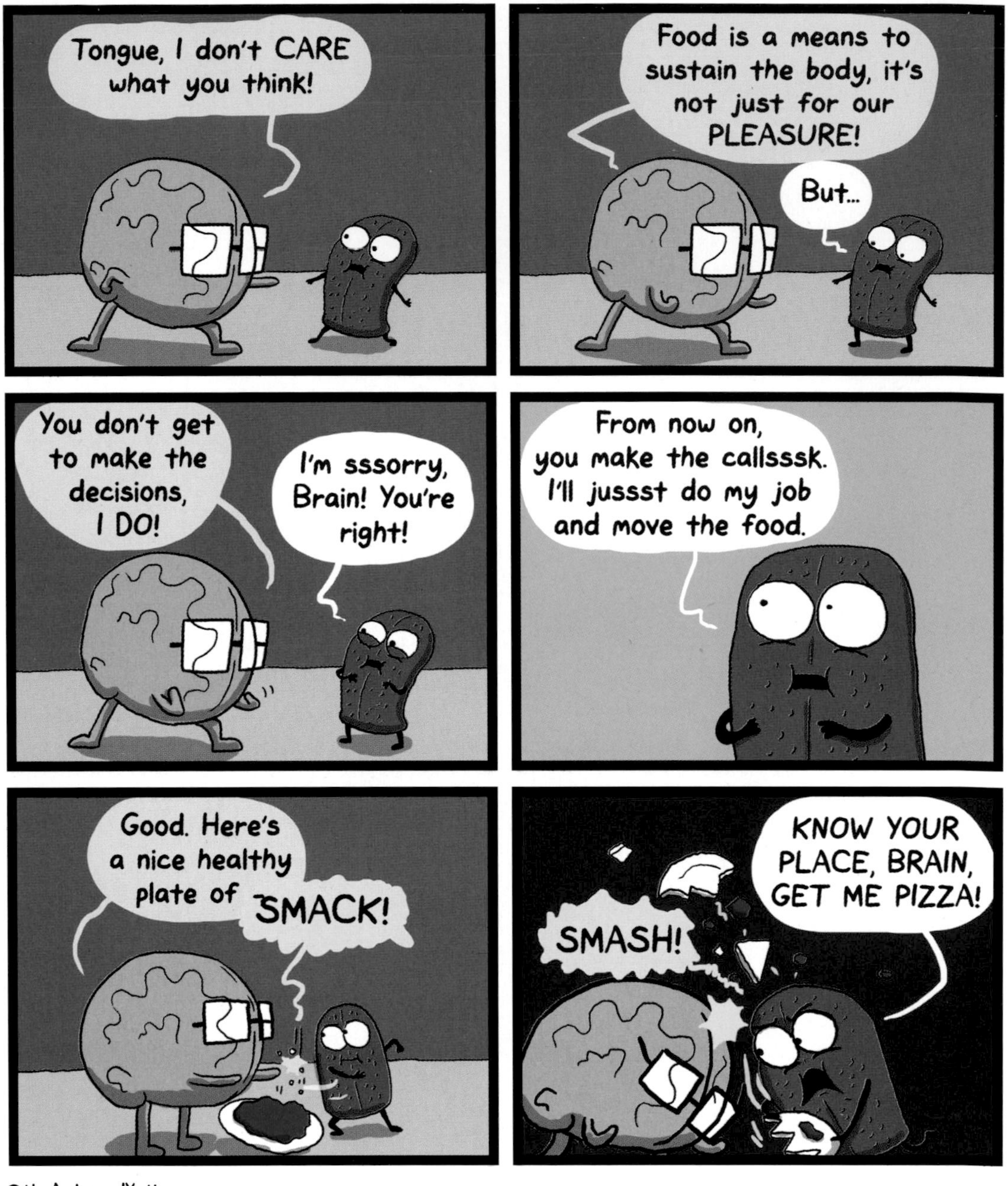
Tongue, I don't CARE what you think!
Food is a means to sustain the body, it's not just for our PLEASURE!
But...
You don't get to make the decisions, I DO!
I'm sssorry, Brain! You're right!
From now on, you make the callsssk. I'll jussst do my job and move the food.
Good. Here's a nice healthy plate of
SMACK!
SMASH!
KNOW YOUR PLACE, BRAIN, GET ME PIZZA!

@theAwkwardYeti

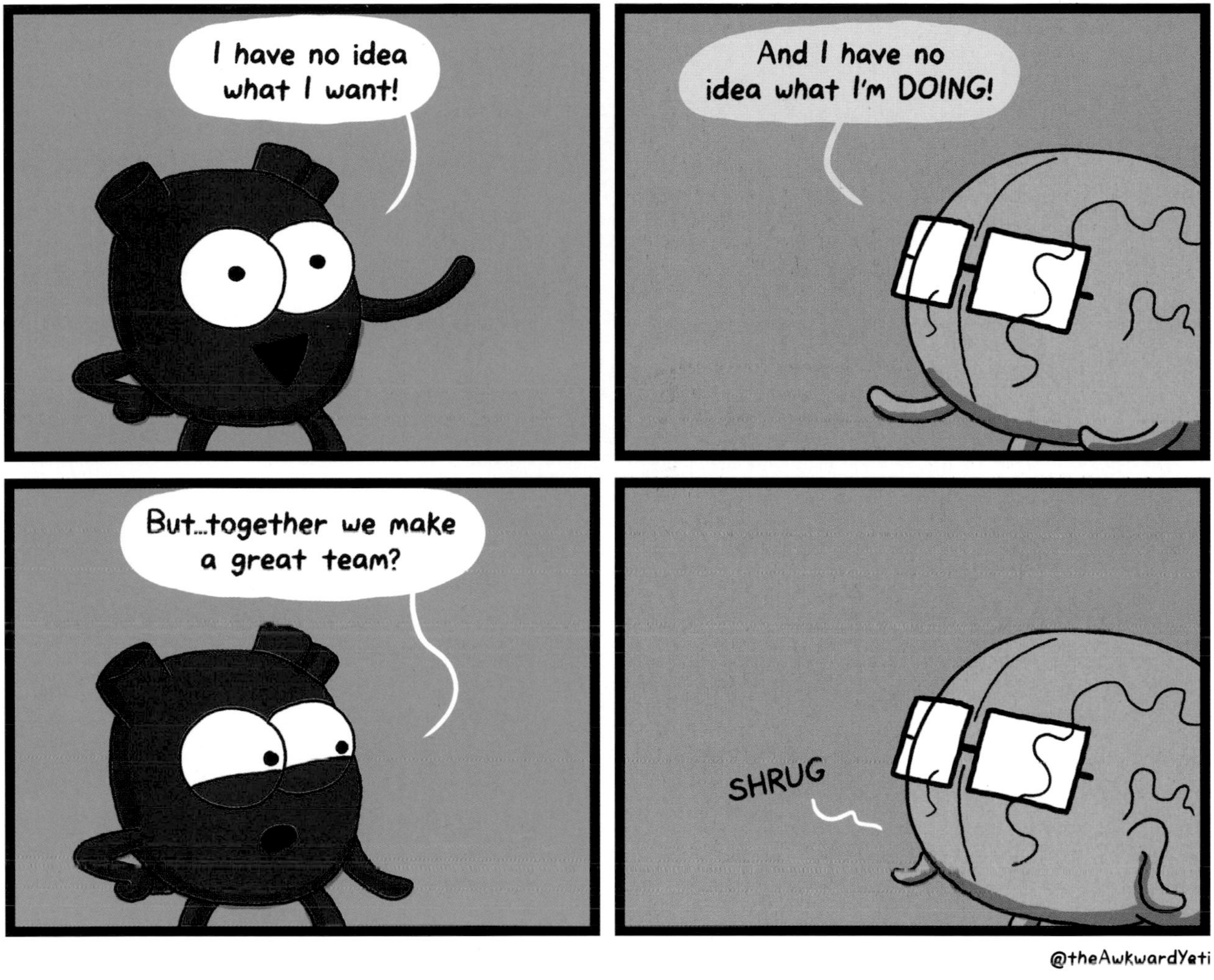
I have no idea what I want!
And I have no idea what I'm DOING!
But...together we make a great team?
SHRUG
@theAwkwardYeti

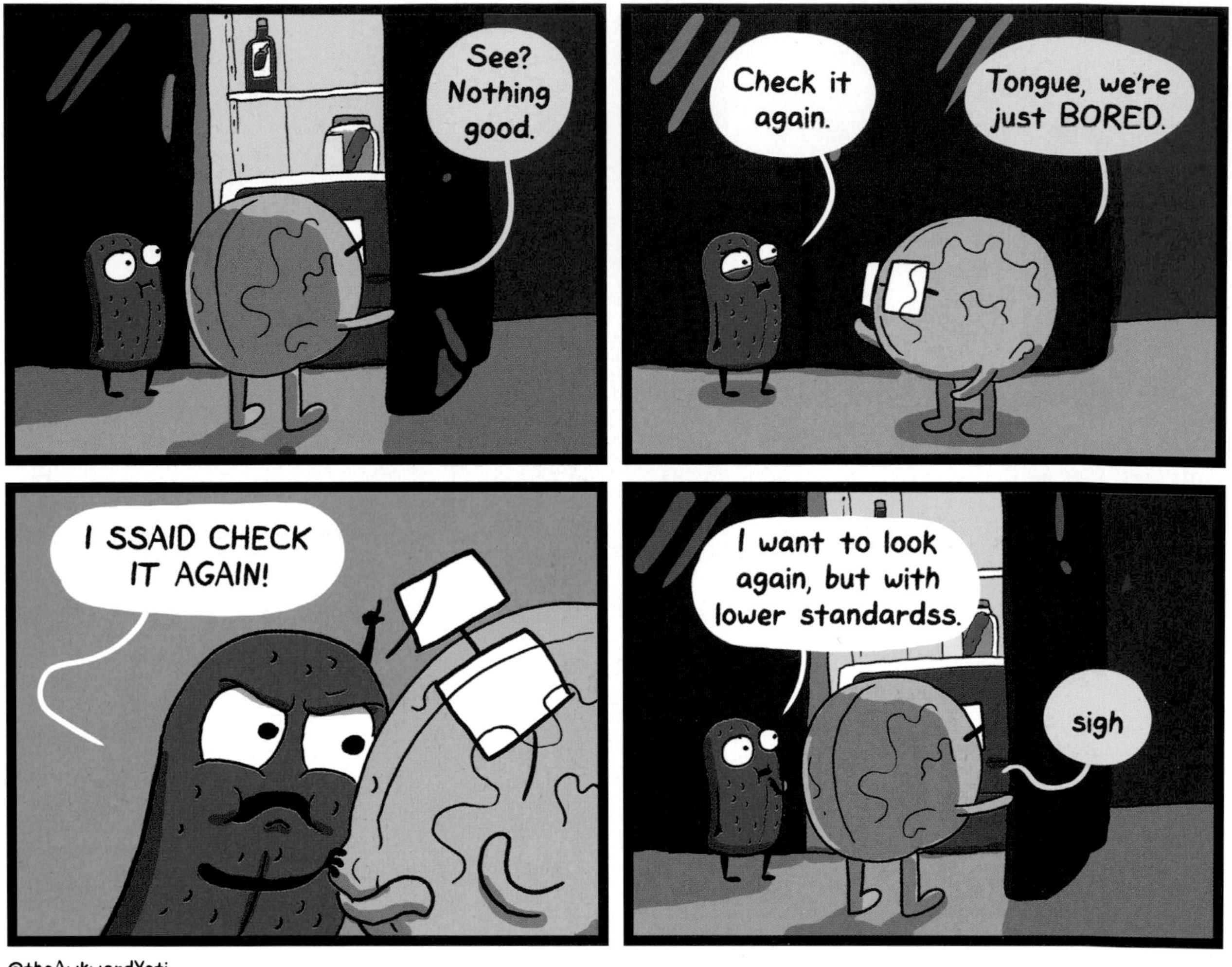
See? Nothing good.
Check it again.
Tongue, we're just BORED.
I SSAID CHECK IT AGAIN!
I want to look again, but with lower standardss.
sigh

@theAwkwardYeti

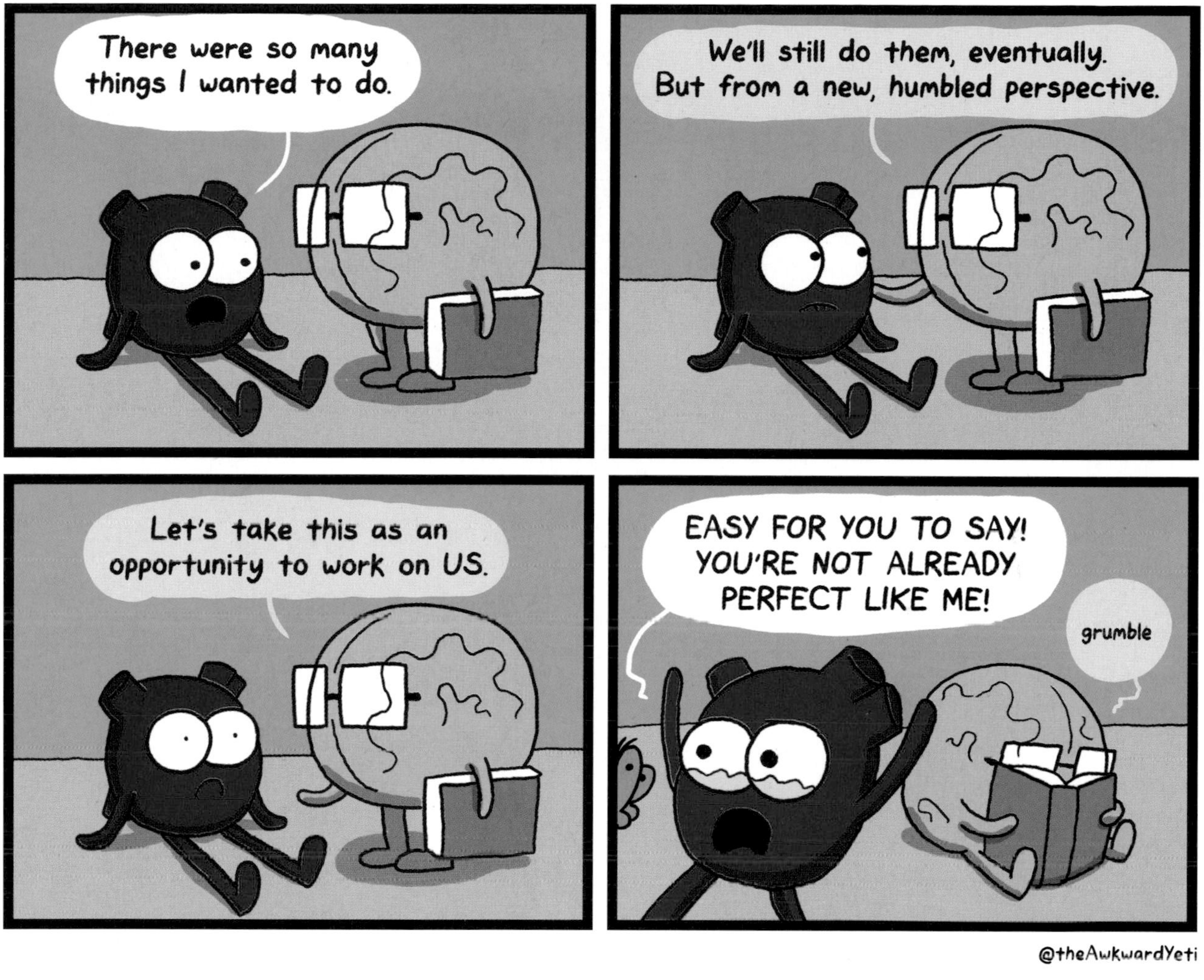
There were so many things I wanted to do.
We'll still do them, eventually. But from a new, humbled perspective.
Let's take this as an opportunity to work on US.
EASY FOR YOU TO SAY! YOU'RE NOT ALREADY PERFECT LIKE ME!
grumble
@theAwkwardYeti

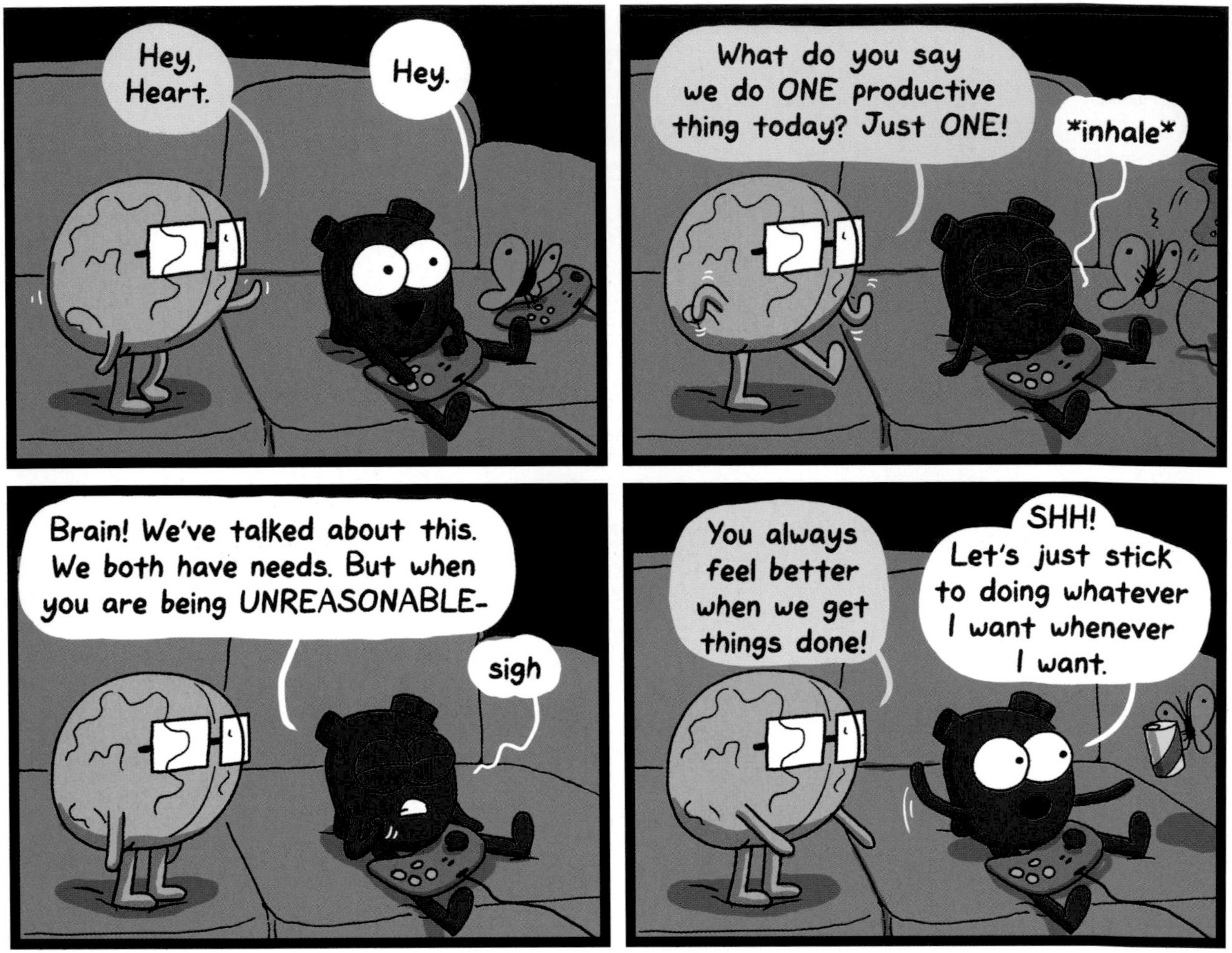
Hey,
Heart.
Hey.
What do you say we do ONE productive thing today? Just ONE!
inhale
Brain! We've talked about this. We both have needs. But when you are being UNREASONABLE-
sigh
You always feel better when we get things done!
SHH!
Let's just stick to doing whatever I want whenever I want.

@theAwkwardYeti

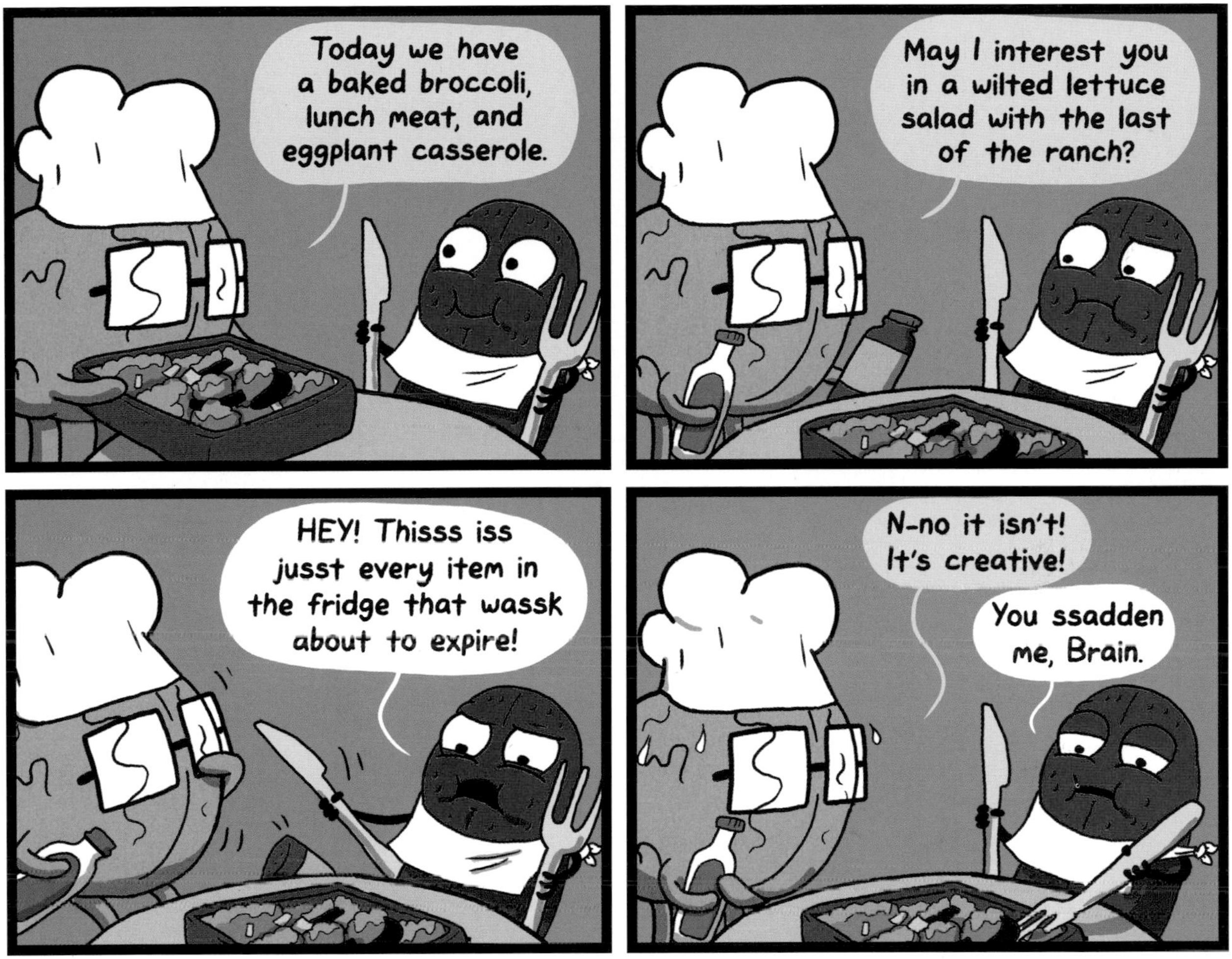
Today we have a baked broccoli, lunch meat, and eggplant casserole.
May I interest you in a wilted lettuce salad with the last of the ranch?
HEY! Thisss iss jusst every item in the fridge that wassk about to expire!
N-no it isn't! It's creative!
You ssadden me, Brain.

@theAwkwardYeti

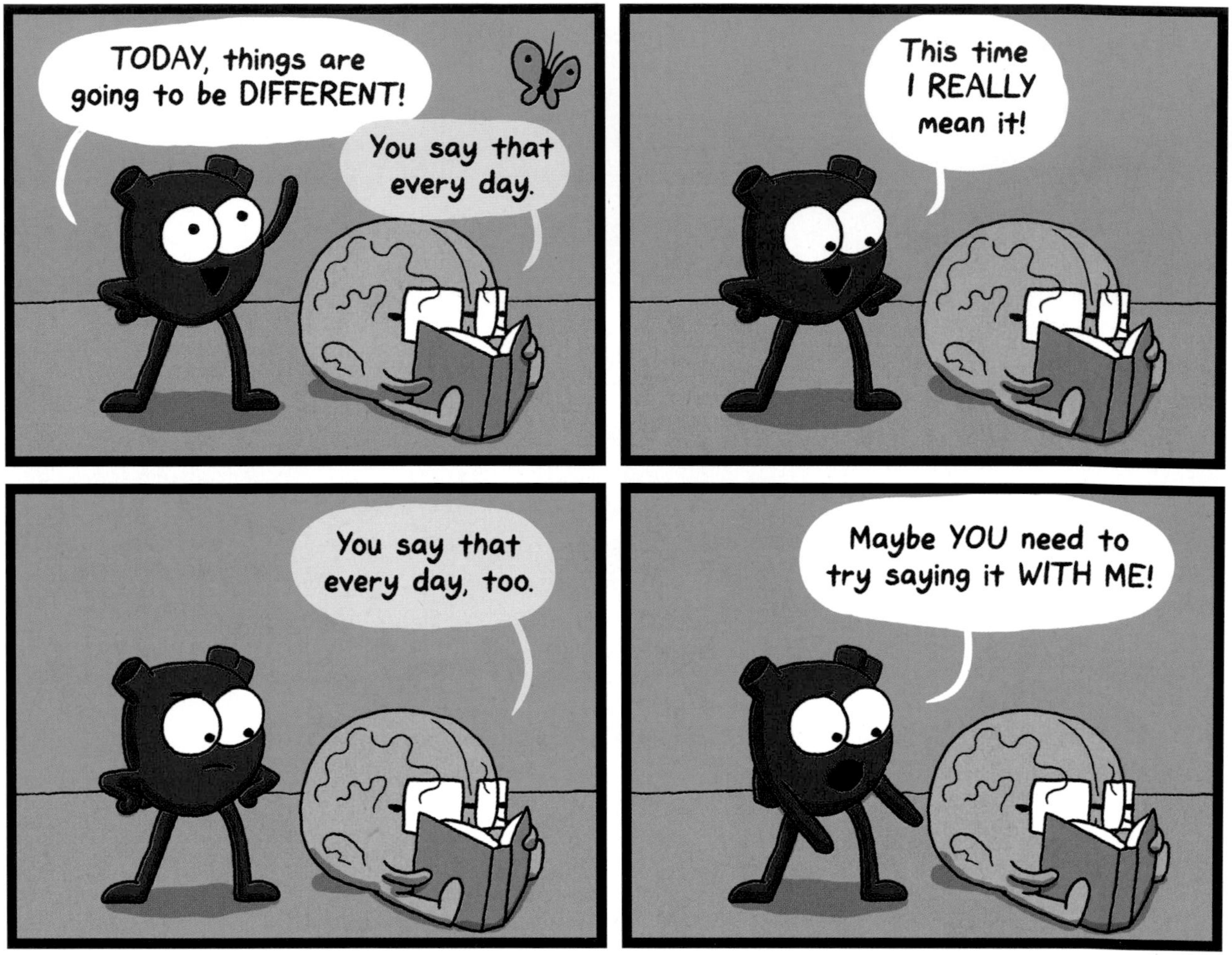
TODAY, things are going to be DIFFERENT!
You say that every day.
This time I REALLY mean it!
You say that every day, too.
Maybe YOU need to try saying it WITH ME!

@theAwkwardYeti

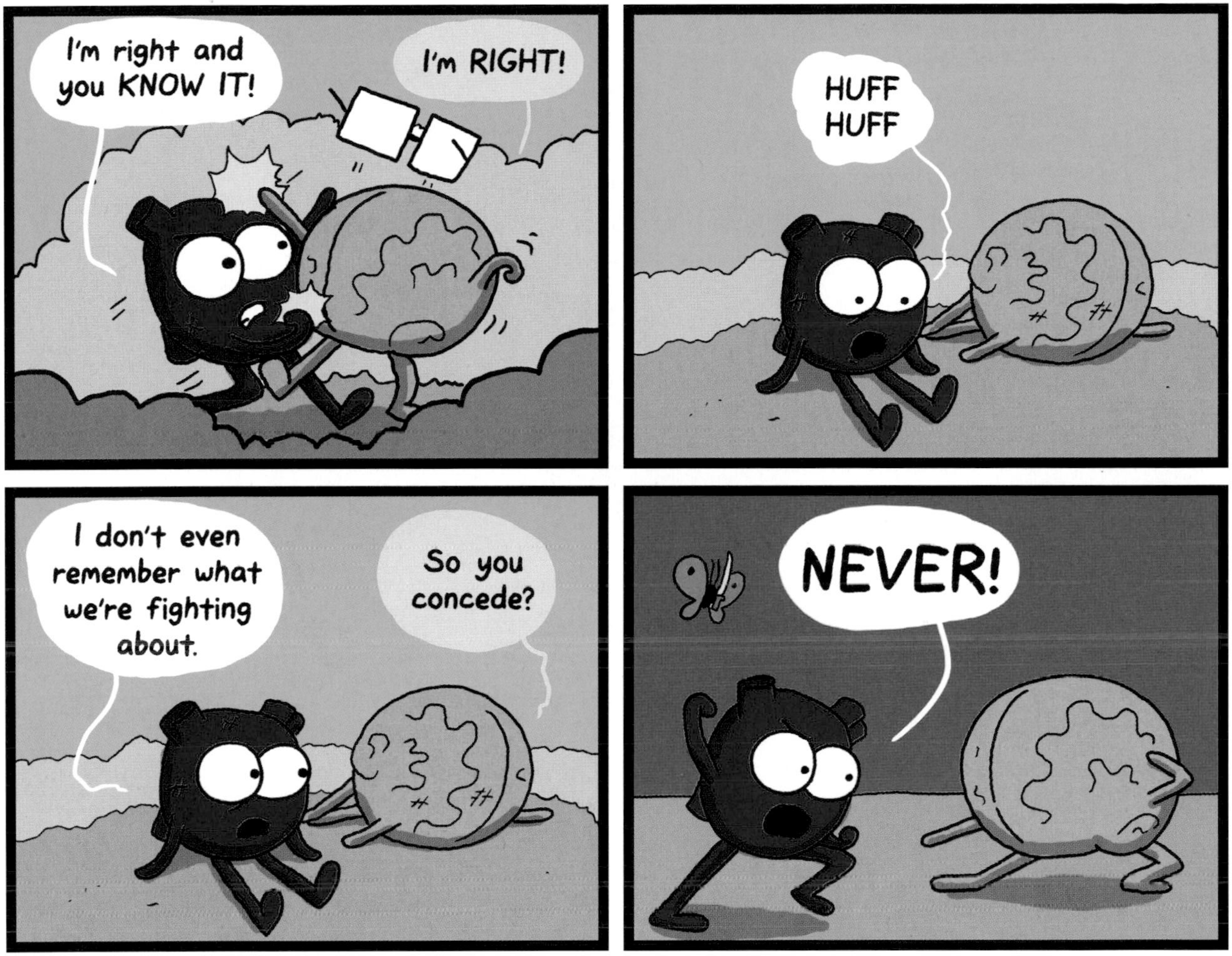
I'm right and you KNOW IT!
I'm RIGHT!
HUFF HUFF
I don't even remember what we're fighting about.
So you concede?
NEVER!

@theAwkwardYeti

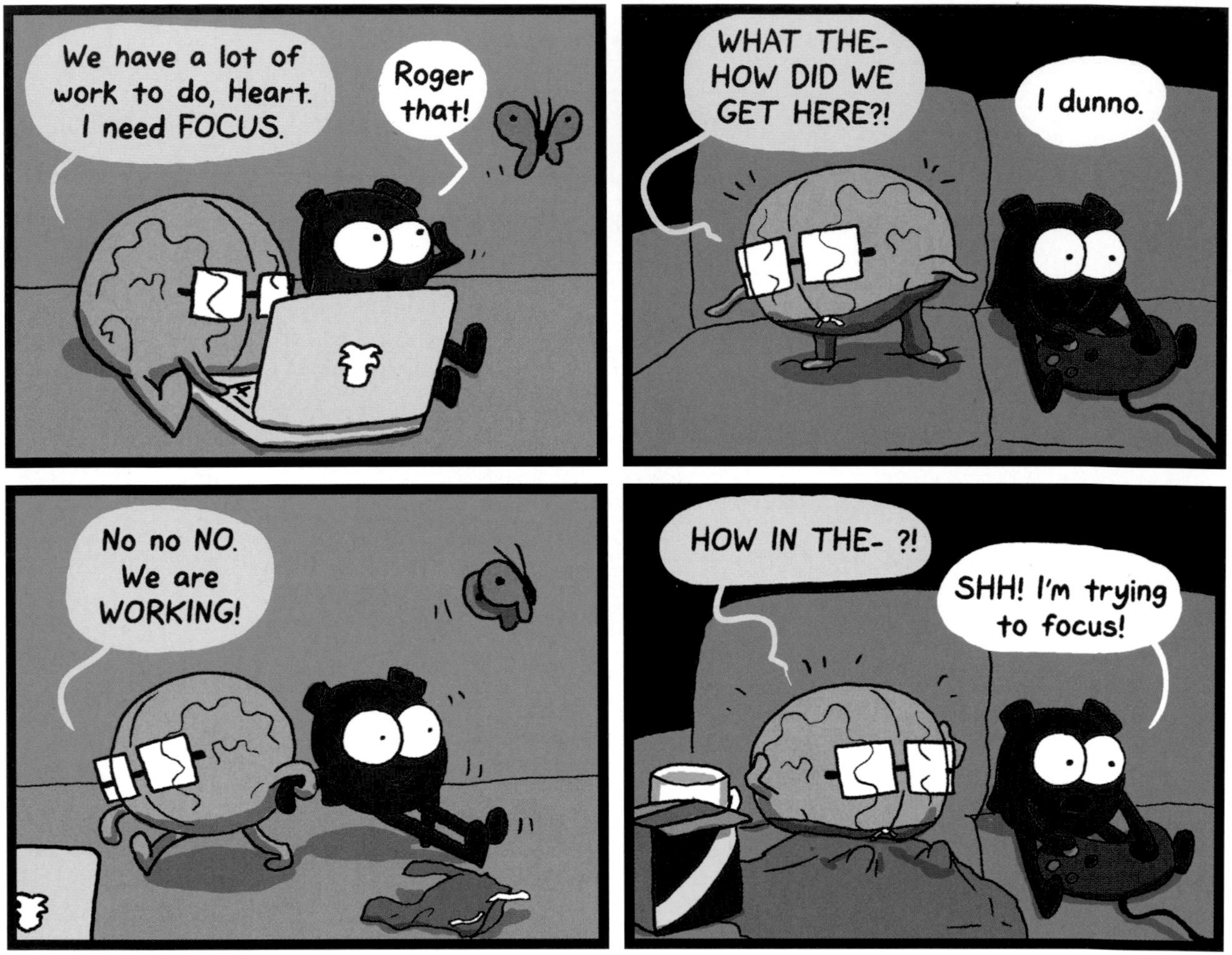

We have a lot of work to do, Heart. I need FOCUS.
Roger that!
WHAT THE- HOW DID WE GET HERE?!
I dunno.
No no NO. We are WORKING!
HOW IN THE- ?!
SHH! I'm trying to focus!

@theAwkwardYeti

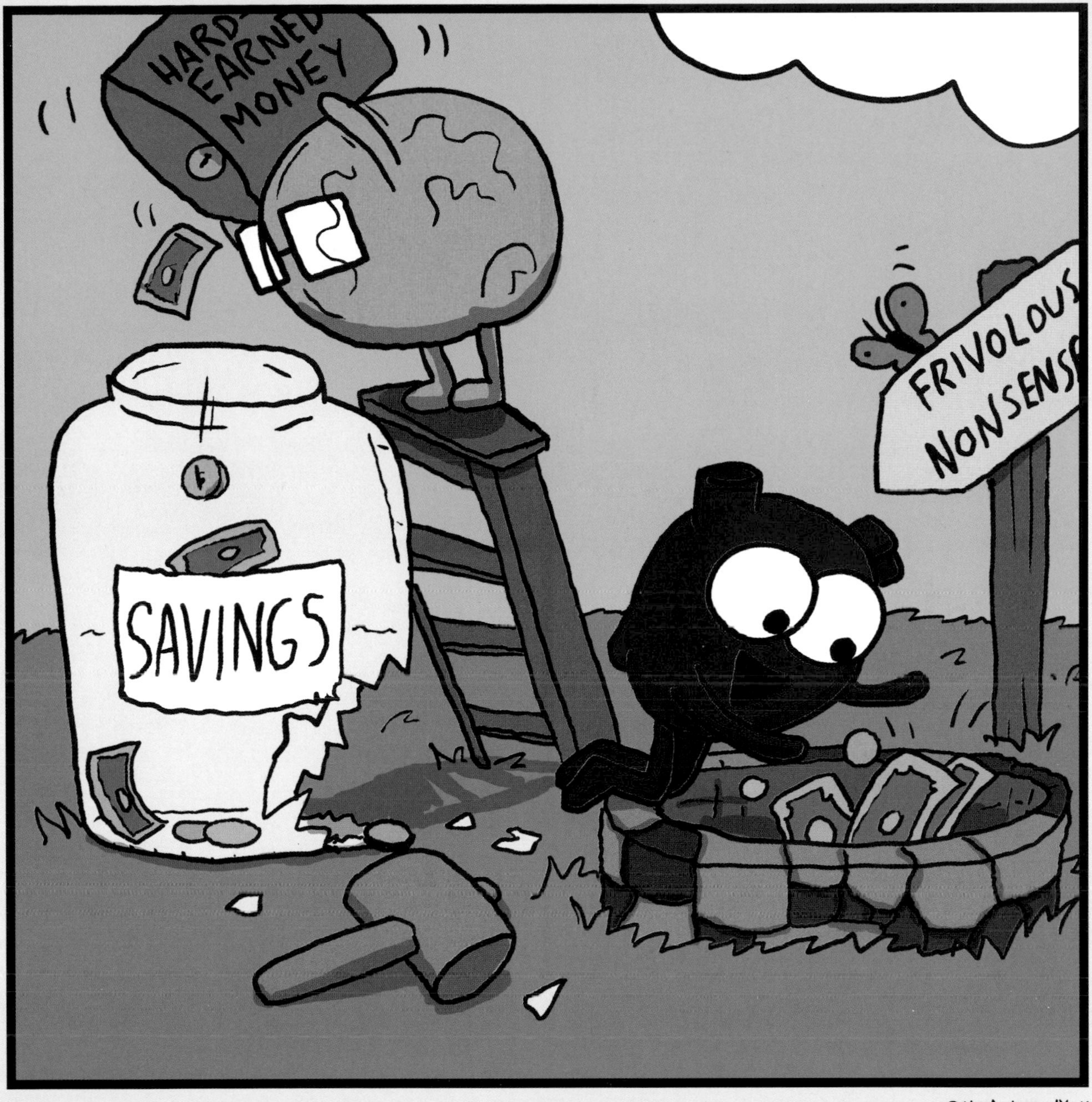
HARD-EARNED MONEY
SAVINGS
FRIVOLOUS NONSENSE

@theAwkwardYeti

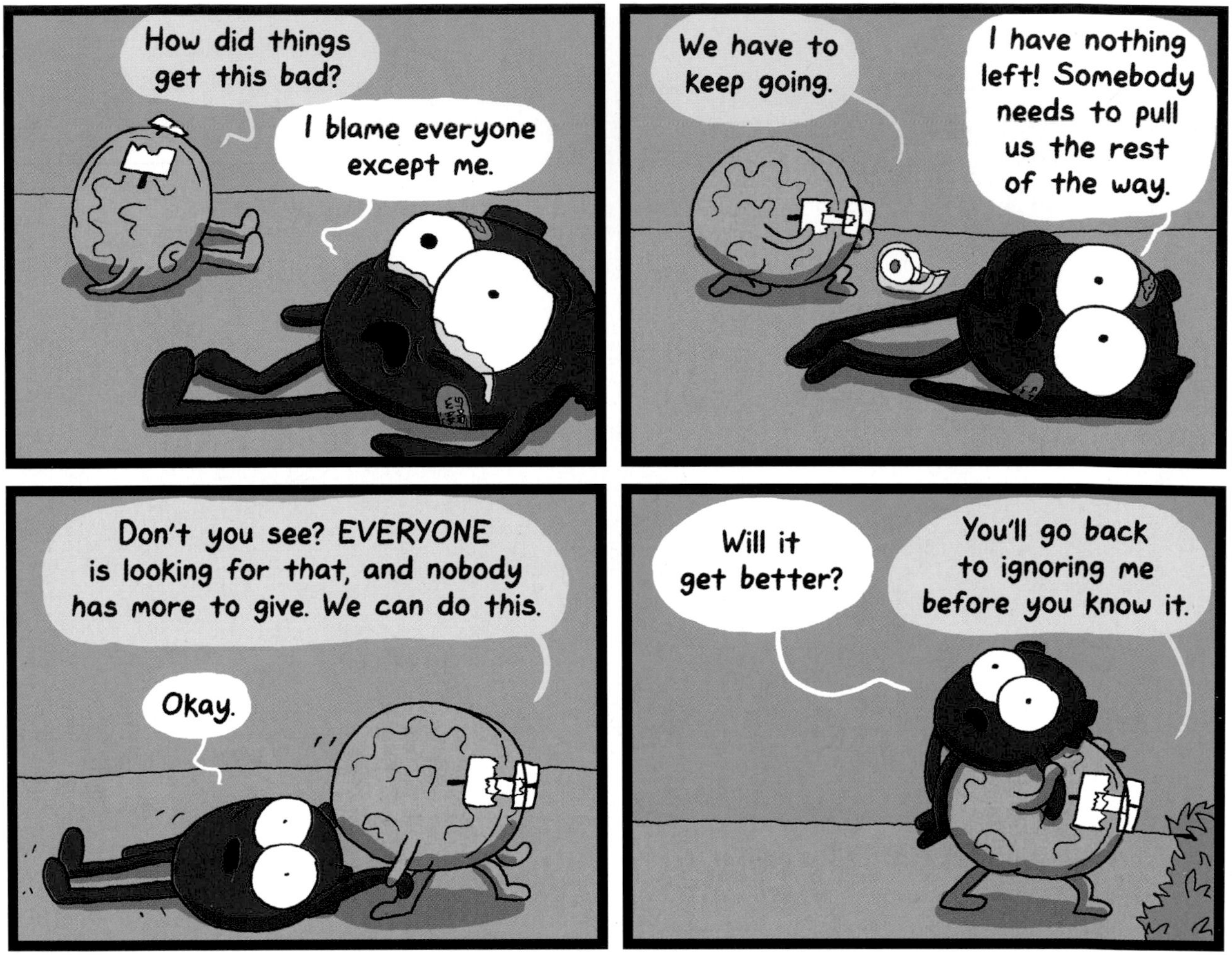
How did things get this bad?
I blame everyone except me.
We have to keep going.
I have nothing left! Somebody needs to pull us the rest of the way.
Don't you see? EVERYONE is looking for that, and nobody has more to give. We can do this.
Okay.
Will it get better?
You'll go back to ignoring me before you know it.

@theAwkwardYeti

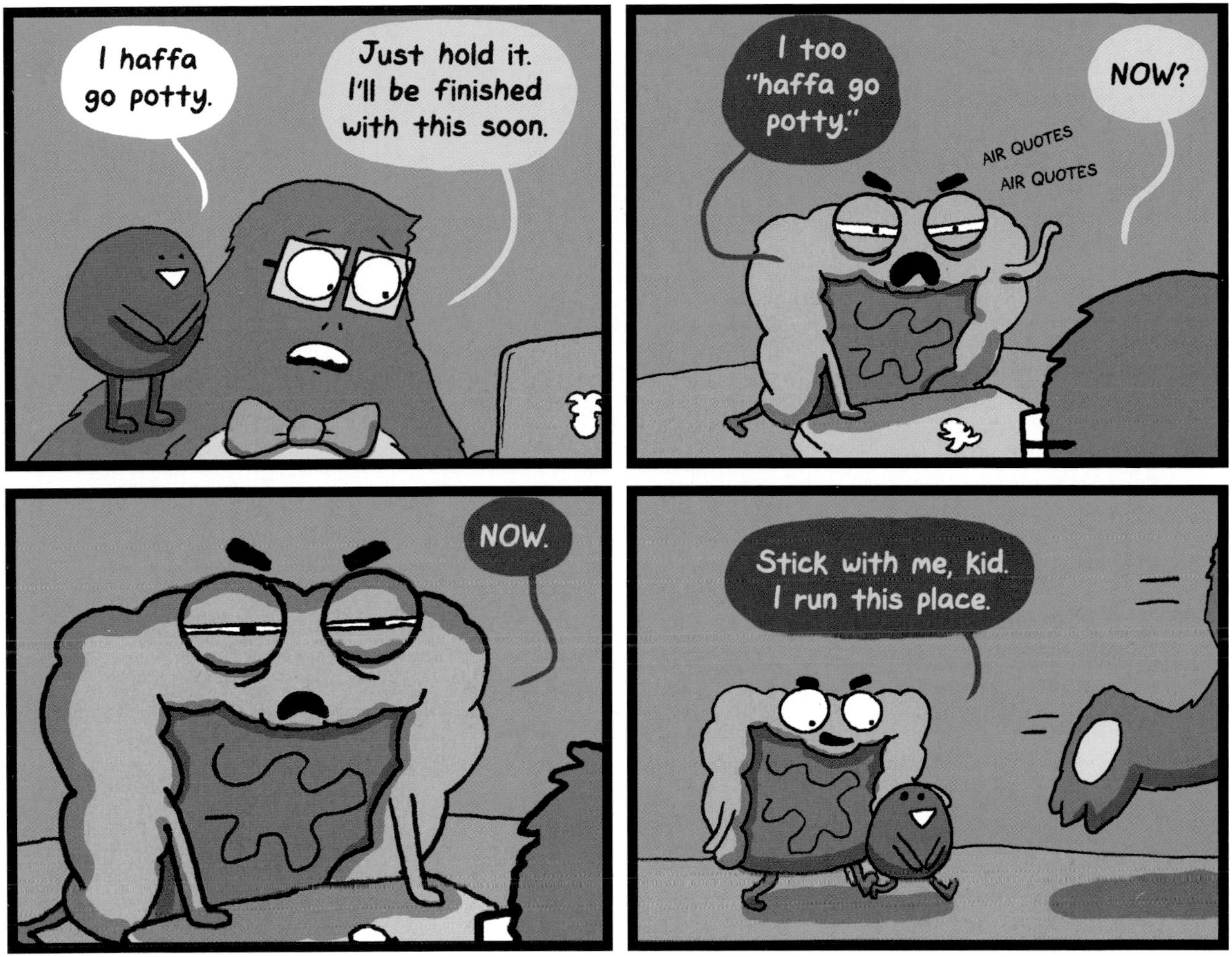
I haffa go potty.
Just hold it. I'll be finished with this soon.
I too "haffa go potty."
NOW?
AIR QUOTES
AIR QUOTES
NOW.
Stick with me, kid. I run this place.

@theAwkwardYeti

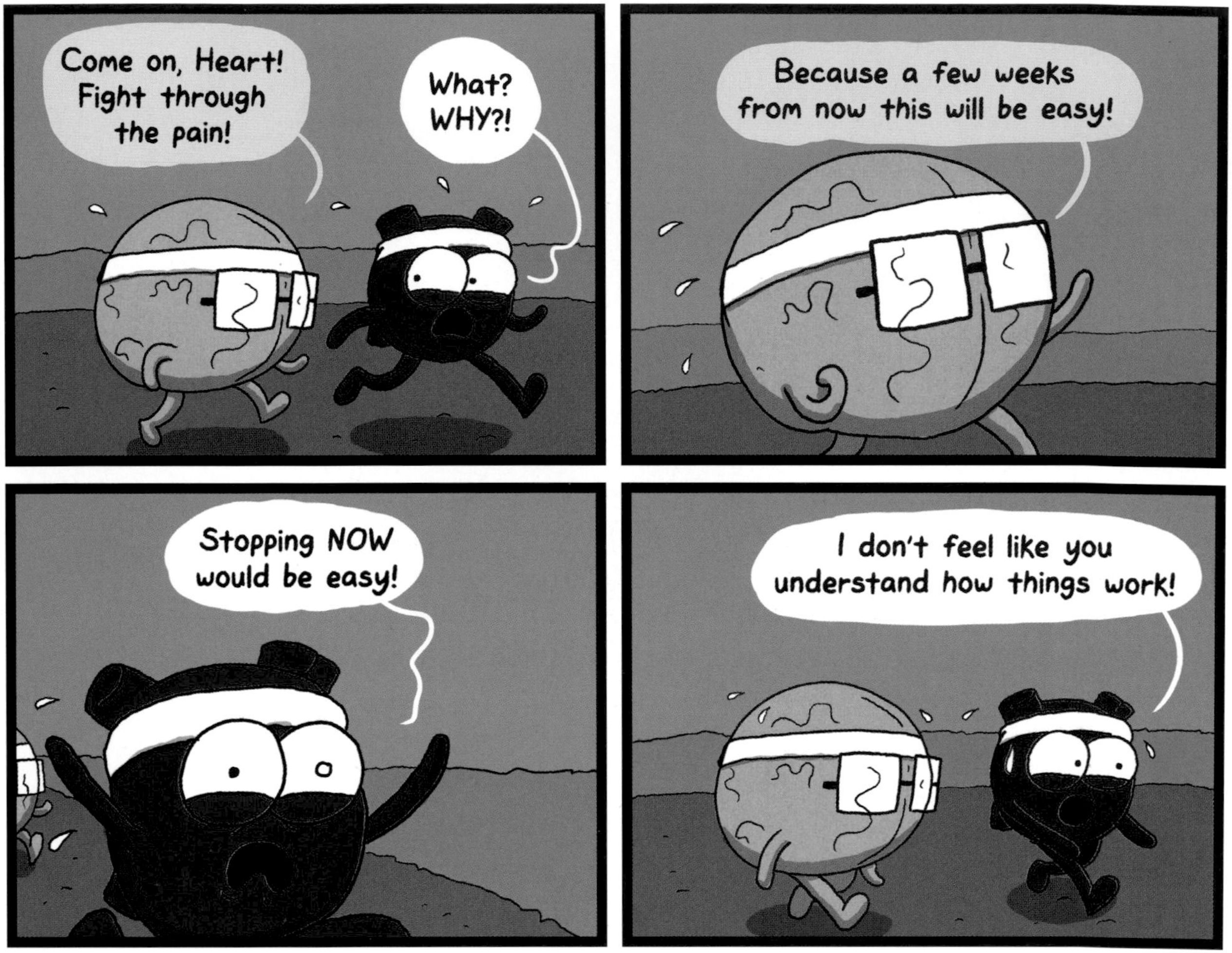
Come on, Heart! Fight through the pain!
What? WHY?!
Because a few weeks from now this will be easy!
Stopping NOW would be easy!
I don't feel like you understand how things work!

@theAwkwardYeti

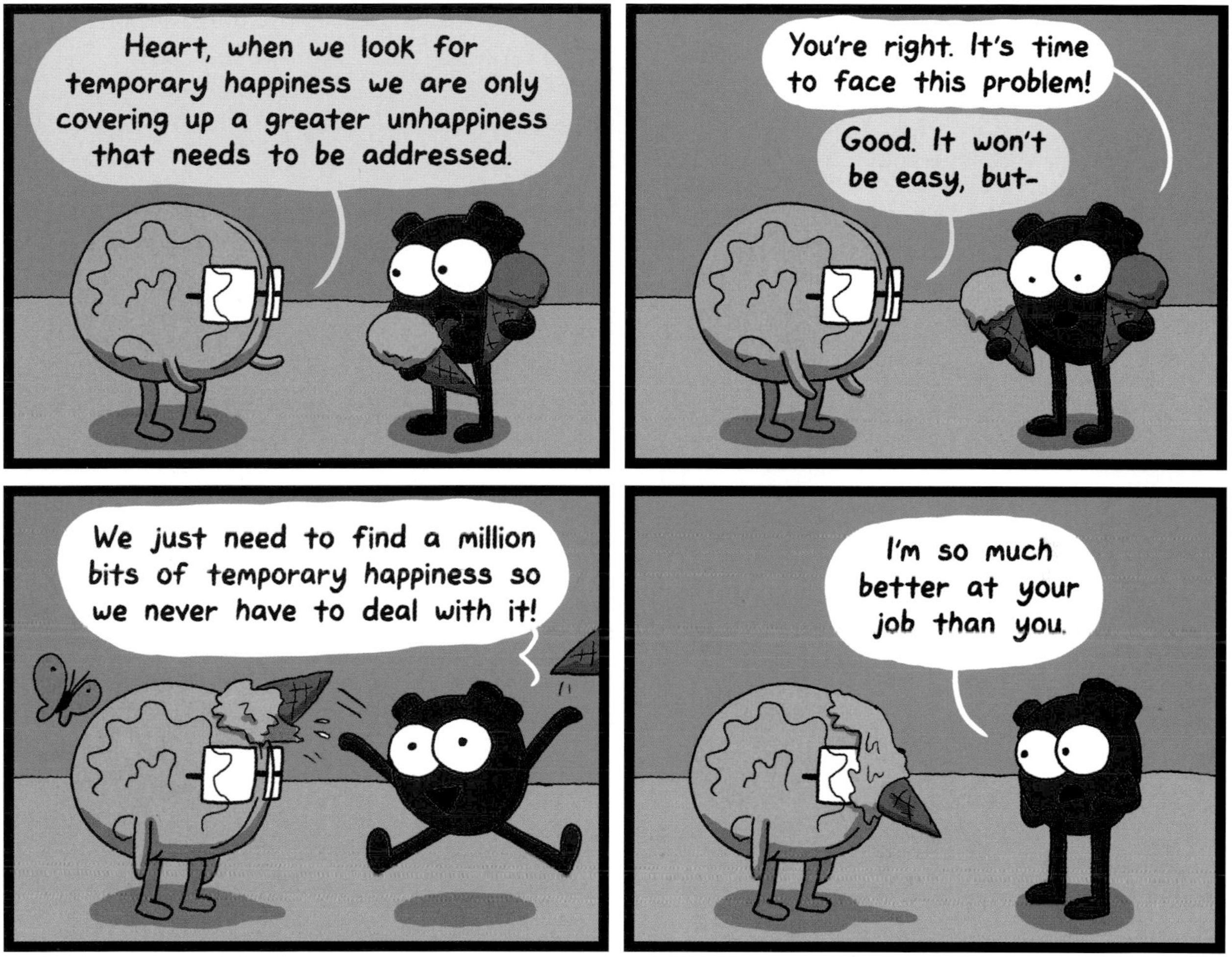
Heart, when we look for temporary happiness we are only covering up a greater unhappiness that needs to be addressed.
You're right. It's time to face this problem!
Good. It won't be easy, but-
We just need to find a million bits of temporary happiness so we never have to deal with it!
I'm so much better at your job than you.

@theAwkwardYeti

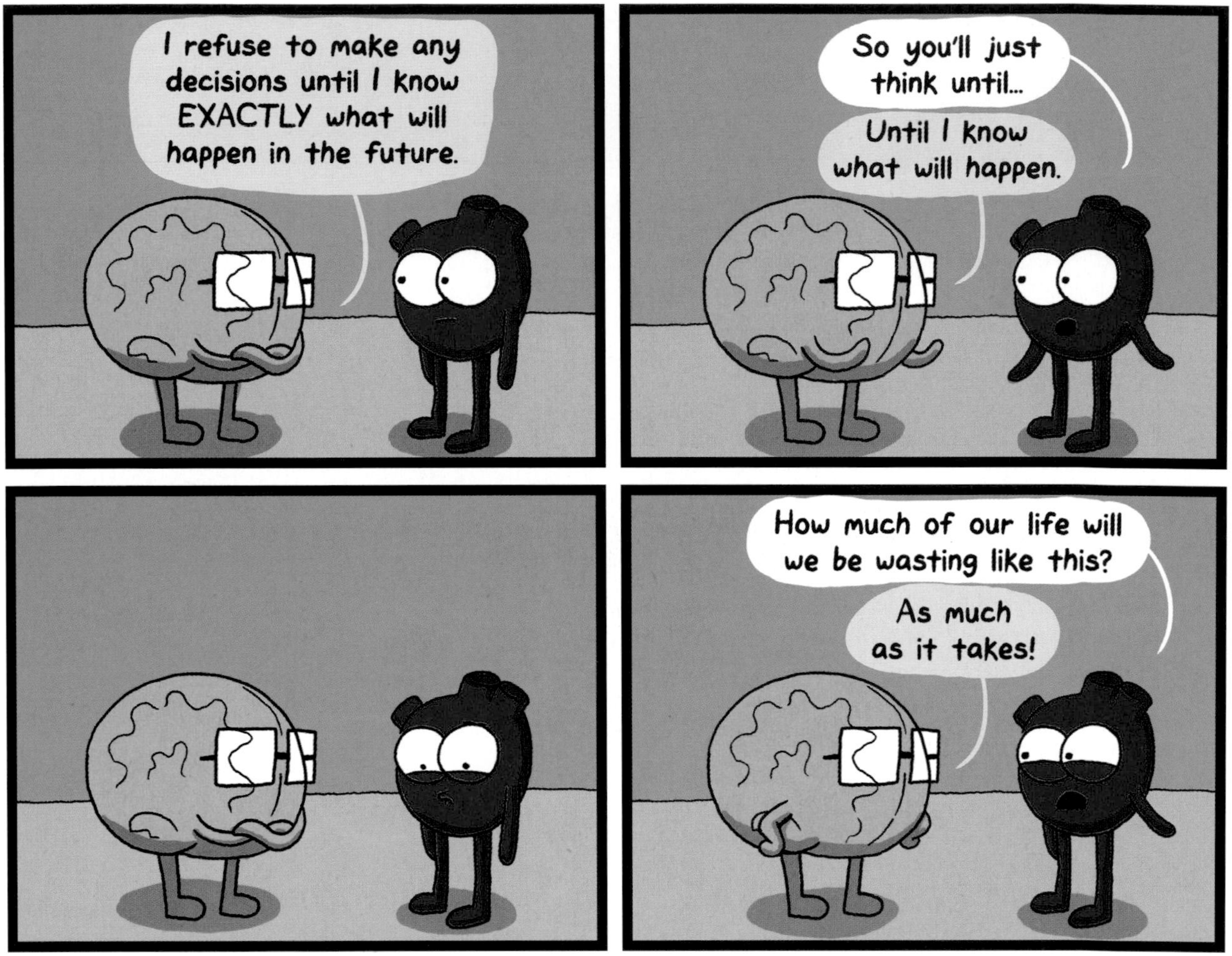
I refuse to make any decisions until I know EXACTLY what will happen in the future.
So you'll just think until...
Until I know what will happen.
How much of our life will we be wasting like this?
As much as it takes!

@theAwkwardYeti

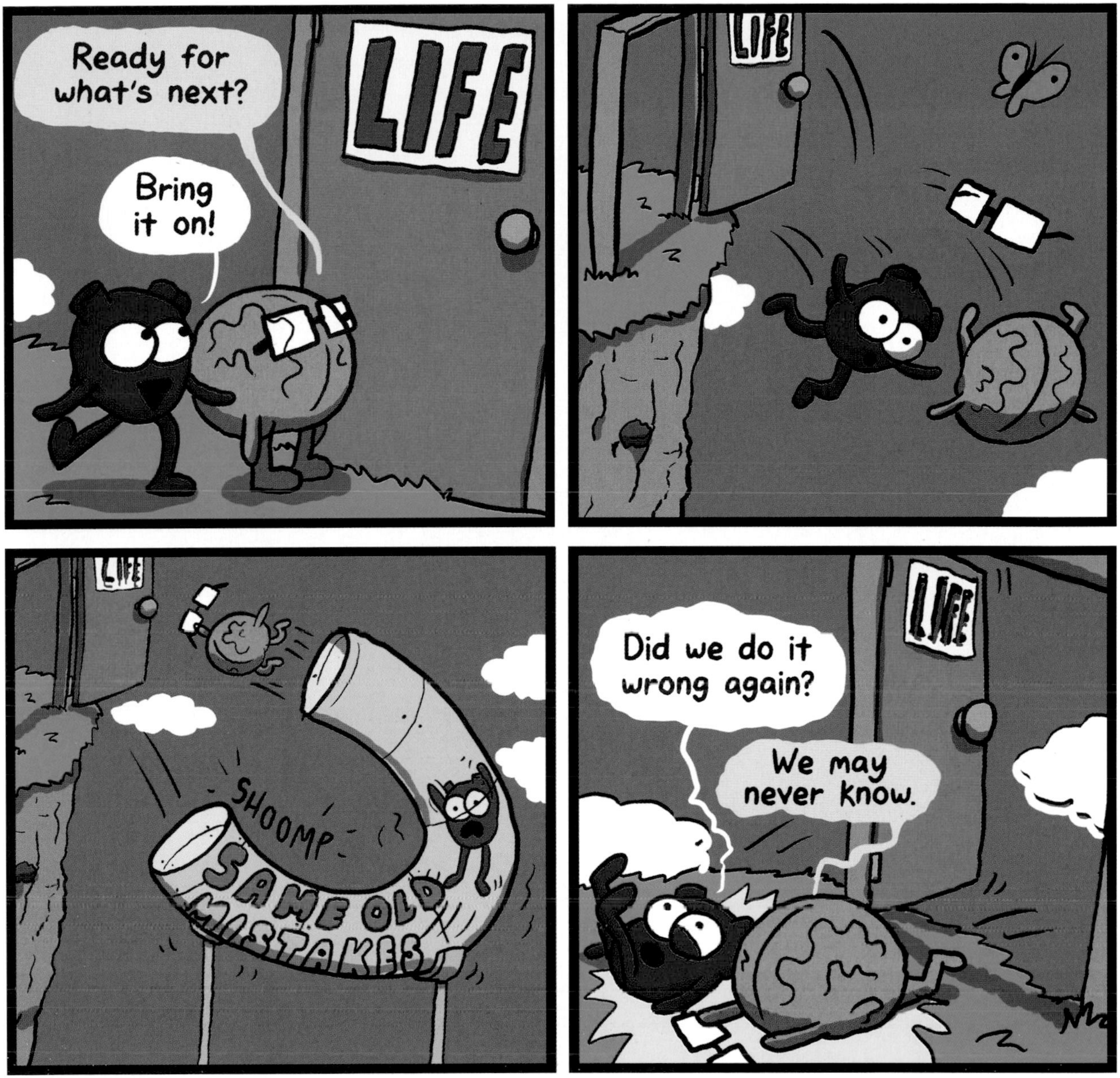
LIFE
Ready for what's next?
Bring it on!
LIFE
LIFE
SHOOMP
SAME OLD MISTAKES
LIFE
Did we do it wrong again?
We may never know.
@theAwkwardYeti

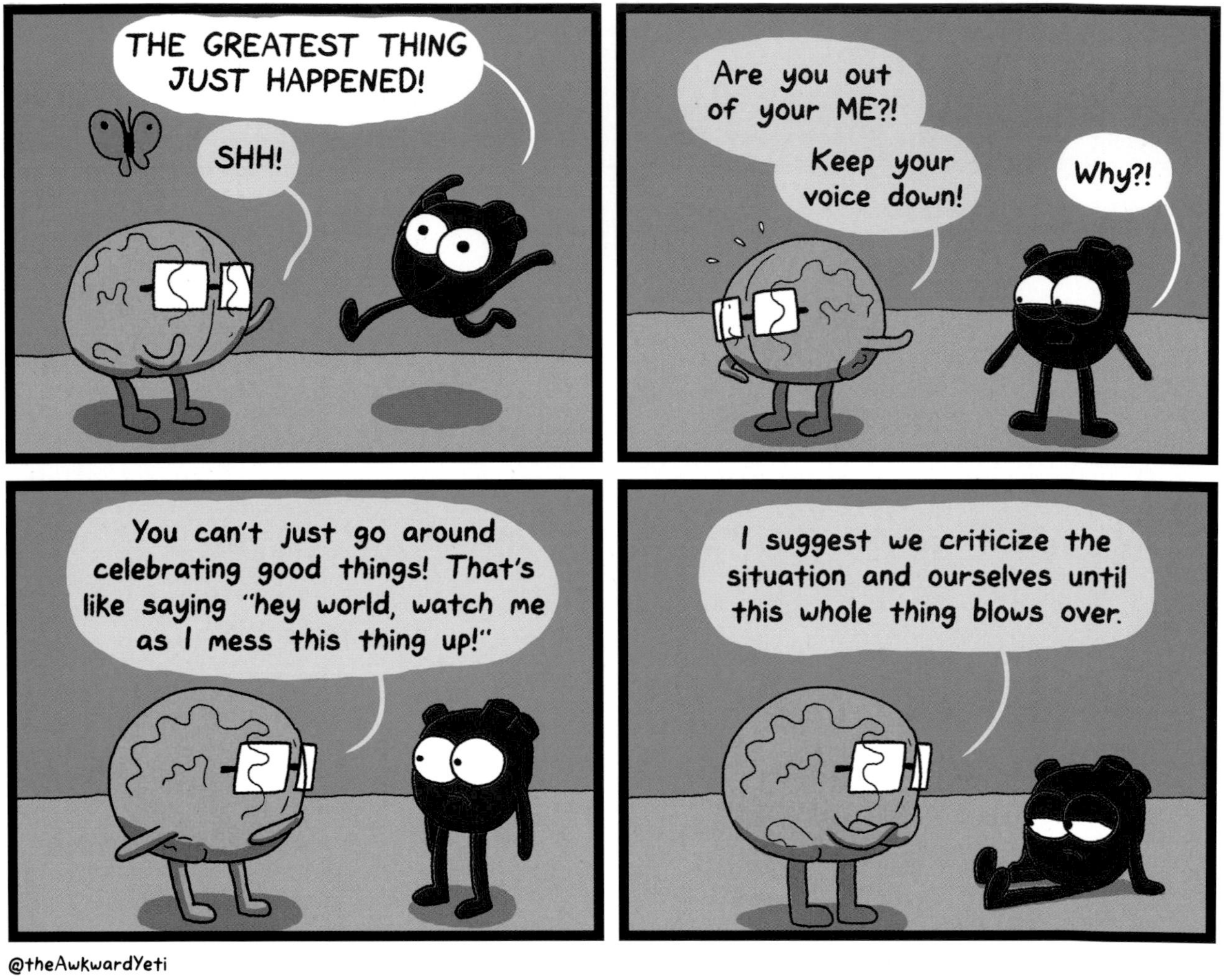
THE GREATEST THING JUST HAPPENED!
SHH!
Are you out of your ME?!
Keep your voice down!
Why?!
You can't just go around celebrating good things! That's like saying "hey world, watch me as I mess this thing up!"
I suggest we criticize the situation and ourselves until this whole thing blows over.
@theAwkwardYeti

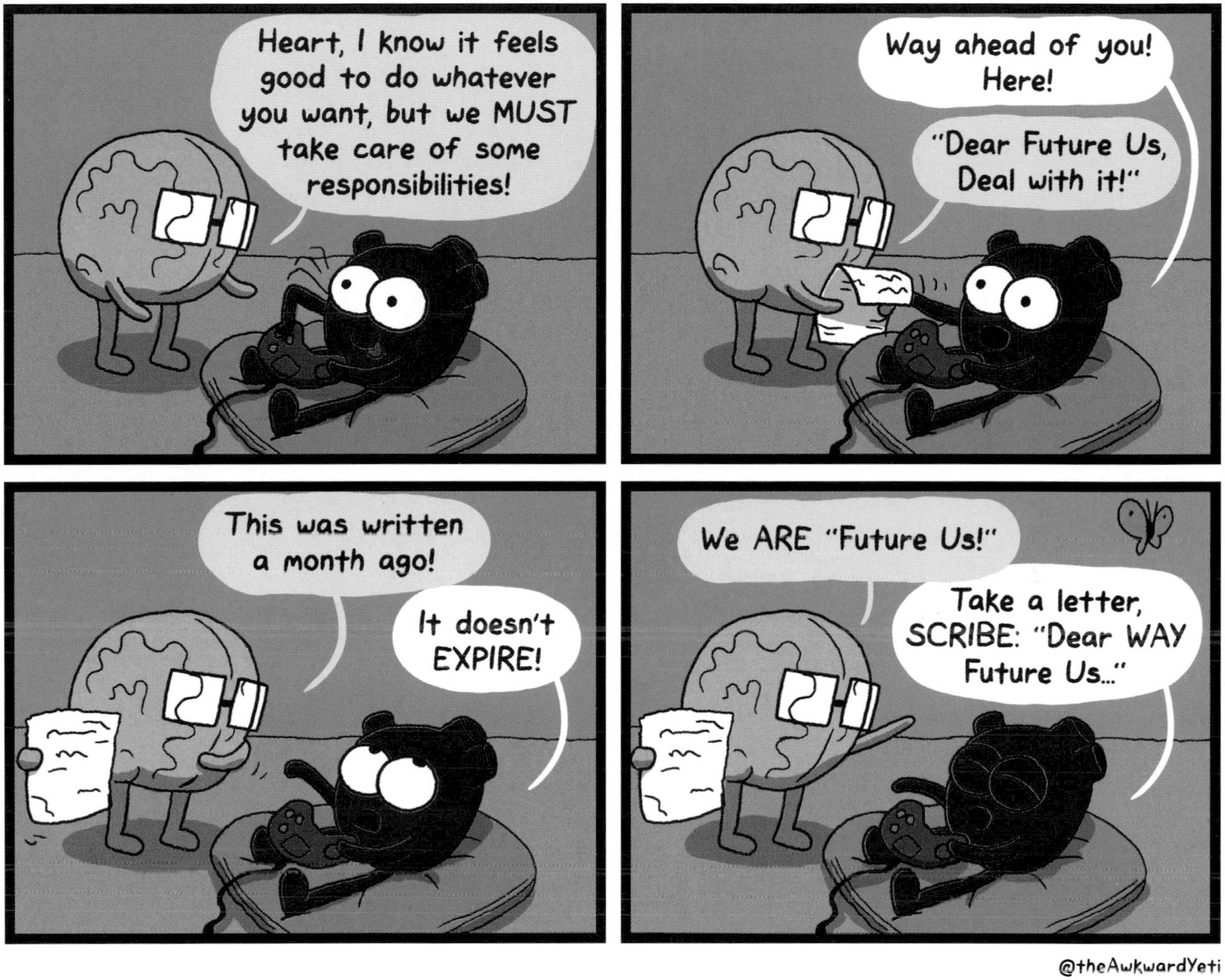
Heart, I know it feels good to do whatever you want, but we MUST take care of some responsibilities!
Way ahead of you! Here!
"Dear Future Us, Deal with it!"
This was written a month ago!
It doesn't EXPIRE!
We ARE "Future Us!"
Take a letter, SCRIBE: "Dear WAY Future Us..."

@theAwkwardYeti

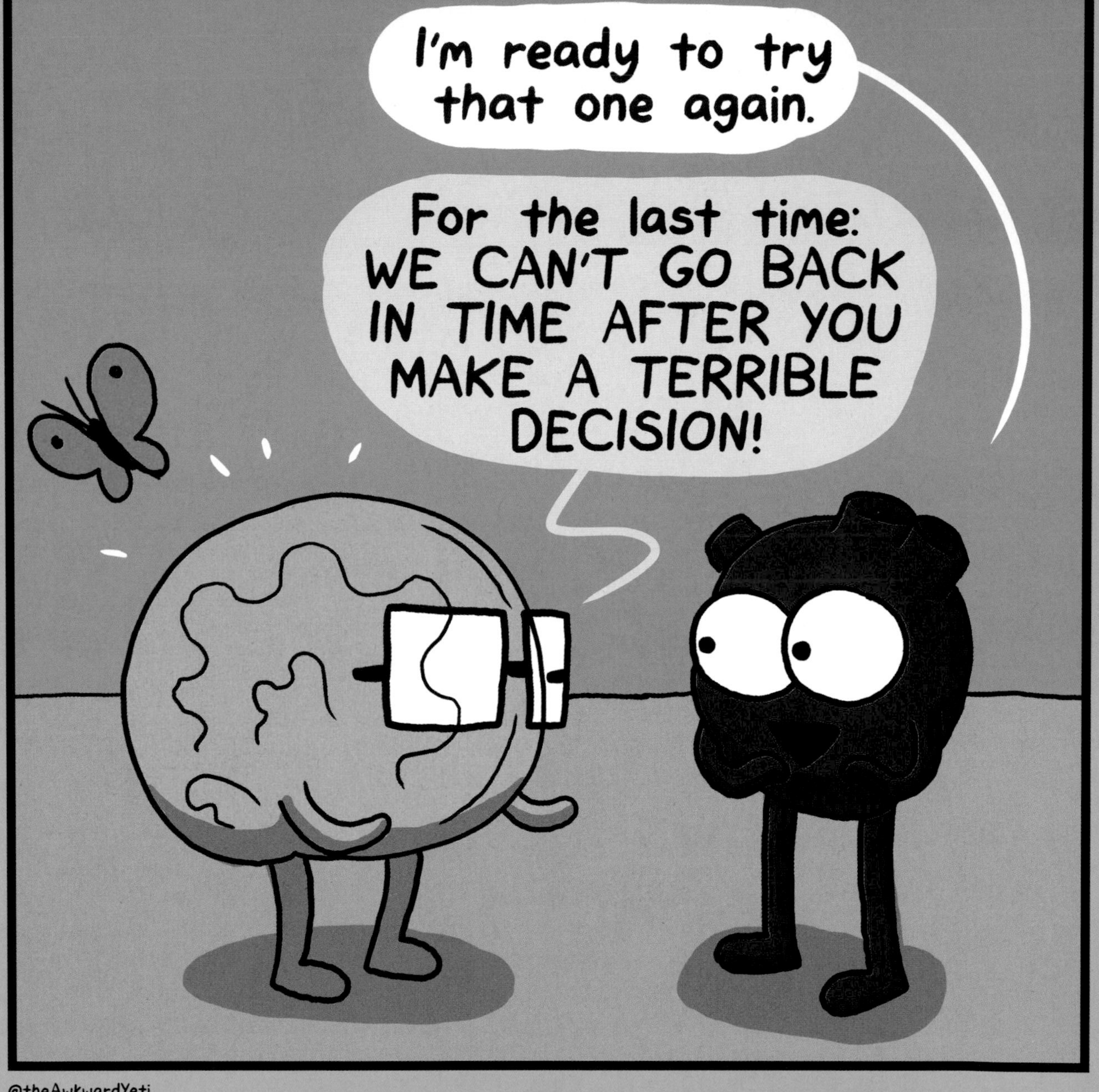
I'm ready to try that one again.
For the last time: WE CAN'T GO BACK IN TIME AFTER YOU MAKE A TERRIBLE DECISION!

@theAwkwardYeti

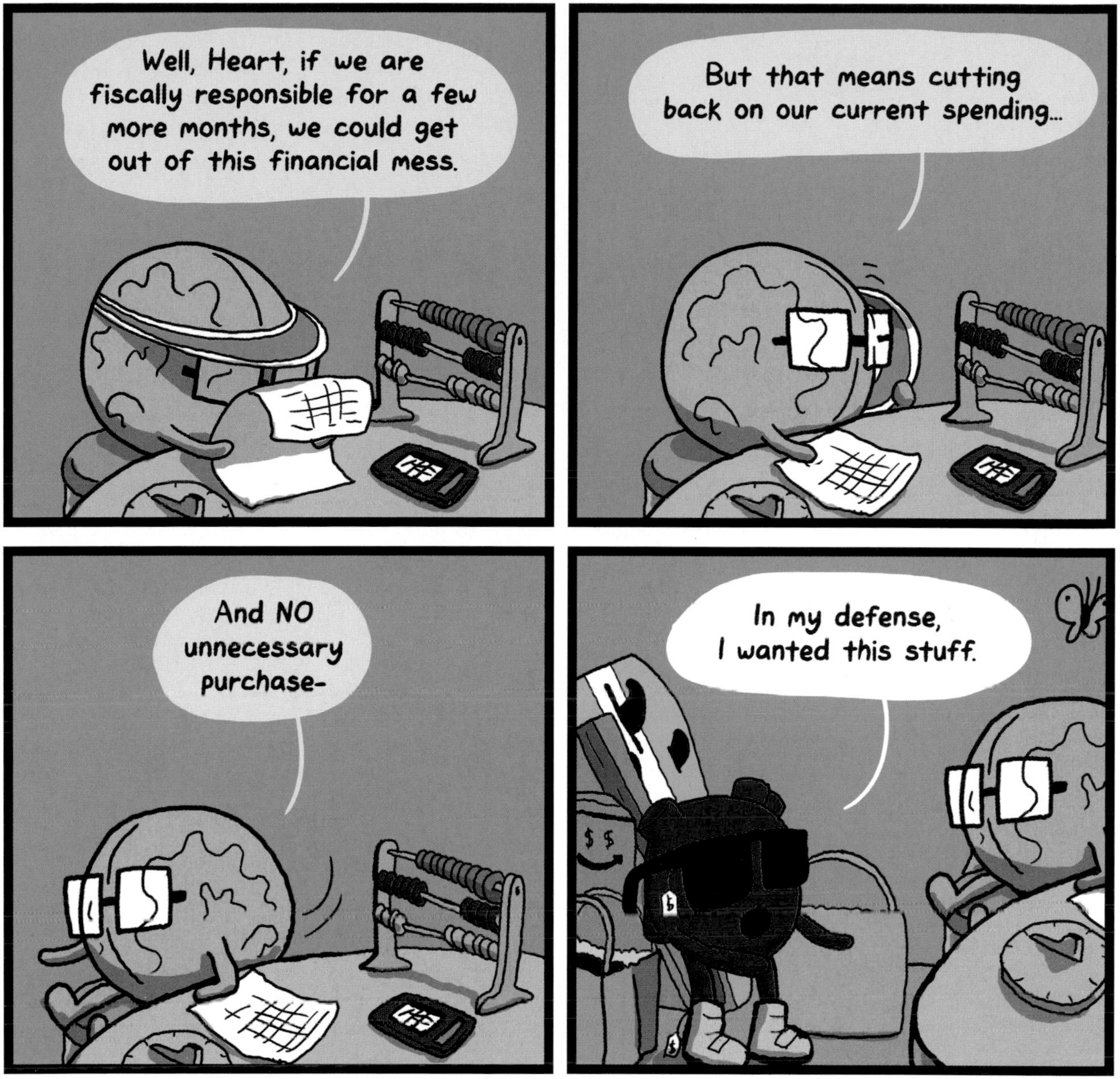
Well, Heart, if we are fiscally responsible for a few more months, we could get out of this financial mess.
But that means cutting back on our current spending...
And NO unnecessary purchase-
In my defense, I wanted this stuff.

@theAwkwardYeti

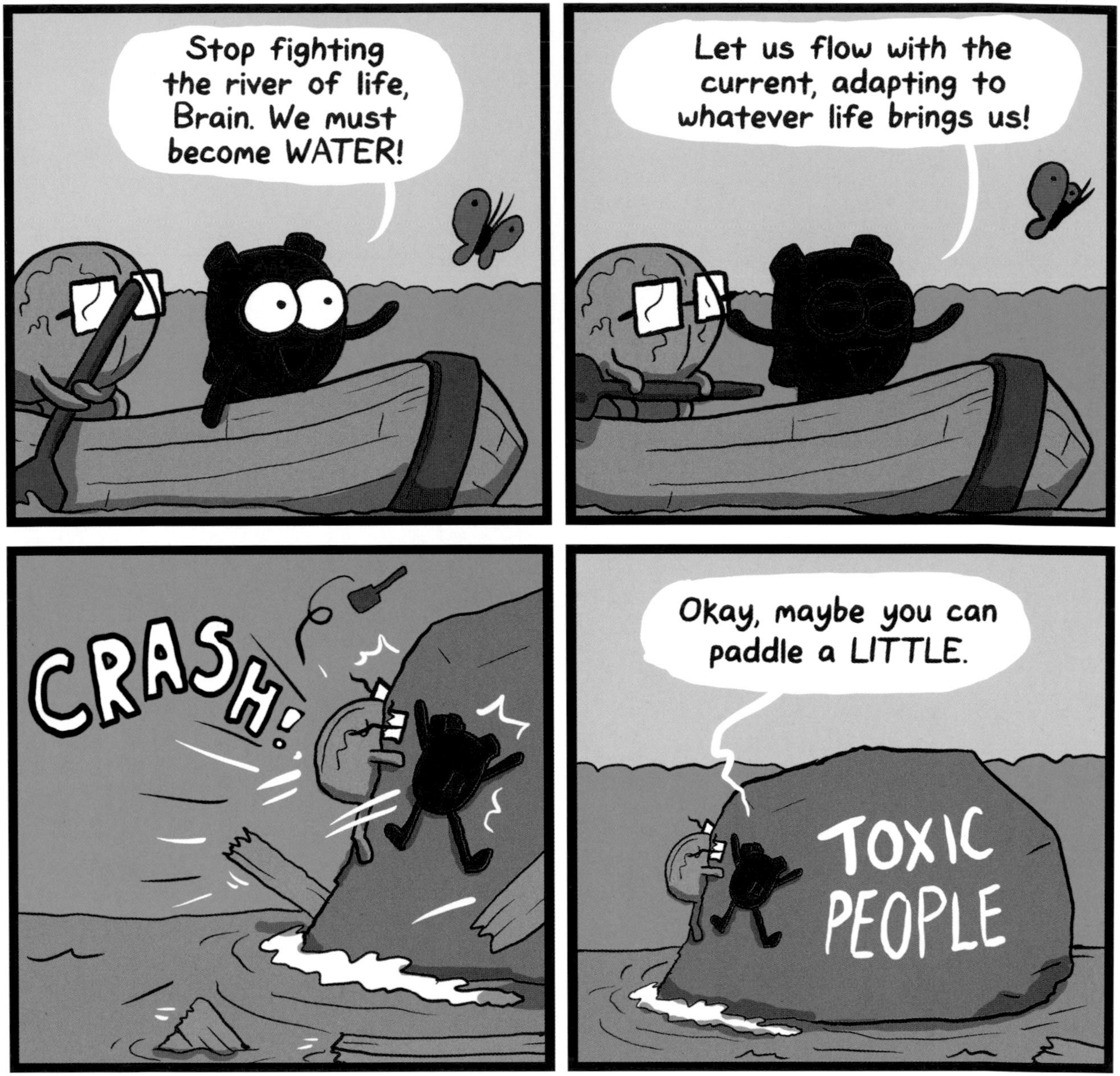
Stop fighting the river of life, Brain. We must become WATER!
Let us flow with the current, adapting to whatever life brings us!
CRASH!
Okay, maybe you can paddle a LITTLE.
TOXIC PEOPLE

@theAwkwardYeti

PART 3

ONWARD TO GOOD THINGS

"It's times like these we learn to live again"
—Foo Fighters

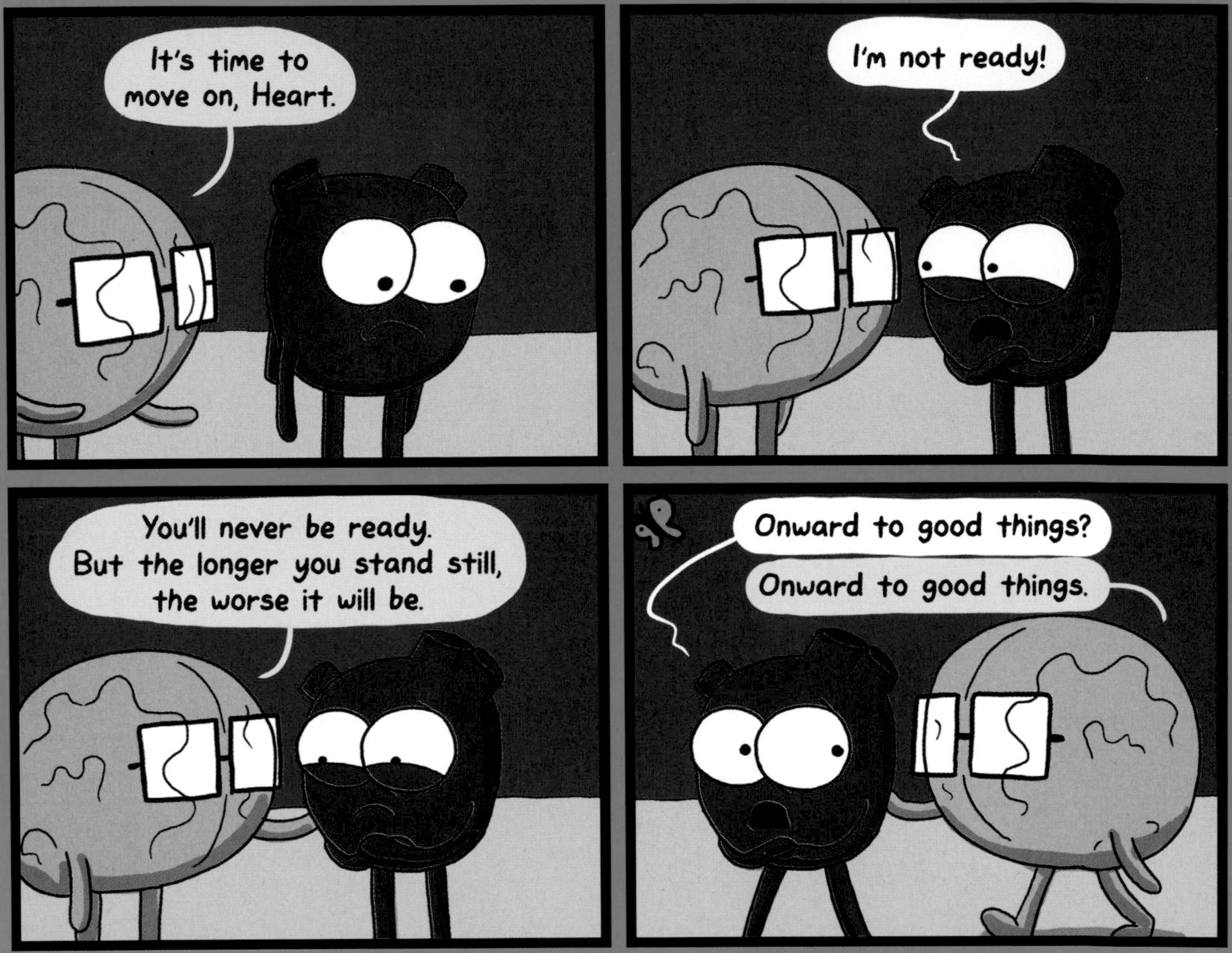
It's time to move on, Heart.
I'm not ready!
You'll never be ready. But the longer you stand still, the worse it will be.
Onward to good things?
Onward to good things.

@theAwkwardYeti

I want it to be BETTER, so it WILL BE.

Did you know that things don't have to be so bad?

I didn't know that. I was so busy sabotaging my life that I forgot that there are actually real ways to move forward, heal, and enjoy life, regardless of circumstances.

"But Nick, didn't you get a degree in psychology? Didn't you know that there were proven methods?" Okay, first of all, wow, that is presumptuous of you to assume I retained any information from college. Secondly, I grew up with a bit of distrust for getting help (there are reasons for this, but they aren't worth adding pages to the book to explain).

Once I did finally concede to getting help, I realized I was still very much in control of how successful I could be. I saw therapists with mixed results, did online workshops, and started using medications (something I formerly refused to do) to treat the ADHD that had been hurting many areas of my life. I kept thought journals, practiced gratitude, and started training my brain through repetitive reframing (putting a positive spin on yourself or your situation and repeating it daily until your subconscious catches on) and visualization (imagining yourself in a positive future and being physically present in it helps to reinforce and speed things up for your very, very stubborn subconscious).

So there it is, the happy conclusion. I'm fixed! I'm perfect now.

All right, obviously not. I'm a mess. But I am a much more manageable mess. And that gives me a lot more hope for the future than I have had in a long time. Life is going to find more ways to knock me down, but I am handling these situations better than I ever have before. That's motivation to keep working on myself, loving who I am—flaws and all—and fueling the positivity and levity that helps the days go by a little easier.

Let's do one another a favor and learn to forgive mistakes and embrace growth, starting with ourselves. I believe in us.

NICK SELUK

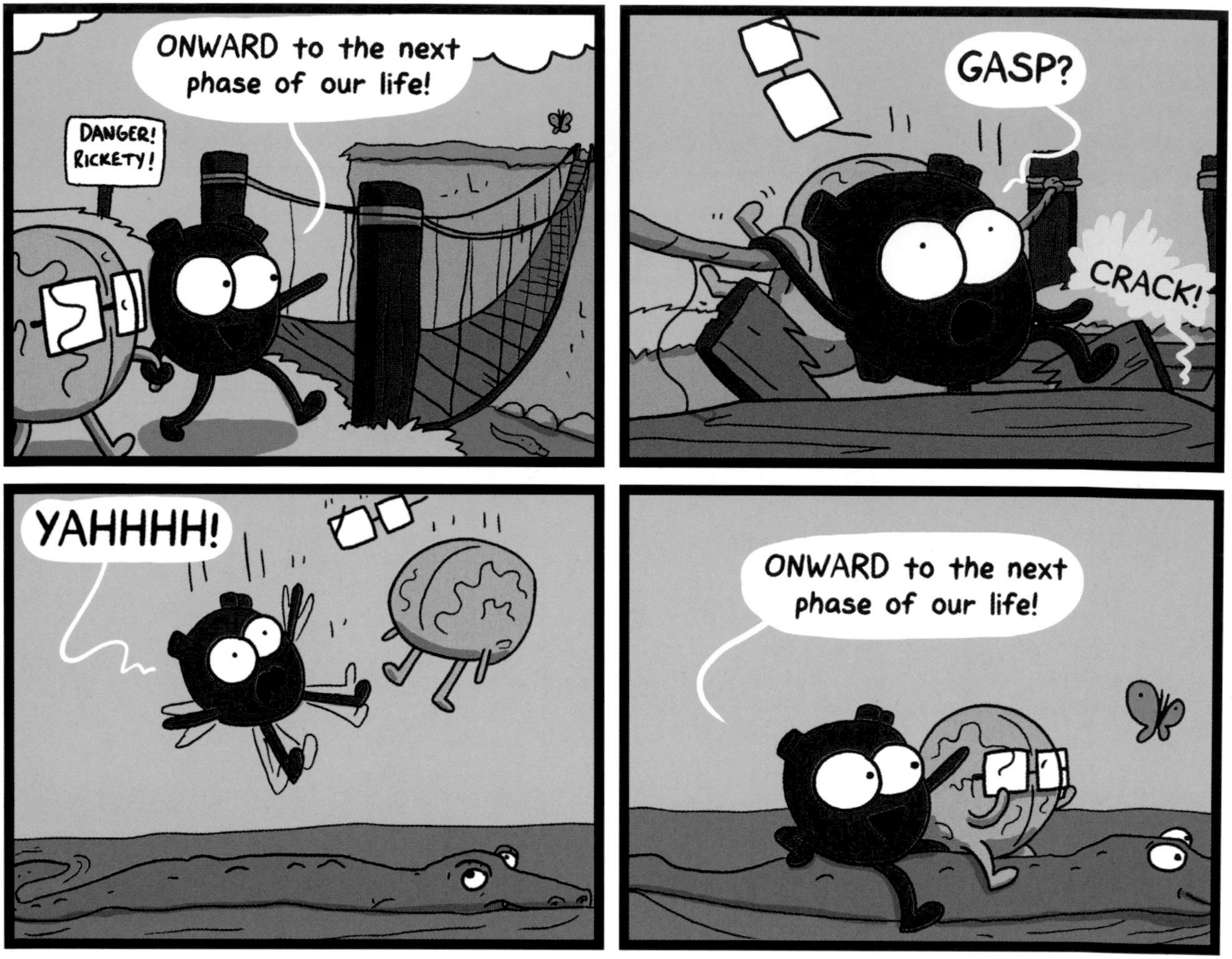
ONWARD to the next phase of our life!
DANGER! RICKETY!
GASP?
CRACK!
YAHHHH!
ONWARD to the next phase of our life!

@theAwkwardYeti

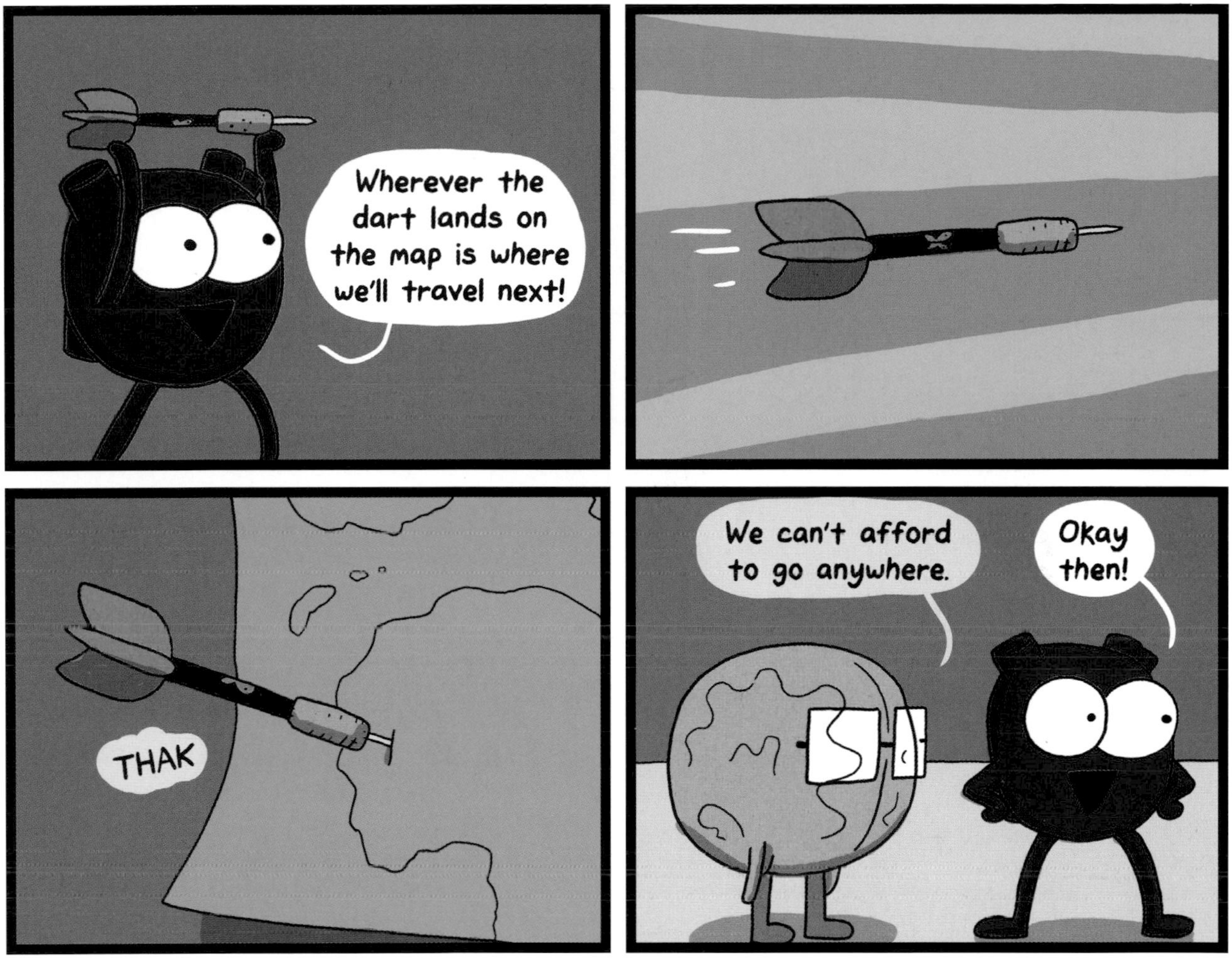
Wherever the dart lands on the map is where we'll travel next!
THAK
We can't afford to go anywhere.
Okay then!

@theAwkwardYeti

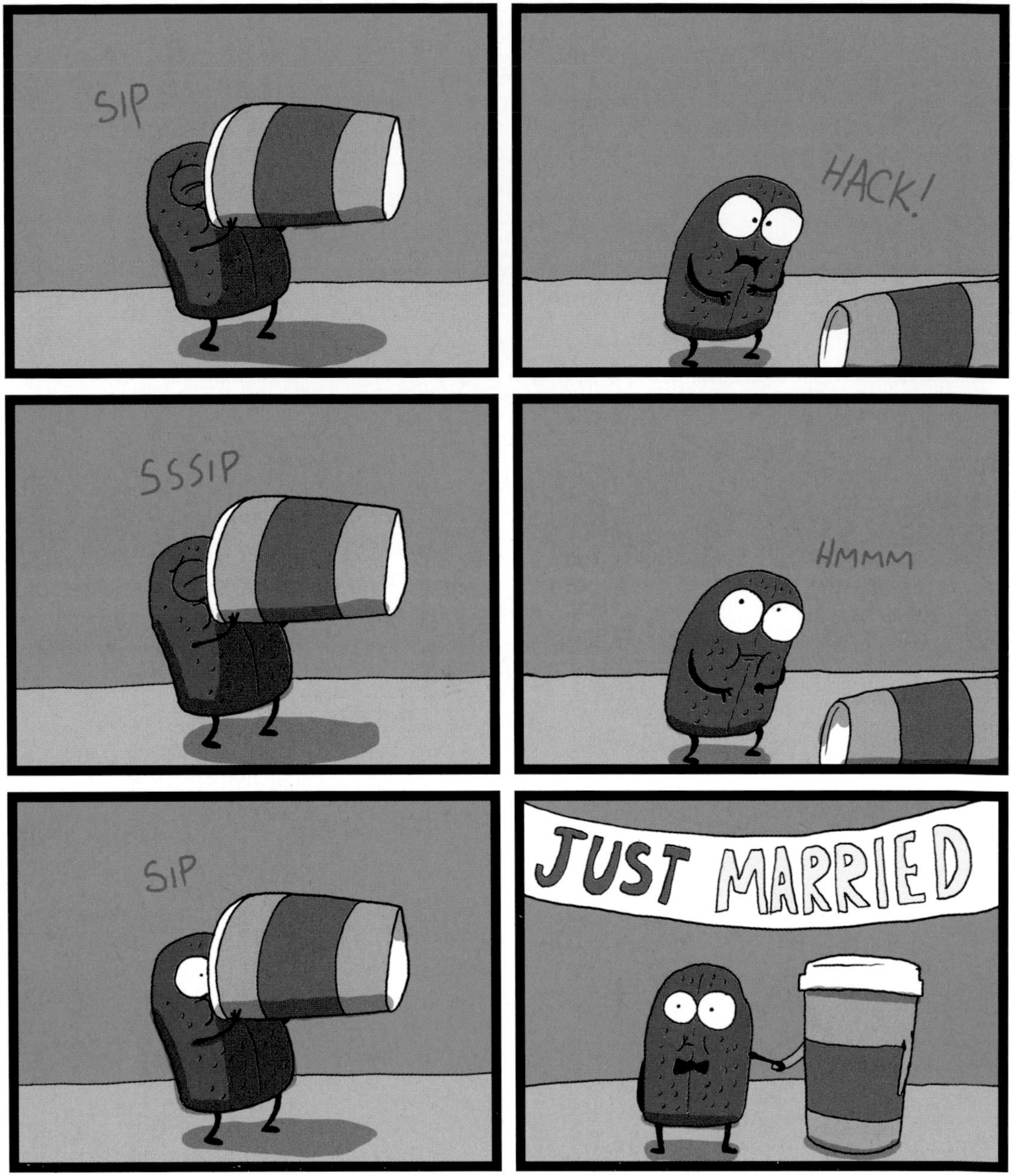
SIP
HACK!
SSSIP
HMMM
SIP
JUST MARRIED

@theAwkwardYeti

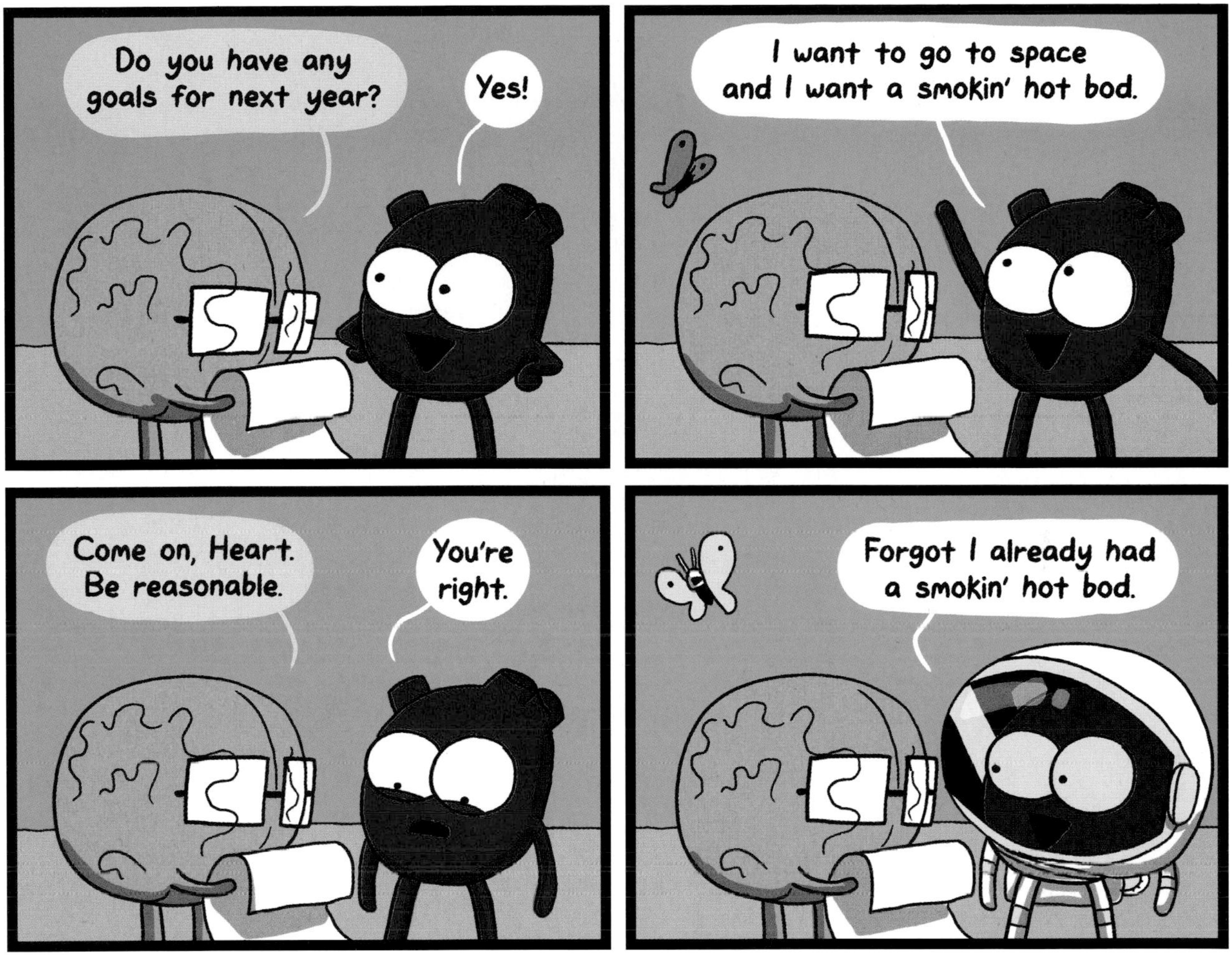
Do you have any goals for next year?
Yes!
I want to go to space and I want a smokin' hot bod.
Come on, Heart. Be reasonable.
You're right.
Forgot I already had a smokin' hot bod.

@theAwkwardYeti

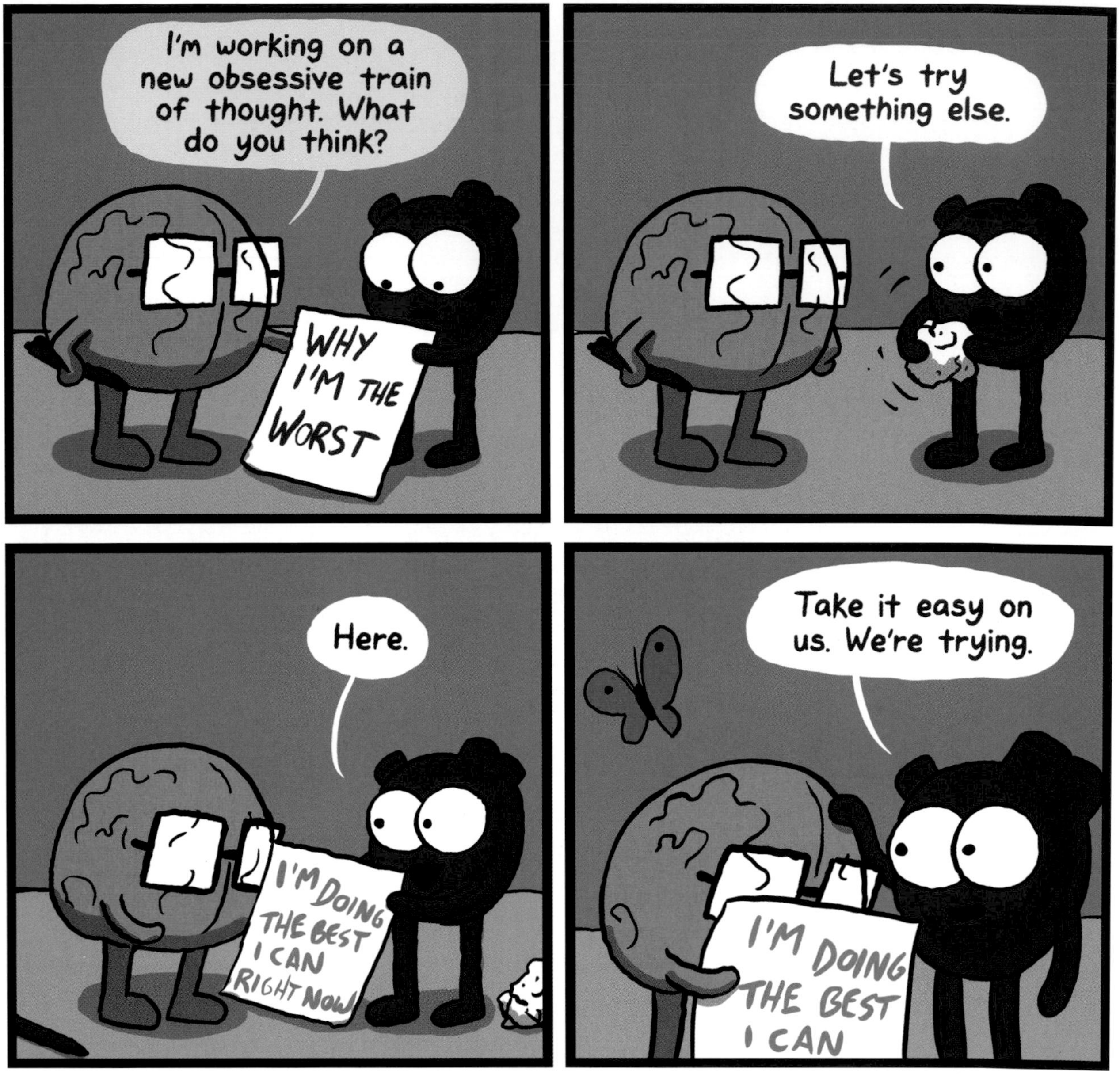
I'm working on a new obsessive train of thought. What do you think?
WHY I'M THE WORST
Let's try something else.
Here.
I'M DOING THE BEST I CAN RIGHT NOW
Take it easy on us. We're trying.
I'M DOING THE BEST I CAN

@theAwkwardYeti

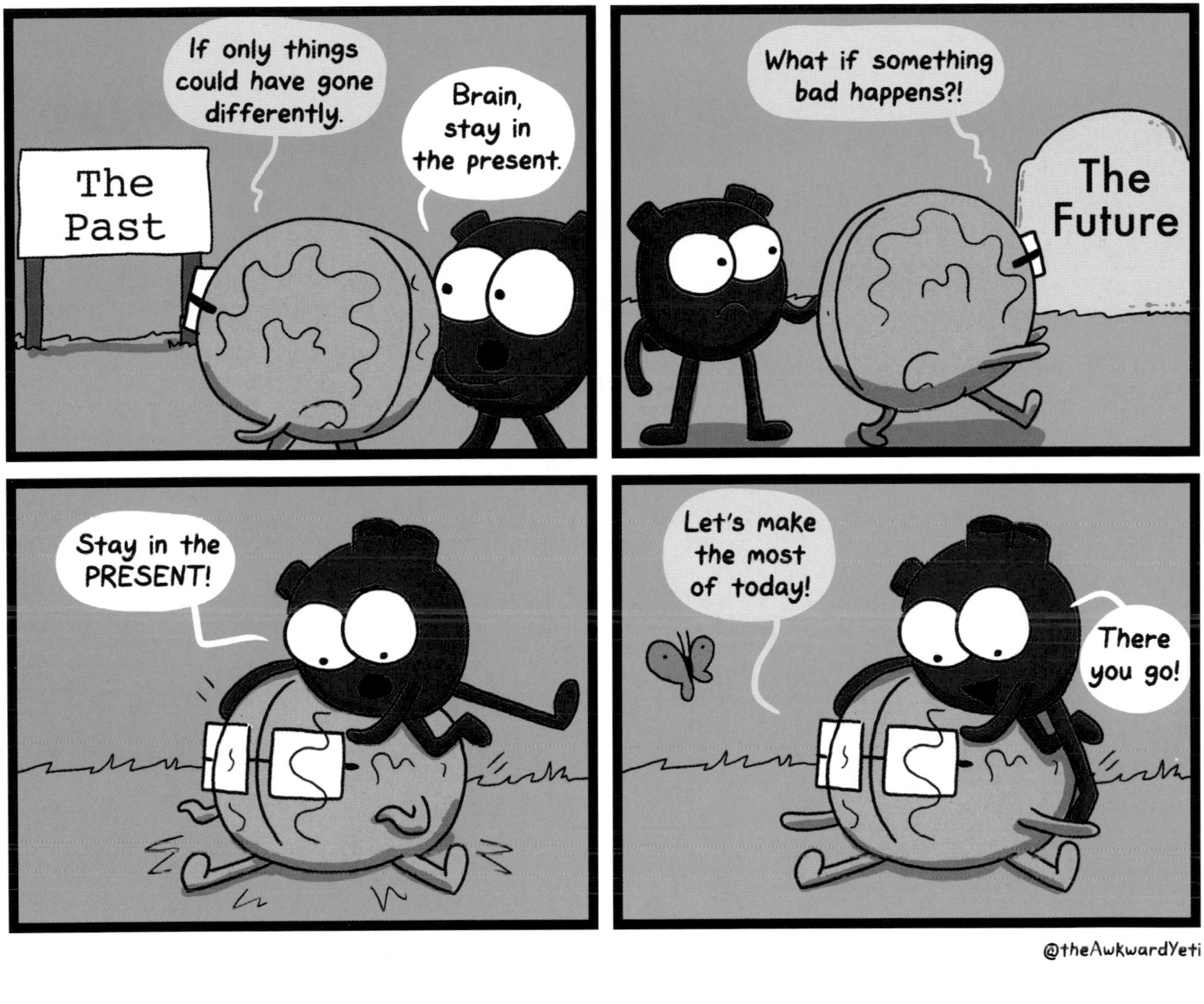
If only things could have gone differently.
Brain, stay in the present.
The Past
What if something bad happens?!
The Future
Stay in the PRESENT!
Let's make the most of today!
There you go!
@theAwkwardYeti

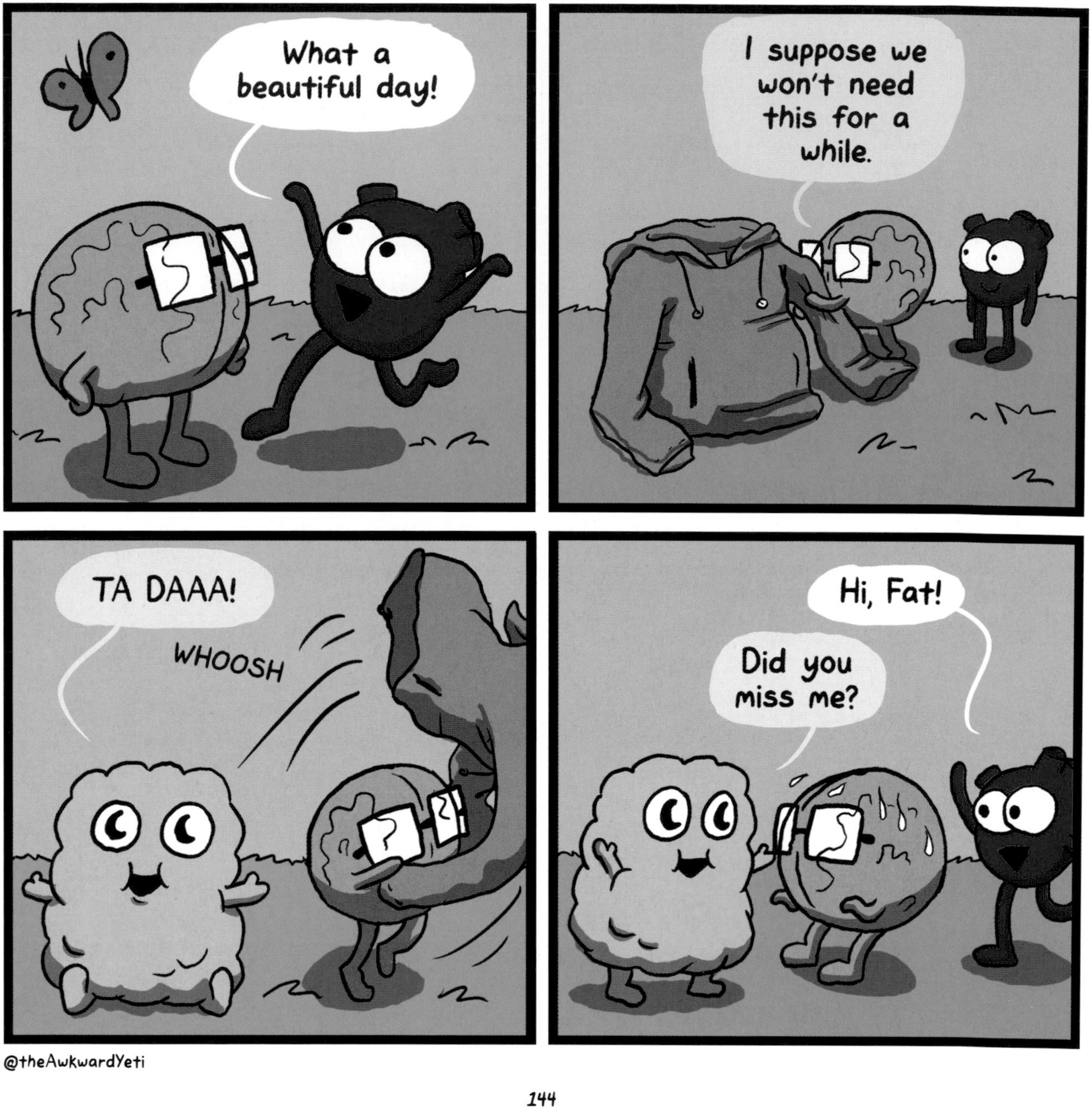
What a beautiful day!
I suppose we won't need this for a while.
TA DAAA!
WHOOSH
Hi, Fat!
Did you miss me?

@theAwkwardYeti

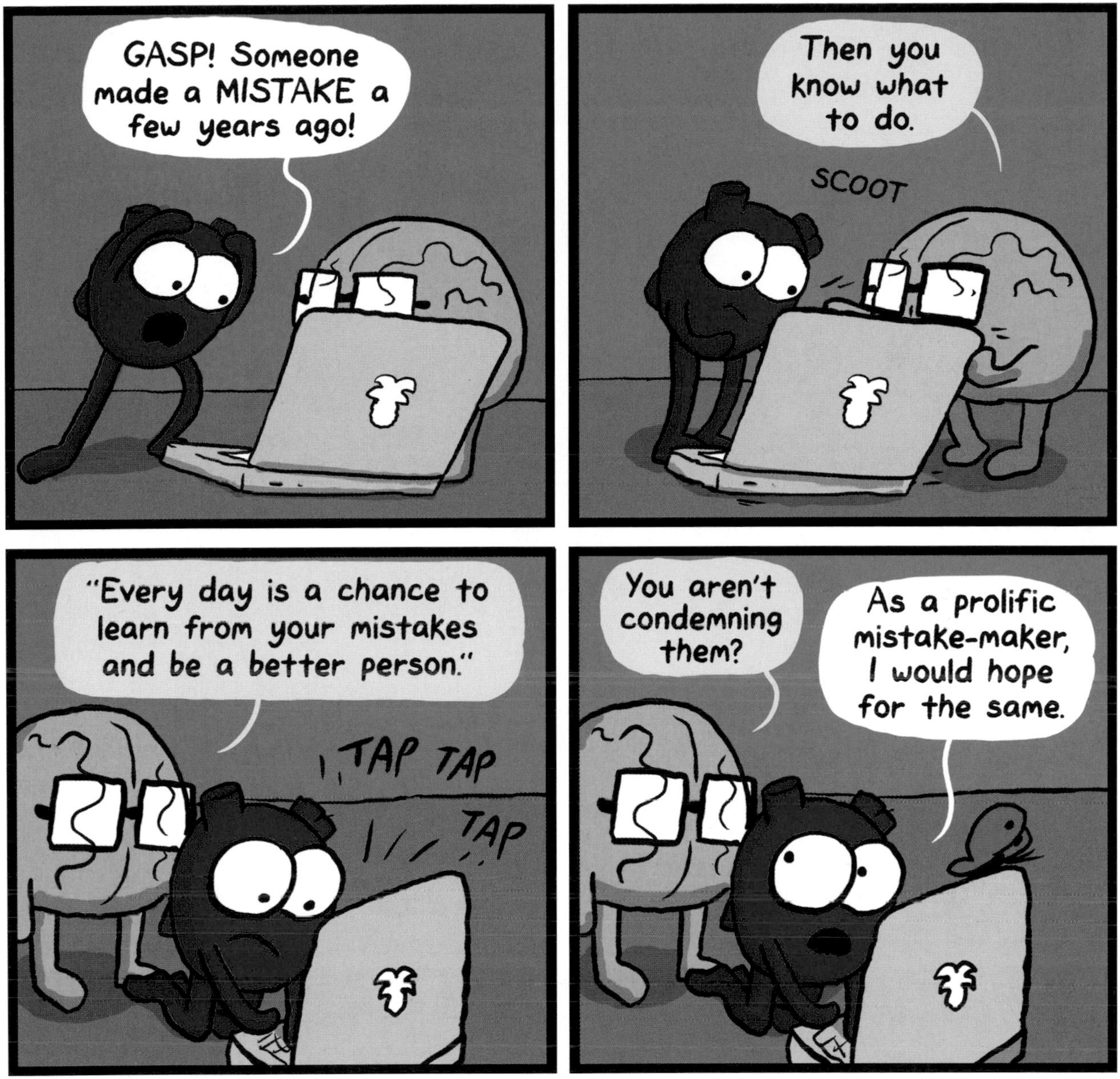
GASP! Someone made a MISTAKE a few years ago!
Then you know what to do.
SCOOT
"Every day is a chance to learn from your mistakes and be a better person."
TAP TAP
TAP
You aren't condemning them?
As a prolific mistake-maker, I would hope for the same.

@theAwkwardYeti

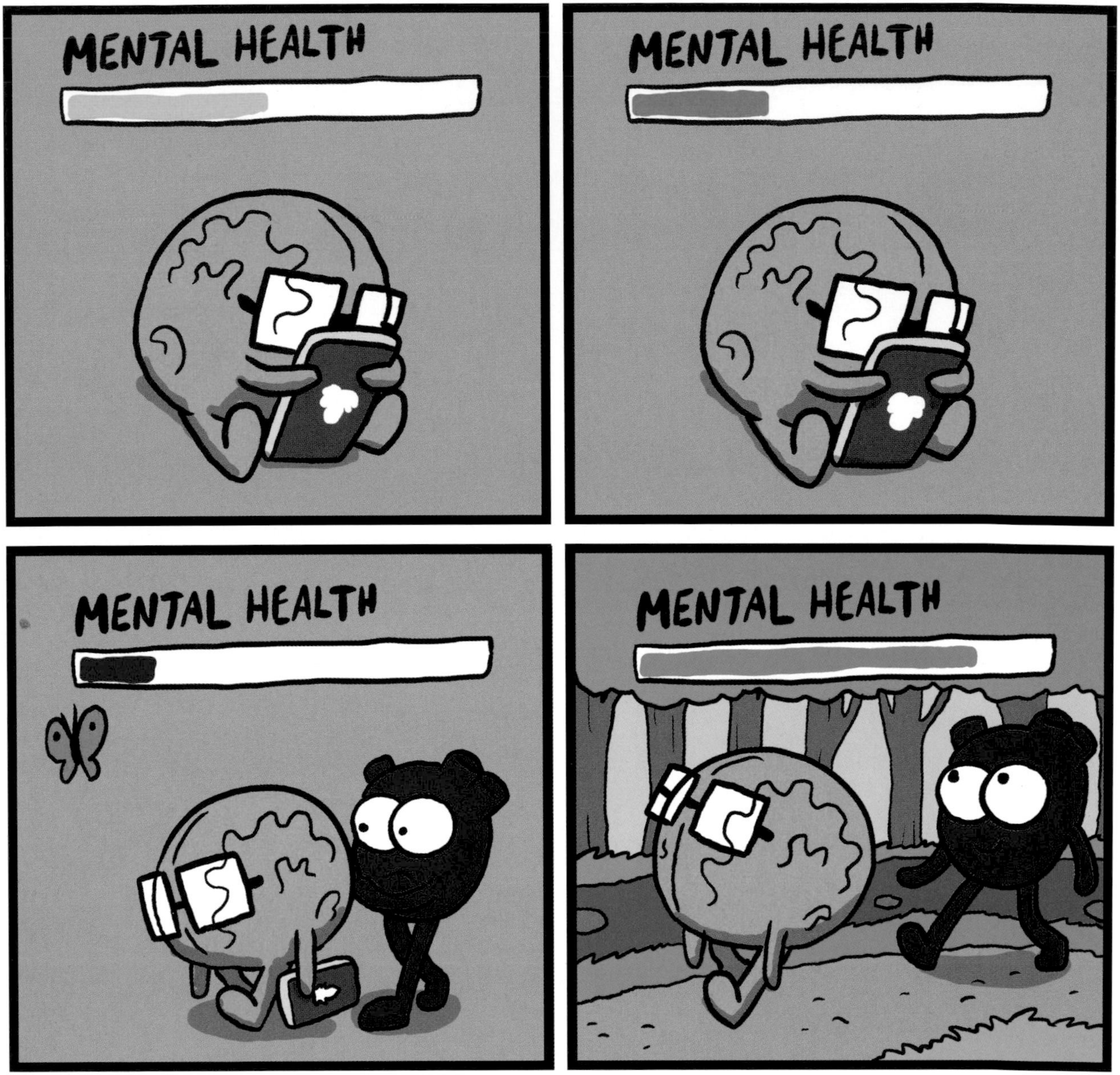
MENTAL HEALTH
MENTAL HEALTH
MENTAL HEALTH
MENTAL HEALTH
@theAwkwardYeti

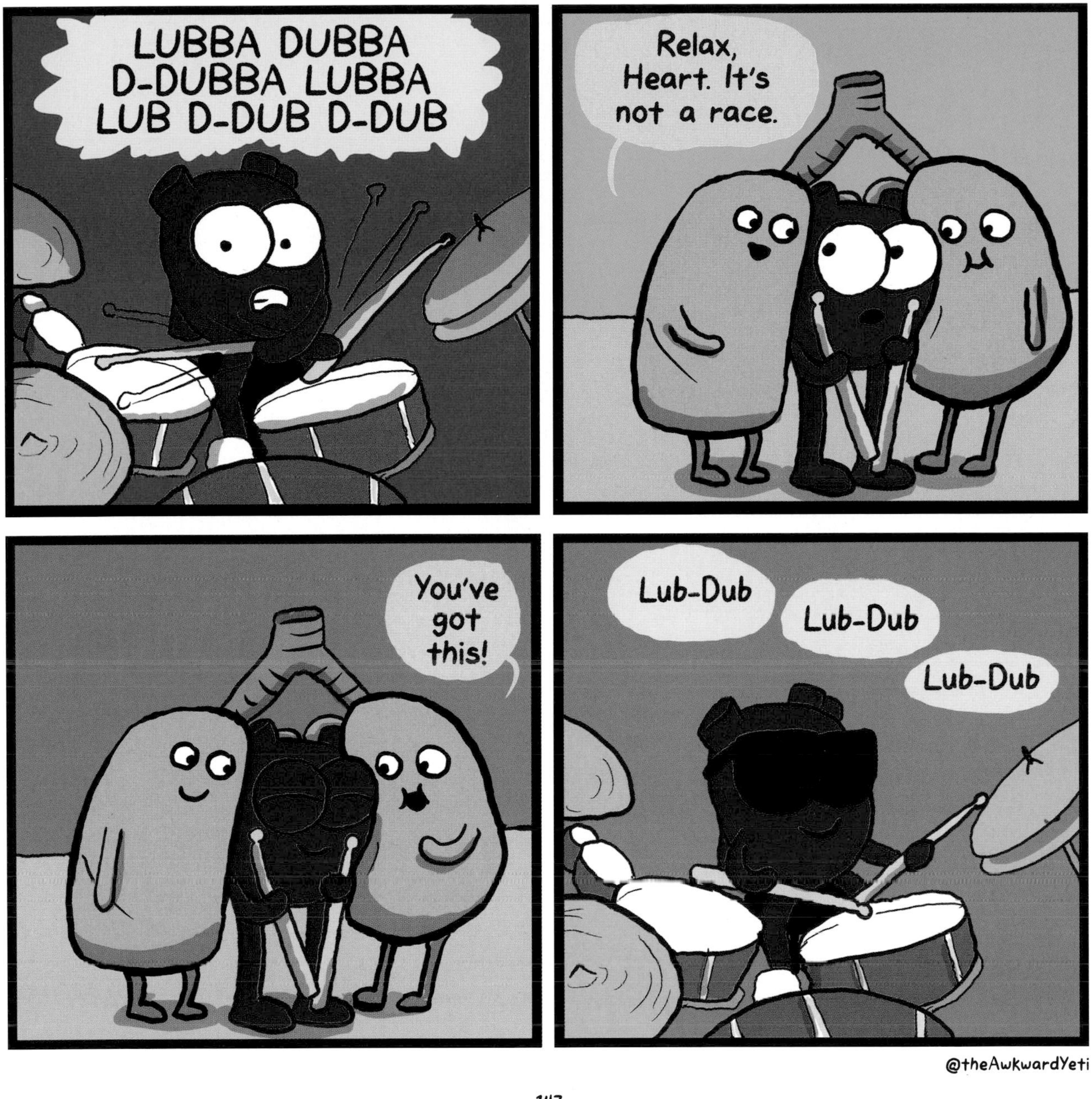
LUBBA DUBBA D-DUBBA LUBBA LUB D-DUB D-DUB
Relax, Heart. It's not a race.
You've got this!
Lub-Dub
Lub-Dub
Lub-Dub

@theAwkwardYeti

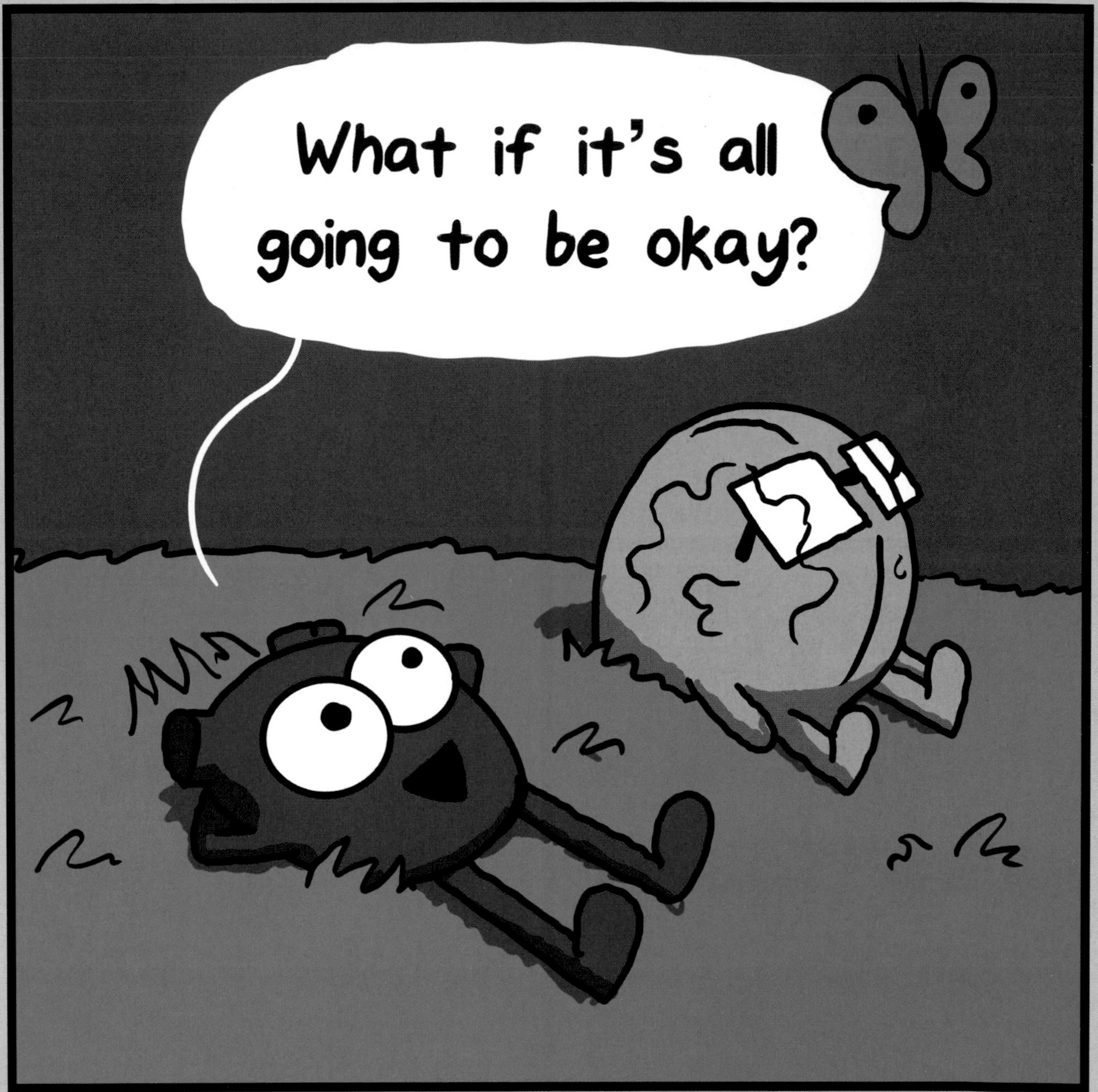
What if it's all going to be okay?

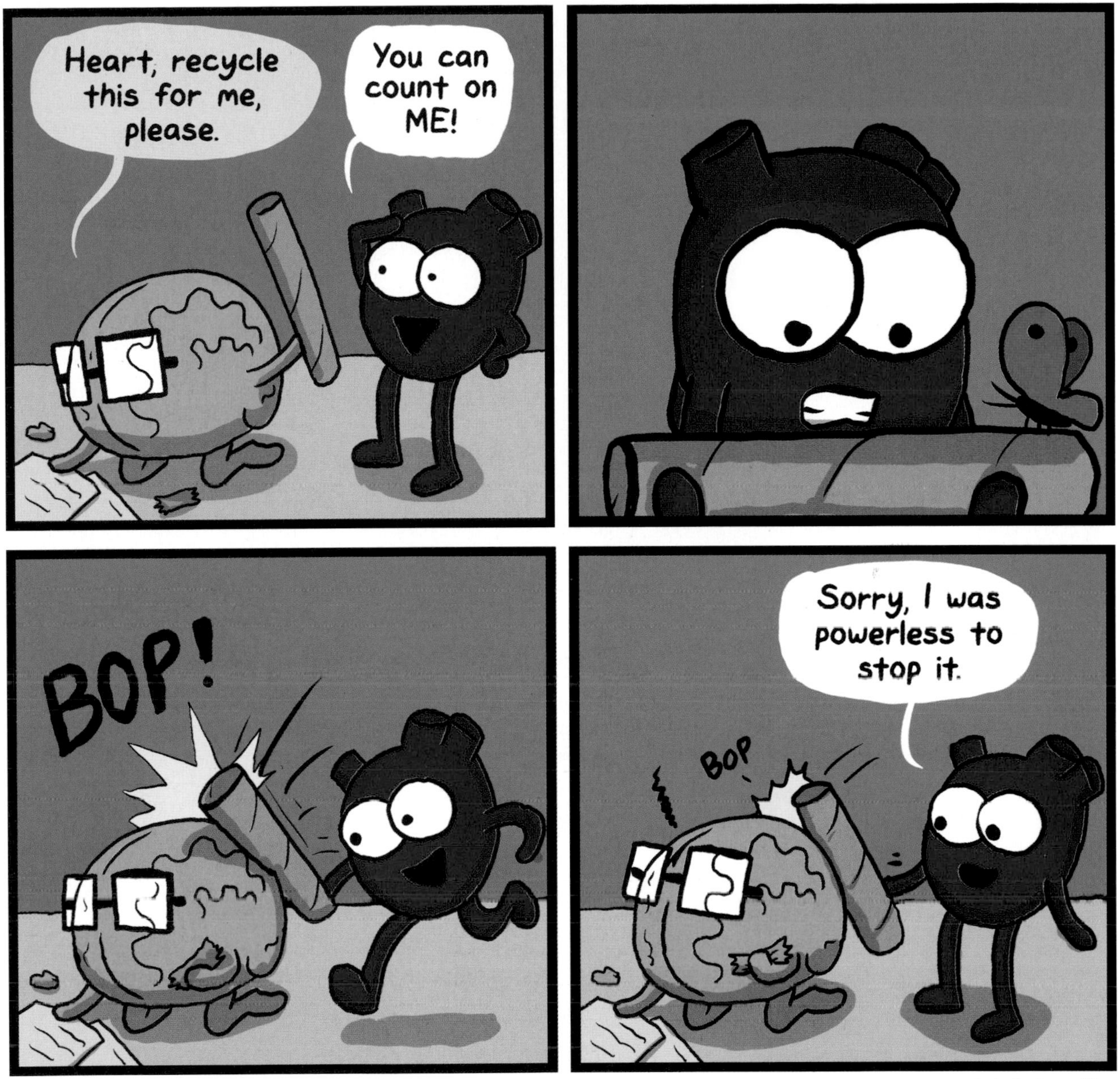
Heart, recycle this for me, please.
You can count on ME!
BOP!
BOP
Sorry, I was powerless to stop it.

@theAwkwardYeti

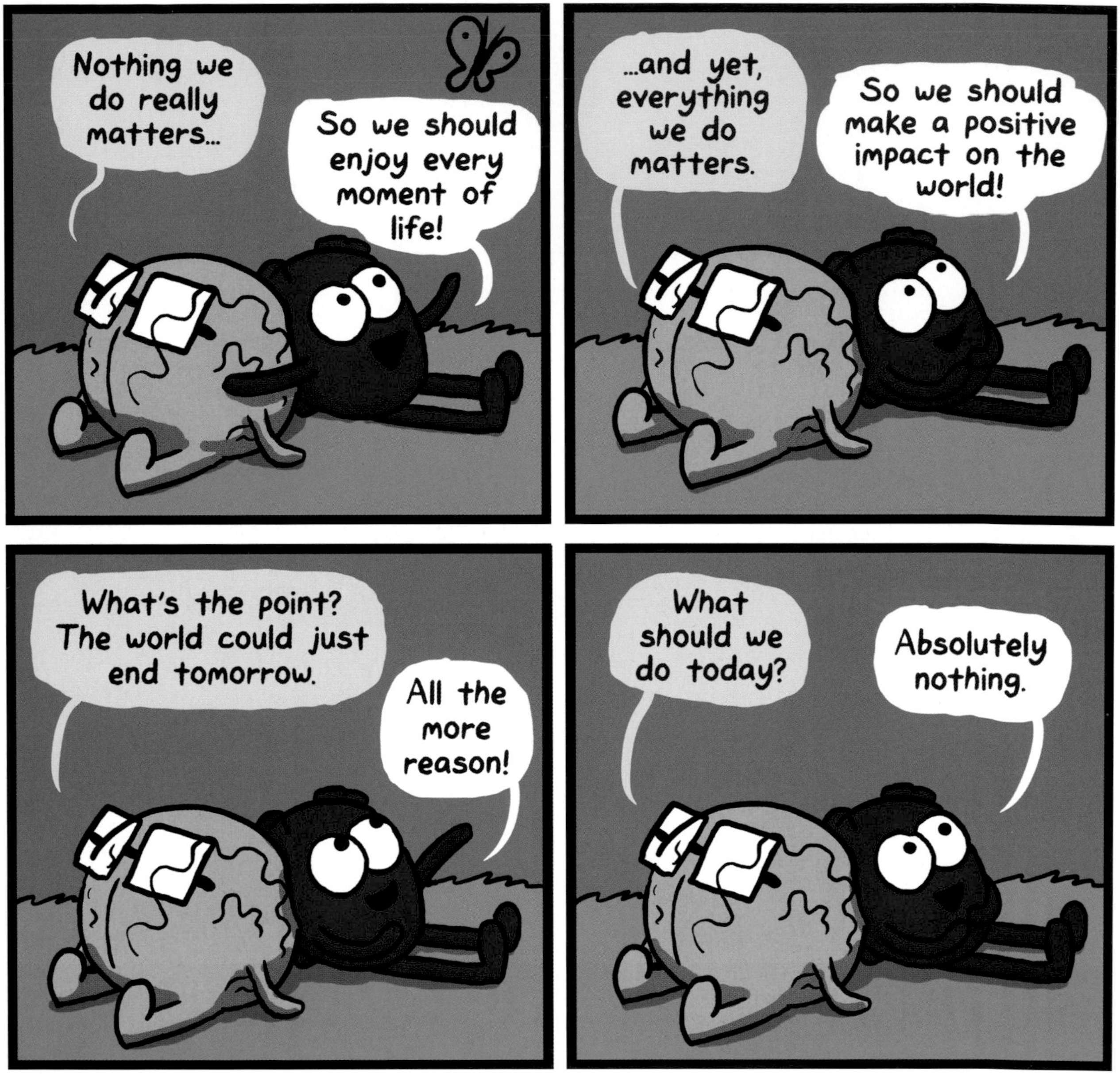
Nothing we do really matters...
So we should enjoy every moment of life!
...and yet, everything we do matters.
So we should make a positive impact on the world!
What's the point? The world could just end tomorrow.
All the more reason!
What should we do today?
Absolutely nothing.

@theAwkwardYeti

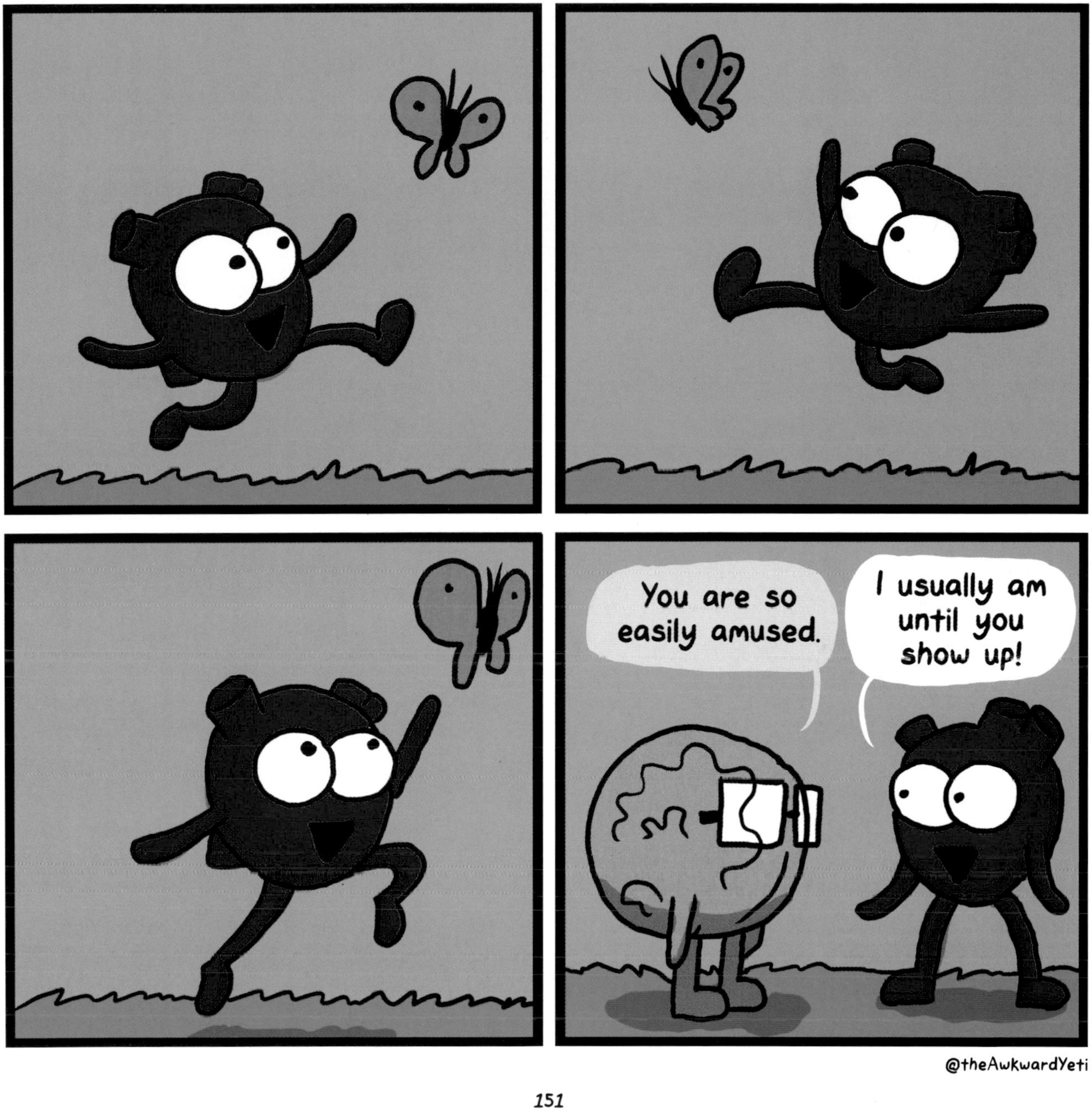
You are so easily amused.
I usually am until you show up!

@theAwkwardYeti

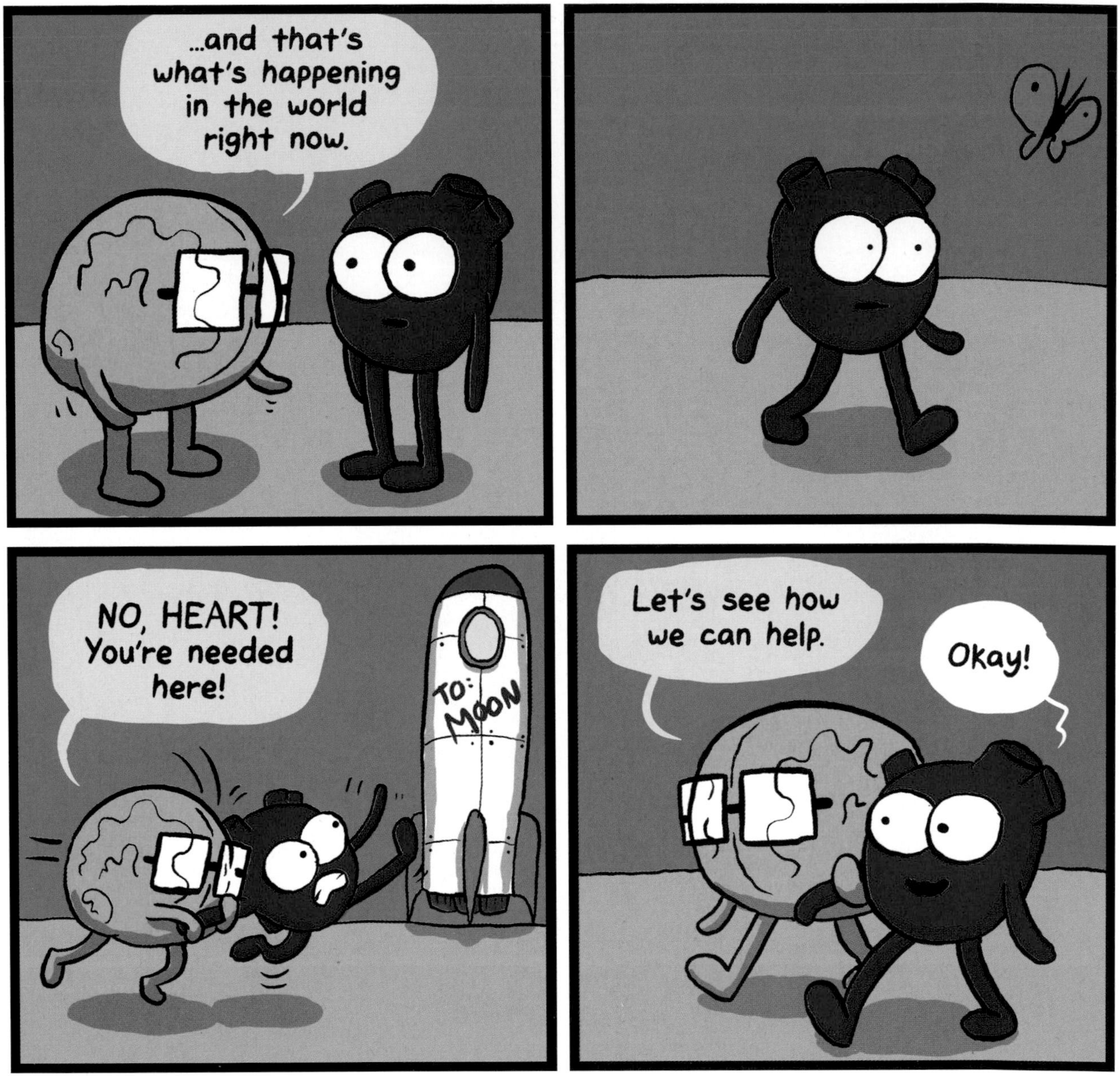
...and that's what's happening in the world right now.
NO, HEART! You're needed here!
TO: MOON
Let's see how we can help.
Okay!

@theAwkwardYeti

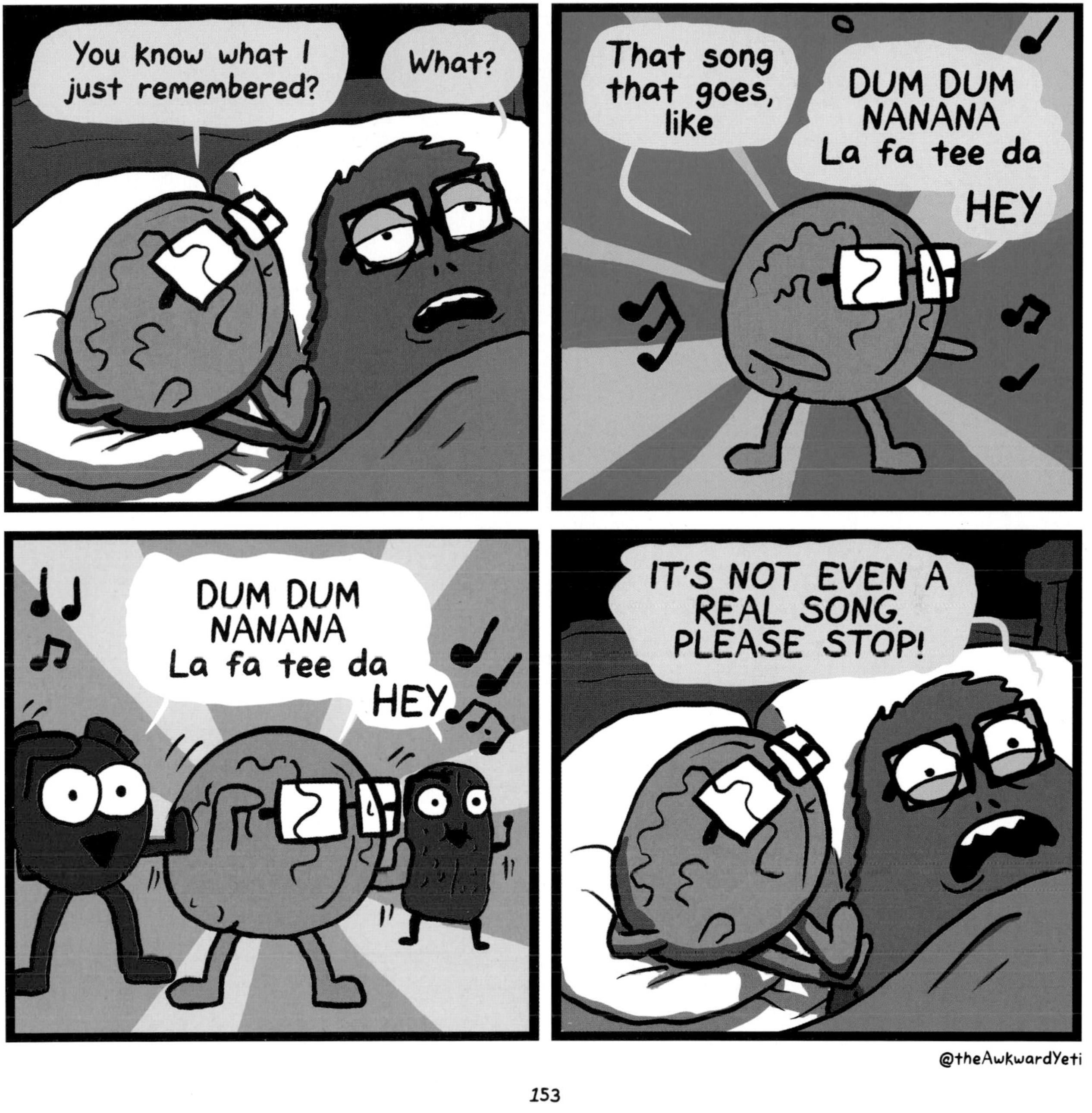
You know what I just remembered?
What?
That song that goes, like
DUM DUM NANANA La fa tee da HEY
DUM DUM NANANA La fa tee da HEY
IT'S NOT EVEN A REAL SONG. PLEASE STOP!
@theAwkwardYeti

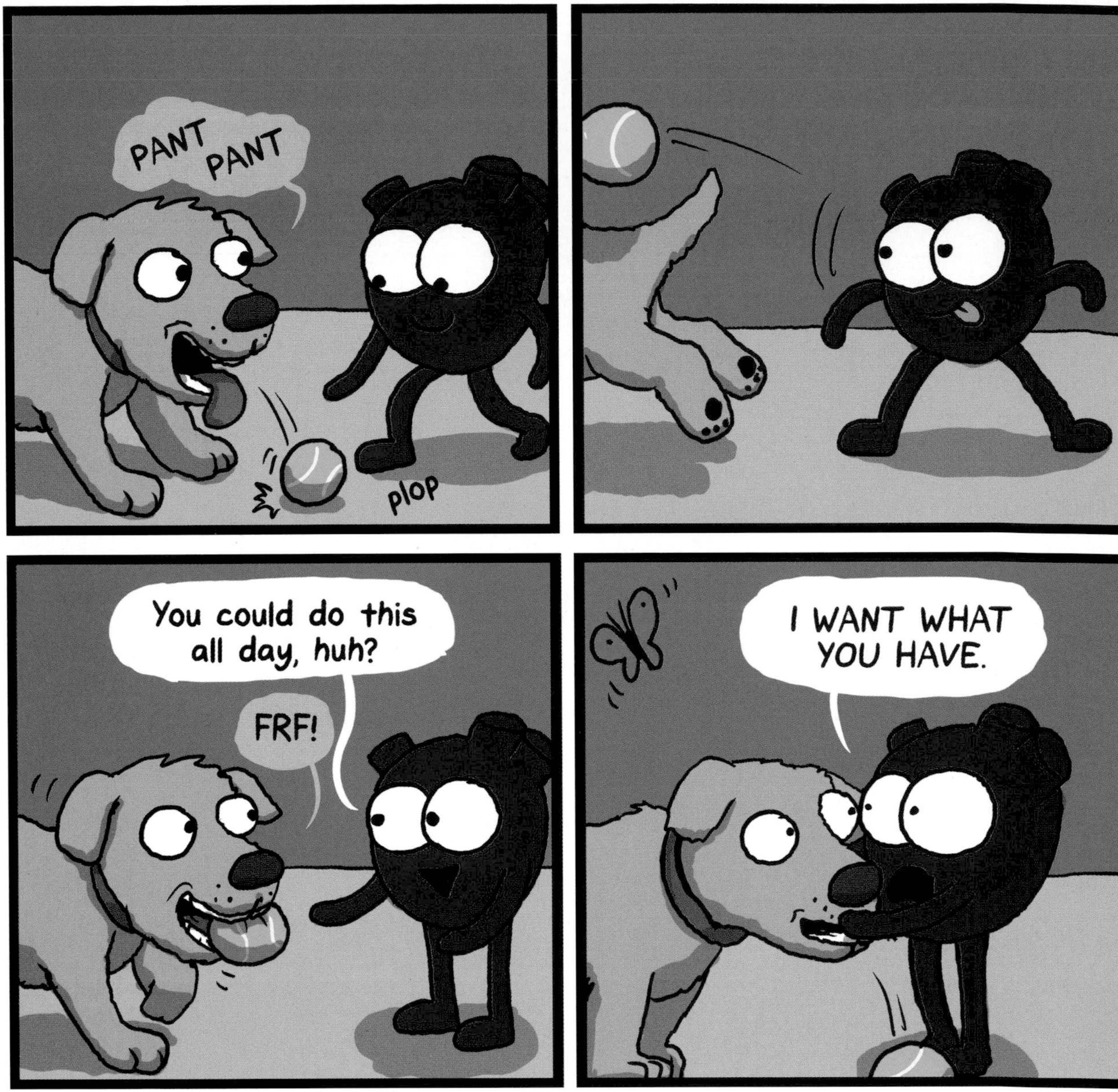
PANT PANT
plop
You could do this all day, huh?
FRF!
I WANT WHAT YOU HAVE.

@theAwkwardYeti

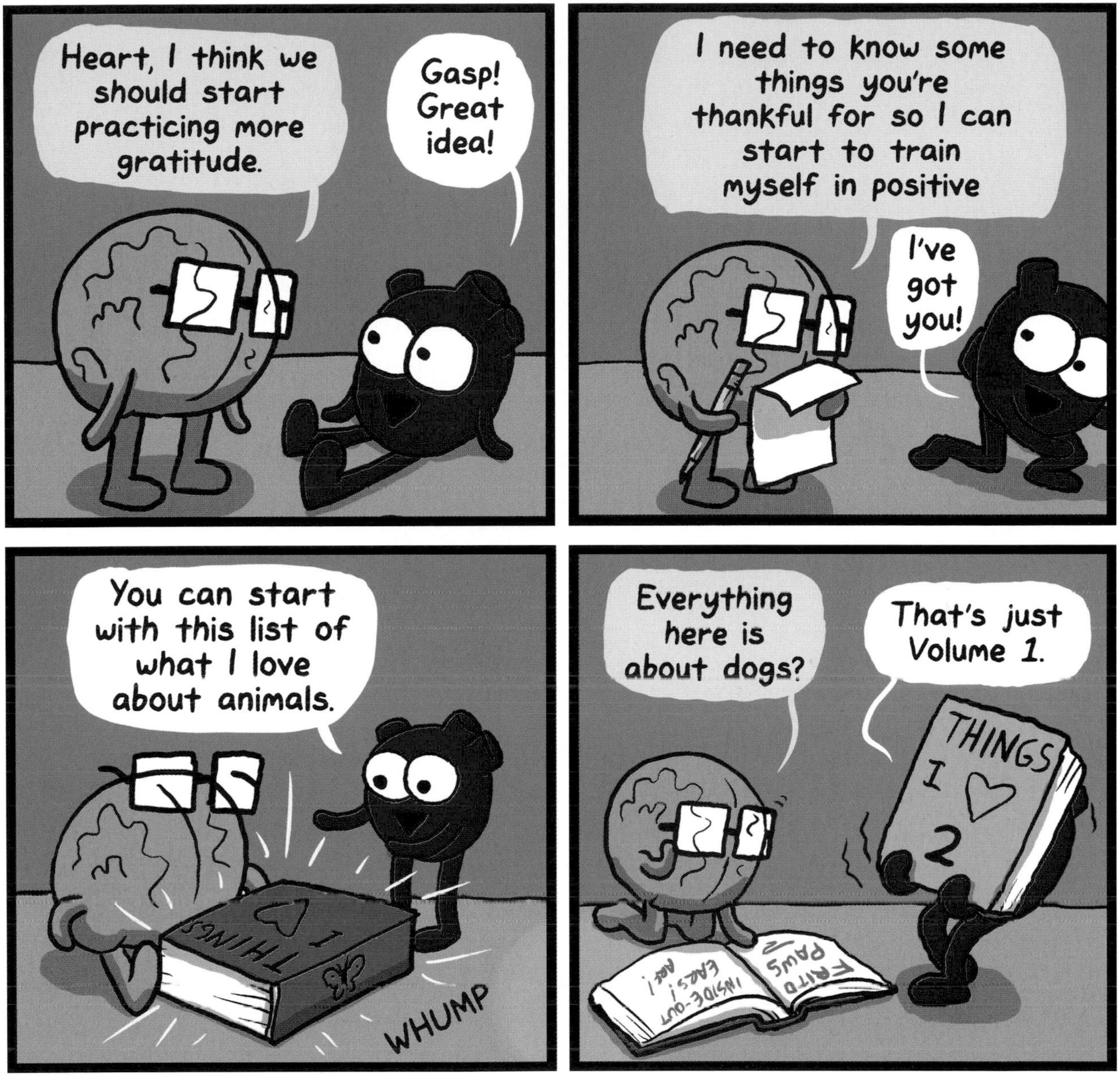
Heart, I think we should start practicing more gratitude.
Gasp! Great idea!
I need to know some things you're thankful for so I can start to train myself in positive
I've got you!
You can start with this list of what I love about animals.
WHUMP
Everything here is about dogs?
That's just Volume 1.
THINGS I ♥ 2
FRITO PAWS

@theAwkwardYeti

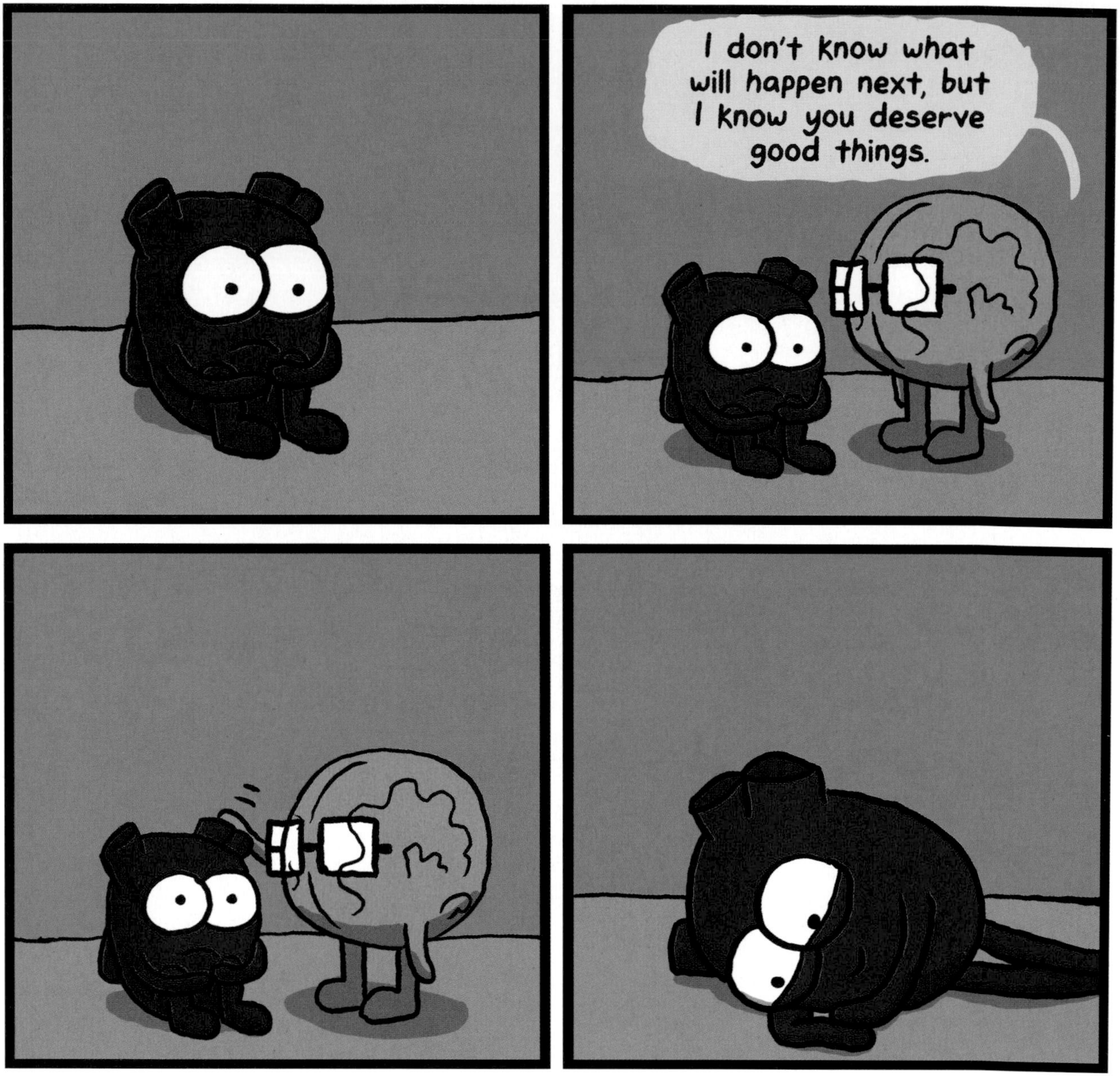
I don't know what will happen next, but I know you deserve good things.

@theAwkwardYeti

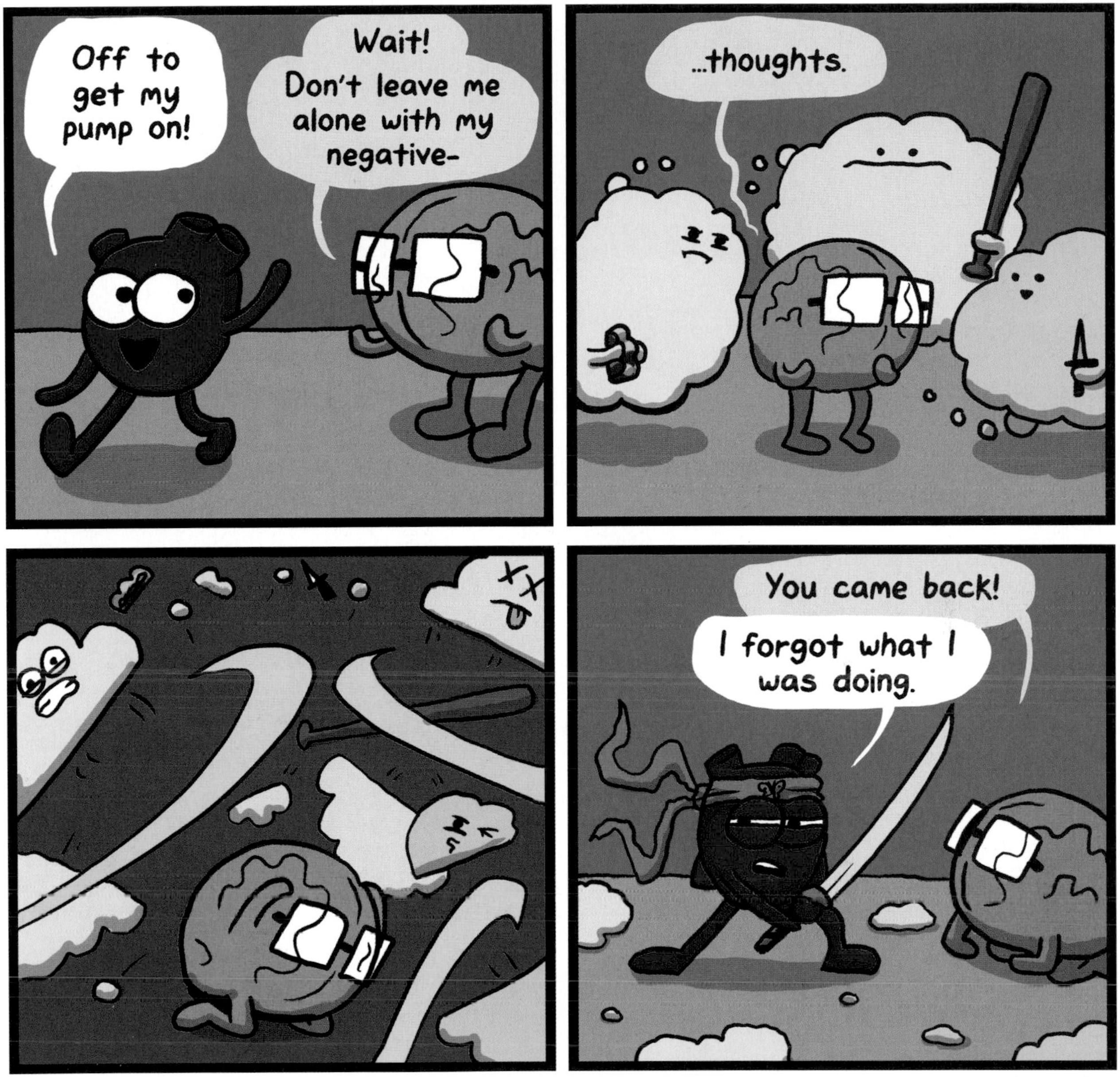
Off to get my pump on!
Wait! Don't leave me alone with my negative-
...thoughts.
You came back!
I forgot what I was doing.

@theAwkwardYeti

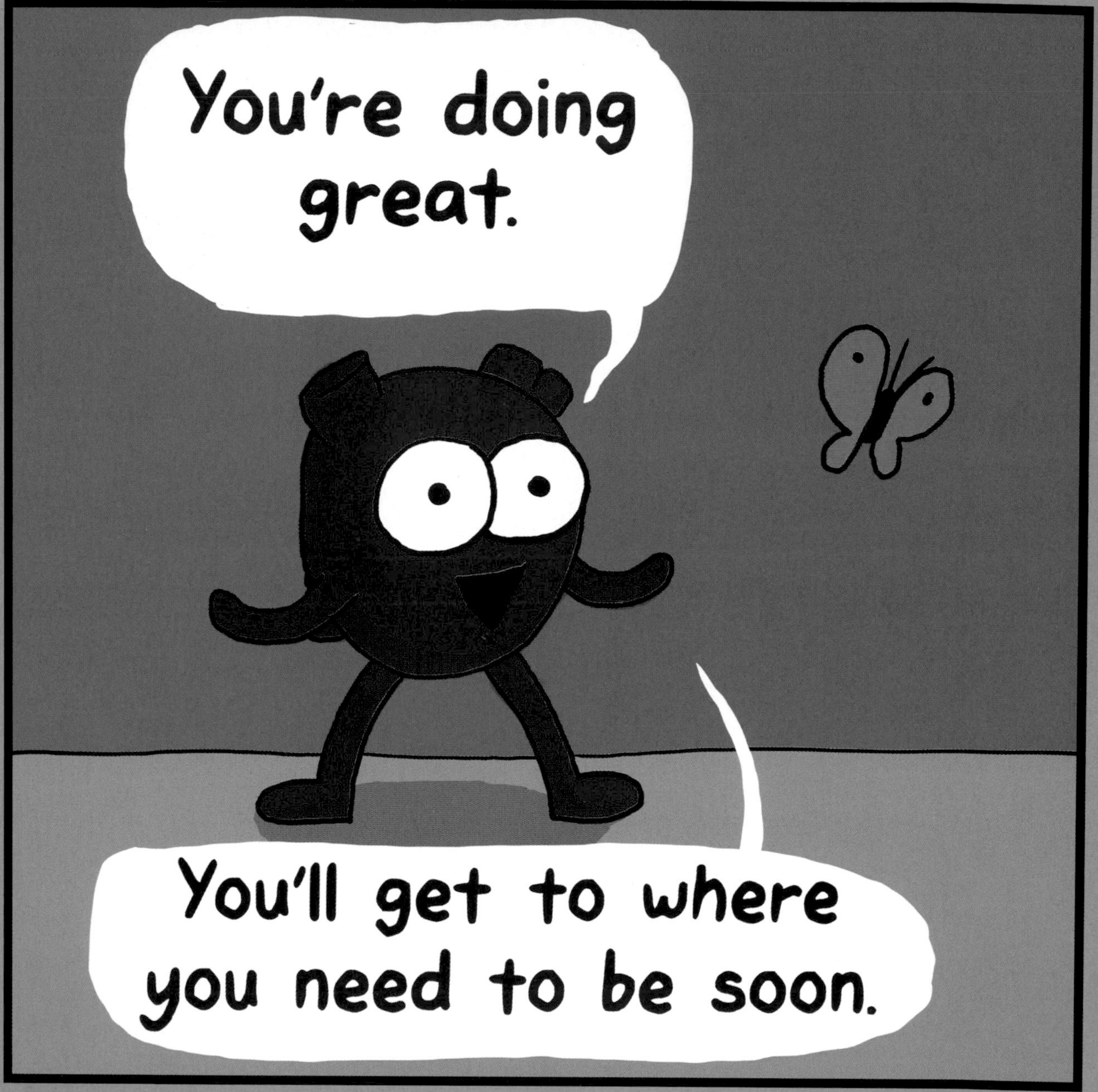
You're doing great.
You'll get to where you need to be soon.

@theAwkwardYeti

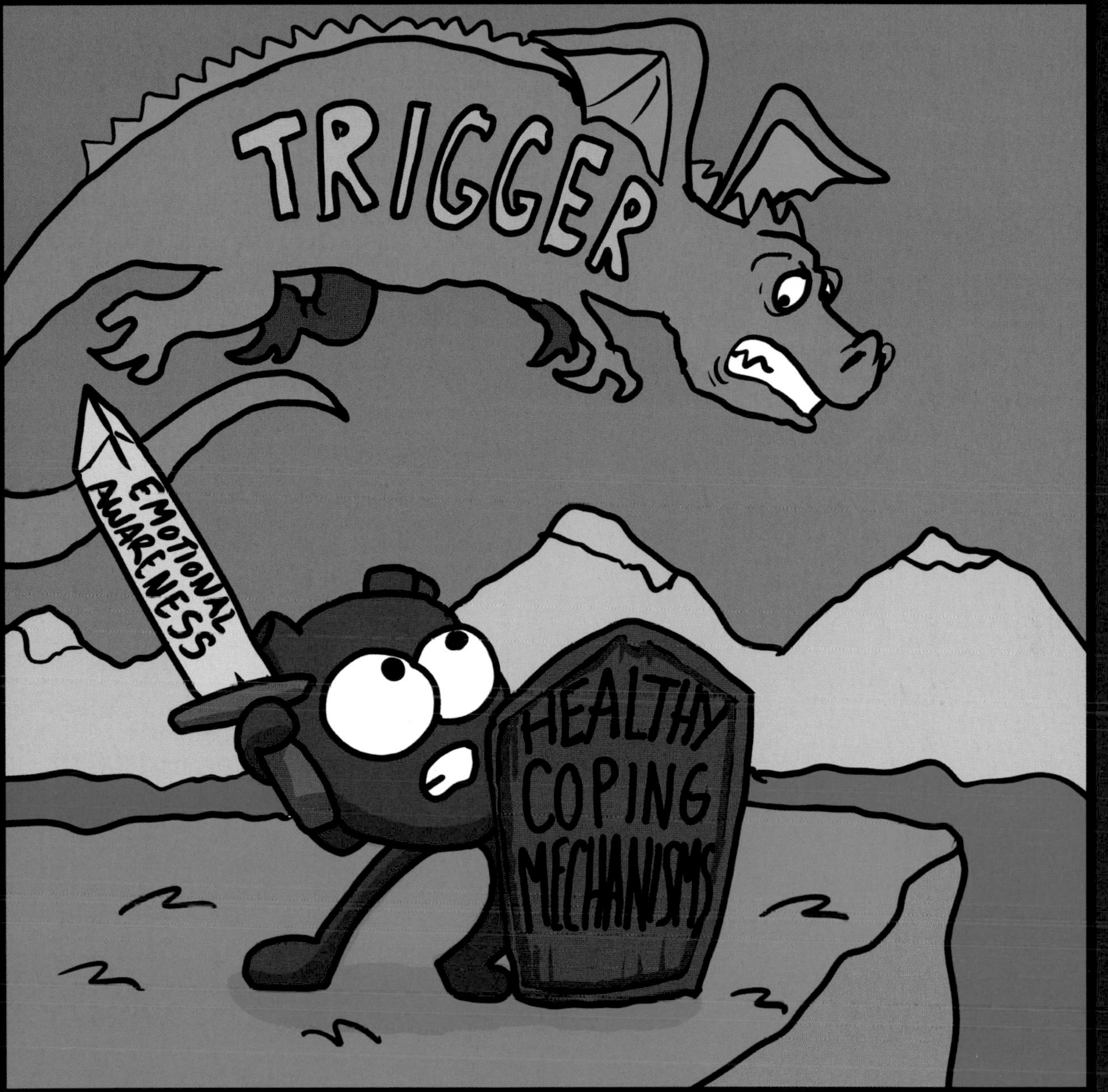
TRIGGER
EMOTIONAL AWARENESS
HEALTHY COPING MECHANISMS

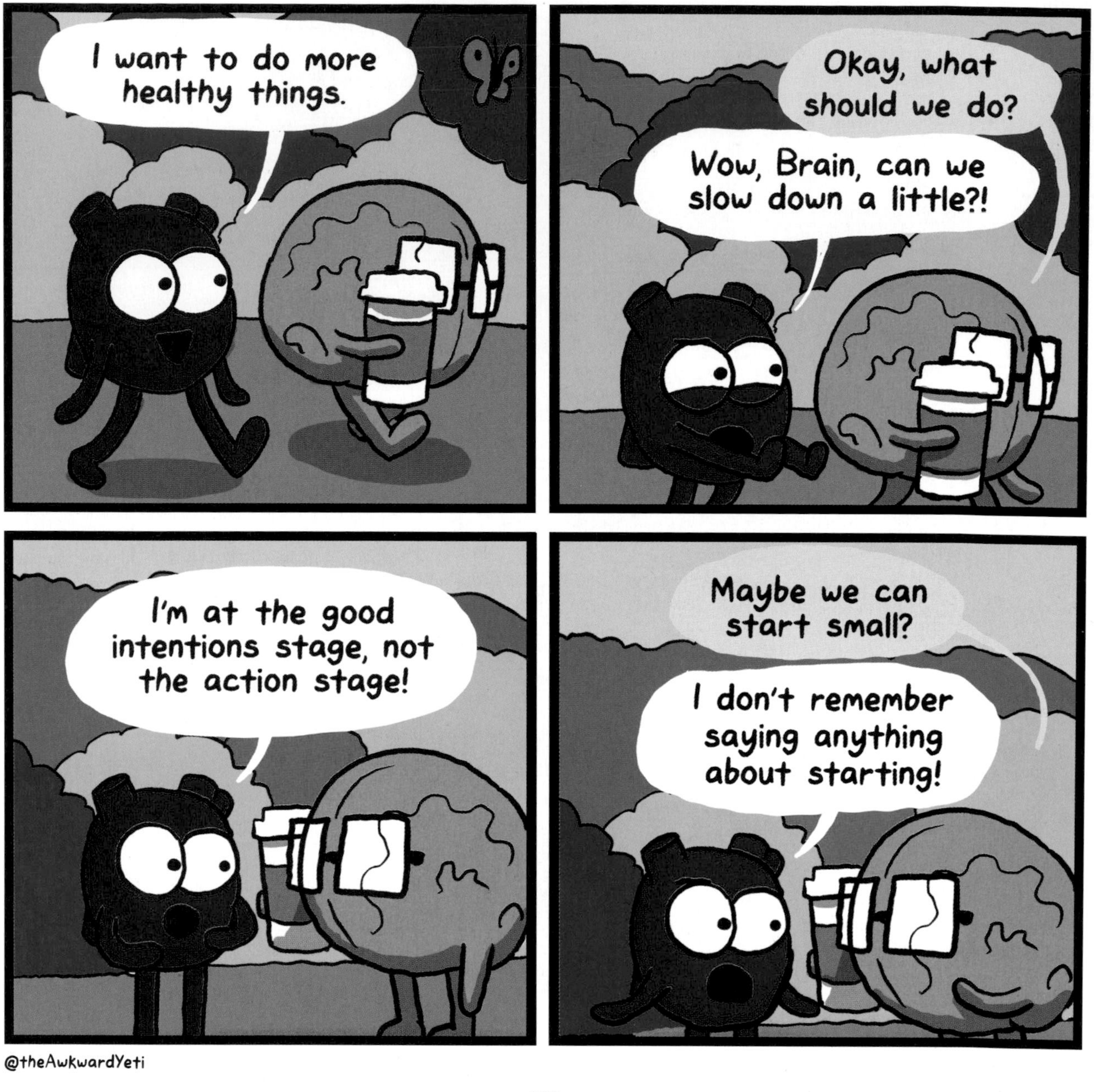
I want to do more healthy things.
Okay, what should we do?
Wow, Brain, can we slow down a little?!
I'm at the good intentions stage, not the action stage!
Maybe we can start small?
I don't remember saying anything about starting!
@theAwkwardYeti

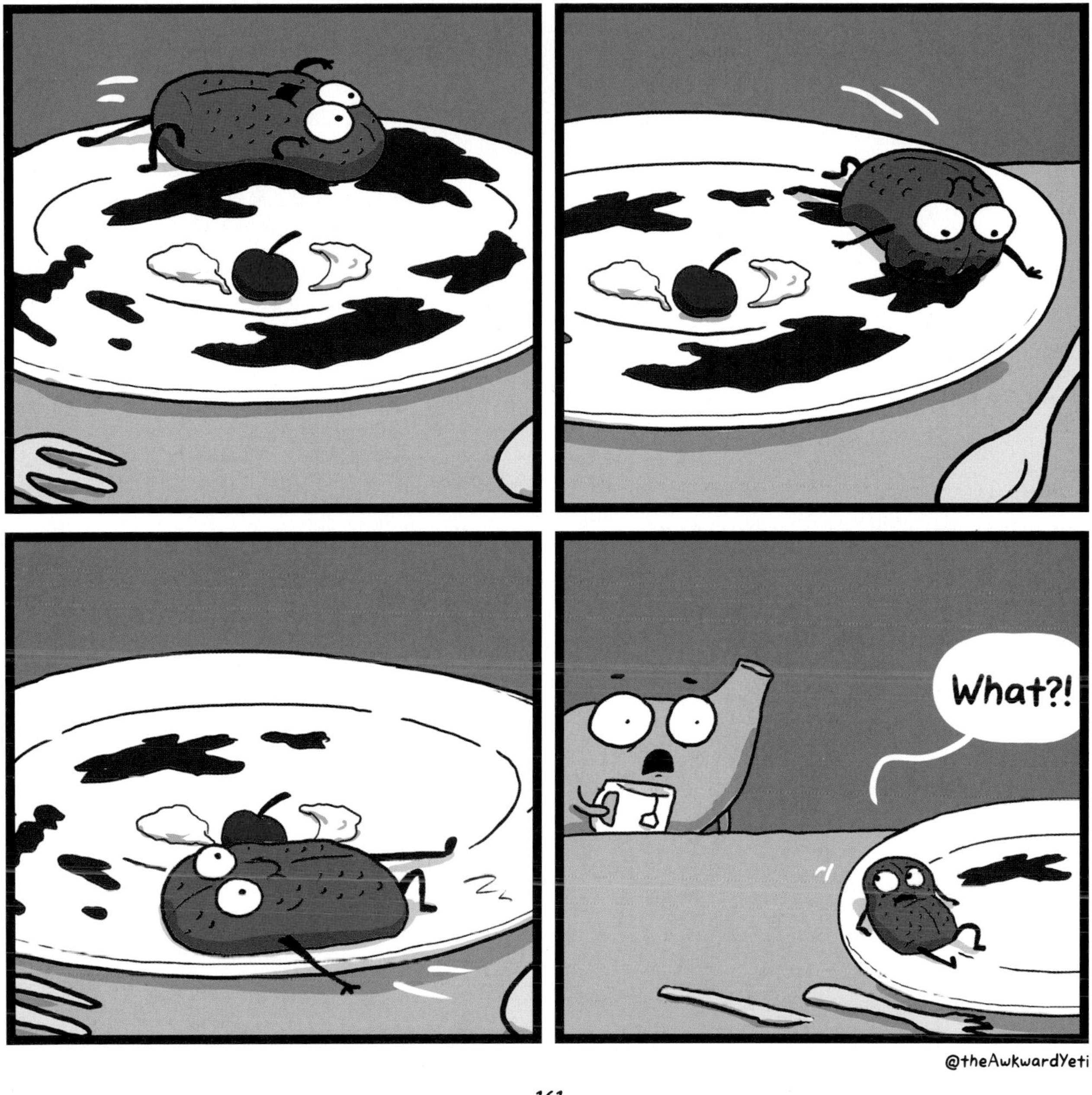
What?!
@theAwkwardYeti

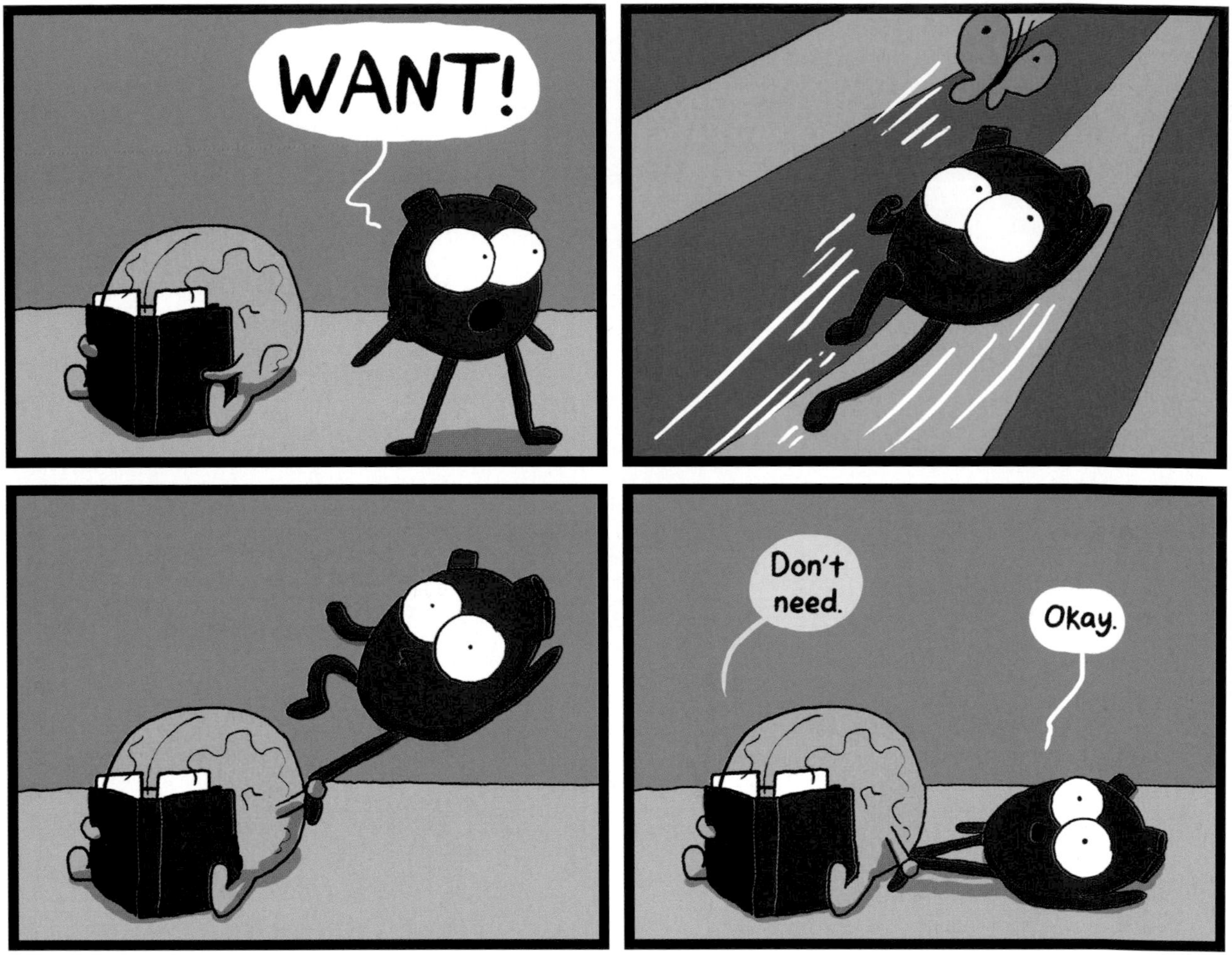
WANT!
Don't need.
Okay.

@theAwkwardYeti

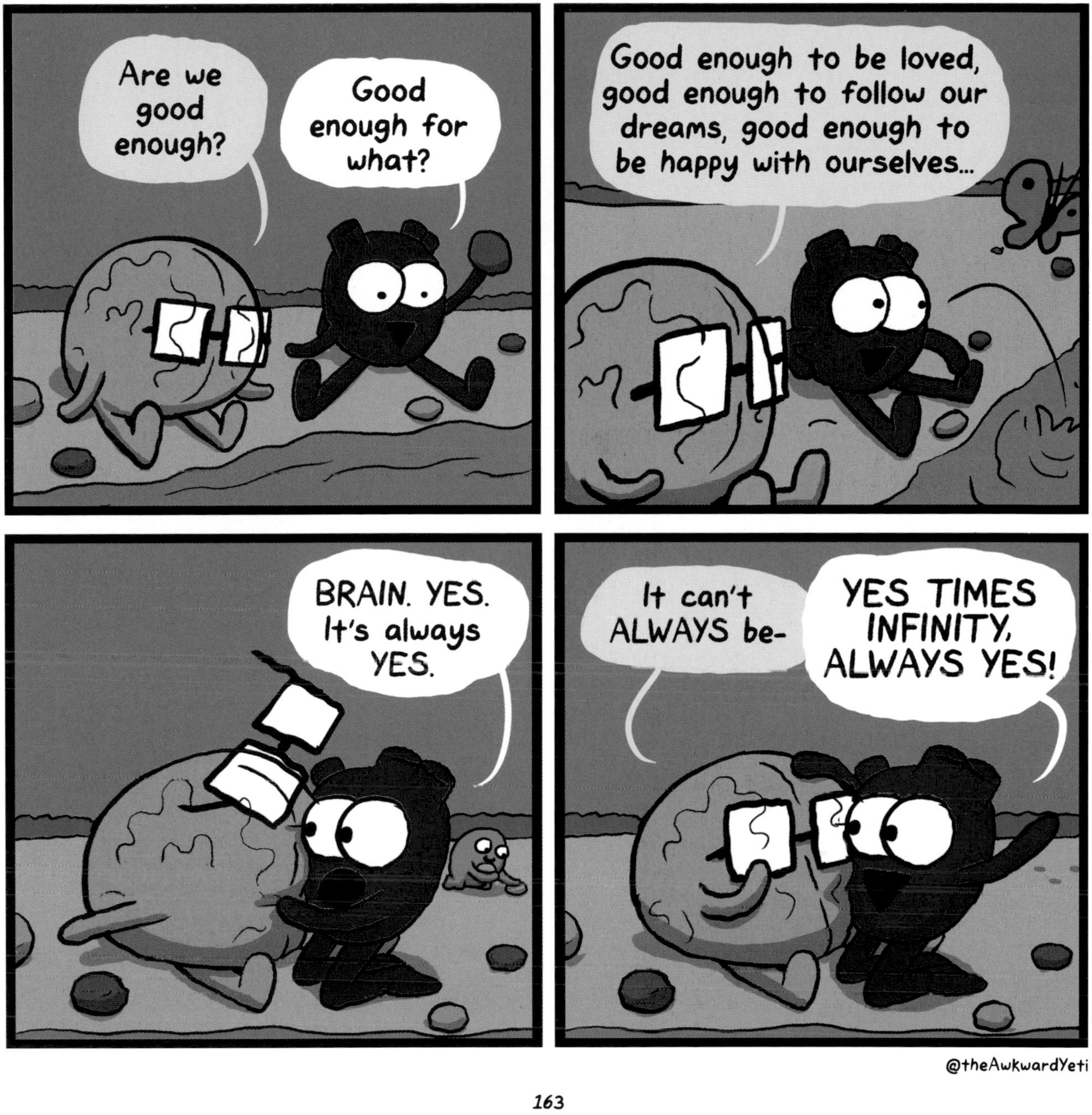
Are we good enough?
Good enough for what?
Good enough to be loved, good enough to follow our dreams, good enough to be happy with ourselves...
BRAIN. YES. It's always YES.
It can't ALWAYS be-
YES TIMES INFINITY, ALWAYS YES!

@theAwkwardYeti

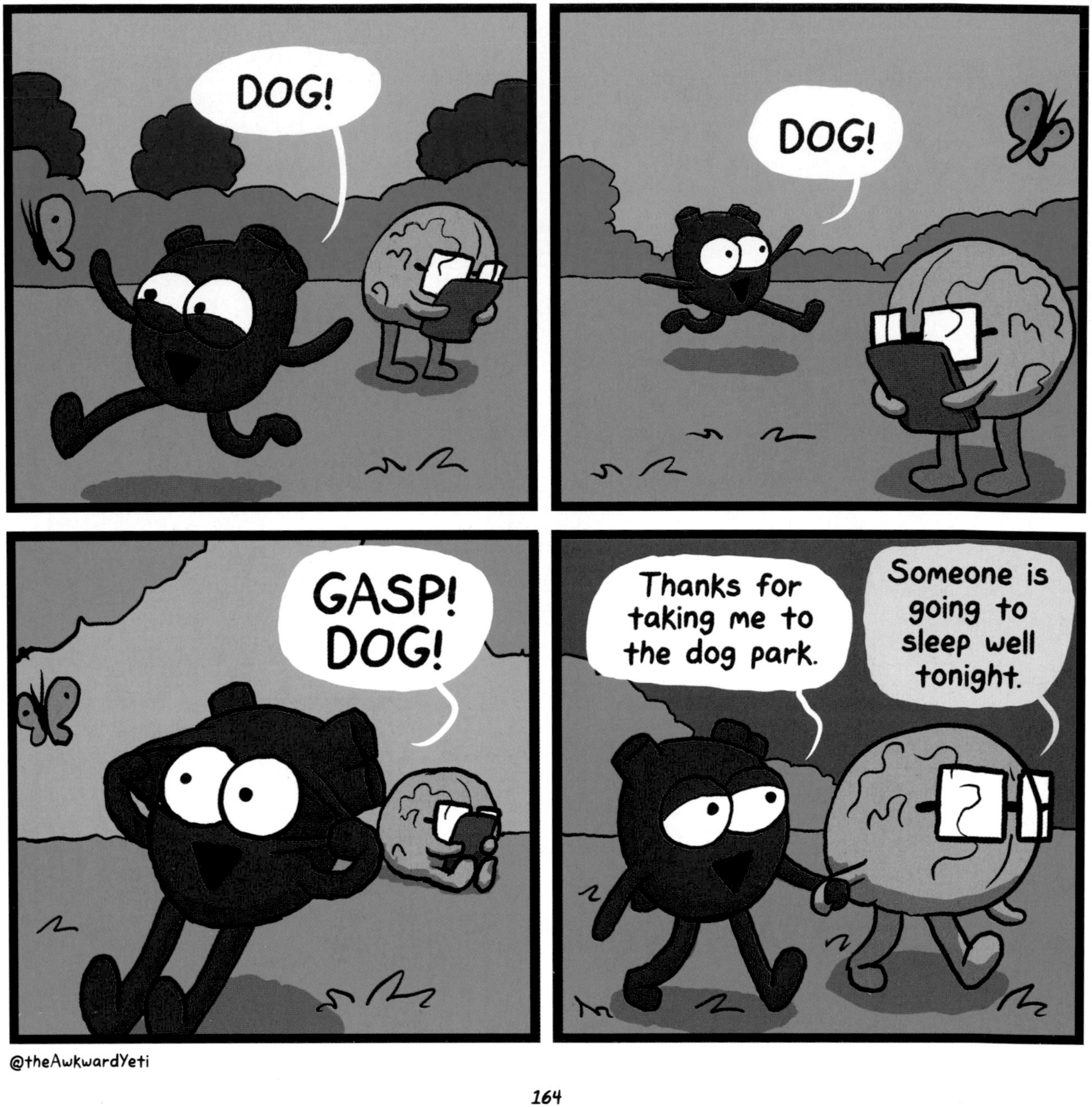
DOG!
DOG!
GASP! DOG!
Thanks for taking me to the dog park.
Someone is going to sleep well tonight.

@theAwkwardYeti

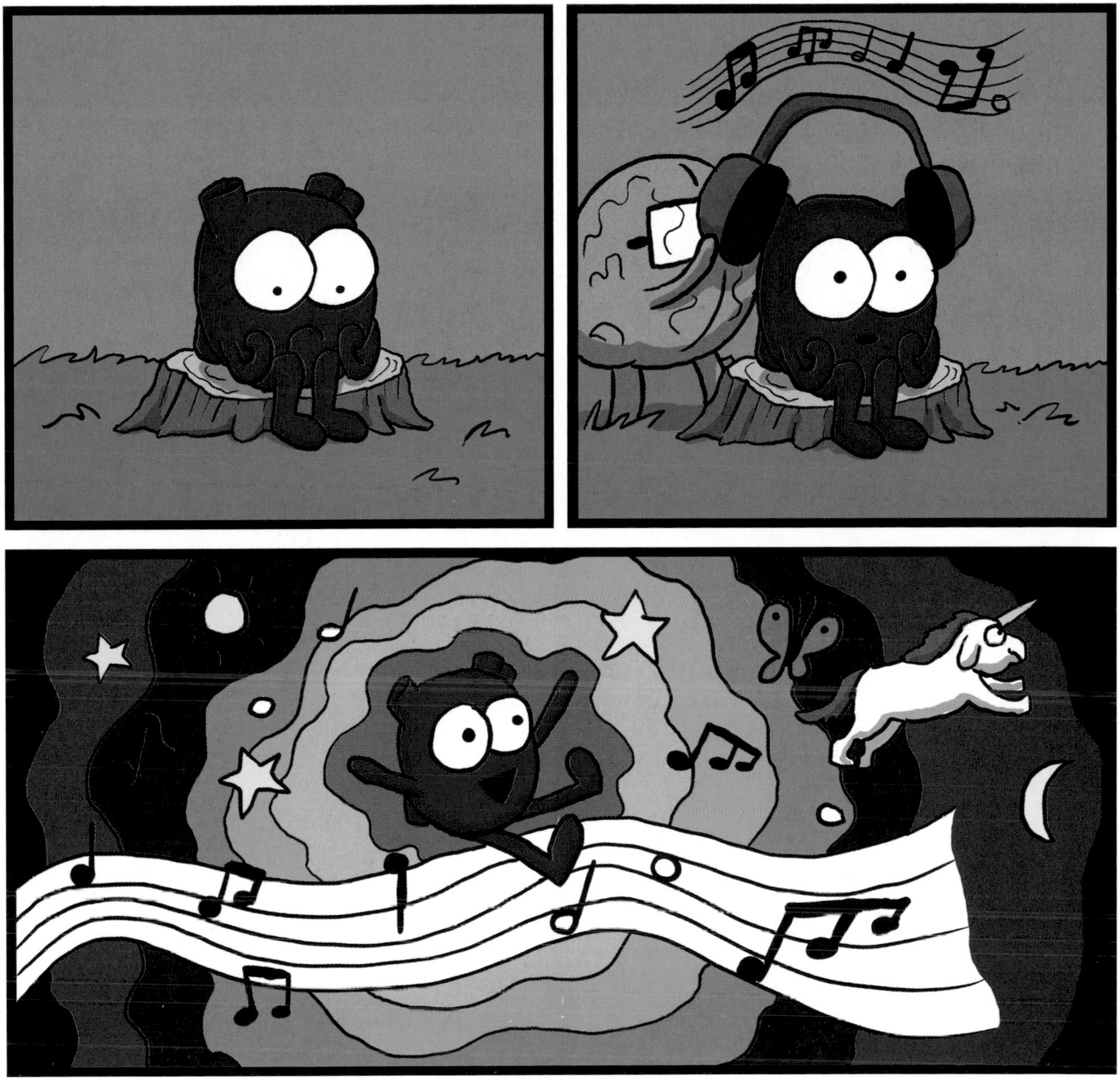

@theAwkwardYeti

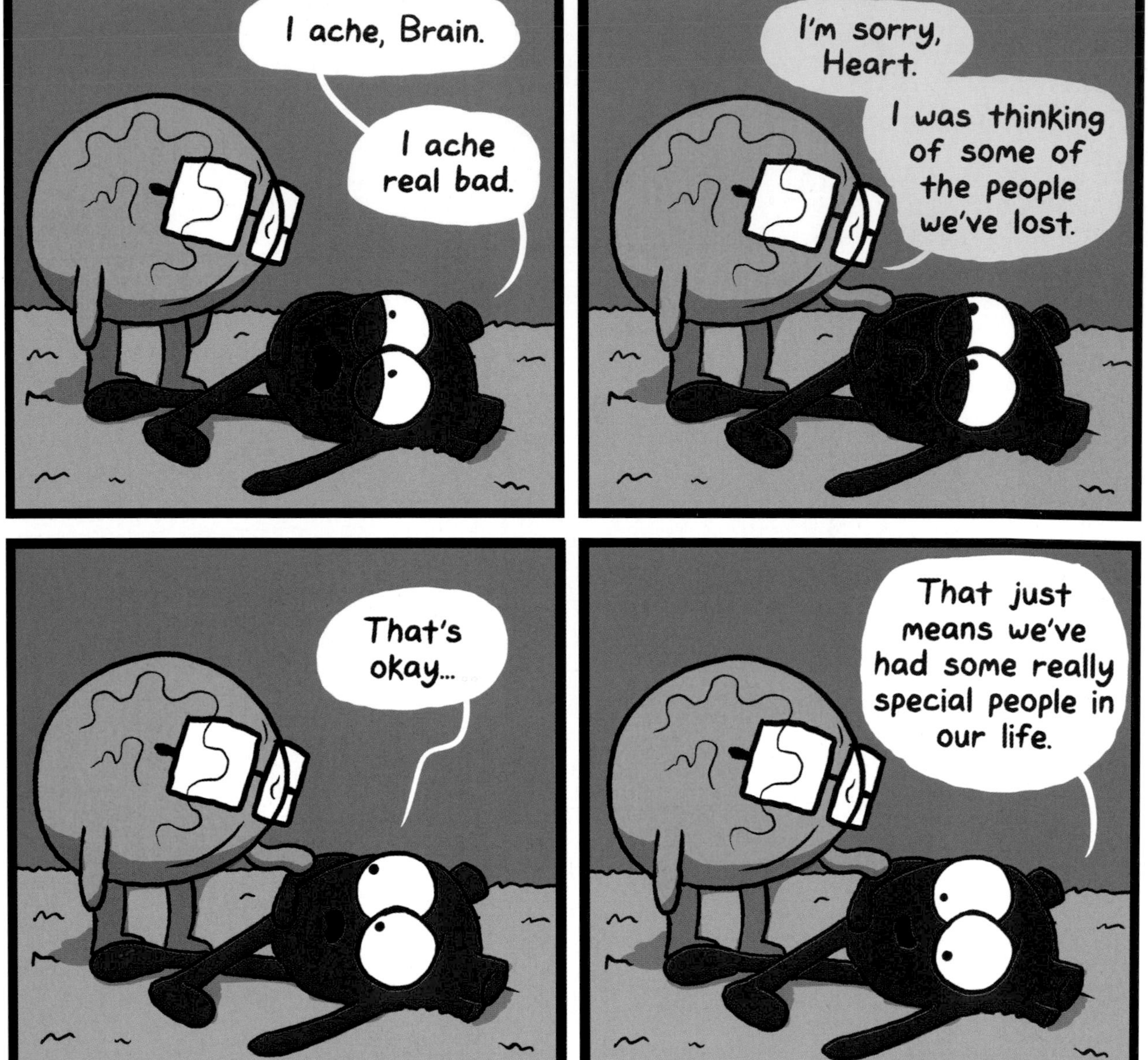
I ache, Brain.
I ache real bad.
I'm sorry, Heart.
I was thinking of some of the people we've lost.
That's okay...
That just means we've had some really special people in our life.

@theAwkwardYeti

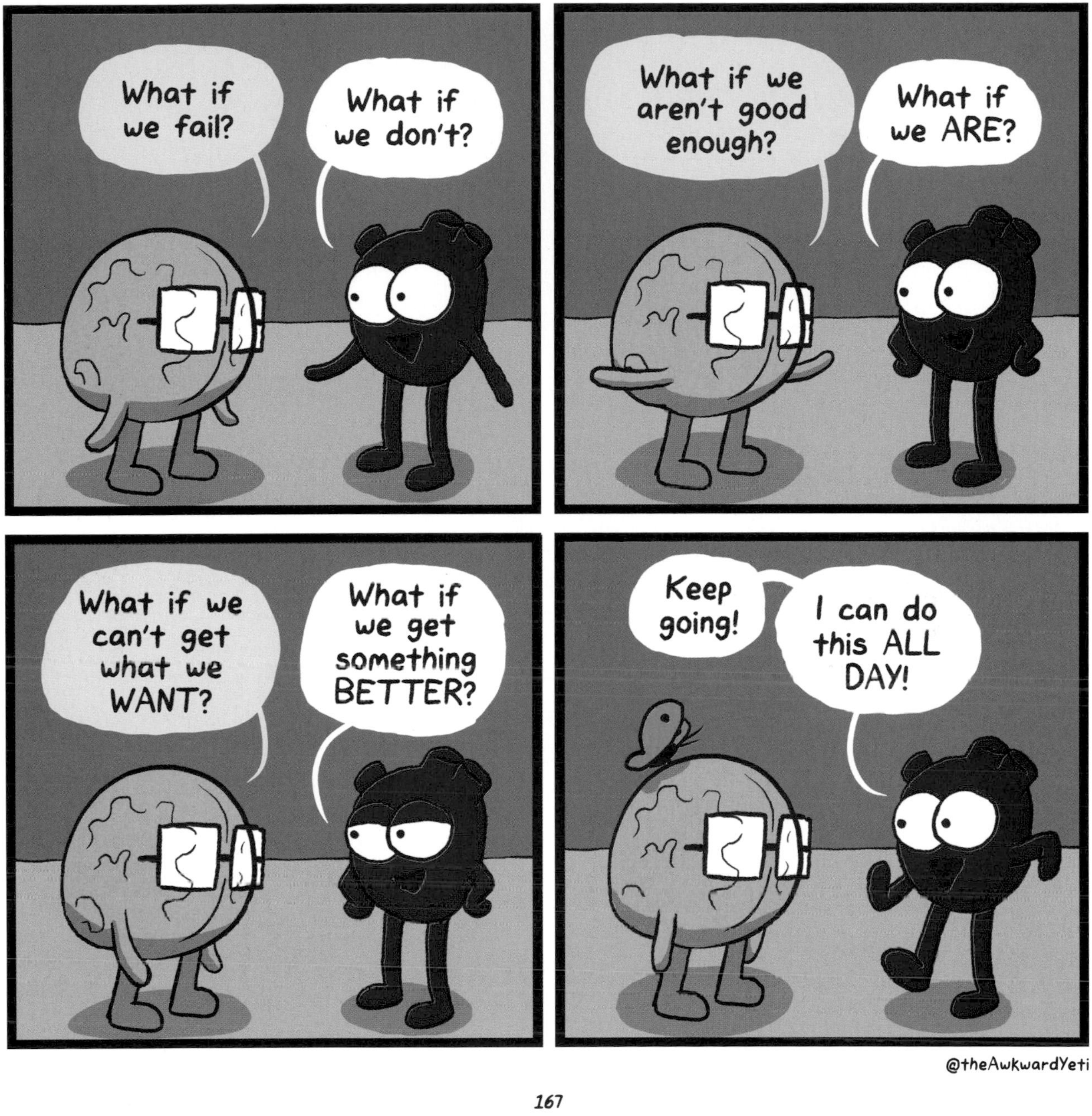
What if we fail?
What if we don't?
What if we aren't good enough?
What if we ARE?
What if we can't get what we WANT?
What if we get something BETTER?
Keep going!
I can do this ALL DAY!

@theAwkwardYeti

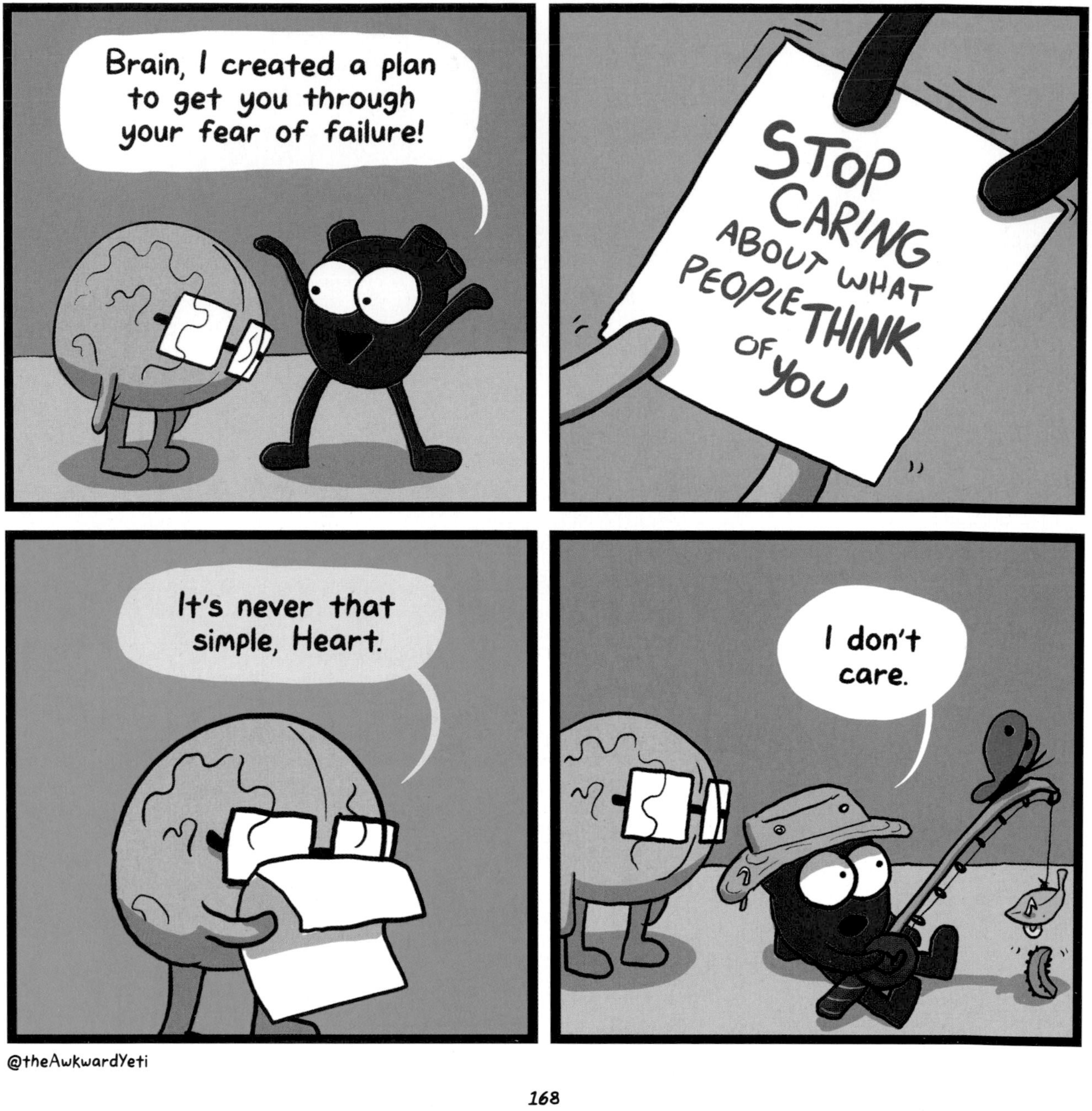
Brain, I created a plan to get you through your fear of failure!
STOP CARING ABOUT WHAT PEOPLE THINK OF YOU
It's never that simple, Heart.
I don't care.

@theAwkwardYeti

Do what you love, always.

Find and pursue the best combination of your love and natural talents.

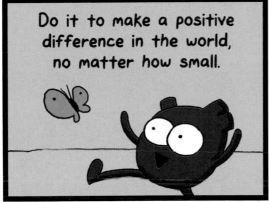

Do it to make a positive difference in the world, no matter how small.

Work harder than the next person.

Adapt. Everything is always changing.

The worst case is you'll know you tried.

@theAwkwardYeti

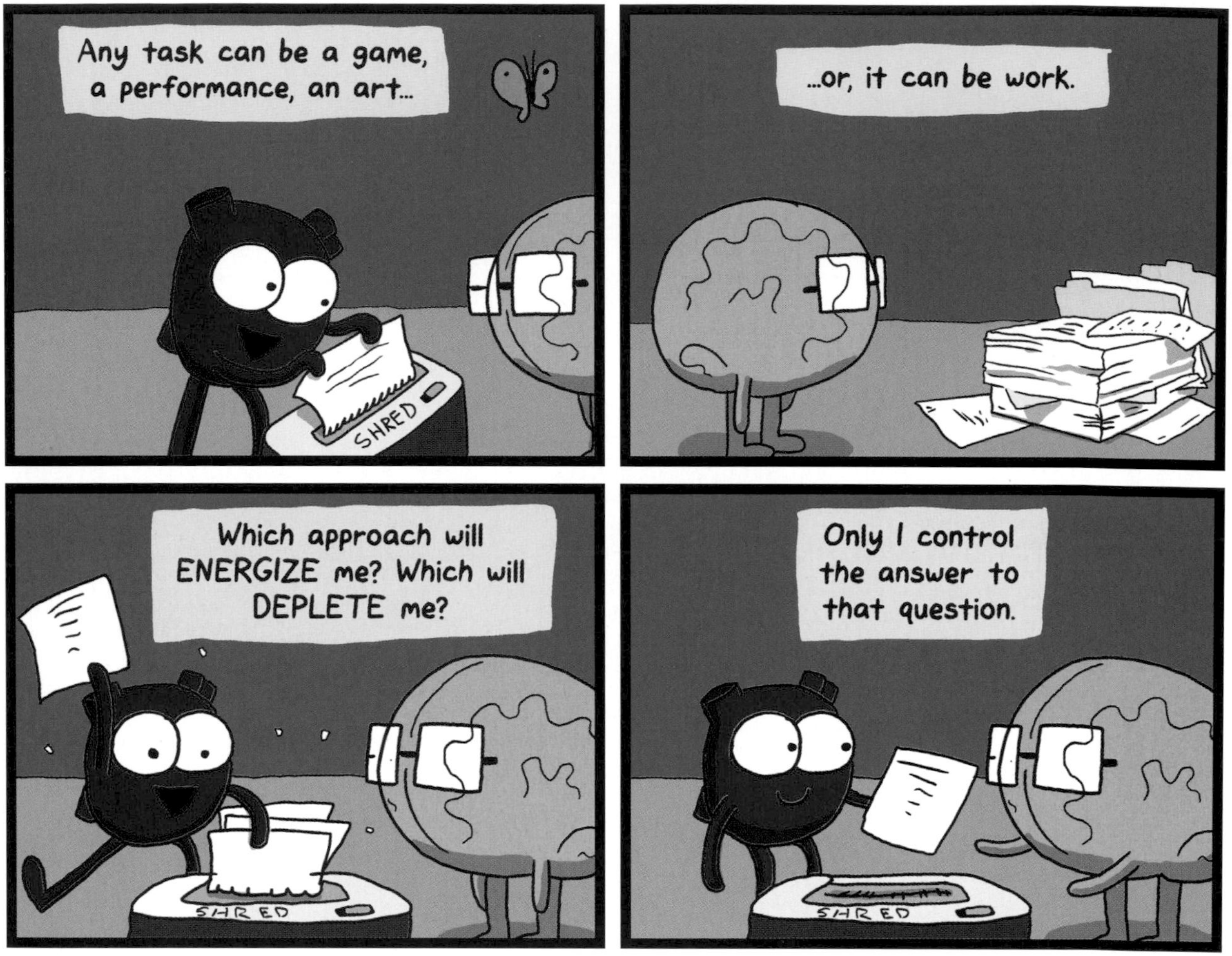
Any task can be a game, a performance, an art...
SHRED
...or, it can be work.
Which approach will ENERGIZE me? Which will DEPLETE me?
SHRED
Only I control the answer to that question.
SHRED

@theAwkwardYeti

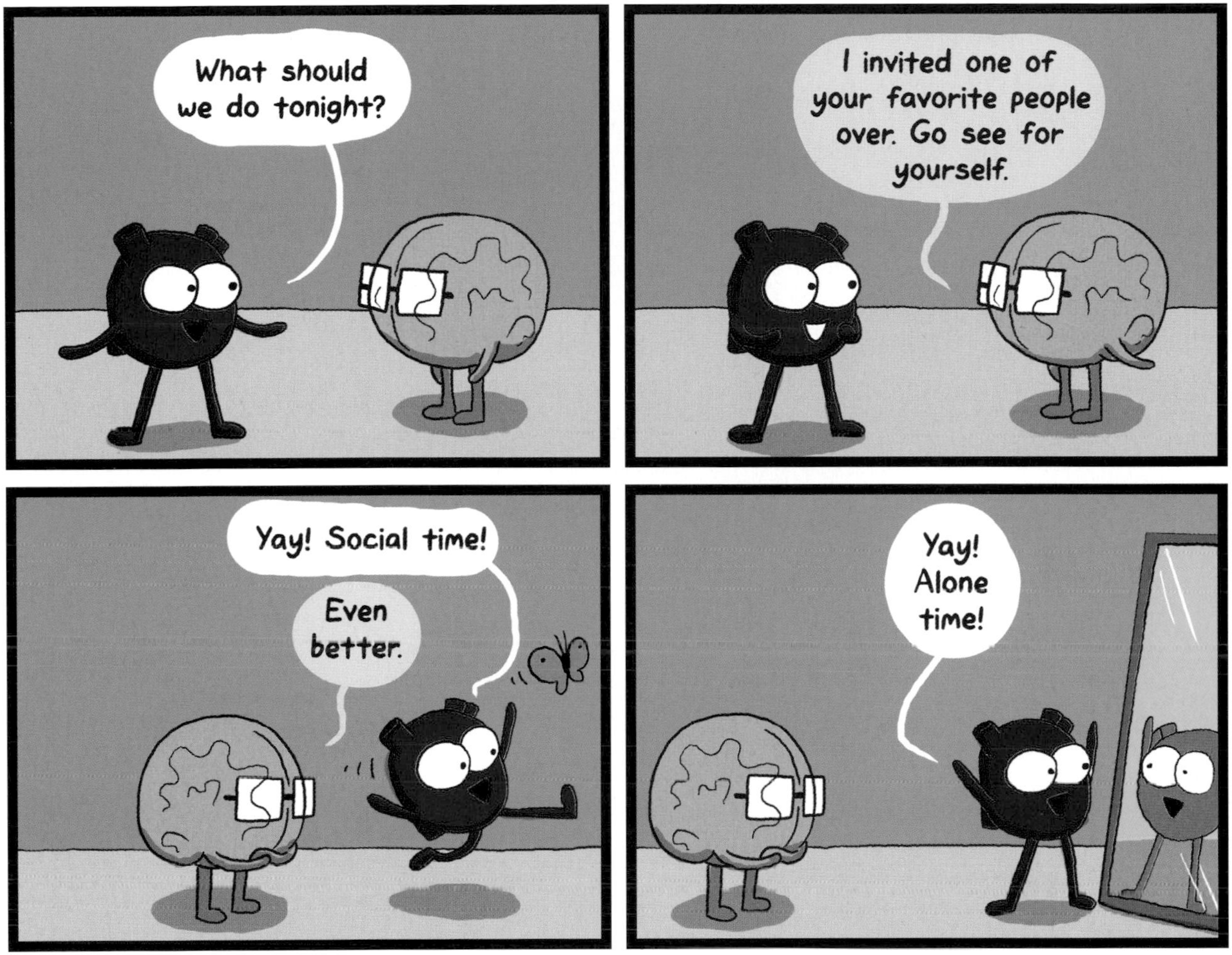
What should we do tonight?
I invited one of your favorite people over. Go see for yourself.
Yay! Social time!
Even better.
Yay! Alone time!

@theAwkwardYeti

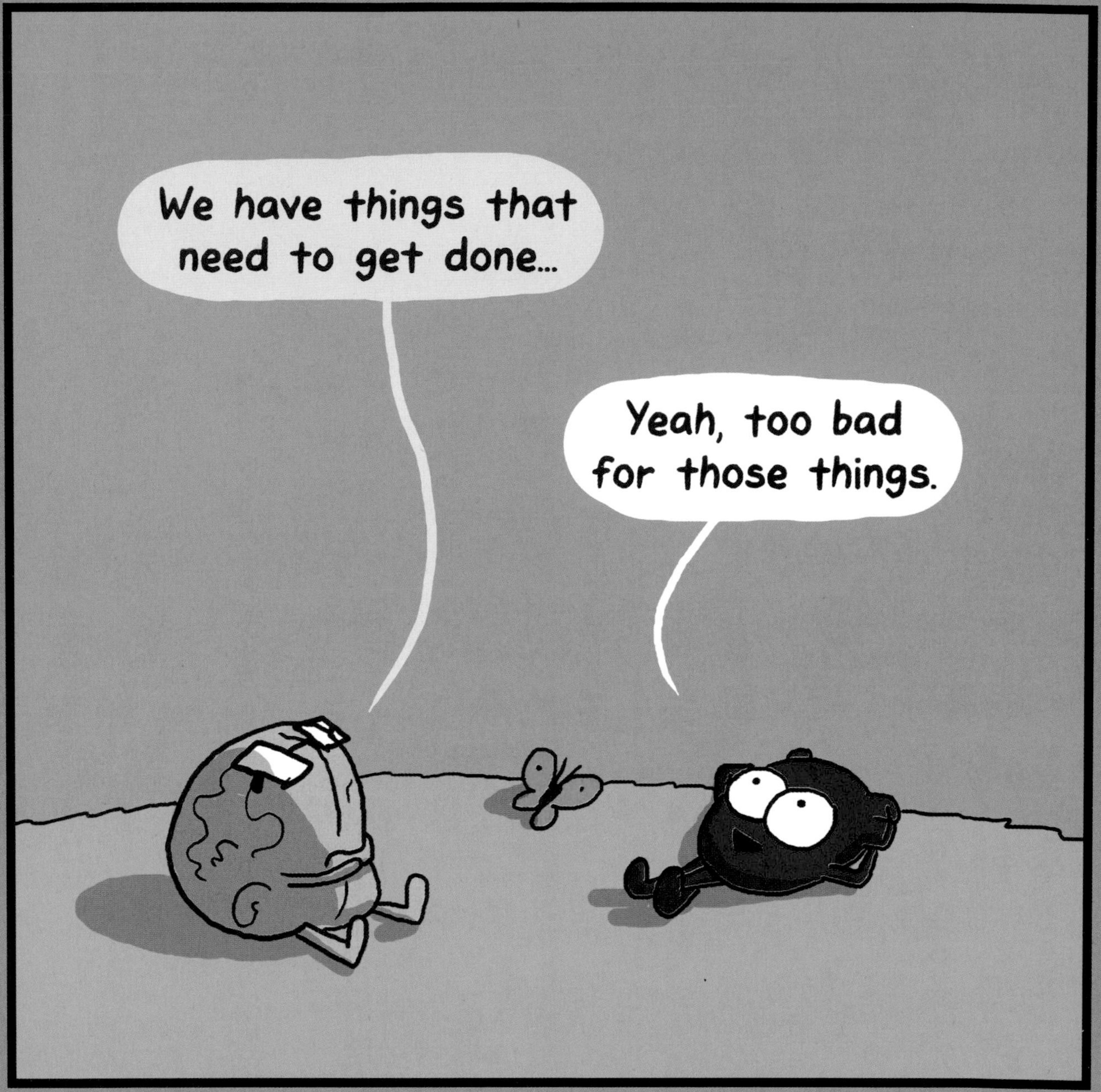
We have things that need to get done...
Yeah, too bad for those things.

@theAwkwardYeti

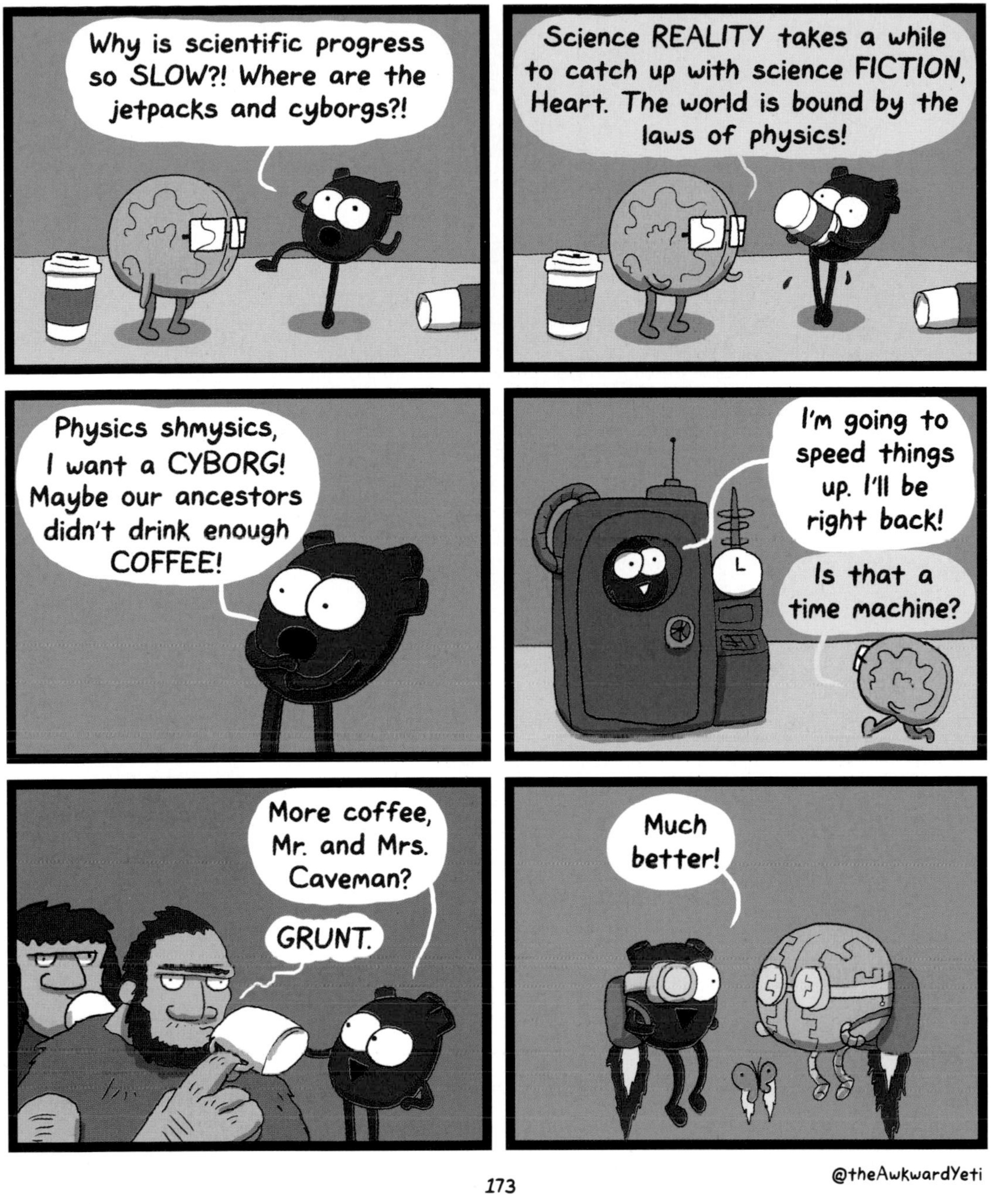
Why is scientific progress so SLOW?! Where are the jetpacks and cyborgs?!
Science REALITY takes a while to catch up with science FICTION, Heart. The world is bound by the laws of physics!
Physics shmysics, I want a CYBORG! Maybe our ancestors didn't drink enough COFFEE!
I'm going to speed things up. I'll be right back!
Is that a time machine?
More coffee, Mr. and Mrs. Caveman?
GRUNT.
Much better!
@theAwkwardYeti

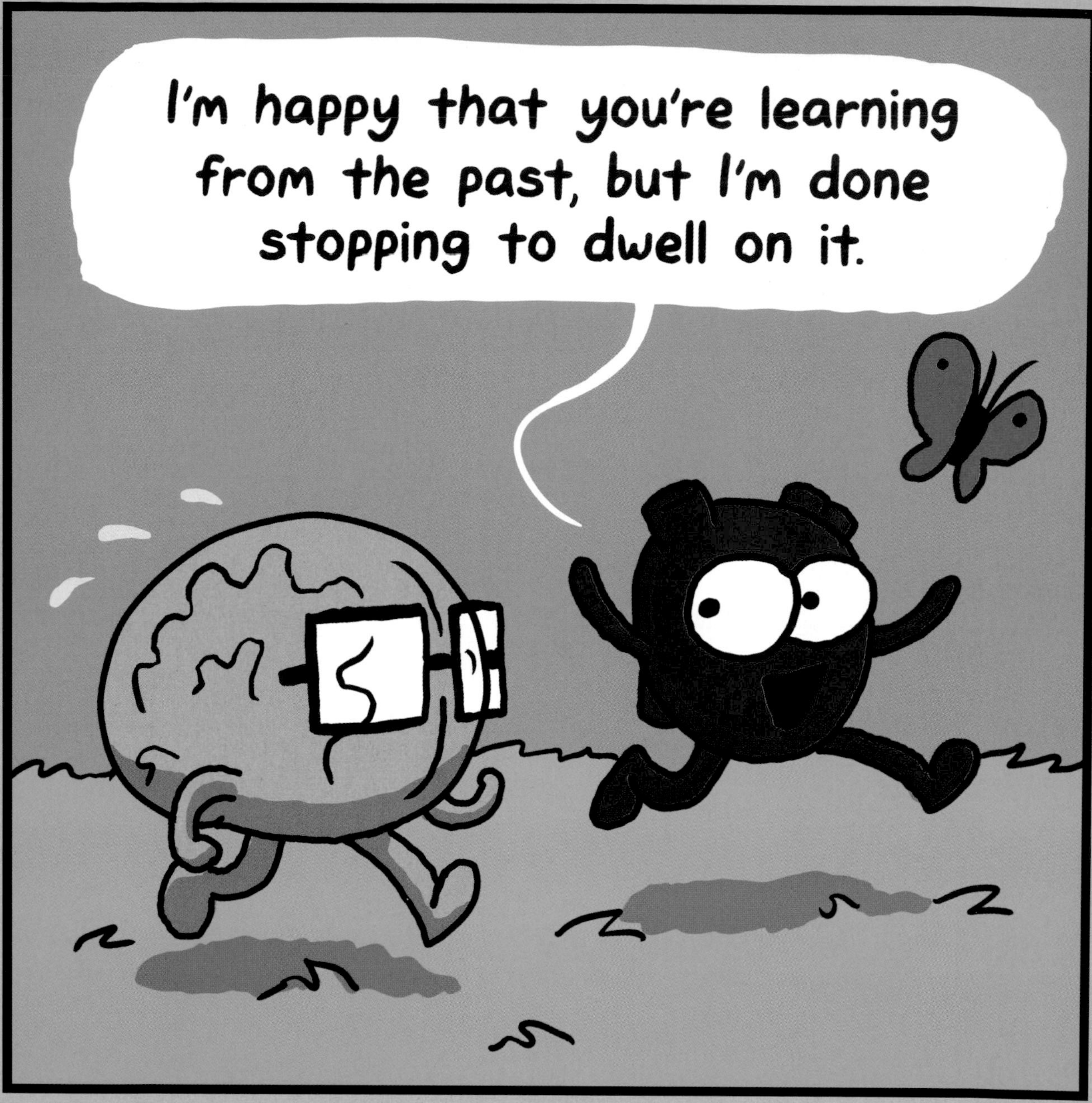
I'm happy that you're learning from the past, but I'm done stopping to dwell on it.

@theAwkwardYeti

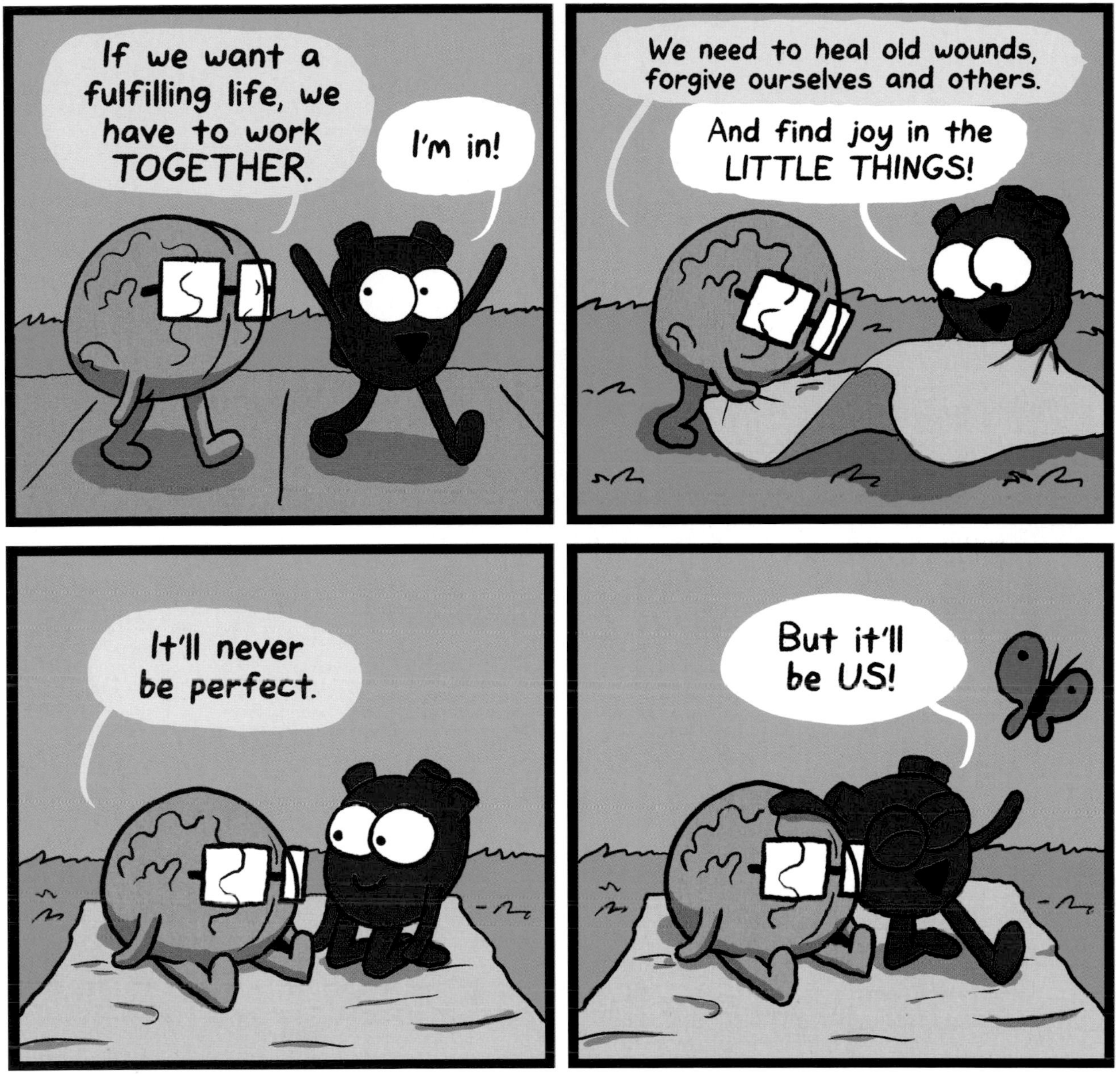
If we want a fulfilling life, we have to work TOGETHER.
I'm in!
We need to heal old wounds, forgive ourselves and others.
And find joy in the LITTLE THINGS!
It'll never be perfect.
But it'll be US!
@theAwkwardYeti

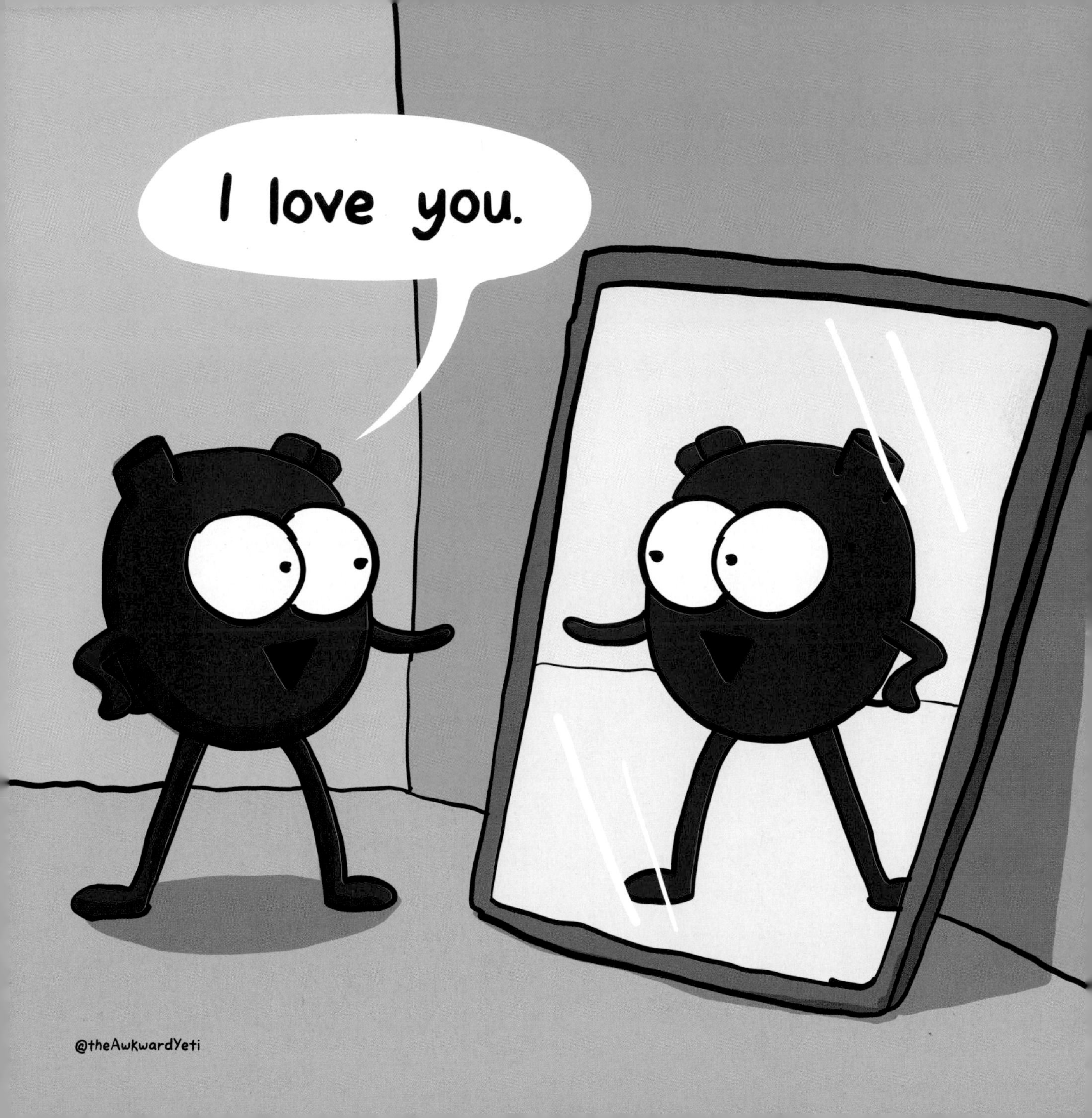
I love you.
@theAwkwardYeti

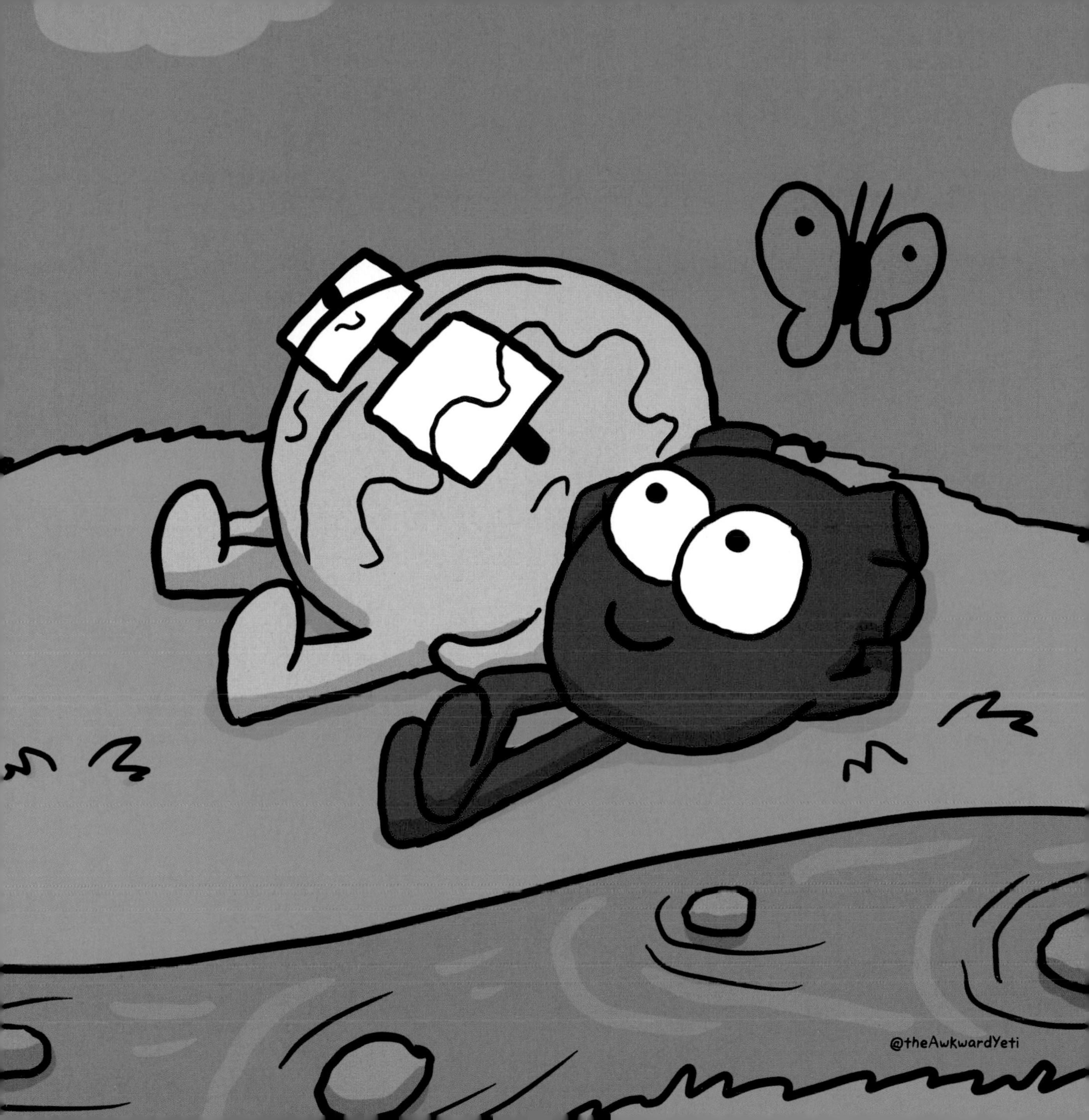
@theAwkwardYeti

Other books by Nick Seluk from Andrews McMeel

the Awkward Yeti™ Presents
HOW I BROKE UP WITH MY COLON
FASCINATING, BIZARRE, AND TRUE HEALTH STORIES

the Awkward Yeti™ Presents
Heart and Brain
BODY LANGUAGE
It's okay, I get irritable sometimes, too.

the Awkward Yeti™ Presents
Heart and Brain
GUT INSTINCTS
"My heart loves this strip, and my brain wishes I had thought of it first."
—Stephan Pastis, author of Timmy Failure and creator of Pearls Before Swine

the Awkward Yeti™ Presents
Heart and Brain
ADULT RESPONSIBILITIES
UTTER NONSENSE
This way, Heart.

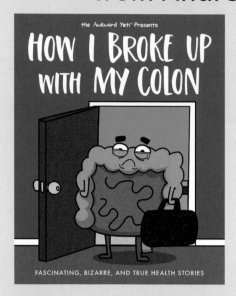

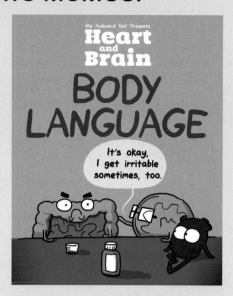

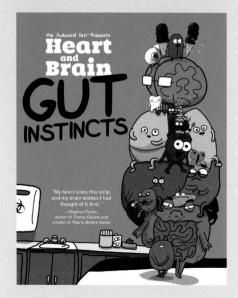

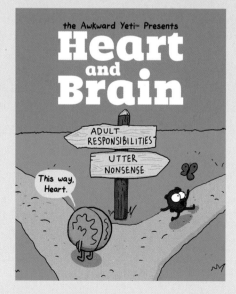